FROZEN

FROZEN

*My Journey into the World of
Cryonics, Deception, and Death*

LARRY JOHNSON
WITH SCOTT BALDYGA

Vanguard Press
A Member of the Perseus Books Group

Published by Vanguard Press
A Member of the Perseus Books Group

Set in 11 point Dante

Cataloging-in-Publication data for this book is available from the Library of
Congress.
ISBN: 978-1-59315-560-5

Vanguard Press books are available at special discounts for bulk purchases in
the U.S. by corporations, institutions, and other organizations. For more
information, please contact the Special Markets Department at the Perseus
Books Group, 2300 Chestnut Street, Suite 200, Philadelphia, PA 19103, or call
(800) 810-4145, ext. 5000, or e-mail special.markets@perseusbooks.com.

10 9 8 7 6 5 4 3 2 1

CONTENTS

INTRODUCTION

You're about to read a really bizarre story. I won't be able to explain all the things my colleagues at Alcor Life Extension Foundation did, or why I made all the decisions I did during the seven months I worked there. Some of those decisions, including why I first went to work at Alcor, may seem strange to you. As you'll read, though, I've been an adrenaline junkie most of my life and the job as clinical director for Alcor promised to be unlike anything I'd ever done before, and never boring for me. Boy, was I right about that.

At first, the idea of working at Alcor fit the bill perfectly. Although the important cryobiological research I was promised during my initial job interview never materialized, soon it didn't matter—the more I got to know my colleagues and the history of the place, the more immersed in it I became. Meanwhile, by slowly earning the trust of my eccentric coworkers, I became privy to many company secrets and was promoted to acting chief operating officer.

At some point, though, when I began to realize that really dark and possibly illegal things were being done at Alcor, I decided I owed it to everyone—the frozen Alcor "patients," their families, the surrounding community, even the hard-core Alcorians sincerely hoping for another life beyond this one—to document the abuses that were going on under the roof of that strange enterprise. I observed unconscionable environmental and animal experimentation practices. My complaints about apparent OSHA (Occupational Safety and Health Administration) and EPA (Environmental Protection Agency) infractions kept falling on deaf ears. Worse,

I soon began hearing persistent rumors about the suspicious, premature deaths of several Alcor members. So I began digging and have never quit.

I'd never before seen myself as a whistle-blower, but that does seem to be what I've become. I began copying Alcor documents and, later, recording conversations with my colleagues. Ultimately, I wore a wire every single day of my last three months there. I had to do this, and you'll read why. I'd never imagined myself in that role, but I respect the truth, and people who aren't afraid to speak the truth, even to the powerful.

During my time at Alcor, and in the six years since I had to flee Scottsdale, maintaining my self-respect by finding the truth and making it widely known have become, next to my wife and family, the most important things in my life. That's why I wanted to write and publish this book. Thank you for reading it.

LARRY JOHNSON
July 1, 2009

PROLOGUE

My wife and I were in the living room packing frantically, rushing to get out of town, when suddenly there was a thunderous pounding on the door. Beverly started screaming. I ran to the bedroom, grabbed my 9mm Beretta from under the bed, and rushed back to the living room. The banging was so powerful, the molding was breaking off from the wall; they were literally bashing their way in. I inched toward the door. Beverly was on the floor, crying hysterically, her hands over her ears. I put my eye to the peephole but the door was vibrating too violently for me to see who was there. Shouts came from the other side.

"Johnson, you motherfucking traitor! We'll get you, you son of a bitch!"

I backed up, aimed my gun at the door, shaking in its hinges, and screamed, "If you come through that door I'll put a bullet through your head!" I meant it. At that moment, I really believed I was going to have to kill someone.

"You traitor, we'll kill you! You too, Beverly. You will both die!" The banging stopped. Footsteps ran down the outside stairs.

Beverly was crumpled in a heap on the floor, sobbing. I stood, trembling, looking down at my wife.

What have I done?

ONE

CARNAGE AND CHAOS IN SIN CITY

July 5, 2002, was just another day for me as a paramedic in Las Vegas.

I awoke at my usual five o'clock to the sound of the weatherman announcing that the outside temperature was already ninety-nine degrees. Still feeling the toll of yesterday's twelve-hour shift, I knew I was in for another long, hot day.

I showered in a flash and was quickly ready to leave home. Careful not to wake my wife, Beverly, I tiptoed outside, walked downstairs into the garage of our apartment building, and said good morning to the other love of my life: my Harley.

One of my greatest pleasures is riding my Fat Boy. Ever since I was nine years old I would hop on any kind of motorbike and roar through the desert to recharge my batteries. It was a perfect escape and helped me stay sane. I've always been happy to be left on my own, and there is nothing like the rush of freedom and solitude I feel when I ride.

During my early-morning rides, whatever was clogging my head would spread out, thin, and be swept away behind me. After cruising some of my favorite desolate desert roads, I chose a route that would take me up Las Vegas Boulevard, the Strip. I hopped off the 215 at the last exit before Interstate 15, down by the airport. There's something eerie about cruising the Strip at five or six in the morning. Somehow I felt like I was getting away with something, like I wasn't meant to be there, not at that time, and definitely not alone.

At that time of the morning I might see the occasional hooker or random drunk stumbling along the sidewalk, but Las Vegas Boulevard itself was usually empty. I could cruise quietly or roar straight down its throat, depending on my mood. I was in little danger of getting sideswiped by a tourist in a rented minivan.

Of course, the casinos never closed, but at this time of morning they were at their quietest—slumbering giants shaking themselves awake, stretching open their jaws to swallow up every dollar from every sucker from every other town in America.

I could see the sun coming up while many of the casinos still had their lights on. There wasn't another soul around.

I passed Caesars Palace and saw the spot where two months earlier I had jumped on a guy who had attacked a cop, all three of us wrestling for the cop's gun. The guy was out of his mind on sherm—a cigarette or joint dipped in embalming fluid. The effect of smoking this popular street drug is said to be like that of the powerful stimulant PCP. It was a vicious struggle but the cop and I eventually subdued him. If he had gotten that gun, I probably would have ended up as no more than a stain on the Caesars Palace sidewalk.

Mount Charleston is a huge chunk of rock that rises out of the sand north of the Strip. This morning it shimmered with the reflection of the rising sun. Spectacular blues, oranges, and a battleship gray were dissolving into a soft purple. Even in the July heat, snow somehow survived on top of Mount Charleston. Whether or not it could be seen from the Strip depended on the previous winter's snowfall, but I had seen it up there myself, year-round, enduring even the desert heat in the protective shadows of the crags and cliffs. I always found that stubborn snow encouraging.

The ride was working its magic, as it usually did. I was being washed clean; the aches and pains from the previous day's shift were sliding away. Seeing Mount Charleston in the distance never failed to refresh my spirit. It helped me prepare for whatever stresses the day would present—and there would be stresses.

It takes a certain type of person to be a paramedic. I've worked in half a dozen cities in the American Southwest and Texas. But in Las Vegas, particularly, I'd witnessed some of the most disturbing human behavior on the planet.

I'd had bits of my ear chewed off by crazed drug addicts who broke through their restraints in the back of an ambulance; scraped sick, homeless drunks off scorching asphalt in 110-degree heat, their charred skin sticking to the pavement; mopped high-diving, high-stakes losers off casino sidewalks; talked teenage rape victims off seventh-floor balconies, and run hundreds of calls to neighborhoods in which I otherwise would never have shown my face. More than once I'd hit the deck when automatic-weapon fire sprayed through my ambulance, bullets ripping the air over my head—gang members usually don't want their rivals to receive medical attention. Somehow I had always made it through the constant mayhem of shootouts, fistfights, knife fights, and ambulance crashes.

It was tough on my body, always carrying heavy gear or even heavier bodies. The emotional strain, though, was worse. Paramedics worked with pain and death every day. We developed mental calluses but still found ourselves continually surrounded by suffering, sorrow, and heart-wrenching loss. Sometimes I could help; sometimes I couldn't. Sometimes I saved a life; sometimes I watched a grown man scream hysterically in the street as his daughter died in his arms.

In Las Vegas, I was constantly wading through the seamier side of humanity. On good nights, I'd be stationed outside Caesars Palace and tourists would ask me to pose with them for pictures in front of the ambulance like I was Siegfried or Roy. Mostly, though, I responded to 911 calls in the tougher North Vegas neighborhoods, poor areas with a lot of gang violence that doesn't make it onto the TV news. Sadly, I worked with the worst people at their worst times.

We often arrived on a scene before the police. Protocol dictated that we did not rush in alone—it wasn't our responsibility to mix it up with gang members, and we didn't carry weapons. It wasn't easy, though, knowing that a bystander might be hurt and all we could do was park at a safe distance and wait for the cops. I'd scrunch down in my seat in case there were shots fired, roll my window down a crack, and wait for the all clear.

In my experience, most paramedics burned out after around five years and switched jobs. I was then in my twenty-fifth year as a paramedic.

It must have been the excitement of not knowing what emergency I could be called to from one minute to the next that had kept me in emergency medicine for five times longer than the average paramedic.

I admit it. I've always been an adrenaline junkie.

When I arrived at work that morning of July 5, 2002, I found my twenty-something-year-old partner, Steve, in the back of our ambulance with an IV in his arm, rehydrating himself after a night of Fourth of July debauchery. Most paramedics lived hard. Twelve-hour shifts were followed by late nights and early mornings of nurse-chasing down at the Emergency Room bar just off the Strip. We had our own hangout, the Las Vegas emergency medical community's equivalent of *Cheers*. Steve had a story to tell nearly every morning. He reminded me of myself back in the day.

There was a strong bond among paramedics, especially between partners. It was similar to that of firefighters, police, or maybe soldiers on the battlefield. You went through hell together, constantly on the lookout to protect each other. I loved that feeling of community and camaraderie. Watching Steve gobbling saline pills and sucking on an oxygen mask, though, reminded me of just how young I wasn't.

Optimistically, we tried to make it to McDonald's for a couple Egg McMuffins before the daily pandemonium began, but like most mornings, the calls came in as soon as we hit the street. Just another day of carnage and chaos in Sin City.

Our third back-to-back morning call involved lugging a three-hundred-pound heart attack victim through the impossibly narrow confines of his mobile home. Struggling with his bulk, I noticed a membership brochure on the man's kitchen table for something called Alcor Life Extension Foundation.

Life Extension Foundation? I thought. What's that all about?

Later that morning, Steve and I heard the news over the radio in our ambulance: Ted Williams had died.

This really upset me. Ted Williams was one of my personal heroes. Even though I had grown up awfully far from Boston, his legendary baseball career had proven to me that with enough hard work and dedication, anything was possible. One of my childhood's prized possessions was a Little League Ted Williams baseball bat. I still have it, along with my Sears Ted Williams bicycle.

"Ted Williams?" Steve asked. "Who's that?"

"You're kidding," I said. "Ted Williams was one of the greatest hitters of all time. Not to mention an American war hero."

Steve shrugged.

I shook my head. "Man, am I that old?"

In December 2002, I began looking for a new job in earnest.

After twenty-five years as a paramedic, I was really burnt out. My wife, Beverly, saw it. As much good as riding my Harley did, as good a shape as I was in, I was still a few years north of forty. I had always been told I looked young for my age. I'd even been accused of having a boy-next-door quality to me. Those days were behind me now, though. Like an athlete over forty, I was constantly sore. I knew in my bones that it was time to make a change.

I also wanted to live closer to my father. My mom and dad had divorced when I was very young. Even before my parents split up, my dad was either gone all day working for the phone company or gone all night working as a pianist. I had never had an opportunity to be around him much. My father was getting up there in age and if I was going to change careers I might as well change cities. Dad was now retired, remarried, and living in Phoenix. Dad's wife was a kind woman named Mary Jane. Unfortunately, she was also very sick and needed a lot of care at home. Dad loved her dearly and stayed by her side day after day.

So I began the process of a change in careers. One field I was interested in was biotechnology research. I had to be realistic, though. Adrenaline had been a part of my daily routine for twenty-five years. How happy would I be sitting in a quiet lab every day watching liquids inside test tubes turn from green to blue? Yeah, I was burnt out from paramedicine but I still craved excitement. Only now I was searching for intellectual stimulation rather than the peculiar thrill of wrestling with sherm-crazed felons. My dream job, then, would be an exceptionally interesting biological research position—in Phoenix, close to my dad. A tall order, for sure.

A few weeks into my job search, I ran across an advertisement on Monster.com looking for a paramedic or nurse to be a "team leader" for a company researching life extension via the cold-temperature sciences. This struck me as interesting. The company was called Alcor Life Extension Foundation.

That was the name of the company on the pamphlet I had seen the morning of Ted Williams's death. What a coincidence.

I hadn't followed the scandal surrounding Ted Williams's death too closely, but I did remember that there was some family squabbling about his final remains and I remembered something about him being frozen. I Googled Alcor and Ted Williams and sure enough—it seemed as if Ted Williams had been brought to Alcor.

Huh. What were the odds? I felt like the universe was telling me to look into this job.

Unlike most job ads, there was a phone number. Maybe they were really anxious to fill the position. I called and spoke to a man named Charles Platt. In what sounded like a distinguished English accent, Charles asked, "Larry, have you heard of cryonics?"

"It has something to do with freezing organs for long-term storage, right?"

"Well, yes," Charles said. "Alcor is a cold-temperature research facility located in the Phoenix suburb of Scottsdale, Arizona."

Wow, a research facility outside Phoenix!

"We work closely with our sister facility in Rancho Cucamonga, California, called Critical Care Research or 21st Century Medicine," Charles said. "Together we develop and experiment with drugs and freezing procedures to preserve human organs in the hopes of one day reanimating our patients."

"Reanimating?"

"Yes. The goal of cryonics is bringing our patients back to life."

"Oh. Well, Charles, it sounds fascinating but I'm really more interested in mainstream biological research, like maybe the preservation of organs for transplants."

Undaunted, Charles told me that what they were doing at CCR in Rancho Cucamonga was right up my alley then. They were making great strides in cryobiological research, he said, particularly in freezing and unfreezing kidneys, hearts, livers, and corneas for transplants. This type of research was going to save lives. CCR was also working toward being able to freeze endangered plant species to combat extinction. And one of CCR's scientists was working on an ice-resistant concrete treatment to keep runways and roads bone dry during the worst ice storms, a real life-saving advancement if it worked. I had seen enough road accidents as a paramedic, enough people killed driving in icy conditions, to know how valuable that would be.

Plus, Charles told me, he was sure I'd be equally impressed with the groundbreaking work at Alcor itself. I should come to Scottsdale, Charles said. Alcor would fly me out. I could tour the facility and we would discuss Alcor's needs in detail. Right there on the phone, without even having seen my résumé, Charles asked what would be a good date for me.

––––––––––––

That conversation with the distinguished-sounding Mr. Platt sparked my interest, so I decided to go online and research recent work in the cold-temperature sciences. What I found was amazing. Much like bold discoveries that have been made in quantum mechanics, advances in the cold-temperature sciences were challenging accepted views of reality. The behavior of certain metals at extremely low temperatures contradicted the very laws of physics! At super-cold temperatures, scientists were discovering, some elements were sliding around without any friction at all. Matter acted in ways it simply shouldn't. I found this fascinating.

The practical applications included improved hospital machines, fuel for the space shuttle, food preservation, organ and embryo storage, scalpels that cut without drawing blood, superior fire retardants, and new plans for fusion energy plants. Cryobiologists were even bringing children to the infertile. And as Charles had mentioned, doctors were now able to perform lifesaving organ transplants that were previously impossible.

Clicking from Web page to Web page, I learned that cryogenics, a branch of physics, was the study of low temperatures themselves and how they affected materials. Cryobiology was the study of the effects of low temperatures on biological matter or organisms, and cryonics was the application of these cold-temperature sciences with the intention of freezing people or animals in the hopes of one day reviving them.

It was that "reviving" bit that was sticking in my craw.

I visited Alcor's Web site. The front page seemed to me heavy on the marketing, like it was meant to entice the average browser to look past the fantastic, science fiction aura surrounding cryonics, which at first sure sounded implausible. I decided to cut to the chase and found the Web page that listed Alcor's board of advisors. If they had any "legitimate" scientists involved, I figured, maybe it wasn't completely far-fetched.

Man, was I in for a shock. When I read the credentials of the people on Alcor's list of scientific advisors and conference speakers, I was astounded.

They included MIT and UCLA professors, research scientists from UC Berkeley and Cambridge, and JPL (Jet Propulsion Laboratory) and NASA advisors. The ranks of Alcor's scientific advisors included Marvin Minsky of the MIT Media Lab and the MIT Artificial Intelligence Lab, and Ralph Merkle, one of the top people in robotics and nanotechnology research.

Stem cell researcher Michael D. West, one of the leading figures in modern biotech, had recently spoken at the Alcor Conference on Extreme Life Extension in November 2002, as had artificial intelligence pioneer Ray Kurzweil, who, I read, had won the $500,000 Lemelson–MIT Prize, the world's largest cash award in invention and innovation. Kurzweil had also received the 1999 National Medal of Technology, the nation's highest honor in technology, from President Bill Clinton in a White House ceremony. Another luminary who had spoken at that Alcor conference, Gregory Benford, was an advisor to both the U.S. Department of Energy and the White House Council on Space Policy, as well as a science fiction author who had won the Nebula and John W. Campbell Awards, and the 1990 United Nations Medal in Literature. Yet another speaker—and Alcor advisor—was Aubrey de Grey of the University of Cambridge, one of the world's leading researchers on anti-aging. These people were all at the top of their fields. I was hugely impressed.

There sure were a lot of world-famous scientists a hell of a lot smarter than me lending their names and reputations to Alcor. And the cryobiological research I could be part of at CCR seemed both thrilling and important. Okay, I thought, I'd visit Alcor, and withhold any judgment on the mysterious cryonics part of the job until I had seen the place. All in all, I thought, what a lively, exciting, rewarding field to be a part of.

TWO

JUST ANOTHER RESEARCH FACILITY OUTSIDE PHOENIX

In the United States of 2003, the days of breezing into an airport thirty minutes before departure were over. My flight to Phoenix was scheduled to leave at 10:15 a.m. Seven in the morning found me already arriving at the airport. This was a Saturday, only a few days after New Year's Day, and even sixteen months after the horror of 9/11, security at Las Vegas's Mc-Carran Airport was very tight.

In the terminal, frustrated people queued up in long lines. Open your luggage. Empty your carry-on. Take off your belt, take off your shoes, lift up your arms, step over there.

It took me two hours to get through check-in and the various security procedures. This put me at the Southwest Airlines gate an hour before the departure time for my flight to Phoenix. Young National Guardsmen were everywhere with combat boots and M16s.

Flying has never bothered me. For six years during the 1990s I worked as a flight paramedic for a large emergency helicopter service based out of the Methodist Medical Center in the Oak Cliff area of Dallas, Texas. That's where the movie theater is where Lee Harvey Oswald hid out after shooting JFK. It's also the hometown of my favorite guitarist, Stevie Ray Vaughan. Eventually I became flight program director for another Dallas helicopter service. I have responded to hundreds of calls as a helicopter paramedic, maybe a thousand. I was the chief flight paramedic at Waco,

Texas, called in by the ATF to chopper out injured agents during the Branch Davidian siege. I've had my share of bumpy rides.

And, flying Southwest was far safer than riding my Harley down half the streets in North Vegas. Still, I was anxious.

Forget about the German shepherds and teenage guardsmen with automatic weapons inside the airport—I was nervous before I even left home. I'm not real good at job interviews. I can take charge of a bloody accident scene with body parts strewn across a freeway, but put me in a chair and start asking me about my accomplishments and hobbies and I start stuttering and sweating.

The cold-temperature sciences may very well be a lively and exciting field to be a part of, but I have seen corpses "down" in the Nevada desert for hours that had more color in their faces than Charles Platt's did. He was sickly looking with sunken eyes and a yellow discoloration to his skin. He also trembled constantly. The paramedic in me registered that this man wasn't getting all the nutrients he needed. Charles Platt seemed like a hepatitis-positive fish whose gills were flapping their last gasps on land.

A crudely drawn sign quivered in Charles's jaundiced hands. The words resembled my name enough for me to recognize it, but the sign looked like it had been scribbled by a disturbed, messy child.

Charles's eyes darted around, as if on the lookout for danger. He turned slowly, the way a man twenty years older would, and introduced a man he was with as "our chief financial officer and vice president, Michael Riskin."

If meeting Charles Platt made me want to run and fetch the man a wheelchair and an IV, meeting Michael Riskin made me want to run and fetch a cop. Riskin was just about the sleaziest-looking person I had ever met. He easily could have made a living bouncing around the various *Law & Order* and *CSI* shows playing "Criminal #1."

Riskin seemed older than Platt, between sixty and sixty-five. He was of medium height, with a spare tire around his belly. His hair was greasy black streaked with gray, his face coarse and covered in pockmarks. I'm a big Rolling Stones fan and it struck me that Michael Riskin looked a bit like Keith Richards, only rougher. Riskin out-Keithed Keith, if that's possible.

Though respectively sickly and greasy looking, Charles Platt and Michael Riskin both greeted me with warm smiles and were very pleasant. I've learned not to judge people based on their appearances. Both men wanted me to feel welcome and comfortable, and I appreciated that.

They led me outside the Phoenix Sky Harbor Airport to the Alcor vehicle, a late-1990s Chevy Suburban. I noticed a Boston Red Sox license plate on the front bumper. Interesting. That was Ted Williams's team.

Charles took the wheel, while Riskin sat in the passenger seat. As a driver, passenger, or bouncing body in the back, I'd gone off the road in a rocketing ambulance a few times. I'd crash-landed inside stalled helicopters that fell out of the sky like bricks. It took a lot to scare me, but still, no experience inside a moving vehicle had terrified me as much as that car ride with Charles Platt! Before we even left the parking lot, Charles was driving like a maniac. He drove way too fast, his hands—and thus the wheel and the whole car—vibrated and jerked as we raced along.

I kept my silence. First impressions and all. I felt I couldn't just say, "Hi, I'm here for the job and, by the way, why are you driving like a lunatic?"

In the passenger seat, Riskin was perfectly calm. I couldn't believe it. Maybe he was so used to driving with Charles he was completely desensitized. We made an odd threesome: Charles, tearing the hell out of the road and trembling like a ninety-year-old palsy sufferer; Riskin, serenely gazing out the passenger window; and me in the backseat, hanging on for dear life, trying to remember the last time I went to church.

Charles made light, how-was-your-flight chitchat. Camelback Mountain was inching by. I talked about my dad living near Phoenix and how much I loved the landscape, how much I wanted to live there. It was true. I did love the Phoenix area, especially north of the city.

Charles went on and on about how glad they were to see me and how they needed a professional like me to help Alcor interact with hospital staff and other medical professionals.

After twenty white-knuckled minutes of high-speed near misses, we arrived at the Alcor facility in Scottsdale. Overall, Phoenix is very pretty and clean, but Scottsdale is like the Beverly Hills of Phoenix—even prettier, even cleaner. There's a lot of money in Scottsdale.

Alcor's facility was located in a huge industrial park southeast of the small Scottsdale Airport, nestled between light-industrial businesses that didn't need walk-in traffic to survive, like the furniture reupholsterer on one side. There was uniformity in the single-story architecture, anonymity in the stucco facades. The only feature that distinguished one front from the next was which particular shade of soft blue, rusty red, or adobe orange each was painted.

Alcor's front was light blue, with tidy desert landscaping composed of rocks, gravel, short prickly shrubs, and lonely cactus plants. In fact, Alcor's building at 7895 East Acoma Drive was, if anything, special in that it was not special at all. From the outside, it was just another business.

The main front door was glass, darkened to the point of being opaque. On the upper right-hand corner of the building, printed in dark blue letters, was the simple word "Alcor." If I didn't know what Alcor stood for, I wouldn't have had the foggiest idea what went on behind that dark door.

I wasn't the only one thankful that our drive was over. Charles became noticeably relaxed as we walked up the concrete path and approached the door. He and Riskin both seemed relieved to be back at home base.

Charles pulled out a set of keys to unlock the door. He may have been calmer than he was back in the airport, but his hands were still trembling as if he had just downed a triple shot of espresso.

I noticed two cameras perched in high corners of the building, aimed down at the front yard. As Charles opened the door, a buzzer went off.

No one's going to sneak up on these fellows, I thought.

I followed them into the building and noticed a couple of rows of eight-by-ten photographs mounted on the wall to my left. There were probably twenty of them in total, some in color, others in black and white. I asked Charles about the pictures.

He told me these were some of the people in cryonic suspension here at Alcor. Unlike most Alcor members, these were allowing Alcor to disclose their identities for the purposes of publicity and recruitment.

The reality of what Alcor did struck me. These people's bodies were frozen, somewhere in this building, in the hopes of one day being revived. What kind of people signed up for that? I studied the pictures.

Many of the photos were of smiling, pleasant-looking elderly people. Some were old wedding pictures. Others were yellowing portraits of military men in uniform. One young man with long, curly hair was holding a bass guitar. Charles pointed him out as if he was famous, but I didn't know the name: Randall Robertson. Charles told me Randall had suffered from several illnesses after contracting AIDS from a blood transfusion.

Beneath each photograph was a brass plate engraved with dates, like on a tombstone: "1962–1998" and such. Underneath those numbers were the words "First Life Cycle."

I asked Charles what that meant.

Charles smiled and explained that Alcor did not consider these people dead; they had simply finished their first life cycle. Now Alcor was looking after them until they could be reanimated into their second life cycle. They weren't deceased, they were merely suspended. Alcor referred to them as patients.

Each brass plate also had the letter "A" engraved on it, followed by a four-digit number, such as "A-2051."

Once a person was awarded full membership at Alcor, Charles said, he or she was assigned one of those A-numbers. The A stood for Alcor. The following four digits were the cryonics equivalent of a social security number. Charles indicated that the number would follow the person around for hundreds of years. Most Alcorians, as he called them, valued their privacy. Those who did not wish their names to be made public were referred to only by their A-number.

One of the pictures was of a very severe-looking Middle Eastern man whose name was listed as FM 2030.

I asked Charles what FM stood for.

"Futureman," Charles said. "That's his name. Futureman thought he'd be reanimated by the year 2030 so he could enjoy his one hundredth birthday. Hence the number."

But something had caught my eye on top of the short divider wall in front of me. At first it looked like a trophy but then . . . *Cool!* I thought. *An Emmy Award!*

I went straight for it. I had never seen one in person and wanted to check it out. It had been awarded to a Dick Clair for writing on *The Carol Burnett Show* in 1978.

Charles smiled paternally, like he took vicarious pleasure in Dick's accomplishment. I looked over at Riskin. He also flashed me a proud smile. Charles said Alcor was looking after Dick's Emmy Award until the day he would reanimate and reclaim it.

Noticing the impression the Emmy Award had on me, Charles started rattling off a list of what he claimed were celebrity Alcor members, including Larry Flynt and his late wife, Althea, casino zillionaire Don Laughlin, and Walter Matthau's son, Charlie; Timothy Leary had been a member until just before his death; Peter Sellers and Walt Disney had both expressed interest to Alcor's cryonic predecessors; and, Charles claimed, Michael Jackson had made contact with Alcor as well. That was quite a lineup.

The Emmy was blanketed in a layer of dust, and I thought, *You might want to clean that off before Dick reanimates.* There was a fax machine and Xerox copier behind the short divider wall, and the only spots on those machines not covered in dust were the buttons, which were smudgy with black fingerprints. I noticed stacks of teetering boxes in the corners of the room. I left my handprints in the dust next to the Emmy as I turned away from the divider wall.

Riskin excused himself and disappeared down a hallway. Charles led me to a small glass table in the middle of the lobby. We sat down opposite each other.

Charles told me that Alcor was very protective about its procedures. Other cryonics organizations were jealous, he said, and would love to get their hands on Alcor's secret formulas. The less "outsiders" knew about what went on inside Alcor, the better. I was being given a very unique opportunity, Charles told me.

Charles outlined the history of Alcor to me, elaborating on the techniques they used to cryo-protect their patients. I was struck by how well spoken Charles was on the subject of cryonics. In this area, he seemed like a real smart guy.

I was distracted, though, by the clutter on the tabletop. In particular, my eye was drawn to a Domino's Pizza box sitting on the table between us. It was too early for lunch, so unless folks around Alcor ordered pizza for breakfast, that box had been sitting there overnight at least. The glass tabletop was fingerprint city, covered with crumbs, dust, and greasy smudges. I didn't see any napkins. Instead, there were several computer magazines smeared with tomato sauce, scattered willy-nilly around the table.

It's a good thing their patients are dead before they get wheeled in, I mused, half expecting to see a cockroach saunter across the table picking pepperoni out of its teeth. Charles didn't excuse the mess. There was no quick, embarrassed expression of "Sorry, but we're awfully busy around here." So this must be S.O.P. No big deal, though. I chalked it up to these guys' being the absentminded genius types.

Riskin entered the lobby with another man trailing behind him. I stood up as Riskin introduced me to "Alcor's president and CEO, Dr. Jerry Lemler."

A little short and a little pudgy, Jerry had thin, graying hair and a thick, graying beard that hung three or four inches below his chin. He wore dark-framed glasses and appeared to be in his early fifties. With his eyes cast down over his belly and toward the floor, Jerry Lemler greeted me with a very timid "Hello."

My grandfather used to tell me you can judge a man's character by his handshake. If that was true, Alcor president and CEO Dr. Jerry Lemler might have been the weakest man alive.

Charles cut short the small talk, suggesting we begin my tour of the facility. Riskin agreed and the two boxed Lemler right out of our little tour group. Trailing behind the three of us now, Lemler quietly suggested that maybe we could all grab lunch before they took me back to the airport. Without looking back, Charles said, "Maybe, if we have time, Jerry."

It was clear to me that these two didn't respect or like Lemler and that they sure didn't want him accompanying us on the tour. The stiff arm to Lemler was so well choreographed, I thought, that Platt and Riskin must have done it to him before. If Lemler noticed the slight, he didn't speak up.

Charles led me down a hallway, then another, deep into the belly of Alcor. The facility was large and I quickly became disoriented. Charles began the tour by showing me the Alcor operating room. The OR was square, about twenty-five feet per side. The walls were painted a clinical white. It looked like a typical small surgical suite except for the hard white plastic mortician's table crouched in the middle of the room where a standard operating table would normally be. That seemed appropriate, since this was a room dedicated to operating on, well, dead people. Unlike standard operating tables, mortician's tables have high walls on both sides to funnel blood down and away from the body during autopsies. Two large surgical lights towered above. They were harsh, where-were-you-on-the-night-of-August-16th-type lights. As I stood at the foot of the mortician's table, I glanced to my left and noticed several roller pumps commonly used in hospital surgical suites to pump blood or medicine through the body.

To the immediate left of the mortician's table was a clear box made of what looked like Plexiglas, about two-and-a-half feet square. Clear piping led away from it, down to a large tank of liquid nitrogen. Inside the box was a piece of metal hardware I recognized as a halo, which physicians use to stabilize patients with neck injuries. The patient's head is placed inside the halo, and then screws are tightened to the point where they make contact with the skull, immobilizing the head and stabilizing the neck. It looks like a medieval torture device but is very effective.

What puzzled me about this particular halo was that it was embedded inside the small Plexiglas box. *Where does the rest of the patient go?* I asked Charles about the setup. He told me it was their cephalic isolation box.

"Cephalic, as in cephalon?" I asked.

Charles nodded. Most patients wished to have only their heads cryo-suspended, Charles said, so Alcor hired a retired local surgeon to come in and decapitate them. Then the head, or cephalon, was placed into that Plexiglas box and perfused with a special formula of drugs while liquid nitrogen was simultaneously pumped in. This began the cooling process.

A little macabre to be sure, but I thought it was fascinating. That cephalic isolation box was ingenious. I asked who had designed it.

It wasn't only Charles's hands that trembled. Now his lips were twitching. The way Charles next said, "our facilities engineer, Hugh Hixon," was enough to suggest there wasn't much love lost between Charles and Hixon.

Looking at that box, though, I could tell this Hugh Hixon guy was one heck of a creative engineer. To envision the design of that box, amass the unrelated parts, build it, and then actually make it work—that was brilliant.

My appreciation of Hugh Hixon's work seemed to speed up Charles's tour. Apart from the door we had entered, there were three others leading out of the OR. One led down a short hallway to a restroom, another led to a small storeroom, and the third led to the lab area.

Given the state of the front reception area, I opted not to visit Alcor's bathroom. I told Charles I didn't have to "hit the cephalon" just yet, but he didn't laugh.

Trembling, Charles broke out his keys once more and unlocked the storeroom door. Its shelves were packed full with hospital supplies. In fact, Alcor seemed better stocked than many major hospital emergency rooms I had worked in. Apparently, money wasn't an issue where supplies were concerned. There was everything in there from sutures to syringes, needles to scalpels. I recognized a vaginal speculum on one of the shelves, an instrument used by gynecologists. I couldn't imagine why they needed one of those at Alcor. There were also intravenous solutions with use-by dates that, curiously, had expired years before.

We entered what Alcor called the dry lab. Like the front lobby, the dry lab was cluttered with cardboard boxes. Whatever—Einstein was a slob, right? Black plastic Pelican storage cases, popular among campers and survivalists because they are watertight and sturdy, were stacked to the ceiling.

Charles told me they stored all of their transport team equipment in the Pelican cases. I asked if I could look inside. Charles appeared happy that I was taking an interest.

He chose one and opened it. Inside were at least fifty ziplock bags filled with vials of drugs. The bags were numbered with a red marker, "1, 2, 3," etc. When I asked Charles why the bags were numbered this way he told me that most of their emergency transport team members were volunteers. These were the people who went to hospitals and homes when Alcor members had deanimated, to begin the suspension process. Though they were all dedicated Alcorians, Charles said, they were not trained medical personnel. He joked that most of them had no idea how to pronounce the names of the drugs in those baggies, never mind what they were used for.

Alcor had found it easier to simply label the bags and instruct the volunteers to inject the drugs in numerical order. Meanwhile, Riskin was poking around the insides of the Pelican case quizzically. It was obvious that he, like the average Alcor volunteer, did not know much about the contents.

I examined several of these baggies. Oddly, I noticed that all of the drugs were expired, just like the intravenous solutions back in the storeroom. I thought to myself, *I wonder if the FDA or DEA would have a problem with these drugs being expired. Then again, these drugs are being administered into the deceased, so—but wait, if Alcor considers their patients to be alive, shouldn't they provide drugs that haven't expired and thus lost their potency?*

It was a wild circle of logic. I wondered which government agencies oversaw these types of organizations. Frankly, the frontiers-of-science mystique really intrigued me. Somehow, despite all the oddities I was encountering, and a few early alarm bells, I was sort of digging this place.

We made our way through another door into the wet lab. There was a large restaurant-style sink divided into three basins with a water sprayer dangling over it. Opposite the silver sink were several industrial-size refrigerators with stainless-steel doors. Everything was sheathed in reflective metal, very futuristic looking.

Charles opened one of the refrigerators and said this was where Alcor kept its temperature-sensitive drugs. I stuck my head into the cold. Again, most of the drugs were expired. I also noticed several metal trays full of a drug called Diprivan. (Coincidentally, this was the same drug that early press reports said was found in Michael Jackson's home afer his death in June 2009.)

Diprivan is a milky white liquid usually kept in twenty-milliliter glass containers. It is a sedative-hypnotic agent. It puts someone out but not totally out, sedating them and at the same time clouding their memory so they don't remember anything. But what does a company whose patients are already pronounced dead by the time they get them into their OR need with a drug that sedates them and then fogs their memory? As Charles was shutting the refrigerator door, something else caught my eye.

"Wait," I said. "Why do you have that?"

Charles closed the refrigerator door, muttering something about pharmacology being out of his element. Riskin seemed to be intently studying his shoes. I had made Charles nervous and now I was sensing that he was by nature a paranoid person. I didn't want to push it, but I remained curious about what I had seen.

The drug I had noticed was called Vecuronium, a muscle-skeletal paralytic, another powerful drug used by physicians, especially anesthesiologists, as well as senior paramedics. In the field, Vecuronium is indicated for patients who need to be intubated. That's when a tube is placed directly into the trachea to help a patient breathe. When Vecuronium is administered, the patient becomes paralyzed within seconds. This allows the physician or paramedic to intubate the trachea without the patient choking, gagging, vomiting, and fighting like hell to the point of endangering himself. As you can imagine, being intubated while conscious is a horrific experience. The drugs used as paralytics must be highly potent.

In the wrong hands, though, Vecuronium is deadly. During my tenure as a paramedic I had had to administer Vecuronium to dozens of patients and it scared me sick every time. If you inject someone with Vecuronium and then do not have the equipment and training to breathe for them immediately, you've killed them.

The fact that Alcor stored sedatives was curious, but—paralytics? What would a company that deals with dead people need with drugs that will stop a patient from breathing within seconds of being administered?

Charles turned to me, clasping his hands together in a trembling image of prayer, and asked, "Would you like to see where we keep our patients?"

It was the icing on the cake. So to speak. Isn't that what everyone on this tour really wanted to see? *Step this way to the coolers, folks! Just past the gift shop.*

We walked back through the OR, past a set of wall lockers, down a hallway, and arrived at a door. This place was a maze. Charles flipped on a light and announced that we were standing in the Cool-Down Bay. There was a large ice machine against the wall. That made sense.

Charles explained that after a patient's head was removed, perfused with Alcor's cryo-protectant chemicals, and initially cooled in the OR's cephalic isolation box, they drilled two burr holes into the skull and slid in microphones to monitor the brain with a computer rig they called the Crackphone. A hook-type handle was installed into the neck for easier handling—from that point on they carried the patient's head around, up-side down, like a bowling-ball bag.

The head was then lugged into the Cool-Down Bay and lowered into a waist-high cylindrical cooling tank called the LR-40. They used duct tape to seal the LR-40's lid, and then liquid nitrogen was pumped in for the cool-down to −321 Fahrenheit.

Before I could ask about the ominous-sounding Crackphone, Charles fumbled with his keys once more and unlocked the gray door at the opposite end of the room. I noticed another camera overhead, pointing down at the door.

"Here it is," Charles announced. "The Patient Care Bay. This is where the patients reside."

I have never in my life been the jumpy type but I almost went through the damn ceiling when I heard the thin, shrill voice call out from beyond the door.

"Who's there?"

"It's Charles. And I'm not alone."

Charles walked through the door. I followed. As I entered the Patient Care Bay, a figure appeared. I would have believed it if I were told right then that one of Alcor's patients had reanimated and was making a break for it.

Dr. R. Michael Perry was skinny. Malnutrition skinny. He reminded me of pictures I'd seen of POWs. He had his arms crossed in front of him, hugging himself, long fingers clutching bony elbows. His hair stood out at odd angles, unkempt and messy. Together with his rumpled, dirty clothes, Mike Perry gave me the impression that he had just gotten out of bed.

It was hard to estimate Mike's true height because he stood slumped over due to his hunched back. It seemed a little too perfect, a little too "Igor," but it was the God's honest truth that Mike Perry, the Alcor employee who looked after the frozen patients, was hunchbacked.

Introducing us, Charles told me that Mike was a mathematician and held multiple degrees, including a PhD in computer science. He was, Charles smilingly said, a genius.

Despite the praise, Mike just lowered his head and scurried out of the room, mumbling. I will say, for an emaciated brainiac who walked with his arms folded, Mike made good time. He was unnaturally fast and stealthy, like a lab rat that was successfully endowed with superhuman intelligence and then picked the lock on the cage. Mike was, to say the least, an eccentric guy.

As the muttering trailed off down the hallway, Charles told me Mike's title was "Caretaker of the Patient Care Bay."

I spotted a blue container on the right side of the room that resembled a big freezer chest. Mostly, though, it looked like something Dr. Frankenstein would have kept in his basement to lock up his failed experiments.

The chest was wrapped in a thick, padded chain with a heavy padlock. A confusion of wires snaked out from under its lid and ran down to some sort of electronic hub, which in turn was connected to a computer. The computer monitor displayed a graph with straight lines running through it, like an electrocardiogram monitor. Attached to one of the wires coming out of the freezer chest was a pale yellow tag with "A-1949" written on it in black marker. I recalled the A-numbers I had seen under the photos on the Alcor Wall of Fame. Actually, another A-number had been blackened out with a magic marker and A-1949 had been written beneath the crossed-out number. *Recycling the tags identifying their patients' heads?* I thought. *They must have one damn thrifty comptroller!*

I asked Charles about the container. Placing one hand on the computer monitor and leaning up against the table in frustration, Charles sighed. He explained that the CryoStar was a high-tech intermediate-temperature storage unit where patients' heads were sometimes stored midway through the freezing process. The CryoStar was intended to afford extra-careful protection while a head underwent drastic drops in temperature.

The CryoStar was giving them problems, though. Charles explained that it was designed to maintain a constant temperature down around −126 degrees Celsius (−196 degrees Fahrenheit). This was supposed to limit cracking the patient's brain, but the CryoStar was malfunctioning, randomly fluctuating plus or minus 10 degrees. Relatively speaking, this was a huge temperature swing.

"Sorry, Charles, did you say 'cracking the patient's brain'?"

"Unfortunately, that happens," Charles said. "There are two heads in the CryoStar right now," he continued. One had been a close personal friend of his. The other was patient A-1949.

"And over here, Larry, are the dewars." Charles turned my attention to a half-dozen tall, shiny metal canisters lining the left side of the room. They were highly polished reflective steel, standing more than ten feet tall and about five feet in diameter. I saw my face mirrored in them, all skewed and unreal, like in a fun-house mirror. Each sported a giant Alcor logo. The dewars looked like something out of a 1980s science fiction movie. Charles was reverential as he discussed them; the way he gushed over them, they were evidently the pride and joy of Alcor. I looked around for Riskin, to note his attitude toward the tall silver tubes, but he had disappeared.

Charles went into great detail about the dewars. I learned that the name originated with Sir James Dewar, the nineteenth-century Scottish chemist and physicist best known for his work with low-temperature phenomena. He was a professor of experimental natural philosophy at the University of Cambridge, England, in 1875, and then professor of chemistry at the Royal Institution of Great Britain in 1877, where he was appointed director of the Davy-Faraday Research Laboratory. Wow, it was as if Charles had swallowed a memory chip. He had this tour spiel down cold.

The dewar bottle was a container for storing extremely hot or cold substances. It consisted of two flasks, one inside the other, separated by a vacuum. The vacuum greatly reduced the transfer of heat, preventing a temperature change. The walls were usually made of glass because it was a poor conductor of heat, and its surfaces were lined with reflective metal to reduce the transfer of heat by radiation. Sir James's containers were most famously used in the distilling of Scotch whisky. Alcor, however, put them to quite a different use.

Bizarre as this seems now in the retelling, I learned that at Alcor, each dewar housed either four whole-body patients or a combination of whole bodies and severed heads. At the time, I was simply fascinated by the engineering behind it. Charles explained that before being placed in a dewar, a full-body patient was deposited into a sleeping bag and then suspended upside down in a pod made of sheet metal. The pod was about seven feet tall and wedge-shaped, made to a measurement one-fourth of the inside diameter of a dewar. If one stood on a ladder and looked straight down onto a dewar with the lid off, Charles said, you would see the tops of four triangular pods, "like looking down on a pizza with four slices." I had to chuckle at Charles's metaphor; it must have been deep-dish pizza.

The reason whole-body patients were placed upside down was to help protect their brains. If something catastrophic happened and there was a massive liquid nitrogen leak, the patients' heads would be the last things exposed. Made sense.

I asked how many suspended patients they had in total. Charles told me the number was in the fifties. They had designed this room very carefully. The south wall was two feet thick, concrete reinforced with steel.

"These walls were built," Charles said, "so that no one could drive a car through them, in case someone tried to break in to harm or steal the patients."

I asked about the smaller, squat silver tank on the back wall.

This was the Neuro Vault, Charles explained. After they lifted the patient's fully cooled head from the LR-40 cooling tank, they placed it into a stainless-steel container called a Neuro Can (it looked like a lobster pot to me), and that pot was placed inside the Neuro Vault for temporary storage. The dewars were the final destination for long-term storage, but it was better to open them as infrequently as possible, Charles said. It was a big, delicate job opening the dewars. There was a crane permanently mounted on the roof to muscle those big canisters around. Heads were stored in the Neuro Vault until they absolutely had to open a dewar. Charles said they also stored samples of their patients' DNA in the Neuro Vault, as well as some cat and dog heads.

"Cat and dog heads?"

"Some members want to have their pets with them when they are reanimated into their next life cycle," Charles said. Charles wasn't sure, but he thought there was a monkey brain in there, too.

"So," Charles said, clapping his hands together, "that's the tour. Hungry for lunch?"

Charles had zero perspective on exactly how funny that question sounded. After twenty-five years as a paramedic, I didn't exactly have a weak stomach where body parts were concerned. The casual way Charles talked about all this, though, was just plain odd. Still, I was impressed with his knowledge and dedication to cryonics.

Lead on, Charles, I thought. *Decapitated TV writers and monkey brains always perk up my appetite!*

As we left the Patient Care Bay, I noticed Mike Perry hugging himself and watching me from underneath the camera in the neighboring Cool-Down Bay. At some point during Charles's explanation of the dewars, Perry must have crept back in there to study me.

Charles noticed and said, "Mike is real protective of our patients."

I followed Charles through many twists and turns, back to the front lobby. On my own, I was sure I would have had a hard time finding the way out. Riskin and Lemler were silently waiting at the table still adorned with the empty pizza box. I looked over at the wall of pictures. Those pleasant folks were in the dewars now, residing between animations. I looked at bassist Randall Robertson. For some reason I pictured an Alcor technician shaving off those long, curly locks. They'd do that, right? Before they chopped off his head? Otherwise, I figured his hair would have shattered when it was brought down to −321 degrees Fahrenheit.

At lunch we talked about my background as a paramedic. Jerry Lemler was very interested in hearing about basic emergency medicine techniques.

Charles and Riskin were more interested in hearing about my experiences as chief helicopter paramedic at Waco during the siege of the Branch Davidian complex. People usually shook their heads in horror and disbelief when I told stories about the Waco siege. Charles Platt and Michael Riskin had a different attitude, though. They told me they admired the Branch Davidians for holding fast to their beliefs and standing up to the U.S. government.

I had held the brains of ATF officers in my hand, American heroes who took fifty-caliber rounds to the head from fanatical cult members ready to kill and die for their messianic leader. I had dealt with the Davidians first-hand, zealots who considered themselves prisoners of war, including their poor brainwashed children. After encountering the Branch Davidians personally, I didn't find anything in them to admire or emulate. I told Riskin and Platt exactly that. They nodded solemnly and said they respected my feelings.

Charles wanted to hear my thoughts on how to organize the Alcor emergency teams into more professional groups. They seemed aware they all gave off an odd sense to outsiders. That's where they seemed to hope I'd come in. They needed someone like me, as a bridge to the mainstream medical community.

First of all, I suggested they change the title of the job—transport team leader—they were interviewing me for. I told them that hospital personnel weren't familiar with the title, and it would give them pause. Better to call the job director of clinical services. Every hospital and ambulance company had a job with this title. It was a title doctors and nurses in an ICU would understand.

"Done," Jerry said. The other two nodded their heads.

Next I asked if the volunteers had any sort of uniform or name tags identifying them as Alcor employees. In order to work in the medical community you really need to look the part. By nature, hospital administrators are a hard-boiled, suspicious lot. They see a lot of shenanigans. You can't walk into a hospital wearing street clothes, carrying all kinds of equipment, and then ask to take possession of a deceased patient you are not even related to. You will not get a warm reception. In fact, with all the recent fears of terrorism and with babies being stolen out of nurseries, I told them, hospitals were now monitored more closely than ever.

Platt told me they had already thought of that. Alcor volunteers, he said, have made name tags that read "Organ Recovery Team."

I sat back in my chair in disbelief. Lemler and Riskin kept right on eating. "You can't do that!" I said.

In no uncertain terms, I told them they were going to get into a lot of trouble. That was misrepresentation, plain and simple. Organ recovery teams were trained professionals with a wide range of licenses and certifications. That would be like me walking into a hospital with a name tag reading "Larry Johnson, MD." I didn't go to school for that; I didn't earn that. If ICU nurses struck up a conversation with these cryonicists, they would figure out pretty quickly they were not real organ recovery personnel. Dressing up your volunteers to look professional is one thing. Misrepresentation is something else, and completely wrong. If Alcor's volunteers were caught impersonating an organ recovery team, I told them, they wouldn't be allowed into another hospital in the country. Period.

The three of them looked at each other, shocked, not knowing what to say. Finally, Jerry stammered something about that's exactly why they needed someone like me at Alcor, someone who knew how to interact with the medical community.

Okay, I thought, *so at least they do want to clean up their act, professionally speaking.*

Charles changed the subject. If I took the job, he explained, I would be free to pursue my own interests in cold-temperature research with their sister facility, Critical Care Research, in Rancho Cucamonga, California. That sounded fantastic to me. I told them that was probably the biggest reason I was interested in the job. Jerry told me I would have all of CCR's resources at my disposal, and plenty of time to participate in their current projects, or pursue my own research. I thought about that road treatment for ice storms. It sounded like awfully fulfilling work.

I would also be asked to train Alcor volunteers on emergency medical procedures, Charles said, and I'd assist their emergency response teams, transporting patients from their place of deanimation to the Alcor facility. I'd help prepare the bodies, administering drugs and assisting in the washout procedure in which the member's blood was replaced by Alcor's cryo-preservant chemicals. Then I would lend a hand in the OR during the final phases of cryo-suspension. I was intrigued, actually, wondering what all this really entailed.

"I guess more than a director of clinical services, I'd be a 'paramedic to the dead,'" I joked.

They all stopped chewing. "Oh no, Larry," Jerry Lemler said. "Those patients aren't dead. They're deanimated. Awaiting their second life cycle."

On the way to the airport, Charles flat-out asked me for a commitment. Just like that.

I already knew they were offering an employment and pay package just about equal to what I was used to as a paramedic—but without the daily physical pounding. I told Charles the truth. Alcor was definitely new, exciting, and fascinating—thus extremely appealing to a guy like me—but I would have to talk it over with Beverly. We pulled up to the curb at Sky Harbor Airport. I leaned across the seat, took hold of Charles's shivering yellow trout of a hand, and told him I would call him later. He said he'd be looking forward to it. Without looking back, I shut the door and walked into the terminal. Once inside that airport, damn if I didn't just sprint to the nearest bar and order a vodka martini.

My brain was buzzing. The unhealthy look of the Alcorians stuck out to me, from the trembling COO to the hunchbacked Keeper of the Dead. Patients. Life Cycles. Deanimation. A-1949. The heads in the CryoStar, the bodies in the dewars, the DNA samples in the Neuro Vault—floating on top of the cat heads and monkey brains. The cephalic isolation box. Fractured brains and Crackphones. The dust, the pizza box, the paralytic drugs, the vaginal speculum. Vaginal speculum?

Man, what a day!

As soon as I got home I grabbed Beverly, rushed her to one of our favorite restaurants, and blabbed about my Scottsdale adventure for two hours straight. Bev let me get it all out with only the occasional intelligent question. She's a great listener, one of the many things I have always loved about her. As I relived the day's events with her, I realized how excited I was by the prospect of working at Alcor: pioneering research on the furthest edge of modern biotech with brilliant—albeit eccentric—colleagues.

During a pause in my story, Beverly said, "You're really excited about this. And it sounds like maybe this is another type of adrenaline rush for you. Maybe you're trading the danger and excitement of paramedicine for this strange, fascinating world of cryonics."

I smiled at her. She knew me. She was right. "Is that bad?" I asked.

Beverly laughed and said, "At this point, anything that gets you off the street as a paramedic is okay with me."

They were some strange birds, these Alcorians. But bizarre as they were, what if they were really onto something? I mean, we're talking about immortality. They told me I would be free to pursue my own research. They had all these world-leading scientists from MIT, Cambridge, and UC Berkeley advising them, even a scientific advisor to the White House, all of them publicly supporting Alcor. And they certainly were well equipped and well funded. Sure, they were messy and disorganized—and isolated—but that's why they were looking to hire someone like me. Honestly, the more I thought about it, the more intriguing it became. It was the only job I had run across that just might fill my need for excitement. It was electric.

Best of all, though, Alcor was right outside Phoenix, literally a few miles from where my dad lived. That part of it was almost too good to be true.

I asked Beverly what I should do. She laughed again.

"As if anyone could ever tell you what to do." Bev smiled. "It's your call, Larry. But you know, in my book, any change right now would be a good change. I hate seeing you so beat-up all the time. And you know how much I love Phoenix."

We sat in silence for a moment.

"Still," Beverly said, "it's your decision. Whatever you decide, I'm behind you."

———————

Early the next morning, after reading through the fine print of Alcor's job offer, I fired up my Harley and took a good, long ride through the desert. My head cleared but the excitement remained. When I got home, Beverly asked what I had decided. I smiled at her and shouted, "What the hell!" By living in Las Vegas we had learned to gamble. We'd spin the wheel and see what happened. Beverly was even happier than I thought she would be. We danced around the kitchen, feeling like a couple of teenagers. We did it—we were leaving Las Vegas, on our way to a new beginning. Hey, if nothing else, it sure wouldn't be boring!

THREE

WELCOME TO ALCOR

Millions long for immortality who don't know what to do with themselves on a rainy Sunday afternoon.
—SUSAN ERTZ, AUTHOR, *Anger in the Sky*

"Alcor? Aren't they the ones that freeze people?"

Our new apartment manager was a no-nonsense, middle-age woman. Beverly and I liked her a lot.

"Well, yes, it's called cryonics," I said.

"What will you be doing there, exactly?" She squinted at me past the cigarette in her mouth.

"Research," I told her. She raised an eyebrow at that, so I added, "Just playing with test tubes. Nothing too creepy. I won't be mucking around with the corpses or anything. Ha-ha. Ha."

I hadn't anticipated how "normal" people would react to hearing that I worked at Alcor. I guessed I'd get used to it. Plus, I haven't exactly always needed the approval of strangers to make me feel like I was doing the right thing. I had spent most of my life in New Mexico, Arizona, and Texas: I'll do my thing, you do your thing, live 'n' let live, don't tread on each other.

For his part, my dad didn't waste any time taking advantage of Beverly and me being in town. He came over to our place the day we arrived and then spent the entire weekend with us, with the exception of going home now and then to tend to his wife. My dad's second wife, Mary Jane, was very ill and couldn't leave home much. He never complained about taking care of her—I knew he loved Mary Jane dearly—but I could tell he was both comforted and delighted to have Bev and me living so close to him. Beverly got on great with Mary Jane. Maybe, I thought, we could help take some of the strain off my dad.

Dad took me aside that first day and said, "Larry, one of the biggest regrets in my life is not being able to spend much time with you when you were growing up."

"I feel the same way, Dad," I said. "But now that can change."

Dad smiled. "We got a lot of time to make up for."

We hugged each other. It was a really nice moment. Dad had brought a guitar over to our apartment. He's a fantastic musician. In between helping us unpack boxes, Dad would pick up the guitar and sing us a song. Who knew unpacking could be fun?

Bev was equally excited to be living in the Phoenix area. Each time we had visited my father in the past, Beverly had gone on for a week afterward about how clean and pretty Phoenix was. She was going to love this.

Our two-bedroom apartment was in North Scottsdale near the Princess Resort, on the north side of the Scottsdale Airport, about two miles from Alcor, maybe a ten-minute drive. It is hard to live anywhere in Scottsdale without being close to a golf course. North Scottsdale is a haven for wealthy retired couples. Although Beverly and I were far from retirement age, and even farther from wealthy, the area appealed to us because it was quiet and well kept. Our apartment was modest but comfortable.

On the morning of January 26, several days after our move, I sat down at my computer with my usual cup of coffee. Beverly continued to unpack the endless stacks of cardboard boxes. Following my morning routine of checking my e-mail, I decided to look around on the Internet for more information about Alcor.

Before my tour and job interview, when I had researched Alcor, I had been immediately taken with the cryobiology side at CCR, and impressed by the scientists on Alcor's board of advisors. After the tour, I was so excited by the prospect of living close to my dad, and intrigued with the fascinating things I had seen inside Alcor, that I hadn't dug any deeper for more on Alcor.

Nowadays people often ask me why I went to work there in the first place. Looking back, maybe I would've hesitated had I been exposed to the weirder side of cryonics—if anything could've been weirder than that tour. To me, though, the science and creative engineering were fascinating. How close to actually being able to do all this were they? Where did science meet fiction? How did Hugh Hixon concoct those brilliant machines? What if we really could be reawakened and see what things are like a couple hundred years from now? And, I imagined, what if one day it could be possible to "cryonically suspend" and actually save patients like those who had died on me so tragically in the street? That was awfully exciting to me.

And, the truth is, daily life as a paramedic had sucked me right back in as soon as I returned to Vegas from Scottsdale. When I thought about Alcor during those quick three weeks before Beverly and I moved, I put that new and exciting job opportunity up against feeling terribly burnt out as a paramedic. I hated the look in Beverly's eye when my back would spasm, when I would give her curt answers about how my day on the ambulance was. Alcor was a lifeline out of that grind in Vegas. Lots of people would have been grossed out by the reality of cryonic procedures, but that kind of stuff rarely bothered me. I'd worked with that kind of physical, anatomical reality all my adult life.

Plus, I've always been impulsive. As Beverly had guessed, Alcor implicitly held out the promise to fulfill my need for high levels of daily excitement. It was sort of like going to work at a high-tech circus, but with the added hope of a real contribution to modern medicine via the promise of mainstream cryobiological research at CCR. As a teenager, I didn't always check to see how deep a narrow gorge was before I jumped it on a motorcycle. I suppose that that recklessness has always been a blessing and a curse for me. It's helped me save lives but it's also gotten me into trouble.

One of the first things I found while Googling Alcor that morning was a Web site called CryoNet.org, an online bulletin board for cryonicists. I found postings dating back to the 1980s. There was everything from nerdy pseudoscientific babble debating cryonic suspension techniques to lengthy descriptions of what these lonely people had had for breakfast to head-freezing jokes to name-calling accounts of arguments with morticians and cryobiologists. Some were intelligent and well-written; some were infantile and defensive. Others were downright shocking, revealing some cryonicists to be troubled, paranoid people.

One posting read:

> . . . just as the animal whose smell is wrong is savagely bitten and forced away, so too do we cryonicists feel the cruel slings and arrows of humanity.

In response to this, a man named Michael Darwin had posted a piece he titled "The Lone Wolf." Darwin wrote:

> I kill dogs and I hurt them. It is my job and I was made to do it. To do it well I have had to love them, and to know them better and deeper than most men ever know each other. I respect them more than I do most humans, and I've loved more of them than I have human beings. . . . And, like it or not, being at odds with the mainstream can kill you. I am a homosexual, an atheist, a manic depressive, possess an aesthetic sense and worldview most people find unbearable, and am brilliant at sensing the softest, most vulnerable part in a person and using that to cause enormous pain.

Michael Darwin didn't sound like much fun at parties—or someone I'd ask to dog-sit for me. I knew cryonics drew fringe people but this Darwin guy and some of the others sounded awfully disturbed. The most surprising thing, though, was the sheer number of postings. There were thousands of them, and this was only on a single Web site. I found a similar site called Cryonics Café. I remember thinking these people seemed to have no lives outside of cryonics.

Oh well. Couldn't be any worse than dealing with Branch Davidians and North Vegas gangbangers.

Three days later, I was out of bed by five and ready for my first day of work at Alcor. Charles had called me earlier in the week and told me that he would be driving down to Phoenix from his home in northern Arizona to join me on my first day. He asked me to be at Alcor between nine and ten.

I arrived at Alcor at precisely nine o'clock. In a strip of commercial storefronts, Alcor was located on the far right as I faced the building. Relative to its industrial park neighbors, Alcor occupied a very large space, taking up what would normally have rented as three separate properties. On the left, its closest neighbor was the furniture reupholsterer. On the far right, a twenty-foot-wide asphalt driveway and parking area led around to the rear of the building.

The only other vehicle in the front parking lot was the Chevy Suburban sporting the Boston Red Sox license plate. Since that vehicle belonged to the company itself, I figured I had been first to arrive at work this morning. I tried the front door anyway. It was locked. I settled back in my truck to wait, a ZZ Top CD keeping me company.

Within minutes, a small sedan pulled into the parking lot. The driver was a young woman in her mid-twenties with a very pretty face. I wasn't sure what color her hair was at first because she was wearing a crash helmet. It was a white plastic bicycle helmet. She didn't see me. As I watched, she turned off her car and removed the helmet, placing it on the seat next to her. Then she exited her car, shook out long brown hair that fell to her slim waist, and marched quickly across the parking lot toward the front door. She had a runner's build and in fact rushed along as if she were being chased, moving in straight lines and turning sharply on her heels like a robot set to fast-forward. The young woman unlocked the door and disappeared into the Alcor facility.

The whole helmet thing had caught me off guard. As I sat there, wondering what the heck she was doing wearing a bicycle helmet while driving her car, I missed the opportunity to introduce myself—and to get inside my new place of employment.

Now that I knew someone was in there, I decided to try the front door again. As I approached, I was struck again with the quiet anonymity of

Alcor's building. Anything could be going on in there and who would know it? That simple word, Alcor, on the front of the building made it sound more like a power tool distributor or aluminum siding manufacturer than a place where they'd lop off someone's head and drop it into a vat of liquid nitrogen. I chuckled at that thought. This was going to take some getting used to.

The door was still locked. *Knock-knock.* No answer. *Knock-knock-knock.* The young woman seemed to have been completely swallowed up inside. I knocked a little louder. Then I banged. Then I started feeling foolish.

I looked up at the two cameras I had noticed during my tour. I waved at them, pointed at myself, pointed at the front door, and waited, but still, nothing.

I looked down the driveway on the right-hand side of the building. Bordering the asphalt was a thin landscaped area, maybe five feet wide. High, scraggly bushes were planted so close together that you couldn't see through them. They were there for privacy, I assumed, but didn't seem long for this world.

I walked down the driveway to the rear of the building. There was another parking lot back there, much smaller than the front lot. The back of Alcor's building was primed for deliveries with a large metal roll-up door serving as a loading dock. To the left of this was a back door with a placard reading: "NOTICE—CHEMICAL HAZARD."

The small parking lot was shaped like a shallow bowl so that rainwater would flow into a drain at the center. A discoloration on the asphalt caught my eye. It was a trail of chalky white residue, originating right outside Alcor's back door and terminating at the storm drain. I could see similar drains behind several neighboring businesses down the strip, but the only one with a residue trail was the one outside Alcor's back door.

Whatever the ghostly stuff was, it had apparently been borne by a liquid, and most of it had flowed down the drain. It didn't take Sherlock Holmes to deduce that someone had taken a step out Alcor's back door and upended a large quantity of liquid that carried the white stuff in it.

I decided not to bang on the back door, partly because it would be an odd way to greet a new colleague, by sneaking around the back of the building, and partly because I didn't want to get that chalky stuff on my shoes. I returned to the front entrance.

Back at the dark glass door, I cupped my hands and peered inside. I could just make out the eight-by-ten photographs I had seen during my initial visit. There was Futureman, staring at me from Alcor's Wall of Fame, stoically waiting for the year 2030.

A shadow congealed and approached. As the spectral figure drew near, I recognized Mike Perry, Alcor's hunchbacked patient caretaker. All the knocking in the world hadn't drawn anyone out but once I started snooping around, Mike materialized. I motioned for him to unlock the door. It took a moment for him to recognize me. He cracked the door a few inches and stood there, squinting. Once again, Mike's hair looked as if he had just woken up. His frayed clothes reminded me of the hand-me-downs hospitals kept on hand to give to the homeless after a night of sobering up in the ER.

"Good morning, Mike," I said. "I'm Larry Johnson. I hope you remember me. Today's my first day at Alcor and Charles Platt told me he'd meet me here around nine o'clock."

Without a word, Mike stepped backward. He watched my every move as I walked by him and sat down at the small table in the lobby. Just as on my earlier visit, an empty Domino's Pizza box lay atop the table. Again, greasy fingerprints were smudged across the glass tabletop and stray science magazines. I wondered if this was the same mess or a recurring one. I looked up for Mike, half ready to question him about it, but he had vanished. I noticed yet another video camera high up in a corner. They sure were serious about security at Alcor. Although Mike had disappeared, I had the feeling I wasn't alone. I'd have sworn someone was watching the camera feed at that exact moment.

At 9:30 a.m. someone else finally arrived. It wasn't easy to see who it was because of my angle to the door, but sure enough, when the person fumbled with his keys to unlock the front door, I figured it was Charles.

Smiling, Charles said in his English accent, "Larry, I am so glad to see you are here."

He still had that cold and clammy handshake I remembered from our first meeting. Under his arm he carried a beat-up khaki travel bag a little smaller than a human head.

Charles smiled again and repeated, "Yes, I am so glad to see you are here."

I followed Charles deeper into the building, down a hallway I hadn't seen during my tour three weeks earlier. We entered a closet with a desk crammed into it. Charles sat his khaki bag down, squeezed behind the desk, and told me this was his office.

Filing cabinets lined a few of the walls, making the tiny room feel even smaller, and there were metal shelves on the other walls, messily crowded with office supplies. Charles shared his tiny room with a small army of Wite-Out bottles, hundreds of pens and pencils, dozens of staplers, and piles upon piles of cryonics literature. Alcor pamphlets spilled off the shelves and pooled on the floor. More stacks of Alcor's ubiquitous cardboard boxes were teetering in every corner. Like the rest of the Alcor Life Extension Foundation facility, this room was a wreck.

A computer monitor covered in dust sat on a shelf, its screen divided into four quadrants. Two of the views were of Alcor's front yard—closed-circuit feeds from the two cameras I had seen outside. The other two quadrants showed high-angled shots of interior hallways and doors. Cables ran from the screen down to an oversized video recording machine.

Charles motioned toward the door. "Come on, Larry, I'll show you where your office is." I had barely enough room to turn around. *Great,* I thought, chuckling to myself. *The COO already has dibs on the broom closet, so what does the clinical director get? A bathroom stall?*

Most of the lights in the building were still off, so Charles flicked switches as we walked down a hallway. On the left-hand side of the corridor I noticed a cubicle office with a small desk and computer facing the open door. The computer was off, the room's occupant not at work yet.

We came to a large open area with two desks, many tall filing cabinets, and more of the brown cardboard boxes stacked everywhere. The walls were a clinical off-white and the floor was covered in what looked like dirty gray tiles.

"Here we are," Charles said. "This will be your new office. It used to be our marketing area."

"Charles," I asked, "how do you market something like cryonics to the average person who might find it, well, a little bizarre?"

Charles laughed good-naturedly and mimicked a call: "Hi there, Mr. Peters, my name is Charles and please don't hang up because I'd like to talk to you this morning about a unique opportunity to freeze your head!"

I thought that was pretty funny. I immediately liked the way Charles was able to poke fun at the strangeness surrounding cryonics. I also appreciated the fact, as I interpreted it, that he was trying to put me at ease.

"Good question!" Charles continued. "Let me know if you have any ideas. Our marketing department did not last long at all. Not every idea around here is brilliant."

I peeked into one of the cardboard boxes. Sure enough, it was filled with promotional merchandise. There were rulers, notebooks, and pencils stamped with the slanty, futuristic-looking Alcor logo, along with faux leather binders, T-shirts, sweatshirts, you name it. I saw coffee mugs printed with an image of a burning phoenix rising up from the ashes over the slogan, *Alcor: If you can't beat 'em, outlive 'em.*

My Alcor promotional binder with the signature slanted logo.

One thing I really liked about the room was that it had nice big windows and a clear glass door facing the street. Desert landscaping always made me feel at home. Even better, when I rode my Harley to work, I would be able to keep an eye on it through that window.

Like cops, paramedics develop a sort of sixth sense as a result of years and years of working in dangerous neighborhoods. As I was looking out through the clear glass door, I got the feeling someone else was in the room. I turned and sure enough, there was Mike Perry standing in the corridor, quietly listening to our conversation. He held a large transparent plastic bowl and was stirring something in it that looked like green Cool Whip. I smiled at him. Mike swallowed a spoonful of the creamy green stuff, mumbled a few unintelligible words, and shuffled off.

"Charles," I said, "is Mike all right? I mean . . . um . . . "

Charles sighed. After ten minutes at Alcor I was already questioning the resident oddities. "I know what you mean, Larry, but Mike is fine," Charles said. "Like most cryonicists, he's just a little off center."

"What's that he's eating?" I asked.

"Mike is very health conscious," Charles said. "Preserving the body for cryonic suspension is of utmost importance to us all. The healthier we are at the time of our deanimation in this life cycle, the better our chances for a successful reanimation in the next. You won't find many Alcorian smokers," he cited as an example. "For some of us," Charles continued, "that means a special diet and lots of supplements. That green concoction is Mike's homemade vegetable mix. It's the only thing he eats. I'm not sure if he makes it from scratch or gets it from Saul Kent's vitamin company, but he says it provides him with all the nutrients and vitamins he needs."

Saul Kent, I knew from the Alcor Web site, was one of the directors of my new company. He also sold vitamins through his "Life Extension Foundation," separate from Alcor.

By the looks of him, though, I thought Mike could use a little variety in his diet.

"You'll get used to it," Charles said. "You'll get used to Mike."

"I am so glad to see you are here." Now it was Alcor's president and CEO, Dr. Jerry Lemler, standing in the doorway, addressing me in his meek little voice. It didn't escape me that Jerry greeted me with the exact same words as Charles had. I got the feeling Charles and Jerry weren't sure I was going to show up at Alcor that first day. Maybe there was a company pool going. From the way these two were acting, it seemed like the smart money might have been against me.

Jerry held out his hand and, unlike the first time we had met, this time he made eye contact. "Come see me as soon as you get settled in, Larry. I've got something very exciting for you to get started on." Jerry winked at me. Then he looked at Charles, lowered his head, and marched out of the room. Jerry certainly seemed more relaxed with me than he had the first time we met.

Charles put a box down and shook his head. "There he goes, President Jerry. Off to pick the lint from his navel and then bill Alcor for tweezer rental."

"Excuse me, Charles?" I said. I knew from the way Charles and Riskin had excluded Jerry from my initial tour that they worked around him, but in my professional experience, insulting a superior like this—especially to a new employee on his first day—was bizarre.

"Never mind." Charles smiled. "You'll form your own opinions about the Alcor officers soon enough."

Charles would have been quick to admit that he was not much good at physical labor. In truth, I felt like I was dragging Charles's added body weight along with the furniture he was helping me shuffle around. But he did his best and we chatted pleasantly. Charles seemed to take a paternal attitude toward me right from the start. I felt like he was looking for someone to take under his wing.

Panting from a few minutes' exertion, Charles said, "I bet Joe Hovey is here by now. Joe is our financial comptroller and accounting manager as well as a former vice president. Why don't you find him and get your paperwork started, Larry."

"Okay, Charles, will do." I think Charles mostly wanted a break from struggling with filing cabinets.

———

If this man goes down, do not try to catch him. That's what the paramedic in me thought the minute I walked into Joe Hovey's office. A balding, seriously overweight man around sixty years of age, Joe was a cardiac arrest waiting to happen.

Joe was an Alcor old-timer in charge of all financial transactions. He was the company's treasurer and secretary and, from time to time, a vice president. As I filled out federal and state tax withholding forms, Joe asked about my new apartment, how my move went, and how my wife was doing. Joe was friendly enough, but I was struck by the strange, fake-jovial tone of voice he used. He smiled the whole time I was in his office, but that smile seemed to be painted on. Like a clown's grin, his eyes didn't come along for the ride. Immediately I got the feeling that Joe was used to saying something more pleasant than what he was thinking. Combined with the fact that he must have packed about 350 pounds onto a five-foot-five frame, the whole effect was quite unsettling.

"We try to go out to lunch together every Friday." Joe smiled. "Of course, you're invited this Friday if you'd like to come."

"That'd be great, Joe, thanks."

Joe told me I'd be getting drug tested and that he'd be asking me for a urine sample soon. That would be fine with me, I told him. I had nothing to hide.

Charles was waiting for me back in my office area. As we continued rearranging the room, Charles's hands never stopped trembling. Whenever he went to pick something up he'd just about juggle it.

Soon a sixtyish-looking gentleman with white hair and thick glasses entered the room. He was wearing khaki pants and a matching khaki button-down, short-sleeve shirt.

"Look at that," Charles said sarcastically. "Only ten a.m. and already Hugh has punched in. Good morning, Hugh. Larry, this is Alcor's facilities engineer and senior board member, Hugh Hixon. Hugh, meet Larry Johnson, our new clinical director."

"It's a pleasure to meet you, Hugh," I said, extending my arm and walking toward him. "I remember you're the man behind the design of the cephalic isolation box. That device is just brilliant."

Hugh paused, staring down at my hand over the top of his glasses. With his head aimed at the ground, Hugh said, "Ah . . . um . . . er . . . "

I stood there with my hand outstretched like a fool and eventually lowered it. Hugh didn't shake my hand; he really didn't seem to know what to do.

Charles stepped in. "Hugh here has degrees in chemistry and biochemistry," Charles said. "He's been with Alcor for over twenty years and has participated in more than forty-five cryo-suspensions." Hugh shuffled his feet as Charles continued. "Before that, Hugh was in the Air Force and retired as a captain. He was a munitions officer, so careful, Larry, Hugh knows how to blow things up."

"Shut up, Platt," Hugh said. Then, still without looking me in the eye, Hugh said, "Um, okay," and left the room.

"It'll be like that for you today," Charles told me. "You're the first Alcor executive or director who's not also an Alcor member, signed up for cryonic suspension. They'll all want to check you out today."

Charles excused himself to make some phone calls. I decided to check in with Jerry Lemler to see about the project he had winked at me about.

———————

As I left my office area, half looking for Jerry's office and half just exploring, I passed that little cubicle office on the left side of the hallway again. This time the computer was turned on and whoever had been using it evidently had no qualms about looking at pornography at work. It wasn't just nude women, it was very X-rated. Close-up, deep stuff. But there was no one in the room. I quickly moved past.

As I walked the corridors, looking around, I realized that boxes were piled in the corners of nearly every room in the building. Either they ordered far more supplies than they ever needed, or they simply weren't good about unpacking. I came to an office that had a small, skinny window next to the door running from the floor to the ceiling. The lights were off inside, so when I glanced through the little window, I was surprised to see a female figure inside. There in the middle of the dark office, standing completely still, was the pretty young woman I had seen earlier in the parking lot, the crash-helmet girl. She had her head tilted back as if she were looking at the ceiling. I ruled out prayer. Nobody at Alcor seemed religious about anything but cryonics. From the robotic way she had moved that morning, I wouldn't have been surprised to learn that the young lady was downloading data straight from a satellite, into her brain.

I felt a little like a voyeur, so I moved on and found Jerry's office on the opposite side of the hall from Helmet Girl. I knocked.

"Come on in, Larry," Jerry said through the closed door. Maybe Jerry didn't get many visitors.

Jerry didn't get up as I entered. In fact, he was sitting with his back to me. After a moment, he swung around in his chair dramatically, a warm smile on his face. He didn't appear to be working on anything back there. I think the swivel-chair swoop maneuver was executed strictly for effect, a sort of "And"—swoosh—"heeere's Jerry!" He seemed to be playing Ed McMahon to his own Johnny Carson.

Jerry made a grand, sweeping motion with his hand. "Have a seat, Larry," he said.

Now that we were in his office, Jerry acted much more confident and comfortable than he had been earlier. His desk was typical scatterbrain-scientist. Papers were strewn everywhere, pens, pamphlets, scribbled-in notebooks. There was a forest of megavitamin bottles, probably twenty bottles of Saul Kent's Life Extension Foundation supplements, scattered across the desk. As we spoke, Jerry picked up various bottles and swallowed handfuls of pills. With that kind of volume, I doubted if he even needed real meals to fill his stomach.

Most people have pictures of their loved ones on their desk. Jerry's desk was crowded with pictures of himself: Jerry, eyes flashing and fist raised, speaking from behind a podium. Jerry, arms crossed in a white lab coat, posing in front of the dewars, chin high and eyes glaring down at the camera, the film all grainy and dramatic.

Jerry followed my eyes and said, "That picture is from an interview I gave to *GQ* magazine." I noticed a letter on the desk. Jerry signed his name: "Sooner AND Later, Jerry Lemler."

There were framed covers of books that Jerry had self-published. One prominent picture on his desk was a shot of Jerry standing in a scrubby-looking desert locale. He was dressed in khakis, a stereotypical "White Man in Africa" costume.

After what he probably considered a long enough time for me to drink in his office, Jerry told me there was a pet project of his that he wanted me to work on. He started by saying there were currently six hundred Alcor members signed up for suspension.

"Six hundred and twenty," I interrupted, recalling the number Charles had told me.

A darkening look flashed across Jerry's face. Lesson number one: Jerry didn't like to be corrected.

"Sure, Larry, to be precise, there are 620, yes. But the point is, I like to be as prepared as possible. There's something I've always wanted done around here but no one was ever qualified to do it until now. Until you."

Jerry smiled, as if he took personal pride in my qualifications. Then came an uncomfortable pause. Lesson number two: Jerry liked to be thanked.

"Thanks, Jerry," I said. "I'll do my best. What do you have in mind?"

"I want you to write me up a Patient Assessment Report," Jerry said. "I want you to assess our current members in terms of when we can expect them to finish their first life cycles. This is for the sake of Alcor's emergency preparedness. We need to know which cities need fully trained volunteer teams the soonest. Your report will have very serious repercussions as to where we store our equipment and initiate volunteer training programs."

Jerry Lemler, president of Alcor Life Extension, my new boss, and an MD to boot, had given me my first assignment as director of clinical services. He wanted me to take a hard look at the Alcor members signed up for cryo-suspension and, utilizing my medical expertise, come up with a report of who, in order, would kick the bucket first.

"You want me to predict the dates of death for 620 people?"

Jerry smiled paternally, as if correcting a child's guess that two plus two equaled five.

"Larry, you need to remember, what you call death, we call the end of the first life cycle. What you call death, we consider a temporary condition, a handicap. Those of us with the foresight to commit ourselves to cryonic suspension will be reborn fifty, a hundred, maybe a thousand years from now. There will be a second life, Larry, there's no doubt about it. You're going to have to start thinking in these terms. It's not death, it's deanimation."

"But that's impossible!" I interrupted. Jerry's smile drooped.

"No, Jerry, I don't mean cryonics is impossible, I just mean this Patient Assessment. Not even the most experienced doctor on the planet could estimate the date of death of one single patient, never mind chart 620 in order of—deanimation. A physician can examine someone and estimate they've only got a few months to live and then ten years later they're still alive and kicking. I've seen it happen with my own eyes."

Lesson number three: Don't contradict Jerry.

"Thanks for coming in, Larry," he said, rising from his chair. "Off you go. I have complete faith in your abilities. I'm sure you'll do your best."

"Plus," he said right before he shut the door, "it's something I want."

Patient Assessment. Predicting people's deaths. I might as well use tarot cards.

As I trod slowly down the hall wondering how to start my new job as a death psychic, I noticed Mike Perry watching me from a doorway, stirring his bowl of green Cool Whip veggie mix. Hugh Hixon entered the hallway from an office a little ahead of me, took a few steps, and disappeared into the same room Mike Perry was in. As I continued walking, I recognized the little office Hugh had just exited as the one I had passed earlier with the pornography on the computer. I guessed it must have been Hugh's office.

Mike slinked backward and out of sight. They lowered their voices as I approached. A sharp, rotten smell pierced my nose.

I entered Alcor's kitchen. Mike was standing across from Hugh. The whispering stopped.

"Hi, Mike. Hi, Hugh," I said.

Mike was staring down into his bowl without a word, stirring, stirring. Hugh proved the keener conversationalist of the two.

"Er, uh . . . hello," Hugh said.

I opened a few of the cupboards as an excuse for being there. I saw some coffee mugs and tuna cans. Then I opened the refrigerator. Big mistake. I'd noticed that the whole kitchen had a biting, foul odor to it. Evidently, the refrigerator was ground zero.

It was disgusting. There was food in there that had to be months old, items that had turned colors they were never meant to be. There was a clear container of Mike Perry's creamy green veggie whip. *They actually use this refrigerator for food storage?* I thought. The fact that Mike could eat that health mix after it had been seemingly laid siege by burgeoning colonies of germs was a testament to the contradictory nature of these eccentric geniuses. It was like plucking a beautiful apple off a tree, polishing it, and then dipping it in dog poop before eating it. I started wondering about the unhealthy appearance of my coworkers and figured it might trace back to this fridge, a sort of Typhoid Mary of kitchen appliances.

I don't remember what I said to Mike and Hugh after that; I just got the heck out of there. Right then I decided I would eat lunch out every single day I was there. For sure, I was never going to put a single thing into that refrigerator.

Charles spent much of that first day with me, answering my questions and eagerly volunteering his opinions on my new colleagues. For instance, the young lady with the helmet, Charles told me—the same woman I had seen with her chin raised to the ceiling in the dark office—was Jennifer Chapman, Alcor's director of membership services. I came to think of her as Alcor's "Head Hunter." Jennifer was responsible for assisting applicants with their Alcor memberships.

Charles explained to me that Jennifer had a unique paranoia of driving or riding as a passenger in a motor vehicle. Because a brain injury would diminish the possibility of having what Alcor considered a successful cryo-suspension, Jennifer wore a bicycle helmet every moment she was inside a car. As a paramedic who had been on the scene of hundreds of traffic accidents, I never had the heart to tell Jennifer exactly how much good that little plastic and Styrofoam helmet would do her in a high-speed wreck. To each their own placebo.

Well, at least I had been right about one thing: This place was not going to be boring.

I came home that first night to find Beverly absolutely glowing. She told me all about the great shops she had found. Today had been bathroom day. She had been out all afternoon buying leopard-spotted towels and zebra-striped candles, as she's quite fond of animal prints. Somehow, don't ask me how, she made it all work together tastefully. Sitting in our bathroom was now a very furry experience.

Beverly is a strong and loving woman despite having had some hard times in her life. She was raised by her mother and grandmother because her dad drank a lot and left when she was young. Bev wasn't exactly inspired from a young age to trust men in general and it is only through the strength of her character and her ability to rise above that we have such a great relationship. Our marriage is very important to each of us. Bev's also a very talented visual artist and, like many artists, a sensitive person.

We'd never had lots of money, but things were safe and stable. Now, even though I was making the same money at Alcor that I had made as a paramedic, we had left Vegas behind. We were living in a pretty resort town in a nice apartment. To Beverly, it was the closest thing to living the American dream she had ever enjoyed. I think all these factors combined in Beverly to make it very important to her that our apartment be a sanctuary, a stable, comfortable home. Judging by our new fuzzy bathroom, she was rising to the occasion.

Just like back in Vegas, I had told Beverly she could work if she wanted, or not. It was her choice. I was making just enough to pay the bills and I wanted her to be happy. I knew her, though. She'd settle in and within a few months get restless and go out and find a job. For now, she was having a ball redecorating and she sure had a knack for it. It gave me real joy to see her so excited. She had never looked happier.

FOUR

ACCLIMATING

In those first few weeks, I was continually confronted with the fact that a lot of infighting went on at Alcor. Even though my colleagues seemed wary of me as an outsider, that didn't stop them from dropping insults and catty remarks about each other in front of me. Charles was the worst.

I got the feeling that Charles was trying to enlist me as a lieutenant in his unending wars with Hugh Hixon, Jerry Lemler, and just about everyone else at Alcor. It seemed to me that these people spent more than half their time scheming against each other in an endless power struggle over who really ran the show at Alcor. I soon concluded that there were well-defined camps with very precise lines drawn among them. Charles was right in the center of the fray, but everyone else chose sides, too. Evidently, different factions seized control now and then. Charles told me there was always a new president taking over, or about to take over, backed by some loose alliance of Alcor's officers, board members, and scientific advisors. I discovered there was so much internal squabbling that a name had been coined for all this backbiting: the CryoWars.

Charles was especially eager to dish out embarrassing information on Jerry Lemler. Jerry had dropped out of high school to become a folk singer, Charles told me, and was then part of a Simon and Garfunkel–type duo in New York. That career didn't last long, though. Jerry later admitted to me that he wasn't much of a singer. I learned he was also the former world record holder in the video game Arkanoid.

Charles raised his eyebrows to me once during my first weeks at Alcor and said I should ask Jerry about the time he assisted in an exorcism.

"Jerry desperately wants to be remembered for something," Charles added. "Anything. It doesn't matter what it is, he just wants to go down in history, to be published, to be somebody."

In comparison to Lemler, Hugh Hixon mostly kept his head down when dealing with people outside of Alcor's inner circle. And he was a creature of habit. I say this because I noticed that Hugh wore the same matching khaki outfit every day. Underneath he wore the same ratty T-shirt and always had a distinct whiff about him of someone who urgently needed a shower. Hugh gave Mike Perry a solid run for "Rankest Cryonicist of the Year."

And yet, to me Hugh was probably the most interesting person at Alcor, and undeniably a true engineering genius. I was able to engage him in conversation a few times during those first few weeks, mostly about the cryonic suspension contraptions he had invented. Even though Hugh spoke slowly and quietly, choosing every word carefully, he was often difficult to follow in conversation due to his vast knowledge and sheer brilliance.

I could tell that Hugh loved talking shop but, like his colleagues, he seemed distrustful of me. He wanted to ease into getting to know me, assessing the threat I represented. As Charles had said, I was the only director there not signed up to be frozen, and thus someone to be wary of. To say my coworkers were a closed group was an understatement.

I was also intrigued by Jennifer Chapman. When Jennifer arrived at work each day, after removing her bicycle helmet and leaving it in her car, I noticed that she walked straight to her office and closed her door, usually without a word to anyone. Jennifer's office was the only clean room in the building. With time, I realized it was normal for her to have the lights off in there, and she always kept her door shut. I would walk by Jennifer's office a couple times per day just to check and, sure enough, about half the time she would be in there, in the dark, staring silently up at the ceiling.

Jennifer's job was mainly to answer the phone and talk people into signing up as Alcor members. She was probably in action about five minutes every day. Still, with the exception of going to the restroom or fax machine, she never left her office. Most of the time, she had her lunch delivered by local restaurants, or by a man who I learned was her husband.

Smilin' Joe Hovey also rarely left his office. We didn't go out to lunch as a group that first Friday, as Joe had mentioned we might (in fact, in the seven months I worked at Alcor, we went out as a group only once). And Joe never did come and ask me to take a drug test.

Jerry Lemler's Patient Assessment death list became my busywork in those early days at Alcor. I needed to start somewhere, so I began, logically enough, with the oldest members. I asked myself, "What causes people to die?"

Ailments . . . accidents . . . I took the twenty oldest Alcor members and sent them a questionnaire: Do you have any heart problems? Have you ever had a stroke? What prescription medications do you take? After they mailed it back, I called them with more questions. I expanded on the original twenty members and kept gathering data. After further talks with Jerry, I devised a priority list and placed members in one of three categories. "Category A" was for Alcor members most likely to die in the coming year. "B" was for those who probably had a few good years left, and "C" was for Alcorians who were still very well-animated.

Like every other Alcor employee, my daily inbox wasn't exactly packed. My most important responsibility was to jump into action during cryonic suspensions by communicating with hospital and medical staff, and then lending a hand during surgery. Alcor averaged only a few suspensions per year. So for the vast majority of the time, I was there to try to improve procedures and train Alcor employees and volunteers in emergency medical procedures. Those training sessions were few and far between. I was really only as busy as I chose to be.

I hated to be idle, though. To familiarize myself with the company's lingo, I leafed through back issues of Alcor's regular publication, *Cryonics* magazine, and read postings on the cryonics Internet bulletin boards. There were lots of puns. "The Cure for the Common Cold." "The Ultimate

Recycling." "I'm practicing for my neuro-suspension by eating ice cream really fast."

I read a poem by Jerry Lemler printed in an issue of *Cryonics* magazine spoofing "'Twas the Night Before Christmas," called "'Twas the Night of My Suspension." It was all about Jerry's future cryo-suspension and included:

"The ice had been gathered/ By a skinny pack of elves/ Who had lugged in the chests/ In spite of themselves/ . . . So, they loaded me up/ And the blanket was chilly/ 'You haven't felt nothin' yet!'/ Said the plump man, dressed silly."

I noticed, leafing through the *Cryonics* magazines, that many Alcor employees had a tendency to capitalize the compound "cryo-" words they liked to coin, such as CryoWars and CryoStar. I think they felt those words looked cooler, more sci-fi that way, not to mention more important. And all of them capitalized their job titles every time they used them in print.

During my ample downtime, I also read Alcor's membership handbook, titled *Alcor Life Extension Foundation: An Introduction,* which Jerry had rewritten before I arrived at Alcor. To dedicated Alcorians, it was one part immortality instruction manual, one part Bible. In Jerry's mind, it was one of the things he would be remembered for.

Charles lambasted Jerry's handbook in memos, calling Jerry an atrocious writer, then accusing him of plagiarism. To be sure, there was definitely some pure Jerry Lemler in that handbook.

Jerry wrote as if he slept with an SAT study guide under his pillow, though he didn't talk like that. It seemed Jerry's first priority in writing was to portray himself as intelligent and well-read.

At the end of his second chapter, Jerry wrote, "Perhaps the late Poet Laureate of the United States, the most honorable Robert Frost, captured best the essence of the vital decision we have before us in his poem 'The Road Not Taken.'" Jerry then reprinted the entire poem.

Two pages later, Jerry quoted Emily Dickinson ("I Heard a Fly Buzz When I Died") and Dylan Thomas ("Do Not Go Gentle into That Good Night"). Then, about seventy pages later, he reprinted the Thomas and Frost poems yet again when he quoted the entire eulogy given by an Alcorian at an "Alcor Life Extension Foundation First Life Cycle Ceremony"

(Alcor's version of a wake). The Alcorian delivering that eulogy? Jerry Lemler himself.

He titled one section of the handbook "Can the Twain Meet? (According to Mark)." Chapter titles included "You Only Go Around Twice," "The Iceman Cometh—Back," "Act Two Will Begin—After a Brief Intermission," "Next to Last Rites," and my personal favorite, "How Dead Is That Doorknob?"

The puns kept coming as Jerry wrote, "Remaining indecisive leads precisely to remains—and they are yours!"

Then Jerry described Robert Kennedy as having the "grave responsibility" of overseeing JFK's funeral services. That was, as puns go, unforgivable. This was not a good use of my time.

I investigated the storerooms, familiarizing myself with and inventorying Alcor's surgical supplies. There were vast stores of things I couldn't imagine Alcor ever using, piles of first-aid kits, bandages, and all sorts of other supplies that were most commonly used on the living. Toward the end of my first week I discovered shelves crammed with expensive microscopes that looked like they had never been used. They were still wrapped in plastic. One that looked especially pricey had a little "UCLA" sticker on it.

I had picked another curiosity up off a shelf when a voice behind me said, "Looks like something Hugh Hixon might use on Mike Perry in the middle of a lonely night."

I turned to see a tall, thirty-something-year-old man smirking at me. He was hugging himself, rocking back and forth slightly.

"I certainly hope not," I said. "It's a vaginal speculum, a gynecological tool."

"Christ! I'm probably more right than I thought, then." When he smiled it seemed like he had too many teeth in his mouth. "I'm Mathew Sullivan," he said, "director of suspension readiness." With his dark, wavy hair, big teeth, and catty voice, Mathew struck me as a young, effeminate Tom Selleck. He didn't offer his hand, just kept rocking back and forth.

"Hi. I'm Larry Johnson, your new clinical director."

"I know. We have more directors than Hollywood. We have almost as many directors as we have vice presidents. Give it a month. Our board will make you a vice president. VP of gynecological tools."

"I've been called worse," I said.

"Yeah, but then they'll ask you to take a pay cut." Mathew squeezed himself tighter and laughed a high-pitched, rapid-fire "ha-ha-ha."

"I've read your résumé," Mathew continued. "Pretty impressive. One of five paramedics in the country to be flight director at a major city hospital. Keynote speaker at national emergency medical conferences. They really hire you to teach doctors about emergency medical techniques you've pioneered out in the field?"

"You should hear my Elvis impersonation," I said.

Mathew rat-a-tatted that squealy laugh again. Then suddenly his eyes darted around like he'd just realized how close the confines of the storeroom were. I could see it in his eyes—the walls were closing in.

"Good luck with your little inventory," Mathew said, his eyes flitting to my clipboard. As he was leaving, he stabbed out his finger and said, "Don't forget those."

I turned and followed his finger. There, underneath the shelf where the vaginal speculum had been, were two butt plugs. These things were sometimes used in hospital procedures, to avoid patients making a mess, but the ones in the storeroom were definitely not medical issue. They were big and black, manufactured by the Doc Johnson sex toy company.

Mathew Sullivan's jittery, machine-gun laughter ricocheted down the hall.

There were some things in Alcor's inventory more baffling than butt plugs, though. In my twenty-five years around hospitals and ambulances, paralytic drugs were always strictly controlled. An institution wouldn't want just anybody getting their hands on them. As a paramedic and ambulance company clinical director I'd been responsible for keeping tabs on highly regulated and controlled drugs, as well as making sure none of them was expired. I could only assume that the DEA was well aware of what was in Alcor's storerooms and refrigerators. The fact that Alcor's paralytic and anesthetic drugs were all expired and *not* locked up made me very uncomfortable. But then I figured, very few people at Alcor really had access to them and, well, at least those drugs would only ever be injected into dead people.

I didn't know what the situation was with Alcor and government regulation, but the idea that the company was just winging it with no regulatory supervision at all seemed somehow out of the question.

I found that Alcor had loads of Diprivan, the creamy-looking sedative I had seen in the refrigerator during my initial tour with Charles Platt. Diprivan is moderately priced, not the most expensive, but not the cheapest sedative either. There are other drugs that can be used in place of Diprivan that cost less and achieve much the same effect, so why would the company spend more than it had to on a drug being injected into someone who, to put it lightly, wouldn't know the difference?

But then—why did Alcor store Diprivan at all? Why would anyone need to sedate a corpse?

And then darker questions arose in my mind: Why did they have all these paralytics? Why keep drugs on hand to immobilize dead people? Jerry Lemler was a medical doctor as well as the president and CEO. I asked him why Alcor stored paralytics.

"We store paralytics?" Jerry said. "We don't use paralytics, do we? You should ask Joe Hovey. He would have a record of their purchase."

Joe's eyes narrowed on me while the corners of his chin pulled up into a tight smile. "Gosh, Larry. I can't tell you. I sure don't remember buying them."

Charles usually had all the answers. I found him in his closet office writing an e-mail to Hugh. His fingers were stabbing at the computer keyboard testily. Charles was obviously really letting Hugh have it in the e-mail.

"I don't know, Larry," Charles said. "Hugh's in charge of the labs. He claims to know them inside and out. God knows he has a fit whenever anyone pokes his nose around in there. You should ask Hugh."

So I went and asked Hugh. He lowered his head and hesitated before answering, peering at me over the top of his glasses. "Uh, you'll have to ask Mathew Sullivan. He's in charge of stocking the drugs," Hugh said.

At the mention of paralytics, Mathew grew fidgety. "Larry, drugs aren't my specialty. You should ask Charles. Or Hugh. Or Lemler. Sorry, but I have some calls to make."

I discovered Mike Perry's nest during those first few weeks. Next door to the Patient Care Bay, inside the Cool-Down Bay, there were some un-painted wooden stairs leading upward. At the top of the stairs was a door, and behind that door was Mike's makeshift office. In the future, if I didn't see Mike around, I could usually find him up there. He never strayed far from the Patient Care Bay. He took his job as patient caretaker very seriously.

Mike's office was a little attic space that also housed Alcor's computer servers. He had converted the rest of it into his personal writing area. Mike loved to write. He published books on cryonics and always seemed to be in the process of writing another. His space was overflowing with hundreds of old books: math, science, science fiction, philosophy, nutrition, medical textbooks, survivalist manuals, stacks and stacks of health and life extension magazines, everything the zealous cryonicist author might need to refer to. Almost as numerous as the reference books were Mike's own handwritten notebooks. They were everywhere. I couldn't believe one man could write so much. And there were huge amounts of loose pages scattered around the place, blanketing everything, each page covered with Mike's tiny, messy handwriting on both sides. He wrote as small as a typewriter and probably fit ten average handwritten pages onto one page. His desk was like a New England yard during autumn in serious need of raking.

Underneath the clutter on the old, rickety desk, I could make out the shape of a computer. There were also dozens of tall, grubby bottles of Saul Kent's Life Extension Foundation supplements and vitamins. I didn't stay in the room very long, though, as I felt like I was trespassing. Besides, the place just smelled funky.

Overall, Alcor was very dirty. I never could tell if the floor tiles were originally gray or just filthy. One day, as an experiment, I took an empty pizza box off the table in the front lobby and threw it away. Sure enough, there it was again the next morning, as if reanimated.

I'm pretty low maintenance and it wasn't a big deal, but between the pizza boxes and the overall dirtiness, it was curious that they called themselves a medical research facility and considered their patients to be alive, yet their reception area looked like a frat house kitchen the morning after homecoming.

Scottsdale is desert and there is lots of dust. You have to keep up with it because the desert will keep trying to reclaim your land. Alcor simply wasn't kept well. As clinical director, I felt partially responsible for ensuring there was a clean working environment. It wasn't really my job but, like everyone else there, I had time on my hands. I thought the most logical person to start questioning about the cleaning procedures would be Alcor's lead volunteer, Jerry Searcy.

Crotchety old Jerry was an ornament at Alcor. You could usually find him asleep in the lobby, snoring in the chair by the front door. As a volunteer, Jerry Searcy pretty much did scut work and didn't get paid for it: faxing, copying, tidying up, running errands. Although he wasn't really a mean person, he was very negative. Every other word was "goddamn."

Most people at Alcor were antigovernment, especially Jerry Lemler and Charles Platt, but there was sheer rage on Jerry Searcy's face whenever he talked about the government. Searcy hated the government to the point where I thought he might do something stupid. I wouldn't have been surprised to have turned on the TV and heard that Jerry had just blown up some federal building. A few weeks into my job I had already started antagonizing Jerry simply for amusement. "Hey, Jerry, you see how in the news today they're cracking down on unlicensed firearms all over Arizona?" That'd just set him right off.

"Goddamn it, what's that goddamn federal government doing now to limit my freedoms as a goddamn American?" Of course, I'd been talking about the state government, but I didn't want to spoil his fun.

Unfortunately, Jerry Searcy wasn't able to answer my cleaning question. "What? Cleaning? I don't know anything about no goddamn cleaning."

I moved on to Jessica Sikes, Jerry Lemler's daughter and administrative assistant. When I approached her, she was busy playing a video game on her computer. I asked her who was supposed to clean up around Alcor.

Without taking her eyes off the screen, Jessica droned, "I have no clue."

I asked Paula Lemler, Jerry's wife, but she didn't know either. Paula had the title of special projects coordinator, but it seemed to me that she pretty much drew a paycheck as Jerry's typist. Why he needed both a typist and a secretary, I didn't know. I never did see Jerry's wife or daughter do much work. Jessica's husband, James Sikes, was Alcor's IT guy, in charge of the servers and computers. I couldn't understand how they needed a full-time tech guy for the dozen or so computers around the place. James was never around that much but presumably that never stopped him from cashing his paycheck. Paula didn't punch in every day either, but I'd say Jessica was probably there more than she wasn't. Jerry's wife was paid either on retainer or as a contractor, I'm not sure which. Jerry's daughter and son-in-law were paid as full-time Alcor employees.

Finally, though, Charles had the answer. He told me Jerry had hired an office cleaning service to come in once a week and mop the floors and empty the trash. Then Charles complained about Jerry's choice in cleaning companies.

Eventually, I saw the cleaning people a few of the late nights I spent at Alcor. I heard Charles and Jerry argue about them more often than I actually saw them. Like most problems at Alcor, it was talked about, fought over, memos were written, e-mails fired off, and then nothing was ever done about it. Whatever those cleaning people did, it wasn't nearly enough to keep the gray floor tiles clean—or the walls, or the business machines, or Dick Clair's Emmy Award.

Sometimes I'd think about the bone saws, the decapitations, the lackadaisical OR procedures, the chemicals, the science experiments growing in the fridge, the less than hygienic personal habits of some of the employees, and I'd wonder about the chemical makeup of all that dust floating around Alcor, coating the walls, the floors, the pizza boxes, the kitchen, my office.

The liquid nitrogen inside the dewars and LR-40 head-storage freezer needed to be replenished because some naturally evaporated and vented into the outside air. But what else was escaping into the air, hitching a ride on those vented gases? Dust is supposed to be ninety-something percent human skin. The question at Alcor was: Whose skin were we talking about here?

Beverly continued setting up our new life in Scottsdale. After the response to the name Alcor from our landlady, we decided just to tell people I worked "in medical research." When Beverly went to the bank to open up our accounts, that's what she told them. She used the same line when applying for our auto insurance. When folks happened to ask her who my employer was, she would say, "Critical Care Research." We had discussed that too. Some people in Scottsdale knew of Alcor, but no one seemed to know of its sister company, CCR. It was a white lie but I figured it would avoid embarrassment. My wife is normally a very direct person; she will tell you exactly what's on her mind. I knew it made her uncomfortable to fib but I thought it was for the best.

Beverly and I went for long rides on my Harley every chance we could. It was great. Each of those first few weekends we'd pack a lunch, hop on the bike, and ride. We picnicked by a beautiful little lake we found about an hour north of home, and explored the two-lane highways in and out of Phoenix. And of course, we visited with my dad a few times each week.

Half the time he'd come over to our place to watch TV after his wife had fallen asleep; the other half we'd go over to their apartment and visit with Mary Jane. At his place, my dad would entertain us on the piano. At our place, he'd play the guitar for me while I grilled up some steaks. It felt great, growing closer to my dad. I looked forward to the months and years ahead of getting to know him better.

Things at work grew odder by the day, but the most important thing was that Beverly and I were still thrilled to be in Arizona.

I attended my first monthly Alcor board meeting.

Next to my office area was a little break room with a microwave and coffee machine, and beyond that was the boardroom, with a wide conference table seating about six per side. Because Alcor was a nonprofit company, board meetings were open to the public.

Chairs were brought in, lining the walls, and Alcor volunteers and members filled up the chairs. There was food available, salads and other healthy stuff, but most of the attendees didn't touch it. Some brought little baggies filled with organic carrot sticks and the like. The room got real crowded, chock-full of future immortals.

The board of directors itself looked like a panel of social misfits. Every one of them seemed to be an Alcor ex-president and each was geekier than the last. The man who stuck out the most was Carlos Mondragon. Carlos was spooky looking, with sunken cheeks and dark, beady eyes that seemed to never stop following me. Like most Alcorians, he was skinny to the point of being undernourished, but Mondragon had a particularly big head that didn't fit the rest of his stick figure, two-dimensional body. Carlos reminded me of one of those fish that live in the darkest depths and grow two eyes on the same side of their heads. Always watching, staring, as if he never blinked.

One Alcor member likewise struck me as particularly unique at that first meeting. He was wearing a tight silk long-sleeve shirt with puffy cuffs and silver glitter all over it. It was as if Liberace had beaten out John Travolta for the lead role in *Saturday Night Fever*. From Charles's previous description of this Alcorian, I recognized him immediately as Rick Potvin. Charles had already told me that, apart from being a throwback to the seventies, Rick was a musician from Canada who had moved to Scottsdale for the sole purpose of living fifteen minutes away from Alcor's dewars, which he believed would be handy when he deanimated. Rick had a job selling pianos in Phoenix but his real life's work was snooping around Alcor as a wannabe journalist.

Rick hosted online bulletin boards for cryonicists, including the one I had found called Cryonics Café. He attended every one of Alcor's board meetings, Charles had told me, and would scribble notes furiously, then race home and start typing articles for his Web sites. Rick was prolific. Many cryonicists didn't like him because they considered him such a busybody. His sites sometimes read like online cryonics tabloids. And Rick was always promoting conspiracy theories. Some of them were pretty far-fetched, but sometimes, Charles had admitted to me, Rick got it right. Every once in a while Rick would shut down his bulletin boards after writing something particularly juicy. When the Web sites went back online a few hours or days later, his accusatory, negative postings about Alcor officers or leading members would be mysteriously absent.

It got pretty heated between Rick and Alcor at times, Charles had explained. An anonymous Alcorian once posted a remark on his site to the effect of "You shouldn't piss off the people who are going to be taking care of you during and after your suspension, Rick." Rick sparred back and forth with the Alcorians who threatened him online. They called themselves the Group of Six and considered themselves the protectors of hard-core cryonicists. Rick would call them spineless for remaining anonymous and claimed he was just trying to tell it like it was. The outcome of these exchanges was always the same, though, with Rick deleting his postings that dug a little too deep.

The board meeting was called to order. Jerry Lemler enthroned himself at the head of the table, as if holding court. You could tell he loved these meetings. Jerry introduced me to everyone in the room. Charles Platt praised the work I had done so far. I thanked them and said how fascinating my new job was. That was true.

I could feel the eyes on me, though. Some of them were very unhappy I was in the room at all. Carlos's eyes, especially, bore into me. The unspoken message was, "You don't belong here, you nonmember, and believe me, I'm watching you!"

Jerry told the group he was setting me to work on Project Futurebound. This was news to me. Lemler liked giving fancy names to his dreamchildren. Project Futurebound, he explained, involved me contacting paramedics overseas and setting up emergency response teams in every country on the globe. Jerry cited my résumé and professional manner and declared he had high hopes for Project Futurebound.

Whoa, I thought. *I'm supposed to get on the phone and convince medics in Portugal to inject dead people with heparin against their controlling physician's protocols?*

It surprised me that no one stood up and told Jerry what a dumb idea this was. Instead, they nodded their heads in approval. These were the true believers, I realized, some of the most dedicated cryonicists in the world. They were completely serious about creating strategies that would spread cryonics across the planet.

Alcor's Keith Richards–like CFO, Michael Riskin, addressed the gathering next. He told everyone that Alcor was not doing well financially, and he began blaming his predecessor. Alcor, he said, was still paying for the mistakes of the past. Riskin was very animated and angry.

I gathered from what he was saying that in the early days, no one at Alcor had thought of including inflation in their calculations of the costs of suspending their members. They had charged some early members a total of $27,000 in advance for a neuro-suspension that now in 2003 had a sticker price of $50,000. Many of those members who had prepaid back in the 1970s were still animated. Many of them might be pedaling their first life cycles for another twenty or thirty years to come. In these cases, when they finally deanimated, their suspensions would cost Alcor three, maybe four times as much as the company had been paid.

Even worse, apparently Alcor had no financial wizard who was cleverly investing the money all this time. Somehow this company whose business was selling the future had forgotten to factor in inflation or, it seemed, to try to gain the highest possible interest on the early down payments it had received. I thought about the disorganization in the Alcor corporate structure and the runaround I got whenever I asked, "Who is responsible for such and such?" I pondered how no one seemed to know anyone else's job responsibilities. Most incredible, no one really seemed to be in charge at Alcor. I wondered who was really the boss at Alcor, but such a clear hierarchy seemed to be lacking.

After complaining about Alcor's previous mismanagement for a few minutes, Riskin introduced an idea he had recently come up with regarding Alcorian life insurance policies.

Alcor members paid flat fees for their cryonic suspensions, as well as yearly dues, but they also bought life insurance policies naming Alcor as the beneficiary. This was to help pay for patients' long-term storage. There was an Alcorian insurance agent by the name of Rudy Hoffman who set it all up.

Since life insurance premiums were less expensive for younger people, Riskin explained, this should be an incentive they could use in recruiting young Alcor members. Riskin addressed Jennifer Chapman, encouraging her to spend some time in the coming month aggressively pursuing potential members still in their teens and twenties, telling them their insurance premiums would be much less expensive for the rest of their lives if they signed up now, rather than ten or twenty years from now. He told Jennifer to let them know that if they signed up now, it would cost them something like $15 a month in perpetuity as opposed to, say, $60.

Again, everyone seemed to agree that this was a great idea. If you truly believed in cryonics, if you believed it was the way to everlasting life, you probably would not have had any problems with a little aggressive marketing. If they signed up young or old, what would be the difference? After all, you'd be helping people conquer death and live forever. The ends justified the means. Still, it left a sour taste in my mouth that they would target teenagers.

Then Riskin brought up an item of business involving an Alcor member's cat. As I had learned from Charles during my initial tour, there were several cat and dog heads suspended at Alcor, as well as a monkey brain. Some members believed that their pets might be able to be reanimated at the same time as their own second awakening. These animals had been decapitated and frozen back when Alcor was located in Riverside, California. These animal parts, along with the human bodies and heads, were transported to Scottsdale during Alcor's exodus from California to Arizona (they had run an overnight convoy to avoid the desert heat of the day).

Someone had recently approached Riskin regarding the price of a pet suspension. Alcor hadn't done a pet suspension in years and, as always, the officers were trying to increase profit by upping prices and cutting costs. So Riskin asked what the true cost of a feline neuro-suspension would be.

"Well, I know sixteen cat heads will fit into a single Neuro Can," Mathew Sullivan said. "Adult cats, that is."

From there, Mathew went on about volume displacement of cat heads and the current cost of liquid nitrogen. They talked about pursuing more pet suspensions and the money it could bring in. Someone mentioned his parakeet. Everyone paid close attention as they crunched the numbers, everyone except Mike Perry. He looked bored. I glanced at his notebook. Mike was working out differential equations the way most people doodle. Differential equations!

Before long they had come up with Alcor's new price for cat decapitations. The number was high enough to satisfy Riskin.

When the meeting was adjourned, the Alcor volunteers and local members filed out of the room but the company officers and board members remained seated. Jerry Lemler motioned me to stay. Riskin got up, shut the door, and announced the names of several Alcorians he was taking off the active member list for nonpayment of their dues.

After each public board meeting was finished, Alcor higher-ups shut the door and convened what they literally referred to as the "secret board meeting." Lemler, Riskin, Joe Hovey, and Hugh Hixon were all clear to me about these meetings during future conversations I had with them—the issues discussed during the secret board meetings were ones they didn't want made public. It was convenient to hold these discussions immediately after the regular meetings. This was how Alcor's hierarchy discussed the delicate issues they didn't want others to overhear and still fulfilled the requirement of a nonprofit organization, holding public board meetings.

After the secret board meeting, I went straight to Mathew's office. Mathew hugged himself tightly when I entered, not comfortable with me yet, but I had to ask.

"Mathew, how do you know sixteen cat heads can fit in one of those pots?"

"Well," he said, "a long time ago I took the size of the average cat's head, calculated how much area it would displace as a sphere, then did some mathematics, given the size of the Neuro Cans and the dewars and how many cans fit inside a dewar. Along with the space it takes up, we need to also consider the amount of liquid nitrogen needed to cool that volume displaced by a typical cat head . . . "

"So you never actually shoved sixteen cat heads into one of those pots?"

He laughed that nervous laugh. "No, no, that's the kind of thing you might have expected during the Mike Darwin days, or something they might do over at CCR," he said, "but me, I just do the math."

I walked back toward my office. The thing that was still baking my noodle was how Mathew had whipped the numbers right off the top of his head at the meeting. *Sixteen cats on a dead man's chest . . . yo-ho-ho and ice the man down.*

It made sense that he had already calculated how many cat heads would fit inside one pot. As "Director of Suspension Readiness," part of his gig was figuring out how much money could be squeezed out of lopping the heads off cats. Anytime you think you have an outrageous job, just think of Mathew Sullivan in his office, bent over his calculator, hugging himself, figuring out how many disembodied kitty heads would fit in a lobster pot.

As I walked back to my office area, I thought about how uncomfortable Mathew had seemed to have me in his office. And then there was the feeling I had picked up from some of the board members at the meeting: outright hostility. So far, everyone but Charles and Jerry had been very cold to me. Charles wanted me under his wing and Jerry simply liked talking about himself to anyone who would listen. As a group, though, these Alcorians were distant, reclusive, emotionless, and secretive. To most of them I was a grudging necessity, an outsider not to be trusted. Oh well, I was happy to be left alone. And maybe I could break through with some of them a little bit. Either way, I knew I'd be all right.

When I returned to my office area, Michael Riskin was waiting for me. Similar to Jerry Lemler's Project Futurebound and Patient Assessment

Report, he had a pet project for me. Like all hard-core cryonicists, Riskin's number one goal in life was to prepare for the moment of his death. Beyond keeping the body clean and healthy, this entailed making sure there was an Alcor volunteer team nearby that would be ready to jump into action as soon as he stopped breathing. Riskin, though, refined this concern to an art form of paranoid obsession. He lived in Orange County, California, and visited Alcor only once every two weeks. He was absolutely consumed with having the Los Angeles–area response team up to snuff in order to be prepared for his own death, transport to Alcor, and lickety-split cryo-suspension.

This was a personal concern more than a corporate one. He told me to spare no expense on supplies for the L.A. team. He would consider it a personal favor if I would pay particular attention to their training.

Thinking back to my initial visit to Alcor, it made sense why Riskin was so calm during that nerve-racking drive with Charles from the airport to the Alcor facility. When it came to driving with Charles, Riskin must have figured, what the hell, he was close to Alcor, a lot closer than when he was at home in Orange County. That was probably the best time for him to buy the farm, riding with Charles just minutes away from Alcor's scalpels, Crackphones, and liquid nitrogen.

As Riskin left my office, he said, "Larry, you need to think very seriously about becoming an Alcor member. I say this for your own good. Dues are waived for Alcor employees. Normally, the only other cost is the monthly premium on the life insurance policy, but I don't want you to even worry about that. I want you happy, Larry. How well you train and equip the response teams is directly related to how successful every Alcor member's cryo-suspension will be. I want your mind clear. I feel so strongly about this that if you do decide to join up, I will have the company pay your insurance premiums too. It won't cost you a penny. I want you to think about that."

"Thanks, Michael. That's very kind of you," I said. "I'll give it some serious thought."

He winked at me. Then he asked me to e-mail him a schedule of when I'd be training the Southern California teams on new procedures.

FIVE

TURNING HAMBURGER BACK INTO A COW

I'm Dr. Nero, your Orientation Advisor. I'm here to supervise the initial phase of your assimilation into society, the society that will take care of your needs and desires more efficiently than any you might have thought possible. Now you get a good rest and next week you'll begin a new life.

—FROM WOODY ALLEN'S FILM *SLEEPER*

Han Solo did it. Buck Rogers did it. Sly Stallone did it in *Demolition Man*. Austin Powers and his nemesis, Dr. Evil, both did it. All were "cryogenically" frozen and successfully revived. In the case of cryonics, though, truth was stranger than Hollywood, and it all went back to frog sperm.

In 1947, physics professor Robert Ettinger, the man who would later become known as the father of cryonics, was laid up with leg injuries suffered during World War II. Ettinger did a lot of reading. He found information about French scientists successfully freezing and thawing frog sperm and it started him thinking. If we could freeze men who were deathly ill and suspend their animation in a semipermanent biostasis, we could then thaw them out in the future when medical science had advanced to the point that it could cure what ailed them.

Ettinger put his thoughts on paper. It didn't gain much attention for years until the Doubleday publishing company found a revised edition of

Ettinger's manifesto and sent it to science fiction giant Isaac Asimov. Asimov told the editors at Doubleday the concept was sound and Ettinger's *The Prospect of Immortality* was published in 1964.

We've all heard stories of children who fall through the ice and are brought back to life hours later. Paramedics have a saying: "You're not dead until you're warm and dead." Nature has its own cryonicists. Bears hibernate. There is a North American tree frog that releases a natural antifreeze chemical into its own bloodstream so that it can be frozen all winter, then reanimates itself in the spring.

From an intellectual perspective, early proponents offered, why not explore cryonic suspension? What's the alternative? "Cryonic suspension is the second worst thing that can happen to you," cryonicists said (the worst thing being burial or cremation). Cryonic suspension was called an "ambulance to the future," where "the present rickety human model will eventually be improved to the point where, with periodic overhaul, it will give service indefinitely."

Though few in number, what pioneer cryonicists lacked in science and funding during those first heady days, they nearly made up for with passion and pluck.

The Cryonics Society of California (CSC) was incorporated on December 16, 1966. Comedy writer Dick Clair, whose dusty Emmy sat in Alcor's lobby waiting for him to reclaim it, was the secretary. Dick was notorious for verbally attacking anyone who opposed cryonics.

The CSC president was a very dedicated cryonicist named Robert F. (Bob) Nelson. Unfortunately for Nelson, while I was at Alcor, everyone there considered him an embarrassment who had besmirched the name of cryonics, because of what had come to be called the Chatsworth Incident. They bashed him to pieces in their cryonics publications.

I've since met Bob Nelson, read his book, and had some long talks with him. He's a nice, benign, grandfatherly guy.

Several years before I went to work at Alcor, Mike Perry and another Alcorian drove hundreds of miles to confront Bob Nelson at his home regarding a book he was then writing about the history of cryonics. Bob recounted the experience to me. The way Bob described it, the message was, "We at Alcor are telling you right now to stop writing that book or you'll be sorry." Bob Nelson told Mike Perry and his cohort to get the hell off his doorstep. As nice a person as he was, Bob Nelson wasn't going to be pushed around. Frankly, if I had been at Alcor, I'd have seriously reconsidered sending Mike Perry as muscle.

Bob Nelson first read about cryonics in the *National Enquirer*. It made a lot of sense to him and he dove right in. He described himself as "obsessed." His daughter would ask him, "Daddy, have you frozen anyone yet?"

In January 1967, he got his chance. Afterward, he published a book called *We Froze the First Man*.

In his introduction to Nelson's book, Robert Ettinger wrote that "there is nothing 'natural' about death in the sense that it is inevitable or inherently good; it is not the proper culmination of a progression, not a phase of development, but only a nasty accident." Since, in his estimation, not many cells are dead at the time we normally call a person "dead," Ettinger described folks at this point as "not-very-dead."

Cryonics is "the most profound revolution in human history," Ettinger continued. "In this revolution, the episode of January 1967 constituted a battle. . . . It was the first major victory in our revolution, and Bob Nelson was the commanding general in the field. . . . Bob was the key man, his leadership decisive. . . . it was his initiative, his resourcefulness, his stamina, his determination that carried the day. . . . And history was made." Many books would be written in the future about Bob and his contribution to mankind, Ettinger claimed.

In *We Froze the First Man*, Bob Nelson included a succinct defense of cryonics. In theory, it sounded very reasonable.

> Certainly if a person is ill but in no danger of losing his life, it would be unethical as well as immoral to subject him to a dangerous, unproved treatment; but when a man is dying, when all hope is gone, when his only choice is between burial and cremation, and he has the desire to live and the money to pay for cryogenic interment, then he cannot wait for an obscure biologist to freeze and revive an animal in order to test the process. Freezing offers the only hope that exists today, however slim, and with the rapid strides being made in all

fields of medicine and technology, it is hardly unrealistic to expect that a future generation of scientists will not only have found the cure for all man's diseases, but that they will have perfected methods for correcting any damage caused by the freezing process as well.

In practice, cryonics was a whole lot messier. In fact, Bob Nelson's own account of the first cryonic suspension reads like a dark comedy. Bob flew to Phoenix to meet the first man who was building tanks for cryonics storage, an eccentric wig maker named Ed Hope. It offered an interesting parallel to my own story: picked up at the Phoenix airport by strange characters, driven to a bizarre facility for a day of science fiction come to life. Why these people chose to do this kind of work in the middle of the desert is beyond me.

On the way from the airport, Hope told Nelson his interest in cryonics dated back to thawing out frozen rabbits as a kid.

Nelson candidly reported that his revulsion for death was stronger than his love of life. That's why he got into cryonies. For years, he says, he suffered from nightmares of being buried alive, scratching at the inside of a coffin. Once he became involved in the quest for immortality through cryonic suspension, the nightmares stopped.

Ed Hope had already frozen a woman at her son's request but it was for cosmetic purposes only. The man wanted his mother preserved like Lenin in his tomb. Hope told Nelson that he had tried to keep the true purpose of the storage tank a secret from the welder he had employed to make it but the guy found out and asked, "Have you frozen the woman's soul, too?" The two didn't work together again.

Rather soon, a "national cryonics movement" developed, consisting of people who considered themselves disciples of Robert Ettinger. Most were based in New York and Washington, D.C. Saul Kent helped form the first cryonics societies, in New York. Kent traveled the country organizing and overseeing various cryonics groups, inspired by Ettinger's words. The Life Extension Society found out about Ed Hope's effort to freeze a woman and fed the story to the press. They didn't mention that the freezing was purely cosmetic, that Hope had for all intents and purposes simply embalmed the woman, and the public was misled into believing Hope had put Ettinger's cryonics theories into practice. After a year, the woman's son had his mother removed from Hope's cold-storage tank and buried.

From the beginning, cryonicists aggressively pursued publicity. Getting on TV became a top priority and cryonics became a regular topic on talk shows. Ettinger appeared on *Steve Allen, Today, Mike Douglas, ABC Nightlife, Merv Griffin,* and *The Tonight Show,* when Johnny Carson was host. Another guest of Johnny's that night was Zsa Zsa Gabor. When Ettinger flew out to California to meet Nelson and the CSC members, the first thing he did was stop by Paramount Studios, at the studio's request, to meet with film producers and advise them on the technical side of cryonics for an upcoming science fiction movie.

By cryonicists' standards, Dr. James Bedford was the first man "frozen" (in his book, Nelson calls him by the fake name "Dr. Harold Greene"). Although Alcorians considered Nelson a traitor for subsequent actions he took, and the worst thing ever to happen to cryonics, Dr. Bedford is nonetheless considered a hero.

During that first cryo-suspension, Bob Nelson had to leave the room three times to vomit. Still, Bob picked up a hypodermic needle and pretended to stick it into the dead body while a colleague snapped a publicity photo.

After the first suspension was completed, *Life* magazine was going to make it a lead story in an issue where it was to run six pages. Bob and his cohorts staged a photo shoot where they donned medical coats, connected a mannequin to a heart machine, and took turns jabbing it with needles while a *Life* photographer snapped away.

On January 27, 1967, while *Life* was printing this edition, astronauts Gus Grissom, Ed White, and Roger Chaffee were tragically burned to death when the *Apollo 1* space capsule caught fire on the ground. *Life* stopped the presses to cover this breaking story. There wasn't enough space in the magazine for both stories. The cryonics story was removed when they restarted the presses. According to *We Froze the First Man,* about 2 million copies of the magazine had already been printed and mailed to subscribers. Nowadays, rare editions of *Life* exist with Bob Nelson and cryonics as the magazine's lead story. *Life*'s publicist told Bob Nelson they could not rerun the story in a future edition since 2 million subscribers already had seen it. Bob Nelson wrote that he believed the entire history of cryonics would have been different had the story run in full.

———————

Beginning with the early days of cryonics, there were problems with family members, not to mention some inadvertent dark humor. People backed out at the last moment on religious grounds, and there were often problems with hospital officials. Dr. Bedford's son nearly came to blows with hospital personnel while getting his father's body released for his suspension.

Dr. Bedford's procedure began at the Los Angeles–area nursing home where he had died. The nursing home was run by a couple, out of their home. Nelson said that it was a gothic-looking house that reminded him of the House of Seven Gables.

"Some day," Nelson wrote, "in the not too distant future, patients will be cryogenically interred in respectable hospital buildings, but the macabre atmosphere in which this first freeze was carried out will undoubtedly satisfy the detractors who equate our efforts with those of the team of Karloff and Lugosi."

Not to be deterred, Nelson wrote, "We would have administered to [Dr. Bedford] in a garage." In this determination, it turns out, he was a forerunner to Mike Darwin and Hugh Hixon.

The doctor hired to perform the first suspension started to back out when faced with the reality of it. Nelson and the others had to be "firm" with him.

While the body was pumped full of primitive cryo-protectants—somewhere between fifty and one hundred needle injections of glycerol—Bedford's son called from his father's nearby home in Glendale to say the storage canister had arrived from Ed Hope's wig shop in Phoenix.

Bob Nelson wrapped the body in a quilt, loaded it into the back of his pickup truck, tied it down with rope, and left for the Bedford home. The body was placed into Ed Hope's canister, but Nelson was concerned a reporter would see the canister in the Bedfords' living room and call the Health Department, so they put the body, inside its canister, back into his pickup truck and drove to the home of another cryonicist.

As they were moving Dr. Bedford into the garage of Bob's friend, the wife of the cryonicist whose home they were now using came running out, saw what was going on, and started screaming. It was "straining her capabilities as a hostess," Nelson mused.

Robert Ettinger wasn't present for the body's perfusion (the process by which the chemicals are delivered to the bloodstream) or its insertion into the canister, but he did make it out to California the next day to speak at the press conference.

At six the next morning, Nelson was awakened by a call. The wife was still angry and threatening to throw her husband out of their house unless the body was immediately removed from their garage. Nelson's friend wanted to restore peace in his home and was going to refuse to attend the press conference, so Nelson struck a deal with the wife. She would allow her husband to attend the press conference if Nelson replaced him with two people to "watch the body" during the interim.

At eight a.m. Nelson woke his twelve-year-old son: "I've got a babysitting job for you." Johnny Nelson had had a friend sleep over the night before, so Bob now had two young body watchers.

On the way, Johnny asked his father who they would be babysitting. "The man we froze," Nelson answered. The two boys looked at each other and shrugged. Two bucks was two bucks.

With Johnny Nelson and his friend stationed in the garage keeping watch on Dr. Bedford's body, Bob Nelson had a day full of interviews and meetings of the Science Fiction Authors Club. He grew concerned, though, that his friend's wife would eventually call the cops, so he phoned his secretary, beginning the conversation with, "I know I've asked you to store some pretty weird things at your home in the past few years, but . . ."

The secretary lived atop Topanga Canyon, high in the hills above Los Angeles. Nelson drove up the five miles of steep, twisting canyon roads, afraid at every turn that Dr. Bedford was going to slide out of the pickup bed and roll down the street behind him.

When Nelson finally arrived with Dr. Bedford, he loaded the heavy canister into his secretary's station wagon and darkened its windows to prevent anyone who peeked into the garage—including photographers—from seeing what was in there. Still rattled, Nelson had a drink, drove home, and went to bed.

One of the physicians involved soon got a call from the county coroner, ordering him to sign the death certificate. Unfortunately for the doctor, he didn't know where the body was. He panicked and began calling Nelson's associates, threatening to have them charged with homicide unless they helped him locate the body.

So Bob Nelson got another call and went back to his secretary's house. He loaded the nomadic Dr. Bedford into the pickup and drove him back down the winding Topanga Canyon roads. By now, Dr. Bedford's canister was running low on coolant (Nelson used dry ice, a sort of poor man's liquid nitrogen). Nelson met up with a colleague to refill the primitive dewar with dry ice at a children's playground at the bottom of the canyon. Nelson was amazed no one gave them a hard time. There they were, in the back of a pickup truck, lifting the lid off of what looked like a coffin, pouring dry ice over a dead body with white vapor billowing out, all in full view of children playing on the swing set nearby.

Not surprisingly, in the years following the 1964 publication of Robert Ettinger's book, all this new cryonics stuff served as prime fodder for wags in the press. Les Dennis of the *New York World Telegram and Sun* wrote about the day when you would defrost a blonde with your TV dinner. Finally, wrote Gary Lautens of the *Toronto Star*, someone will be able to tell us whether or not the little light goes out when you shut the refrigerator door.

Some college students at Berkeley heard about it all and decided to form a protest movement—this being the sixties and all. They started the Abolish Death Committee and picketed a funeral parlor.

Bob Nelson continued to freeze people but funded most of it himself. Some of the relatives who promised financial support for the continued maintenance of their loved ones eventually stopped paying. He was able to excavate a large plot inside a cemetery in Chatsworth, California, and have a tank installed in it. Many people who worked on it donated their time, like Nelson, convinced of the value of cryonics. Like liquid nitrogen, dry ice naturally evaporates and will escape through whatever cracks it can find, so Nelson had to replace it regularly. Once every five days, he would load up his vehicle with two hundred pounds of dry ice and drive more than an hour each way to replenish the tank. He paid for it all out of his own pocket. At times, he took personal loans to continue filling the tank with dry ice.

A few people involved were wealthy and gave Nelson enough money to ensure their loved ones were cared for. More tanks were buried in the cemetery, more canisters ordered from Ed Hope. One wealthy Frenchman paid for his deceased eight-year-old daughter to be suspended and stored. However, the ones who hadn't paid Nelson enough, or at all, became a big problem. Nelson felt obliged to care for them but had nowhere to put them. Without telling anyone, Bob Nelson started putting multiple bodies into single canisters. The unpaid ones were stuffed into frozen embraces with the paid ones. Some went head first, some went feet first, and as an Alcorian later put it, "It was like putting together a Chinese puzzle."

Eventually, Nelson just ran out of money and stopped refilling the canisters. The bodies thawed and melted into each other. (Years later, Alcor moved Dr. Bedford's body into one of their dewars, making a big deal about now having in their facility the first man ever cryonically suspended; Alcor didn't take possession of any of Nelson's other unfortunate cryopioneers, just Bedford.) Almost everyone involved sued Bob Nelson. They also sued the mortician who was working with him. The name of the undertaker was Joe Klockgether, the same mortician Alcor was using when I worked there. This mass melting is what cryonicists refer to as the Chatsworth Incident.

After the Chatsworth Incident, cryonicists fled the CSC like rats from a burning building. Two of them, Fred and Linda Chamberlain, formed the Alcor Society for Solid State Hypothermia in 1972. In 1977 the name was changed to Alcor Life Extension Foundation.

In choosing the new name, the Chamberlains figured cryonicists' final destiny would be traveling into outer space, so they wanted to name themselves after a star. They pored over star maps and found Alcor, a star in the Big Dipper.

Jerry Lemler wrote a whole section on Alcor's name in his *Alcor Life Extension Foundation: An Introduction.*

Jerry described "Alcor" as an imperfect acronym for "Allopathic Cryogenic Rescue." Allopathy is "a medical perspective wherein 'any treatment that improves the prognosis is valid.'" In this case, the prognosis is death. The thinking is that nothing is worse than death and burial, so anything else, even with a billion-to-1 odds, is an improvement.

I did a little research of my own on the star Alcor during some of my downtime around the office. Alcor has a companion star named Mizar, which is very bright. Throughout the centuries and in a variety of cultures, it has been a test of visual acuity whether a star watcher can see Alcor despite its bright neighbor. The cryonicists who started Alcor wanted to play off that tradition. "Only with excellent vision can one tell that there are two stars rather than just one," Jerry Lemler wrote. "In the early days of cryonics, . . . Alcor would be a 'test' of vision as regards life extension."

It was perfect. Is your foresight acute enough to recognize the truth? Do you have the unique ability to see Alcor, the guiding star of mankind?

The visionary aspect of Alcor could be looked at from a different angle, though, I realized. The nature of Alcor, the dim star, is to deceive, to hide itself, to conceal its true essence. Like the cryonics facility quietly camouflaged inside the nondescript industrial park outside the Scottsdale Airport, Alcor did its best to not be seen for what it really was.

Some mythologies do not paint the star Alcor kindly at all.

To the Greeks, the "Lost Pleiad" Electra left her companions and became this star, which they called Alopex, "The Fox." The influence of the entire constellation is said to be suspicious and mistrustful. It was believed prone to great ire when roused.

In the Hindu realm, the dim star Westerners call Alcor is a symbol of marital piety. She is the humble and demure wife, dutifully following her husband, Mizar, never leading, always acquiescent. Because of Mizar's position as the groin or loins of the Great Bear (aka the Big Dipper), Alcor's feminine nature and close proximity to her mate are sometimes depicted with more erotic implications. Suffice it to say, she's always right there under him.

In an Arabic story, the star Alcor is the infant in the arms of Mizar, here a female mourner in a funeral procession. The mourners follow the procession and thirst for vengeance, Mizar holding little bloodthirsty baby Alcor in her arms.

And perhaps most appropriate of all, in Norse mythology, Alcor is the toe of a man named Orwandil. The toe suffered frostbite and was broken off and tossed away into the sky by the god Thor. Little, unhealthy, frozen Alcor, tossed off as diseased debris, amputated to protect the whole. At least the frozen part jibed with the Alcor I had come to know.

Most people believe that the brain houses our personalities, our memories, what makes us human individuals. If we could transport our brain through time, cryonicists postulated, and then either reanimate our body, grow a new one from DNA cloning, fix our brain atop a robot body, or download our brain's information into a computer matrix, we could achieve the ultimate in life extension: immortality.

The science of cryobiology—as opposed to cryonics—has led to in vitro fertilization, with sperm and embryos cooled to the temperature of liquid nitrogen, thawed, and combined to create a viable organism. Cryobiologists have also successfully frozen small organs for transplant. The question is, can we successfully freeze and then defrost the human brain despite all its fragility and complexity?

Most scientists think the answer is no. The argument goes that you're better off cloning from a DNA molecule since the freezing and unfreezing process is just too destructive. Dr. Michael Shermer, founding publisher of *Skeptic* magazine and author of *Why People Believe Weird Things: Pseudoscience, Superstition, and Other Confusions of Our Time*, wrote in *Scientific American* in 2001 that "To see the flaw in this system, thaw out a can of frozen strawberries. During freezing, the water within each cell expands, crystallizes, and ruptures the cell membranes. When defrosted, all the intracellular goo oozes out, turning your strawberries into runny mush. This is your brain on cryonics."

Ice crystals under a microscope look like horribly barbed medieval weapons. They physically puncture and tear the body's cells as they grow.

Then there is the immense pressure of expanding ice. Think of roads, broken and buckled by water that seeps into the ground and then freezes. This is the same thing that happens to a brain and skull when frozen. Cryonicists argue that they now have a "vitrification process" that eliminates water and ice, converting the brain tissue into a consistency like glass. The bottom line, though, is they are nowhere near being able to use this process on the human brain. This isn't just my opinion.

Prominent cryobiology researcher Arthur W. Rowe, of New York University's School of Medicine, scoffs at the whole idea, stating, "Believing cryonics could reanimate somebody who has been frozen, is like believing you can turn hamburger back into a cow."

"This doesn't pass the straight-face test," says Kenneth Goodman, director of the University of Miami's Bioethics Program.

Dr. Charles Daschbach of St Joseph's Hospital in Phoenix says of cryonics, "It's not science, it's pseudoscience. The odds [of a successful suspension and reanimation] are somewhat the same that you would have a religious apparition, be struck by lightning, and win the lottery on the same day."

The president of the National Council Against Health Fraud, William T. Jarvis PhD, calls cryonics "quackery's last shot at you."

The Society for Cryobiology actually went so far as to state in its bylaws that membership may be refused to anyone practicing cryonics.

Even if centuries from now the technology is developed to reanimate folks who are frozen, the technology does not exist today to cryo-preserve them safely enough to make resuscitation in the future viable. Cryonicists respond with the argument that nanotechnology will evolve to the point where miniscule molecular machines will be able to repair and replicate our bodies on the cellular level. An army of these microscopic machines will fix the freezing damage as well as whatever killed us in the first place. They argue that even if there is a one in a billion chance to be revived, isn't it worth it?

Imagining successful cryonic suspension and reanimation were possible, though, raises some very serious questions, both philosophical and practical. Was man made to be immortal? Are we psychologically equipped to live thousands of years? Who will care for the suspended patients decades or centuries from now? Would ethics in a future society even allow for reanimation? The pursuit of cryonic suspension is "supreme egotism," said John Baust, director of the Institute of Biomedical Technology at the State University of New York at Binghamton. "The individual who freezes himself or herself to come back in the future makes the assumption he will be a contributor to that society and that they would want them."

Who will pay for their reanimation? Who will choose which cryonauts to reanimate? How will the reanimated assimilate to the culture shock of a future century? What about the depletion of the earth's natural resources if population goes unchecked, and many become immortal? Who will they know when they awaken? How will they earn a living? Might they reclaim their great-great-great-grandchildren's inheritance? Will they be eligible for social security? Rent control?

As bizarre as it may seem at first glance and despite all this anti-cryonics sentiment among the mainstream, as I discovered before first visiting Alcor, there were some very serious scientists behind cryonics, world leaders in the fields of medicine and technology like Marvin Minsky, Ralph Merkle, Michael D. West, Ray Kurzweil, and Aubrey de Grey, to name a few. Jerry Lemler was fond of mentioning how he had shared the stage at cryonics conferences with these luminaries.

The mainstream, "legitimate" fields of cryogenics and cryobiology are the foundation upon which cryonicists stand. In a way, today's cryonicists are simply waiting for tomorrow's technology to catch up with their vision. Frostbitten toes and slushy strawberries aside, there sure were a lot of brilliant scientists putting their hopes in Alcor and cryonics. This convinced me that, despite the skepticism of other notable scientists and all the weird things I'd seen on the job, there was still—hopefully—something positive going on at Alcor, something worth being a part of. Otherwise, why would Michael D. West, Ray Kurzweil et al., keep signing their names to it? This hope helped me get past my own doubts about cryonics. It kept me going.

SIX

GATEKEEPERS TO IMMORTALITY

I was eager to take up Alcor on the offer that had been made during my interview, to participate in what Charles Platt and Jerry Lemler had promised was the valuable research going on at Critical Care Research, aka 21st Century Medicine, Alcor's cryobiology research facility in Rancho Cucamonga, California. I was very excited about the ice-resistant road treatment and organ transplant research. I knew Charles visited CCR regularly and reminded him of the offer. Eventually he took the hint and invited me along for an upcoming visit to the facility. This was, in fact, the same day as the first board meeting I had attended. Charles and I left for CCR later in the afternoon. For a variety of reasons, February 10, 2003, turned out to be a day I'll never forget.

Since that bare-knuckled drive from the Phoenix airport to Alcor during my initial visit, I had avoided at all costs stepping into a moving vehicle with Charles Platt behind the wheel, so I volunteered to drive. As Charles climbed into my white Dodge Ram pickup, he carefully placed his khaki travel bag on the floor between our seats. I remembered how Charles had carried that bag with him on my first day of work, and how he had set it down on his desk in his supply closet–cum-office. In fact, I had seen Charles carrying that bag with him every day he came to Alcor.

"Charles, what's the story with that bag?" I asked.

"This is my Survival Bag," he said. "I keep it with me in case of a natural disaster or terrorist attack."

"Oh."

"Inside are several of my personal medications, a first-aid kit, and a few dollars cash," Charles said.

He unzipped it and showed me his first-aid kit. The entire contents consisted of a handful of bandages.

"I carry it everywhere I go," Charles continued. "To work, on vacation, to the movies, to the corner store, everywhere. I want to be prepared for any eventuality. Earthquake, nuclear attack, chemical spill, biological weapon attack, anything. These things can happen at any time, Larry. You should think about carrying one yourself."

As soon as we hit the freeway, Charles told me part of the reason he wanted us to take this trip together was so that we could talk. As I've said, Charles sometimes exhibited a paternal attitude toward me. We had already spent a good deal of time together. He came down from his home in northern Arizona quite often during my first few weeks. Like me, he didn't have real time-consuming, day-to-day duties, so we sat and chatted a lot. "Together, Larry," he would say, "we can do great things in cryonics." I liked Charles.

"Larry," Charles began, "I know you've only been with us for several weeks but you've been doing a phenomenal job. Everyone thinks so. You've already adopted responsibilities beyond your job description. I've wanted to step down as chief operating officer for a long time but there hasn't been anyone qualified to replace me."

Charles paused for a moment, then continued, "Larry, I want you to take over for me as COO."

"Really?!"

"I will continue to advise Alcor from home, but I don't want to be coming into the office on a regular basis anymore. Frankly, I'm a little burnt out."

It was obvious Charles was stretched pretty thin. Maybe he wasn't always as paranoid as I had seen him, and just needed a break.

"I want you to start shadowing me at work," Charles continued. "I want you to learn how to do everything I do."

"Charles, thanks," I said. "I'm honored that you have that much faith in me."

"It's not going to be easy to get the board to approve this," he said. "You're the first Alcor executive who isn't also an Alcor member. I'm sure you've already noticed that we're a closed group."

"Yeah."

"I want to share my personal observations regarding the other Alcor employees, Larry. If you're going to run the place, I want you to know everything I know."

All the tales Charles told me during that drive bore out in my future experience. I heard them confirmed by other Alcorians or saw proof of them myself. I can't discount that Charles really wanted me on his side, but I also believe he wanted me to be in the know. Alcorian political wrangling aside, Charles really did want the best for the suspended Alcorians in the dewars. He took that sense of responsibility for their well-being very seriously. Some of them had been his close friends before their suspensions.

First, Charles confided in me that he didn't think much of Jerry Lemler. I knew this already. I had noticed that Charles spent a good deal of time writing and distributing e-mails and memos criticizing Lemler's actions as president. I had received many of them in the few short weeks I had been at Alcor. Alcor had had something like four presidents in six years.

"This high rate of turnover," Charles said, "is a testament to the unique characters that are drawn to cryonics. Free-spirited, strong-willed people. Alcor's presidents tend to be a tad eccentric but they are all, if you will excuse the pun, deadly serious about cryonics. They have to be. But Jerry Lemler simply isn't up to the job." Charles explained that Jerry was voted in as president and CEO a very short time after becoming an Alcor member.

Charles believed that the board had made Jerry Lemler president only because he was an MD, thinking it would look better to have a medical doctor as president. "I was against it then, and I'm against it now," he said. "Lemler has no clue how to run an organization like Alcor."

Charles told me that the only previous executive or managerial experience Jerry Lemler had had was "being in charge of an insane asylum." Indeed, I found out later, after Jerry had completed his psychiatric residency training at the Norristown State Hospital in suburban Philadelphia, he had become chief of the medical staff of Lakeshore Mental Health Institute in Knoxville, Tennessee. I never found out if this was really the same as, in

Charles's words, being in charge of an insane asylum, but I have to say I knew a lot of people who would think that running an "insane asylum" was the perfect training ground for a future president and CEO of Alcor.

"Then Jerry got into trouble with the State of Tennessee for a diet-pill scandal," Charles said. "He got caught selling uppers to housewives."

In a petition to the Alcor board regarding Jerry Lemler, Charles wrote:

> I have never seen a public statement explaining in detail why JL [Jerry Lemler] was disciplined by medical authorities in Tennessee. I am concerned that there is a potential embarrassment, here, which a resourceful journalist could uncover.
>
> When JL was in Tennessee, he ran some clinics, which prescribed diet pills. Subsequently, according to documents that were found online, he was subjected to disciplinary action by a local medical authority. . . .
>
> To retain his license, the disciplinary action required him to travel to several meetings. I refused to sign a check reimbursing him for legal fees connected with one of these trips, but I have seen evidence that Alcor paid for some of the others. . . .
>
> So far as I know, JL has never made a full public statement about the regulatory problems that he experienced. . . . Full disclosure is an obvious ethical requirement for anyone who takes the sensitive job as Alcor's CEO. Fortunately no journalists have investigated JL's Tennessee background.

I believed that not only was Charles correct that Jerry had some serious ethical questions to answer about the diet-pill accusations, he had also crossed an ethical line in billing Alcor for the trips he took to Tennessee to satisfy the terms of his probation.

Jerry Lemler's specific case and the official reason for the suspension of his medical license are posted on the Tennessee Department of Health Web site for Licensure Verification:

> The Tennessee Board of Medical Examiners Docket No. 17.18–011107A.

Unprofessional conduct; Gross malpractice or a pattern of continued or repeated malpractice, ignorance, negligence or incompetence; Violation of statutes and rules governing the prescribing of
controlled substances.

Lemler was sentenced to two years' probation and a $1,000 fine.

Charles went on to complain about Lemler's expense account. In
Charles's opinion, Jerry was treating Alcor, a nonprofit company, like his
own cash cow, regularly fattening his friends and himself on $400 lunches
at upscale Scottsdale restaurants—outside his already extremely generous
expense account. Four hundred dollars seemed like a lot of money to
spend on lunch. However, several weeks later, Charles showed me Jerry's
lunch receipts. It was true. The numbers made my head spin.

Charles told me Jerry had also consistently hired his wife, his daughter, and his son-in-law to perform odd jobs around Alcor for big cash payments. They already drew weekly paychecks as full-time Alcor employees
but Jerry also arranged for each of them to receive an extra $500 to $1,000
for every decapitation they participated in. They didn't miss one. Charles
was exceptionally unforgiving on this issue—he referred to it as the "Lemler family bonus scheme."

"Jerry becomes outraged when anyone accuses him of nepotism,"
Charles said, "yet he continues signing the checks." Charles said Jerry's
family performed nonessential tasks, jobs that should never call for so
much pay, yet still their work was substandard.

Then Charles told me that Jerry had published a book about the time
he led an expedition to Turkey and claimed to have found the final resting
place of Noah's Ark. It's called *Journey to Noah's Ark*. That explained the
picture on Jerry's desk with him wearing an Indiana Jones outfit. That was
Jerry standing atop Mount Ararat, on the site of his discovery of the remains of Noah's Ark. Later, Jerry gave me an autographed copy. If I remember correctly, his only proof was finding a hill with a sort of
boat-shaped bulge in it.

Next, Charles told me that CFO Michael Riskin hired himself out as a
sex therapist. I told Charles I found that hard to believe. Charles said it

was true, although from what Charles had heard, Riskin's "sex therapy" sounded a lot like he and his wife just threw spouse-swapping parties in their home.

In his capacity as sex therapist, Charles continued, Riskin had worked on, and/or appeared in, several swingers' DVDs. Later, searching the Internet, I found a movie "Written & Directed" by Michael Riskin and his wife titled *Swinging: From Fantasy to Reality.* The DVD cover featured two women licking a man's bare stomach and grabbing the bulge in his jockeys. The online description of Riskin's movie had this to say about Riskin and his wife: "Co-authors of the popular book *Simultaneous Orgasm & Other Joys of Sexual Ecstasy,* they were professional surrogate partners prior to acquiring licensure and board certification."

Evidently this meant people actually paid Riskin to have sex with them as a professional surrogate partner. What a world.

(Later, I searched the Web and found that the actors appearing in the film written and directed by Alcor's CFO were also the stars of the films *The High Price of Gash, Shower Head, Pump My Humps, Clit Smackin' Good, Ass Crunchers 8, Semen Sippers 5,* and *Interracial Sausage Party.*)

As I continued driving us toward Rancho Cucamonga, I reflected on the connection between cryonics and deviant—or at least freaky—sex. I already knew that Alcorians were often frontiersmen in their attitudes toward sex as well as life extension. Saul Kent, a major player at Alcor and one of the pioneers of the entire cryonics movement, had published a book called *Future Sex* in 1974. In it, Saul predicted that recorded sex environments would one day be loaded into one's home computer, in order to provide an immersive sex trip and achieve what he called "multimedia masturbation." Kind of like a Jungle Room at a by-the-hour sex motel, but in the privacy of your own home. Robert Ettinger, the father of cryonics, also spent some time writing about sex of the future. In his book *Man into Superman,* published in 1972, Ettinger wrote about people using future medical technology to improve on nature's design: "The sexual superwoman may be riddled with cleverly designed orifices of various kinds, something like a wriggly Swiss cheese, but shapelier and more fragrant; and her supermate may sprout assorted protuberances, so that they intertwine and roll over each other in a million permutations of The Act, tireless as hydraulic pumps. . . . A perpetual grapple, no holes barred, could produce a continuous state of multiple orgasm."

Charles, I knew, was himself a prolific and well-known writer. His first novel was called *The Gas*. In it, the government had accidentally released an experimental chemical weapon, a gas that once inhaled made people lose their sexual inhibitions. After that, there's a whole lotta humpin' goin' on. The idea was, if your enemies are busy having sex, you could walk right in and defeat them. Though Charles called the novel science fiction, I had found reviews from disappointed SF readers complaining that too much of the book was dedicated to long, detailed descriptions of deviant sex acts.

To be fair, Charles also wrote many articles for respectable publications like *Wired* magazine. He was probably best known for his interviews of famous science fiction writers. They have been published in many magazines, as well as in book form.

The way Charles spoke about cryonics made him seem like an intelligent guy. He was very confident when he talked about it, I came to realize, because he was so well rehearsed. It was like playing the piano. If you practiced the same song over and over for years, you were going to get real good at playing that one piece, but only that one. Charles spoke intelligently about cryonics because he knew his arguments on the subject inside and out. I had heard him repeat them word for word on separate occasions. But when you took him out of his comfort zone and got him talking about some other field, Charles did not seem very knowledgeable or confident.

When we stopped for gas, Charles opened his Survival Bag to get some cash. What he had referred to as "a few dollars cash" was actually a thick stack of twenties and hundreds, probably $3,000 or $4,000.

Back on the road, Charles told me that Mike Perry and Hugh Hixon lived at Alcor. Not like when people say, "Oh, he's married to his job; he lives at the office." I mean, just like the patients in the dewars, they resided there. Back when Alcor was in Riverside, California, Charles told me, the two lived inside an old Volkswagen bus parked out back. Now, in the Scottsdale facility, they were upgraded to a hidden apartment down a hallway off the front lobby. There was a room with two beds, Charles said, one for Hugh and one for Mike. The most surprising news was that there was a bathroom with a shower back there, although I suspected the shower was grossly underemployed.

Over time, I heard Jerry Lemler express his fears over this issue repeatedly, especially whenever he and Hugh were at odds. Jerry would complain that the area was zoned commercial and if the city found out Alcor had people living on the property, there would be heavy fines. It seemed to me that, for him, it wasn't an issue of right and wrong, legal and illegal—it was the fear of discovery and punishment.

No wonder Mike always looked like he had just woken up.

And the mystery of the pizza boxes was put to rest for me. Charles told me they were Hugh's. I pictured the two of them munching away every night in the front lobby, their own private dining room, Hugh with his Domino's, Mike with his veggie Cool Whip.

Charles told me that Hugh's father, also named Hugh, was in one of the dewars, the second person ever suspended at Alcor. He was one of the military men on the front lobby's Wall of Fame. I wondered how it made Hugh feel, living and sleeping a few steps away from his father's frozen body.

I also learned more about Mike Perry from Charles. After earning his doctoral degree, Mike worked as a computer programmer before becoming actively involved in cryonics. He became an Alcor member in 1984. Mike started volunteering at Alcor in Riverside, California, in 1987 and by 1989 had become a full-time employee.

I was beginning to realize that, like Jerry Lemler's family, people tended to get hired on at Alcor because they became part of the trusted inner circle. If someone was devoted to cryonics and hung around long enough, he would be given a title and get put on the payroll. That's how Mike Perry and Mathew Sullivan were hired, I knew. Mathew Sullivan was living in Ohio when he first got into cryonics. He relocated to Scottsdale, started volunteering at Alcor, proved his loyalty, and soon they gave him the title "Director of Suspension Readiness." Jennifer Chapman, one of the most dedicated Alcor members, was paid extremely well for answering a few phone calls. Alcor hired a non-Alcorian accountant for a short time. She used to come into my office and complain that here she was, a certified public accountant, yet Jennifer, a glorified secretary, was paid more money.

"I suppose the most curious thing about Michael Perry," Charles continued, "is that he removed his own testicles with a razor blade."

I nearly drove us off the road.

"Back in college, he peeled the layers of his own scrotum off with a razor, one by one."

I was in shock. All I could think about was, for all my years in medicine, I didn't know there were layers down there. Then again, I'd never been called in on a case of self-castration.

Later I learned that Mike talked about it freely, and in fact he volunteered the information to a psychologist who published it as part of a study on self-castration and self-mutilation. Mike had some sort of psychiatric problem with his sex drive, so right there in his college bathroom he cut into the flesh of his scrotum with a razor. Only, halfway through the "operation," Mike got hungry, stuffed some paper towels down his pants to soak up the blood, popped down to the cafeteria for a bite, then returned to the boys' room and continued working. According to Mike's own words, he successfully "removed his testicles" in this manner. He cut very deep and severed the nerves running to his penis—intentionally.

It still functioned, Charles said, but "only as a hose." Then Charles added, "But Mike has no regrets about it."

These were my new colleagues.

Critical Care Research, aka 21st Century Medicine, occupied an impressive building in Rancho Cucamonga, California. When I visited, there was a staff of five people. Dr. Steve Harris ran the place and was in charge of the medical research there. Steve was geeky, lanky, and completely content that he had found his life's calling. The rest of the staff was composed of a cryobiologist named Brian Wowk—who wasn't there the day we arrived—Sandra Russell, Steve's surgical assistant, another woman named Joan O'Farrell, and a nerdy fellow named Greg Fahy.

Greg was a cryobiologist who used to work for the Red Cross in Bethesda, Maryland. He did not have the mind-set of a typical research scientist, though. Greg had been into cryonics, hard-core, for decades. He was the one researching the road treatment that would inhibit freezing, and was well-known in his field.

At CCR that day I also met a young volunteer named Todd Huffman, a whiz kid and veritable prodigy who began working with Alcor when he was a teenager. When I met him he had already turned twenty, and impressed me as an absolutely brilliant young man. Like many hard-core Alcorians, however, Todd's background was grim. I think it is not uncommon for people who are extremely unhappy with their present lives to dream of another life, a fresh start in a distant future where everything will be new, exciting, and, most of all, just different. Actually, I think this is a powerful motivation for many cryonicists.

Todd's upbringing was far from average and, in my opinion, far from healthy. His parents were extremely strict. For instance, Todd told me he was never allowed to watch television. Ever.

At a very young age, Todd had become obsessed with the idea of living for centuries and seeing the future. At thirteen, Todd joined a fringe pseudoscience group of people who called themselves Extropists or Extropians. Going back to Sir Isaac Newton, entropy has always been understood as the concept that matter, the universe, and life itself are naturally deteriorating to a state of inert uniformity. Extropy is a term these folks coined to mean the opposite, to express their belief that through his own efforts, especially technology, man can put an end to entropy, inhibit and defeat physical deterioration, and live forever.

Extropians believed man would achieve immortality through recombinant DNA, surgical implants, and the like. Extropians funneled many of their members into Alcor, and that's how Todd became involved. He figured if he couldn't live forever in this life, the consolation prize would be to be frozen for a possible second life.

Todd was an especially active Alcorian. He had become a member of Alcor's Los Angeles emergency response team while still in his teens. Charles told me that emergency cryonic suspensions had been delayed for hours because car rental companies wouldn't rent minivans to Todd since he was too young to sign their rental agreements. On the other hand, Alcor had no minimum age policy. They even let Todd assist during surgery. I frowned at the thought of teenage Todd in the Alcor operating room helping to decapitate octogenarians and AIDS victims.

Personally, I liked Todd. I figured he had gotten a raw deal as a child. Still, I thought Todd was an extremely bright young man and could accomplish anything he set his mind to.

Steve Harris gave me a tour of CCR. There were some small offices but most of the building was taken up by the lab and OR. As they were showing me around, I heard dogs barking.

"They do a good deal of animal experimentation here at CCR," Charles explained.

"I didn't know that," I said.

"Actually, Larry, we have an animal experiment scheduled for today," Steve said. "The dog is already on the table. Would you like to observe?"

"Sure, Steve," I said. "The research you guys do here is a big reason I took the job at Alcor in the first place."

"Smart man." Steve smiled. "Well, let's get to it."

That word, "it," sounded more than a little ominous, and I wondered what was in store. I love dogs. I understood that there was some valid, life-saving experimentation done with animals, but I also knew there was a lot of frivolous, unnecessary animal experimentation performed in the name of science as well. I was really hoping dogs didn't get hurt at CCR. Maybe they were just testing thermometers on them or something.

As I watched Steve anesthetize the German shepherd, I wondered what scientific purpose the experiment would be directed toward. Once the dog was asleep, Steve performed a blood washout, removing her blood and replacing it with the same chemicals Alcor uses for human cryo-suspensions. In only a few minutes the dog had died on the CCR operating table.

Next, Steve Harris sliced opened up her chest, examined her lungs, and—that was it. No one took notes. No one filmed the procedure. Steve Harris left the dog splayed out on the slab for his assistant to dispose of.

"Steve," I said, "why did you do that?"

Steve popped something into his mouth. "Do what? That? I wanted to see how long she'd live," he said.

I grew very quiet. I was really upset. Was this the lifesaving cryobiological research Charles had referred to back in December when he was selling me on Alcor over the phone? Was this the type of work Ralph Merkle and Aubrey de Grey and all those famous scientists were signing their names to?

I knew these Alcorians were strange. I had started to get used to the fact that they were obsessed with achieving their own immortality. Many of them were brilliant and others were arrogant, but the experiment I had just witnessed on that poor dog gave me the first clue that some of them were completely remorseless and without conscience.

What was Steve expecting? What was he really looking for inside that animal's chest? Though he had replaced her blood with the chemicals used in cryonic suspensions, he hadn't even tried to freeze her. What was the point? He said he wanted to see how long she lived—a pretty dubious reason to sacrifice a dog—yet I don't think he even watched the clock. It seemed completely senseless.

I was speechless. It broke my heart.

Charles said, "Well, that's it, Larry. Unless you want to see anything else, we should be going."

"No, Charles," I said. "Let's get out of here."

As we were stepping into my truck, Charles said, "Larry, we didn't drive all this way just to visit CCR. I'm taking you to visit Saul Kent."

I knew the name. Saul Kent was one of the most dedicated and influential Alcorians alive.

———

Saul Kent was filthy rich. He had a real nice house, very big and private, set off by itself in the middle of a wooded area outside Riverside, California. As we drove up, I was impressed.

A maid opened the door and as soon as I followed Charles into the foyer, a strange-looking German shepherd started shuffling toward us. The dog scared me at first, not because I was afraid of getting bitten, but because there seemed to be something creepy about her, something not right in the head. Immediately, I wondered if Steve Harris had gotten his hands on this animal too.

She inched up to me sideways, like a crab, sniffed my hand, looked at me out of the corner of her eye, whimpered, and then limped off. She seemed like she had deteriorated motor functions, or maybe she was mentally impaired. Or both. In fact, she looked to me like a mentally retarded dog that had had a stroke. One thing was for sure, she did not seem happy. Charles told me her name was Dixie.

We followed the maid into a large, open living room, and there was Saul Kent, sitting on a couch. He looked like Michael Keaton in *Beetlejuice*. He had crazy white, Einstein-like hair, and dark circles under deepset eyes. Saul's skin was wrinkled and leathery, dehydrated looking. It was as if some tribe of head-shrinking pygmies had gotten hold of Saul Kent, but just for a few days. This was a man who had made millions selling vitamins and he was one of the unhealthiest-looking people I'd ever met.

Charles and I walked over to Saul.

"Hello, Saul," Charles said. "Good to see you. Thanks for taking the time to meet with us. This is Larry Johnson. Larry, meet Saul Kent."

Still seated, Saul reached up to shake my hand. His movements were slow and efficient. It was as if he used his mind to keep his body carefully in check. In contrast to his unhealthy appearance, Saul had a strong, firm handshake, just about the polar opposite of Jerry Lemler's soft grip. Also very unlike Jerry Lemler, Saul locked his recessed eyes on mine right away. He was staring deep into me, like he was trying to read something behind my eyes and assess any potential threat from me. He seemed hyperfocused, a man who had learned to bring all of his attention to bear on whatever was in front him. To me, Saul Kent came off as guarded, calculating, and plotting.

"A pleasure to meet you, Larry." Saul spoke quietly in slow, measured tones. "I've heard a lot about you."

"Same here, Mr. Kent. Nice to meet you," I said.

"Please," Saul said, "sit."

That was probably the last time he addressed me directly. The maid served us drinks, then disappeared for the rest of the evening.

Charles started right in bashing Jerry Lemler, telling Saul that Jerry had terrible leadership skills and wasn't fit to manage Alcor. From Charles's perspective, Jerry sat around all day long and Charles really ran things but wasn't getting the recognition or the paycheck he deserved.

Saul sat there, staring at Charles, nodding his head rhythmically. Then, right in the middle of this slamfest, Charles turned to me and said, "Larry, what do you think of Jerry Lemler's performance as president?" Saul stopped nodding, neatly swiveled his head, and turned the full force of those deep-set eyes on me.

Charles had set me up. I didn't think much of Jerry's leadership or organizational skills but the guy was my new boss. Honestly, I thought Charles was pretty much right about everything he said. Still, I didn't want to bad-mouth Jerry to Saul Kent.

I felt manipulated. This trip wasn't about introducing me to the research at CCR. It was an opportunity for Charles to vent to Saul Kent about Jerry Lemler and use me to corroborate his accusations.

It might seem odd for me to say this since I'm writing this book as a whistle-blower, but I've never been a snitch. It's only when pushed real hard that I'll narc on people. I told Saul I agreed that Jerry didn't seem to have much experience managing a business, but I didn't lay into him the way Charles did. Mostly I just kept my mouth shut. Saul just stared at me silently.

Charles and I didn't stay much longer. I think once Charles realized I wasn't going to back him up against Lemler the way he had hoped I would, for him, our business there was done. I shook Saul's hand again before we left. His butt never left that couch during our entire visit. As I followed Charles back to the door, I could feel Saul's eyes burning into my back, staring, assessing, calculating.

I was quiet as Charles and I began the drive back to Scottsdale. I couldn't stop thinking about that poor dog Steve Harris had killed. From what I had seen, they weren't conducting valuable scientific research at CCR. They were playing some deluded godlike game. I thought about the barking I had heard at CCR, all the other dogs waiting to die senselessly. It really bothered me. Then I thought about Saul's dog.

"There's something not right about that dog, Dixie," I said.

Charles smirked. "There'd be something not right with you too if someone had drained out all your blood, replaced it with experimental cryo-preservants, kept you alive on machines for hours, and then pumped your blood back in," Charles said.

"What?"

"A former Alcor vice president named Jerry Leaf experimented on Dixie back when Alcor was in Riverside, California," Charles said. "He experimented on lots of animals."

Those cryo-preservants didn't carry oxygen around the body the way blood did. That accounted for Dixie's apparent brain damage. And Charles had just said they had experimented on "lots of animals." I frowned as I drove. By the looks of poor Dixie, for the sake of the other dogs, I almost hoped they hadn't survived.

After driving in silence for a while longer, Charles asked what I thought of Saul.

"He was pretty quiet," I said.

Charles thought for a moment. "Yeah," Charles said. "Saul has his secrets."

Then Charles asked if I had heard of the scandal involving Saul's mother, Dora Kent.

I told Charles I had read something about it online, that Hugh Hixon, Mike Perry, and a few other Alcorian leaders had been arrested during an investigation of her death but that ultimately no charges were filed. Charles said yes, it had been quite a fiasco.

"It almost meant the end of Alcor," he told me. According to Charles, the whole thing was pretty much the fault of an Alcor ex-president by the name of Michael Federowicz. Years earlier, Mike Federowicz had changed his name to Mike Darwin, Charles said, rolling his eyes. In Charles's opinion, Federowicz renamed himself after the pioneering evolutionary scientist because he considered himself as strong a voice in the scientific advancement of mankind as Charles Darwin. By now, that kind of self-aggrandizement didn't surprise me coming from an Alcorian. These people considered themselves the smart ones; everyone who didn't believe in cryonics was shortsighted and, basically, stupid. Mike Darwin, Charles said, had been arrested for Dora's homicide in Riverside. He told me two of the other high-ranking Alcorians who had also been arrested at the time were David Pizer and Carlos Mondragon. Mondragon was the creepy board member I had gotten such a hostile vibe from during my first board meeting.

I remembered the name Michael Darwin as well. Mathew Sullivan had mentioned him to me, and there were those postings on the CryoNet Internet site I had read by someone with that name. He was the one who had written about experimenting on dogs, and how he was good at finding people's weaknesses and then hurting them.

It was alleged by the investigating Riverside County coroner, Charles continued, that Alcor officers and employees killed Dora Kent to begin her cryo-suspension on their own schedule. Charles implied that Darwin was responsible. He said that Jerry Leaf—the one who had experimented on Dixie—had left an eyewitness account in a secret safety-deposit box before he died, describing how Darwin had killed Dora Kent with an injection.

Jerry Leaf, Charles said, had been a highly respected cryonicist himself and ex–Alcor VP as well as a former Green Beret. He was a hero to many at Alcor.

For some reason, Charles said, the county coroner allowed Dora Kent's head to remain at Alcor after their first visit there, even while his investigators confiscated other evidence from Alcor. When the investigators returned a few days later with a search warrant, intending to collect Dora's head, they were told the head was gone. No one at Alcor would tell the detectives where the head was. As a result the Riverside authorities were unable to bring formal charges against Alcor's leaders.

The coroner had an autopsy performed on Dora's headless body, Charles told me. "Lethal levels of barbiturates were found in Dora Kent's body," he continued. "They were found in her bone marrow."

"That's pretty convincing evidence, Charles," I said. "In order for those medications to be found in the bone marrow, the heart must still be beating when the drugs are administered. Even performing chest compressions on a dead body wouldn't get those barbiturates all the way into the bone marrow."

Charles looked at me. He was silent for a moment. Then he looked back out the windshield. "That was a big part of the county coroner's case," Charles said.

I opened my mouth to speak but—I didn't know what to say.

SEVEN

DEEPER

A few days after Charles and I returned from Rancho Cucamonga, I found Mike and Hugh's secret bedroom. I felt a little nervous at the idea of getting caught in there but I just had to check it out when no one was looking. It was one big square, like a college dorm room, maybe twenty feet on each side. The bathroom was right across the hall. It matched the kitchen in its disgusting state.

Mike and Hugh had a video monitor in their bedroom, a closed-circuit feed from the camera pointed at the door into the Patient Care Bay. For them, it was like having a camera on the gates of heaven. To them, those dewars were just about the most sacred objects on earth. And they were the watchdogs, the guardians of the precious horde.

I asked Charles about the Dora Kent incident several times during the next few days. He either wouldn't or couldn't tell me anything more about it.

"Sorry, Larry, that's all I know," he said. "You should ask someone who's been here longer than I have. Ask Joe Hovey. Or ask Hugh Hixon or Mike Perry—they were right in the middle of it all."

I knew there was no chance I'd get anything further out of Hugh, Mike, Joe, Mathew, or any of the other Alcor lifers. Although Charles was willing to open up with me to a point, I still got the feeling most of the others barely tolerated me.

It was disturbing to know that Hugh, Mike Perry, Mike Darwin, and other Alcor officers had been arrested during the investigation into the death of Saul Kent's mother. The bit about barbiturates being found in

Dora Kent's bone marrow really seemed suspicious. But formal charges were never brought, so—creepy, yes, criminal, apparently not.

———————

Charles was tight-lipped a few weeks later when we took another trip together. We drove to Los Angeles to attend a party celebrating the first anniversary of an Alcor member's suspension. The house was in Woodland Hills, in the San Fernando Valley, north of L.A. The suspended man's wife had turned his old bedroom into a shrine. He had been a military hero, so there were medals everywhere and pictures of this Alcorian posing with General Douglas MacArthur. Outside were refreshments and lawn chairs. The people there were all cryonicists but they were by no means as weird or eccentric as the Alcorians back in Phoenix. They seemed like nice, normal people there to pay their respects and console the widow. But a group I met later that evening was a whole different story.

Charles took me down to the touristy Third Street Promenade in Santa Monica, where a group of cryonicists was meeting at a Barnes & Noble bookstore. Young Todd Huffman was there, hanging out with his Extropian buddies.

Like Todd, many people involved in cryonics were also members of other radical scientific organizations. Many of the Alcorians at this meeting were also Extropians and Venturists (another fringe science group associated with Alcor that I would soon get to know a whole lot better). I know Southern California was famous for being home to eccentrics and all, but the crowd at this gathering was way, way out there.

They were all interested in meeting me since I worked at Alcor. Most had read about me in the Alcor newsletters and *Cryonics* magazine.

I mingled, moving from group to group. The mood was very festive, very loud, lots of laughter interspersed with animated arguments. I had run calls to *Star Trek* conventions as a paramedic where people dressed up in alien outfits, sang Klingon opera, role-played the night away, and had loads of high-octane geeky fun. These cryonicists made those Trekkers look like Young Republicans.

Many were in small groups debating what the future would be like. One woman was talking about "mood skin," how in the future people will have implants that allow their skin to change color with their emotions.

Another group was poring over their sketches of flying cars, arguing heatedly over engine placement and wind shear.

Two strangers were staring silently and intently at each other, and I overheard that they were practicing telepathy.

A computer animator was deep in an argument about the ethics of immortality with a rocket-fuel specialist from the famed Jet Propulsion Laboratory in Pasadena—literally, a rocket scientist. They were talking about the depletion of natural resources and their ideas for new government agencies that would be responsible for the reintegration of reanimated cryonicists into twenty-third-century society. They mentioned a reeducation machine, where people would be hooked up to a computer that would upload data straight into their brains, bringing them right up-to-date on twenty-third-century current events.

Someone else was singing the praises of bear liver and tiger hormones as miracle life extension supplements. This guy had apparently been swallowing a boatload of each. Although tiger hormones were illegal, he said with a wink, he had a connection in Thailand. The others in his group were begging him for the contact information but the guy was playing coy, soaking up the attention.

Todd Huffman and another young man were feeling each other's fingertips. They had had magnets implanted under their skin. I'm not sure why, but I think it had something to do with the earth's magnetic field supposedly influencing life extension.

One seemingly drunk young woman was berating an older man for not agreeing that the space shuttle was already obsolete and that work needed to begin immediately on a space elevator to get people and materials up into Earth's orbit.

Another group was comparing the volume of megavitamins they ingested. It was like kids in a schoolyard showing off their scars. Each was trying to outdo the next with how many thousands of milligrams of vitamin C they took three times a day.

Each time I joined a conversation, folks grilled me on recent happenings at "Alcor Central." One redheaded, freckled young woman giggled as she referred to Scottsdale as "Headquarters." They asked extremely specific questions about the recent advances at CCR, quoting chapter and verse from the latest Alcor newsletter. I elected not to tell them about my personal opinion of what was going on at CCR.

One group of Extropians was talking about elective surgeries that would be available in the future. When I heard two guys discussing where they wanted their second penis attached, I figured that was my cue to leave.

"Charles, this isn't my scene. I'll meet you for dinner downstairs in an hour."

I went across the street and had a beer. And then another. This new group of colleagues was a far cry from my rowdy old paramedic crowd. On impulse, I tried reaching my old ambulance partner, Steve, on his cell phone. It went to voice mail. I didn't leave a message. He was probably chasing nurses down at the Emergency Room bar off Las Vegas Boulevard. I missed Steve and my other old partners. I missed the camaraderie.

Charles seemed acutely aware of how odd the average cryonicist appeared to the average non-cryonicist. Whenever someone toured the Alcor facility, Charles would do his best to present the most normal face of Alcor possible. More and more, that face was becoming my own.

Tours of the Alcor facility happened once or twice a week. Mostly these were for potential members, either individuals or families. Sometimes they were for journalists. Charles had a pretour checklist.

First: hide Mike Perry. Charles would shoo him down the hallways, herding him toward his secret bedroom. Mike was used to being treated like Uncle Fester, locked in the basement when company came over.

Next on Charles's list: hide Hugh Hixon. He'd be sent after Mike to their room with instructions to keep quiet.

Third: Charles would check the lobby and make sure Jerry Searcy wasn't snoozing in his chair by the front door. Charles nearly had a fit whenever he escorted visitors inside Alcor and the first thing they saw was some old codger drooling in the front lobby.

Meanwhile, Jerry Lemler would be in his office donning a long white lab coat, admiring himself in the mirror. The only times Dr. Jerry ever wore one were for tours and photo shoots.

Charles and Jerry led the groups and made my office an official stop for most visitors. They brought people by because, they told me, I was the most normal person there. "People can relate to you, Larry," they said, "and you're easygoing." In their own words, I proved that not everyone involved in cryonics was a "weirdo."

Sometimes I felt like an attraction at Disneyland. "And here's Larry Johnson, our clinical director." I'd get up and shake hands with visitors, all smiles. This was quite a bit different from Vegas tourists snapping pictures of me as a paramedic outside Caesars Palace. Neither Charles nor Jerry ever officially coached me on what to say, but I was sure to be on my best behavior, and would say something like, "Nice to meet you. Congratulations on considering cryonic suspension. Let me know if I can answer any questions. Enjoy the tour."

Visitors weren't really much interested in the offices or the executives or the OR or the freezing procedure, though. No one on a tour ever asked me a single good question. No, what they really wanted to see was where the bodies were stored. I'd say that ninety-nine out of a hundred of them came out of a grisly sense of humor or a macabre fascination with death. They were hoping for glimpses of gore. They wanted to see white vapor steaming off decapitated heads.

The percentage of folks who became members after taking the tour was negligible. I had several conversations with Jennifer Chapman about recruitment. She mailed out about one hundred membership applications a week. These were mostly in response to requests submitted through the Alcor Web site. Out of those hundred, she told me, she was lucky if she got back one completed application. And then maybe one out of ten of those applicants would ever return Jennifer's calls or e-mails after that.

Sometimes I'd see children on the tours. There were no kids suspended up to the time I left Alcor but I do remember seeing two-year-olds on the membership list. Since I left, I've read that one baby was made an Alcor member, presumably by a parent or guardian, on the day she was born.

The first tour I witnessed that included a child was an older couple with their young daughter. She was a very cute little kid, maybe four or five years old with tight blond ringlet curls, very Shirley Temple. The father seemed especially gung-ho about cryonics, much more so than the average tourist. The mother was along for the ride and the little girl had no idea what was going on. I overheard the father ask Jerry about cryonic suspension for children. Jerry was complimenting the father for making this decision for his daughter, for making "the most important investment possible in his daughter's future."

"We're talking about immortality," Jerry said. "Surely that's more important than saving for college."

The little girl had a puzzled expression, her little head swiveling this way and that among the grownups, her golden curls bouncing. She gave me a quizzical look and pointed up at me as she left my office, yanked along by her father. Her outstretched finger was the last thing I saw of her.

I overheard Jerry hard-selling them out in the hallway. "So, like I said, that Emmy Award you saw in the lobby belongs to the famous television writer Dick Clair. He wrote episodes for *Mary Tyler Moore, The Carol Burnett Show, Diff'rent Strokes,* and another comedy called *Soap.* Remember the TV shows *Mama's Family* and *The Facts of Life?* He created them! Dick knew all about the facts of life—that's why he's here at Alcor, ha-ha. Let's see. One of our members is Charlie Matthau, the son of Walter Matthau. Charlie is a famous movie director. He tried talking his dad into cryonics but Walter Matthau died in 2000 before Charlie could convince him. A shame. Timothy Leary was signed up but at the last minute he decided to blast his ashes into outer space instead. What a waste. The famous publisher Larry Flynt is a member, as well as a billionaire family of hotel owners in Canada whom we can't name." Jerry whispered something under his breath, laughed, then continued. "Then there's casino mogul Don Laughlin. You know, Laughlin, Nevada? That's his town. Mr. Laughlin is such a dedicated cryonicist that he made sure six of his personal assistants became EMTs and then he had them trained in Alcor's protocols. They work in shifts. Two of them are only a few steps away from Mr. Laughlin at all times. Now that's being prepared! Walt Disney expressed very serious interest in cryonics before he died. What do you think of that, little girl? Disney on ice, he-he-he. And we're not supposed to talk about it but Peter Sellers—you know, the star of the *Pink Panther* movies—he also met with Alcor's predecessors about being preserved. Larry King—the CNN talk show host—has talked seriously to us about cryonics. Many science fiction writers, of course, have been interested and sympathetic to cryonics, including Arthur C. Clarke and Frederik Pohl, even the novelist Gore Vidal. And now, I'm *really* not supposed to talk about *this* but we've also had some very serious talks with Michael Jackson! You know who he is, right? Michael Jackson? The singer? Isn't that exciting?"

Jerry was really turning it on. I had never seen any evidence about Michael Jackson at Alcor. All I could think about, though, was that little girl's curly golden hair lying on the floor of Alcor's OR. The way she pointed at me reminded me of another little girl I had met during my weeks at Waco as the chief helicopter paramedic during the siege of the Branch Davidian compound.

———————

When David Koresh released some of the children—and puppies—from his compound in Waco, I watched those Branch Davidian children march out of their stronghold like little soldiers, very militant, completely expressionless. They were like miniature prisoners of war. Those children had been brainwashed.

We'd had to buy some time waiting for the state agency to come and take the kids off to temporary foster homes. Maybe the Feds had some psychological reason to keep them around in order to work on getting the parents out too. I didn't know. Whatever the case, after those kids came out of the compound, each emergency worker was given a child to watch over for the night. The children were bused over to the old Air Force barracks we were staying in, down the road from the Davidian cult complex. They gave me a cute little girl, probably five or six years old, to look after. Like the little girl on the Alcor tour, this cutie had curly blond hair. "Hi, my name's Larry. What's yours?"

I might as well have been speaking in Swahili. She kept staring down at the ground. I got her a can of Coke, thinking I was making a kind gesture. She just stood there and looked at the can. At first I figured she was pulling some attitude on me, a hunger-strike kind of "screw you and the Coke you rode in on," but as she stared and stared at the aluminum can, I realized she just didn't know what it was. She had never seen a can of soda before.

I opened it for her. Then I opened one for myself and took a swig.

"It's okay," I said. "It's good. You can drink it if you're thirsty."

Again, nothing. She wouldn't even look at me. Cold, no emotion at all.

There weren't any beds in my barracks. There were, however, a bunch of couches and some military sleeping bags somebody had brought in, so I threw a sleeping bag up onto a couch and coaxed the little girl inside of it. Then I fell asleep on the floor.

In the middle of the night, probably two or three in the morning, I sat straight up with this horrible feeling like something had happened. I found my flashlight, shined it up on the couch, and, sure enough, the little girl was gone.

I went running all over the barracks, shining the light around, calling out, "Little girl, little girl," in an urgent whisper, waking people up left and right and then—I heard a toilet flush. I stopped. It flushed again. I approached the bathroom . . . flush . . . flush . . . flush . . . I walked in and there she was, staring down into the toilet, flushing it over and over. She turned to me quizzically, dumbfounded. It was the first time she had looked me in the eye.

She pointed down at the toilet. Then she pointed up at me as if asking me to explain.

She had never seen indoor plumbing.

Apparently, one of the buildings on David Koresh's compound had a basement that the cult members had converted into one huge latrine. Once the FBI and ATF got them out of there, they started digging the place up and basically found a big open sewer down there. That's what they used as a toilet. No wonder this little Branch Davidian girl was so fascinated by the toilet. She'd never seen one before.

I didn't know how to begin to explain plumbing to her, so I didn't even try. I walked her back to her sleeping bag, tucked her in, and lay back down on the floor. It was real disheartening to see the way those kids were raised, what they were deprived of, what life-altering decisions their parents had made for them. Another emergency worker I know had a similar experience. The little Davidian boy he was looking after had never seen a soda can or a flush toilet either. It made me sad. Those kids never made a conscious choice to join a cult.

If that little blond girl on the Alcor tour died and her father had his way, off would come the curls, then her head, and into the freezer it would go, a choice she never could have made for herself.

After that particular tour, I started feeling uncomfortable in my role as an Alcor marketing tool. Still, since Charles seemed so worried that everyone else there came across as weird—maybe weird enough to raise the eyebrows of the local authorities—I became more and more the Alcor poster boy.

Publicity was a double-edged sword around Alcor. They wanted famous people involved. They wanted to spread the gospel. Hell, they wanted every person on the planet to sign up for the deep freeze, an Alcor on every street corner. At the same time, they didn't want any close scrutiny of their operation.

One time the whole place went into a tizzy because some guy was parked across the street, taking pictures. Jerry Lemler came running into my office, hopping from foot to foot, begging me to see who it was. My Harley was parked out back, so I circled the block and came around to check him out, but whoever he was, the guy had split without leaving any trace of what he'd wanted.

It became the talk of the office for about a week. Hugh and Charles fired off e-mails, speculating on who it might have been outside Alcor with a camera. The uproar it caused felt ridiculous and unwarranted to me, but the folks at Alcor seemed simply terrified of outsiders knowing exactly what went on in there.

Local Arizona media ran stories about Alcor on a regular basis. I think Alcor was a go-to filler whenever a newspaper needed to fill a column on a slow news day. Local TV stations probably kept stories on file for whenever they needed to fill a few minutes' airtime. Phoenix's little homegrown freak show was always curious enough to raise viewers' eyebrows, always newsworthy.

One time a CBS network affiliate from Los Angeles came to do a story on Alcor. Charles made sure he was the one who spent most of the time in front of the camera, but he wanted me to be interviewed as well.

So after Charles corralled Mike and Hugh into their secret bedroom and shooed Jerry Searcy from his chair in the front lobby, I was plopped down in front of the cameras.

The lights were bright. Charles positioned himself directly next to the camera and stared at me the whole time, trying to make damn sure I said all the right things. Alcor actually had an official internal checklist of things to look out for during media interviews. On it, Alcorians were reminded that every news organization spun stories to make Alcor look like a den of freaks. We were to be aware of this and act accordingly. We were also urged to keep our answers brief and expect the worst. Don't let them fluster you.

I became pretty nervous with Charles staring at me the whole time to enforce the party line. The bit they used of me on-air shows me saying how I was obsessed with seeing what things would be like one or two hundred years from now.

Most of the edited story showed Charles spewing his rehearsed cryonic propaganda, about how the new vitrification procedure Alcor and CCR were developing protected the brain from freezing damage and how the whole thing really wasn't that expensive. There were quotes about the cost of suspension being a "down payment on resurrection" and no more than the cost of an elaborate funeral. It was basic Alcor PR BS. The viewer also got to see Hugh Hixon in his khakis.

And then they showed a bunch of shots they took of me on my Harley, with a voice-over calling me a "thrill seeker." It was somehow both fun and dorky that the piece's editor played Led Zeppelin's "Rock and Roll" underneath a montage of me on my Harley, including a peel-out and a close-up of me in my side mirror. I feel like a dweeb looking back on it now, but at the time I felt like I had to play my part.

After the interview, Charles circulated a memo praising me for my performance, literally writing, "Larry came across as very laid back, natural, and nonweird." Then he added, "I had to interrupt Jerry Searcy's midday nap and asked him to vacate his favorite chair, and Hugh ate his lunch in the lobby as usual. If we want favorable media coverage, we need a little more cooperation around here."

While my Alcor colleagues all seemed to acknowledge I was doing a good job, I was far from being accepted into their inner circle. Voices were still lowered whenever I approached people at Alcor. Mathew Sullivan and Joe Hovey were especially uncomfortable with me, while Jennifer Chapman usually went out of her way to avoid me. I kept discovering Mike Perry lurking in corners, staring at me.

I was heading off to lunch one day and overheard Charles talking to Hugh in the front lobby. Jerry Searcy was there too, in his chair.

"Forget Lemler," I heard Charles say. "You should ask Larry."

"Ask me what?" I asked, entering the lobby.

Hugh had his khaki pants rolled up and was scratching at his leg. I could tell he didn't want to include me in the conversation but it was too late.

Charles said, "Hugh has had this rash for several days now."

Hugh looked up at me over the rim of his glasses. His fear of illness was overcoming his mistrust in me.

"Do you think it's serious?" Hugh asked.

I took one look and said, "That's scabies."

Charles covered his mouth, scared now that Hugh's rash had been given such a nasty name. "What the hell is scabies?" Charles said.

"What you've got there, Hugh, is a rash caused by little burrowing parasitic creatures," I said.

"What?" Charles was mortified.

"Goddamn scabies," said Jerry Searcy.

"Scabies are microscopic bugs that tunnel into your skin," I said. I could tell Hugh was a little embarrassed and more than a little creeped out about his newfound stowaways, so I left out the part about scabies laying eggs under the flesh.

"You can clear it up with an ointment a doctor can prescribe," I told Hugh. "That'll take care of it in a few days. You'll be fine."

Hugh thanked me before making his escape, probably straight to a doctor. It was a win for me. I had helped Hugh out and gained his confidence.

Charles was still horrified. "Is it contagious?" The wheels were turning and Charles was chugging off to paranoia land.

"Don't worry, Charles," I told him. "Unless you've been sleeping in Hugh's bed or touching that rash directly, you're pretty much safe."

"How does someone get scabies in the first place?" Charles asked.

"Sometimes you hear of people catching them from raunchy motels where the sheets are never changed. Personally, the only people I've ever seen with scabies are homeless people. It often comes from a gross lack of personal hygiene."

Charles nearly fell over laughing. For the moment, he was so happy to get some ammunition against Hugh, it overrode his paranoia. "That's disgusting!" he said.

From then on, I was the go-to guy for everyone's medical questions. Charles had a plethora of ailments both real and imagined he grilled me about. Jerry Searcy would come ask me about his goddamn prostate. Jerry Lemler may have been a physician but he still came to me for medical advice.

I had to patch up Mike Perry a few times. He had a bicycle he would ride down to the local Wal-Mart. It was an old cruiser, a little rusty but real cool, probably an antique and valuable to a collector. Mike attached a basket to the back for when he needed to carry things.

I cracked a joke one time, asking him if it was his first or second cycle. He didn't get it.

Mike couldn't drive a car. Maybe his body wasn't built for that sort of motor control, but I'm pretty sure he was just mentally incapable of driving. I heard he got in a car accident one time while he was driving, suffered a head injury, and that was that. No use risking the ol' cephalon.

Honestly, though, Mike went headfirst into so many light poles on his bicycle I don't think he should have been operating it either. Or at least he should have borrowed Jennifer's crash helmet. I'm not saying Mike Perry was mentally substandard, just the opposite.

When I asked him about the differential equation he was scribbling during the first board meeting I attended, he said he was just trying to work through something he had thought of a few days earlier. He reminded me of the tormented mathematician Russell Crowe played in *A Beautiful Mind*. I'll bet you Mike Perry's IQ was 200, or higher, but he went all the way through smart to the other side. The guy was so smart he was almost stupid, so smart that he had zero sense of humor, so smart that he couldn't get behind the wheel of a car and use his hands and feet at the same time.

I saw him riding that bike a few times and it made me think of the Wicked Witch of the West in *The Wizard of Oz*. All Mike needed was a little dog, and a tornado to get caught up in, spinning around and around, pedaling like mad, all hunched over.

Mike Perry was a bit of a celebrity around Scottsdale. I struck up a conversation once with a local cop. When he found out I worked at Alcor, the first thing he wanted to know was, "Who's that guy on the bike? He's gotta be one of yours, right?"

"Does he look really odd?" I asked. "Hunched over on his bike?"

"Yeah. Is he one of those Alcor people?"

"Oh, yeah. That's Mike. He's just a little off center," I acknowledged, repeating the exact words Charles had used when I first met Mike.

"Off center? He's off the friggin' map! He scares the hell outta me!"

———

After I helped out Hugh by diagnosing his rash, some of the wall he had built between us started crumbling. He began dropping by my office. He would walk in without any kind of greeting, sit down, and off he'd go, talking about something technical he was doing in the lab. He'd have his head down, looking at me over the top of his glasses the way he always did, speaking in a low, monotonous voice. He'd drone on and on. He didn't really have anyone else to talk to and I always had lots of questions. In me, Hugh found the only person at Alcor who could partially keep up with him when talking about laboratory procedures, chemical formulas, and all the gear he had rigged up around the place. He was happy to have someone to talk shop with. For instance, it was Hugh who told me all about Alcor's dewars and CryoStar.

Not surprising, no cold-temperature equipment manufacturer specialized in machines for cryonic suspension. Hugh had to take what was out there on the market and modify it to meet Alcor's unique needs. Hugh told me the CryoStar was originally made for the short-term storage of human organs and sperm. Alcor had gotten its CryoStar from CCR. It had never been tested as a long-term storage unit, never mind for something as susceptible to small temperature fluctuations as the human brain.

Hugh didn't exactly take me under his wing but at least he didn't ostracize me the way the rest of the flock did. I enjoyed my talks with Hugh and always learned something from him.

Charles was amazed Hugh would speak to me at all, and said the idea of Hugh seeking out companionship was unprecedented. I got the message that Hugh was a loner among loners.

Unfortunately, Charles used Hugh's scabies as a low blow in their ongoing feud. These CryoWars raged on every day. No one was very busy with work, so they created ways to pass the time. Often this simply involved arguing with each other.

One time I actually heard Charles, Hugh, and Mathew Sullivan conspiring together in a temporary alliance against Joe Hovey. They wanted to get rid of him. The problem was, they didn't know what he did all day. The corporate structure at Alcor was so disorganized, with no one really in charge, that none of the vice presidents or directors knew exactly what the others did. Charles, Hugh, and Mathew tried talking Joe Hovey into taking a thirty-day vacation. They gave him all kinds of bull about his health and how he deserved a break, but what they were really doing was trying to see if Alcor could survive without him. Joe didn't take the bait.

The Severe Acute Respiratory Syndrome (SARS) scare was in full bloom in the media at the time and it absolutely consumed Charles. He sent e-mails to everyone at Alcor to keep them up-to-date on the latest outbreaks. Bored, Hugh Hixon researched the current cases and came up with a graph predicting the next outbreak.

Just to be contrary, Charles came up with his own graph with different projections. And off they went. They'd bicker back and forth like kindergarten students in a kind of "did not—did too!" e-mail argument. Worst of all, they incessantly copied everyone in the office on those e-mail exchanges.

Each day I would be copied on fifteen or twenty e-mails as they rocketed back and forth. I deleted most of them without even reading them. This was the Alcor members' suspension dollars at work, all done on Alcor's time.

Charles had a girlfriend named Erico. She was a very pleasant Asian lady about Charles's age. Erico had a residence on the East Coast but spent six months out of the year in Arizona with Charles. They got along real well. When she wasn't in Arizona, they spoke on the phone all the time. I met Erico for the first time when she accompanied Charles to Alcor at the height of the SARS scare. Charles was putting together his own SARS emergency preparedness kit. He came to Alcor to raid the place for drugs and was all in a lather.

Erico cornered me while Charles was rushing around Alcor rifling through the drug cabinets.

"Larry," she said, "Charles has told me about you. Will you talk to him? He's scaring me with this SARS thing. He's really going off the deep end."

I appreciated how concerned she was, confiding in me like this when it was the first time she had even met me. I told her I'd try but I wasn't sure what I could do. I already knew that Charles was very paranoid when it came to paranoia. Sure enough, Charles rushed out of the building with Erico in tow before I could talk to him, eager to get home with his new drugs.

A few days later, when Charles hadn't shown up at Alcor or contacted us, I gave him a call. Erico answered.

"Larry, I'm so glad you called. You must speak to him. He's going crazy. He won't leave home. He's too afraid of catching SARS!"

"Oh, geez," I said.

Suddenly Charles's voice came on the phone. He had been listening. "I'm concerned that you're being so flippant about this epidemic, Larry."

"Epidemic?" I asked.

"SARS!" he breathed over the phone. "Don't you know how serious this is? This could mean the end of mankind."

"Charles," I said, "health threats like SARS have to be treated very seriously, but really, these scares are partially created by the media. They make good news. Next year it'll be some other sickness that threatens all life on this planet."

"How can you say that?" Charles said. "I'm so disappointed in you!"

"Listen, Charles, you're leaving me on my own here. I need you at Alcor. What if a member goes down and there's a suspension? I'm not ready to do your job yet. Who would organize everything? Jerry?"

I could hear the gears turning over the phone. "Larry, I need more drugs. I've been doing some reading. What do we have at Alcor that could boost my immune system? I know we have steroids. I know we have Solu-Medrol and epinephrine but I couldn't find them the other day. Do you know where they are? What else could you recommend? What else have we got there that could help?"

Nothing he wanted was controlled or dangerous in the limited amounts I would give him, so I figured, what the heck?

"Okay, Charles, I'll put those together along with whatever else I can find. When will you come down for them?"

"Come down?" I could hear him trembling over the phone. "Larry, I'm not coming down. I was hoping you could bring them up here."

Erico joined in. "Larry, please. Please come."

So I did. The next day I drove up to Charles's home, about one hundred miles north of Phoenix, with some of Alcor's expired Solu-Medrol. He was locked up tight inside his house and wouldn't even let me in. I had to talk to him through the door, like I was contagious. He wasn't going to leave for anything—except Ribavirin.

"Ribavirin, Larry! That's the key! I've been reading that Ribavirin is an antiviral medication that's being used in Canada and Asia. They're injecting children with it right now in Hong Kong. It seems to be the best drug therapy humanity has against the SARS virus." He went on and on like this, raving. Erico came outside to stand by me.

Ribavirin is a very common antiviral. It's sort of like the penicillin of antivirals, a panacea. Whenever doctors don't know what to inject in someone to fight a virus, they reach for Ribavirin. There would be no harm in Charles's getting his hands on some. The problem was you couldn't get it in the United States without a prescription.

"Mexico, Larry! We need to go to Mexico." You can get just about anything short of morphine in a Mexican pharmacy. Erico clasped her hands together as if in prayer, then made a looping motion by her ear, then clasped her hands together again. It was her desperate sign language for "Please, Larry! He's friggin' crazy! Please!"

"Charles," I said, "if I take you to Mexico to get Ribavirin, will that be it? Will you come back to work?"

"Yes! Ribavirin!"

So I drove Charles Platt to Mexico to get Ribavirin. More than trembling, he was actually quaking. It was about a five-hour drive to the nearest border town, Nogales, Mexico. I had spent some of my younger years in Texas border towns, and so I knew the drill.

We parked on the U.S. side and walked into Mexico. I talked Charles out of crossing the border with his Survival Bag stuffed full of cash. We left it in my truck. We had to check four or five pharmacies before we found what we were looking for, and then I scared Charles senseless by taking us off the beaten path to a local bar.

It was the kind of place tourists don't really go. With our pale skin and Charles's English accent, it was pretty obvious we weren't local boys. My Spanish was good enough to order a couple beers and I was never uncomfortable in places like this. I wanted to show Charles a good time but I guess he was too nervous to enjoy the novelty.

In the end, it all worked out fine. Charles got his miracle cure, I bought a bottle of duty-free Kahlua for Beverly and me, and after stuffing himself full of Ribavirin, Charles's SARS paranoia was sated enough to get him out of his house and down to Alcor the following week. It was all part of my job, I figured, as Alcor's COO-in-training.

There was a cat that lived at Alcor, a gray and white tiger-stripe named Aido. That was another dicey cleanliness issue in my opinion—hey, yeah, this is a state-of-the-art medical facility and we consider our patients to be still very much alive but don't worry, we scoop the litter box in the Cool-Down Bay—just outside the door to the OR—quite regularly, thank you very much.

Aido was the fattest cat I'd ever seen. He belonged to Mike Perry, which was funny because they were such opposites, the rail-thin hunchback and his stomach-dragging cat. Mike was real affectionate with Aido. I imagined that one day that cat would be decapitated and frozen, to be reunited with Mike in the year 2525.

Nobody touched that cat but Mike. Aido was attached to Mike, too, but more in a "you feed me" way than an "I love you, Daddy" way. That cat always had this look on his face that said, "Come on over here, pal, lemme claw that eye out for you." I never heard him purr, never even heard him meow. To this day I don't know if that cat had a voice at all. More than once I thought seriously about the possibility that Mike Darwin or Steve Harris or some other Alcorian had experimented on that cat, maybe flushed him with some experimental cryo-preservant cocktail. It was obvious to me that they were capable of that type of thing.

Aido followed Perry around all the time like a shadow, though. "Perry's minion," Mathew Sullivan called him. Mathew cracked to me one day that, like everyone else who hung out at Alcor, the cat had been made a vice president by the board of directors. Aido stayed back in the Cool-Down Bay, walking around like he owned the place, and never came out front. He wasn't allowed, which was probably a good idea. Pizza boxes are bad enough. Pizza boxes and an obese, free-range cat giving everyone the evil eye would have been too much even for Alcor. Actually, visitors would sometimes catch a glimpse of Aido on a tour and mention how scary he looked. Maybe Aido should have been named "Director of Patient Security" or "Vice President of Giving Visitors the Willies."

I wandered into the Cool-Down Bay a few days after our trip to Mexico, looking to strike up a conversation with Hugh and saw an empty tuna can without a label on it. My first thought was that Aido had just finished lunch. In the kitchen, on several occasions I had seen Mike Perry open up the cabinet, take down a can of tuna, and feed it to his cat. I made some kind of joke about how fat the cat was. Hugh told me, yeah, that was true, but after Aido had eaten his tuna, Hugh used the empty cans to mount heads on.

"What?"

After the human heads were severed from their bodies, Hugh explained, they were balanced upside down on empty tuna cans during cool-down inside the LR-40, the way a statue is set on a pedestal. So they wouldn't fall over and freeze to the bottom.

"So, uh, what kind of tuna is it, Hugh?" I asked.

Hugh lowered his head and looked at me over the rim of his glasses, the way he always did. I might have been asking about the price of khaki socks. In his methodical, droning voice, Hugh said, "Oh, well, that'd be, uh, BumbleBee tuna."

More than thrifty, it was surreal. Inside Alcor were disembodied human heads, frozen to the point of shattering, awaiting their second life cycles perched atop empty tuna cans. There's a marketing slogan for you: "BumbleBee Tuna—Your Ambulance to the Future."

EIGHT

SUSPENSION 1: TOURISTS AT A MUTILATION

If anything is sacred, the human body is sacred.

—WALT WHITMAN

I participated in my first cryo-suspension.

When I started working at Alcor in January 2003, there were fifty-something patients sliced and iced in Alcor's vaults, some with, some without their heads still attached. Alcor was founded in 1972. That makes an average of roughly two cryo-suspensions per year. After my first month at Alcor, three members died in the course of the next six weeks. Oddly, Jerry Lemler told me I was good luck. Cryo-suspensions were a time of excitement around Alcor. Everyone finally got a chance to put his or her practice and preparation to the test. This was what they lived for.

At 8:50 Monday morning, February 24, 2003, Alcor's hotline started ringing. There was an actual Alcor hotline, like the Batphone. It sat over by the dusty fax machine behind the grubby divider wall off the dingy front lobby. Every Alcorian was supposed to wear an Alcor membership bracelet at all times with Alcor's hotline number engraved on it.

In those days it was unusual for Charles Platt to be around early on a Monday morning, but he was the one who happened to answer the phone. It was the son of an eighty-one-year-old Alcor member from the San Diego area.

In his case summary subsequently published in an Alcor newsletter, Charles Platt referred to the Alcor member by name: Dr. Thomas Munson. Unlike most Alcorians, Dr. Munson had given Alcor permission to use his real name. "Dr. Munson had been a long-time Alcor member," Charles wrote, "who formerly served as our medical director at a time when few professional physicians were willing to be associated with cryonics."

Earlier that morning Dr. Munson had complained of shortness of breath and nausea. Feeling ill, he lay down to rest. When Tom Jr. checked on him later, he found that his father had apparently suffered a cardiac arrest and was no longer breathing. He called 911.

Paramedics arrived and worked on Dr. Munson but it was no use. They soon ceased resuscitation efforts. According to his father's wishes, Tom Jr. immediately called Alcor. The paramedics were still on scene while he was speaking with Charles, who instructed Tom Jr. to ask the paramedics if they would mind administering heparin, which is the first drug in Alcor's suspension protocol. Heparin is an anticoagulant; it causes the blood to thin and prevents clotting. The paramedics replied that they would be unable to administer any drugs at this time. This upset Charles greatly. I told Charles I couldn't blame the paramedics. They have to follow protocol written by their medical control physician. Once resuscitation of a patient ceases, paramedics cannot administer any more drugs.

"I would hate to have to explain to *my* medical control physician why I administered heparin to a dead guy," I said.

At the top of his voice, Charles screamed in his English accent, "Larry, as far as we're concerned, that man is not dead!" Veins were standing out in his neck.

"Well, Charles, as far as those paramedics, the law, and people in the real world are concerned, that gentleman is dead, as in door nail!" I'm not very good at being yelled at. I left the room and stomped all the way out into the front parking lot.

After a couple minutes spent cooling off, I walked back through the front door. As soon as I entered the lobby, I could hear Charles calling from deep inside the building, "Larry? Where's Larry?" Charles was rushing from room to room. He hurried into the lobby and, in an apologetic tone, said they needed me on the phone right away.

In order to prevent an autopsy, Charles had already directed Tom Jr. to get ahold of Dr. Munson's physician to make a statement that he had seen the ailing Dr. Munson recently and that his death was from natural causes. On the strength of that statement, the coroner's office had issued a waiver eliminating the need for an autopsy. It was quick work on Charles's part.

Now, Charles said, since the paramedics wouldn't comply, he wanted me to talk Tom Jr. through administering the drugs to his father. I followed Charles out of the lobby, wondering where the son had gotten hold of the drugs, but then I remembered the Alcor membership kits. Tom Jr. must have found his father's collection of Alcor's expired meds numbered 1, 2, 3, etc.

The son was very calm, considering the circumstances. He was not a cryonicist himself, yet he was willing to participate in Alcor's gruesome protocol to honor his father's wishes. At Charles's direction, he had already packed his father's head in all the ice they had in the house.

Over the phone, I talked Tom Jr. through the administration of several drugs, including one that was in powder form that needed to be mixed with saline. Although the paramedics would have no part in the injections, Tom Jr. did convince them to leave his father's IV attached. This way, he could push the drugs straight into the IV line's piggyback port and avoid jabbing at his deanimated father with needles. Between injections, I instructed Tom Jr. to perform CPR on his dad for several minutes to aid in circulating the drugs throughout his bloodstream.

Actually, Alcor didn't call it CPR. CPR stands for cardiopulmonary resuscitation. The last thing Alcor wanted was for their members to resuscitate. They called it CPS—cardiopulmonary support.

During the hour I was on the phone with the son, he probably felt the warmth draining out of his father's body. Can you imagine sticking all those syringes into your dead father's IV line, then straddling his body and pumping his chest to circulate the drugs? Considering, Tom Jr. had performed remarkably well.

When I finally hung up the phone, I had to shake my head in disbelief. Charles put his hand on my shoulder and said, "Larry, I'm sorry I lost my temper. You just did a phenomenal job. No one else here could have walked Tom Jr. through the drug protocol the way you did with such professionalism and precision."

"No, Charles," I said, "I'm a damn fool."

"Why do you say that?" asked Charles.

"All those years of getting my ass beat on the street as a paramedic, and all I had to do was phone it in."

While I was on the phone with Tom Jr., Charles had called the emergency response team members in Los Angeles to notify them that an Alcor member was down.

The leader of the Southern California emergency response team was Peter Voss. Peter was an especially hard-core Alcor member who lived in Marina del Rey, a really beautiful spot along the Southern California coast, south of Venice Beach. Peter was very dedicated to Alcor. Unfortunately, he possessed what people call a strong personality (he was a pain in the ass) and was not easy to get along with. If everyone had to follow Peter in the usual way people follow a leader, the Los Angeles response team would have fallen apart within a day because everyone was always pissed off at him. His live-in girlfriend, Louise Gold, was also a member of the team. Louise was tall, athletic, and gorgeous. I had no idea why she was with Peter. Maybe the fact that he made millions of dollars developing artificial intelligence technology had something to do with it. At least one thing I knew they had in common was a passion for cryonics.

Regina Pancake was another Southern California team leader. She was real good with people, which was great because it balanced Peter Voss's abrasiveness. Regina kept the team together. She was paid a monthly stipend to store Alcor's emergency equipment at her business in Culver City, just south of L.A. I don't think those few boxes really took up much space, but I was learning that there were a variety of ways Alcorian insiders turned a profit by "volunteering."

Regina's business was Applied Effects, a special effects company. It made props, mostly for science fiction films. Regina and her company worked on big movies like *X-Men*, *Vanilla Sky*, *The Green Mile*, *The Hulk*,

Men in Black II, Minority Report, Starship Troopers, and *Charlie's Angels.*
Regina also worked on three of the *Star Trek* television series. I went in
there one time and Regina showed me around. I had a blast. It was like a
movie museum. There were ray guns, laser blasters, and model spaceships
hanging all over the place. They had a setup where you could design a futuristic weapon on a computer and then a machine would make it right
in front of you out of plastic. Regina reminded me of an ex-hippie, and I
liked her right away.

Bobby June was the fourth Los Angeles–area team member. Bobby was
a professional musician who had a recording studio in his Long Beach loft.
I always got a good vibe from Bobby and thought he was probably a very
talented guy. Many Los Angeles–area Alcorians worked in the entertain-
ment business.

Todd Huffman was also called. He rushed to the Munson home with a
backpack full of drugs while Regina made for her office to grab the surgical gear.

Meanwhile, Alcor was prepped for surgery. Mathew Sullivan, along
with Jerry Lemler's daughter Jessica and her husband, James Sikes, was
preparing the operating room. Hugh Hixon began brewing a batch of
Alcor's cryo-preservation solution.

Every paramedic has stories of the sickest thing they've ever encountered on the job. I ran a call one time to a truck stop in the Nevada desert.
An unfortunate truck driver had suffered a heart attack sitting in his cab
and died right there. He stewed in his truck for a few days with the windows
up, fermenting in the 110-degree heat, until another trucker pulled up next
to him, took one whiff, said, "What the hell's that?" and called 911.

I didn't get closer than twenty feet from that big rig before I had to turn
back. We had to use respirators to get any closer. There was a puddle of
red goo under the truck. The driver had slumped down to the floorboard
and, after a few days in the desert heat, melted into the thick red gel that
was oozing through the crack of the door.

That liquefied trucker was the most disgusting thing I ever smelled in
my life—until the Alcor cryo-preservation solution.

I can best describe the stench of that god-awful concoction as a combination of raw hamburger and stale blood. The building reeked of it for

days after. I will never be able to smell uncooked hamburger meat again without wanting to vomit.

Dr. Munson's son had already begun the first two steps in the suspension protocol—icing the head and injecting the body with anticoagulants. Ice was applied immediately because the cooler the body, the slower the decomposition. After Tom Jr. used up all the ice in the house, Charles directed him to go borrow more from the neighbors (to this day I wonder what he told them it was for). Anticoagulants were important because once the blood began clotting, Alcor's cryo-preservant chemicals wouldn't be able to push through and circulate throughout the body.

Next, as soon as possible, the goal was to get the body to a facility where the blood washout procedure could begin, replacing the blood with the cryo-preservant solution. This took great quantities of toxic chemicals as well as medical equipment including blood pumps, IVs, and an operating table or, as was the case at Alcor, a mortician's table.

Exactly where this procedure would happen depended on where the member's first life cycle ended. If a member deanimated in the southern reaches of greater Los Angeles, say, Orange County or Long Beach, he or she would probably be brought to a funeral home owned by the undertaker Joe Klockgether.

Joe Klockgether had helped Bob Nelson back in the days of the first cryonic suspensions. Like Nelson, he had been sued after the Chatsworth meltdowns. Klockgether had been working with Alcor ever since it had started. Klockgether helped Alcor obtain death certificates and allowed its teams to perform surgery on the newly deanimated inside his funeral home. Like practically everyone else involved, Joe Klockgether made good money on Alcor cryo-suspensions.

If an Alcorian had deanimated in the northern part of greater Los Angeles, there was a good chance the body would have been placed in a minivan and driven to CCR in Rancho Cucamonga, since Klockgether's funeral home was in the opposite direction. Saul Kent, of course, allowed Alcor to use the CCR facility to perform the initial washout, and Rancho Cucamonga was right on the way to Phoenix from Los Angeles.

If a member had died anywhere other than Los Angeles, he or she would have been at a tremendous disadvantage. Brain cells start dying within minutes. Cryonicists agree that the chances for future reanimation increase significantly if the patient is immediately iced down and the blood washout commences without delay. The exact time limits in question are a matter of contention within the cryonics community, but basically after a few hours, the chances for an optimal suspension diminish steeply. That's why Alcor tried so hard to get its members to move to Phoenix. Another pie-in-the-sky brainchild of Jerry Lemler's was the Alcor House, sort of like the Ronald McDonald House in reverse. Lemler's vision was to build a facility near Alcor for members to come and die.

In Dr. Munson's case, his body was rushed toward the Klockgether Mortuary in Buena Park, California, about three hours from the Munson residence, where Alcor's Southern California surgical team was waiting. The surgical team was led by my least favorite animal researcher, Dr. Steve Harris. His assistants were Sandra Russell and Joan O'Farrell, Steve's fellow CCR employees.

When the body arrived at the Klockgether mortuary, Steve Harris jumped into surgery.

The first protocol of this temporary surgical stop on the way to Scottsdale was to perform a femoral cutdown, slicing open the leg in two places. A tube was slid into each opening, one in the femoral vein, one in the femoral artery. They approached the body as if it were a car radiator. The tube in the vein pumped the cryonic preservative chemicals in, the one in the artery sucked the blood and chemical mixture out. The ultimate goal was to replace all the blood with chemicals, but that was never fully achieved until the body was back at Alcor. At an intermediate stop like Klockgether's mortuary, the partial washout was performed until the technicians were satisfied that the blood-to-chemical ratio was high enough on the chemical side for the body to resume its journey to Scottsdale. This pit stop washout was meant to reduce clotting and cool the body further. The quicker this happened, of course, the better this ostensibly was for the member.

Dr. Steve, however, had a real tough time locating Dr. Munson's femoral artery, and what should have been a simple preliminary washout procedure took a full four hours. The femoral arteries in the legs are nice big fat ones, usually easy to work with. I never found out why Steve had such a difficult time with Dr. Munson.

One of the Los Angeles team members was dispatched to rent a U-Haul truck. This was how most patients were transported from L.A. to Scottsdale. So four hours after arriving for what should have been a two-hour procedure, Dr. Munson was finally loaded into the rental vehicle. Bobby June and Todd Huffman raced the U-Haul toward Alcor with Dr. Munson on ice in the back.

Charles had been able to reach Alcor's contract surgeon, a retired doctor by the name of Jose Kanshepolsky. Had Charles been unable to get ahold of Jose, he would've had to call the second person on the list who decapitated Alcorians for money—a local veterinarian.

Dr. Munson's body arrived at Alcor at around 1:45 a.m. local time.

The body was wheeled in through the back door and straight into the OR. Charles had done a good job making sure everything was prepared. Still, it took forty-five minutes for the operation to commence.

At 2:30 a.m. the surgery began.

To my amazement, about half a dozen Alcorian spectators were allowed to observe the procedure inside the OR. They were the Alcor volunteers who usually came in a few times a month and worked for free. Today they were paid several hundred dollars each, all of which had been prebilled to Dr. Munson.

There was very little for them to do—gofers with nothing to go for. They just hung around, getting in the way.

What really shocked me was their attitude. They were chatting, joking, and patting each other on the back. There was lots of laughter, giddy excitement in the air. It was like a tailgate party before a big football game. Even more amazing to me, many of them had brought cameras and were snapping their own souvenir pictures of Dr. Munson's corpse, taking turns posing around the body.

I realized that for the true believers, the deanimation and cryo-preservation of a fellow Alcorian for his second life cycle was a time of celebration, not mourning. They were helping their brother on his way to a new life, maybe to immortality. It was one big, happy bon voyage. Why not whoop it up?

These were the hard-core Alcorians. Some of them had moved across the country to live and die near Alcor. They all looked forward with glee to the day of their own decapitation. I asked Jerry Lemler about the volunteers shooting photographs, if that was condoned by Alcor.

His response was, "Larry, no one complains when people take pictures at a baptism, do they?"

Charles wasn't very hands-on during Dr. Munson's operation. He was coordinating the efforts, making phone calls, overseeing it all. Since Charles was training me to take his place, I was there by his side, following him from room to room and learning from him. I didn't get my hands dirty, so to speak, during this first suspension but I did get a solid overview of everything that normally happened during an Alcor cryo-suspension. Basically, it was a total mess.

There was a terrible lack of communication, a definite vibe of winging it. They just went in there and sliced somebody up. Try as Charles might to keep things moving smoothly, he was not exactly dealing with medical professionals here. The volunteers were worse than useless, getting in the way, only there to have a good time. James Sikes, Jerry Lemler's well-paid son-in-law, was on hand to be the laboratory assistant. I think the closest thing to medical training that man ever had was taking a computer course from DeVry University.

In the OR, they kept Dr. Munson packed in ice and carried on the blood washout, replacing his blood with the chemicals. In all, they flushed about twenty liters of chemicals through him. Some of the chemicals, as intended, remained in the body. An adult human body holds five or six liters of blood. When it was over, there were about twenty liters of a noxious blood and toxic chemical stew to be disposed of. Think of one liter of milk. Twenty liters is a lot of blood and chemicals.

An even pressure needed to be maintained at all times during the washout. That's why the blood pumps were so important. If the pumps didn't push hard enough and the pressure fell too low, blood would pool and congeal in the body. Pathways would be blocked and the chemicals would not reach all the places they should. If the pump pressure was too high, arteries and veins would burst, spilling blood all around the inside of the head and body. There would be obvious physical evidence of this if it happened. If blood leaked from the member's ears or eyes, then vessels had burst and blood was finding its way into the nooks and crannies of the skull. At that point, you would know the washout had failed and that blood was hiding out inside the head.

Alcor's pumps were old. They malfunctioned. Charles told me it was a chronic problem at Alcor. Dr. Munson's surgery should have gone smoothly but with Hugh Hixon constantly struggling with malfunctioning pumps and volunteers crowding the room flashing snapshots, it was a circus. Alcor's surgical standards were not even remotely up to those of, say, your average hospital. I'd call the bodies under the knife dead. Alcorians considered them alive. Regardless, as an emergency medical professional for more than twenty-five years, I had never seen such a gross lack of professionalism in my life.

Dr. Munson was signed up for a neuro-suspension, meaning his head would be stored separately from his body, so once Hugh was satisfied they had removed enough blood and replaced it with preservatives, they removed Dr. Munson's head. I wasn't around for that; I was off following Charles around, trying to come up with ways to make what I was witnessing more professional and respectful in the future.

After the decapitation was completed, Dr. Munson's head was put into Hugh Hixon's cephalic isolation box. At this point, if a member hadn't paid extra for the long-term freezing of the headless corpse, then the technicians were done with the body. They would have put the decapitated cadaver back into the body bag, wheeled it into the Cool-Down Bay, opened the back door, and a creepy-looking local mortician by the name of Steve Rude (pronounced "Rudy") would have taken the body and cremated it. As I recall, this is what happened in Dr. Munson's case. Depending on the individual arrangements, the ashes would be either returned to the Alcor member's family or disposed of.

All attention turned to Dr. Munson's disembodied head. The washout tubes that were previously in his femoral arteries were now connected to the carotid artery in his neck. They filled his head like a water balloon with cryo-preservants, attempting to flush out and replace whatever blood was still in there.

This procedure was even trickier than it sounds, though. There are many tiny alcoves inside a head where blood can pool. When the temperature was brought down to −321 degrees Fahrenheit, the remaining wayward blood could freeze and those little barbed, microscopic ice crystals would rip up everything around them as they grew, including brain matter. In worst-case scenarios, the force of expanding, freezing blood could actually crack the skull and punch straight through the bone.

Hugh Hixon took samples by grabbing residual drops that snuck out around the washout tubes in Dr. Munson's neck. Hugh looked at these drops under a handheld microscope to see how much blood was left versus chemical solution. The initial readings were always very rich in blood, and became diluted with chemicals as they proceeded.

Hugh would take upward of two hundred sample readings per body. Alcor kept many of these samples on hand. They were logged on paper and stored in the Neuro Vault in case the Alcorian's DNA was needed in the future. It was a failsafe. If, for instance, a plane overshot the Scottsdale Airport runway, crashed through the two-foot concrete-and-steel-reinforced walls of the Patient Care Bay, and took out all the heads and bodies, at least they'd have the DNA for possible future cloning.

When the samples were thrown away, they were called waste. When Hugh placed them in the Neuro Vault for long-term freezing and safe-keeping, they were called fluid samples.

It normally took between four and nine hours before Hugh was satisfied that a washout was complete. Once the head got the thumbs-up from Hugh, a Flash Gordon laser gun–looking tool was used to drill several dime-width holes deep into the skull. Little microphones were slid into the holes until they rested directly on the brain. The wires from the microphones were stapled to the skull and then connected to a modified computer rig that was originally developed to monitor patients during heart surgery. This was Hugh Hixon's Frankensteined contraption that Alcor called the Crackphone.

When the Alcorian brains underwent the extreme temperature drop to −321 degrees Fahrenheit, they would crack and split apart. Always.

There was no avoiding it. Hugh created the drilling/mic-ing/stapling protocol and the computer rig so that these "acoustic events," as Alcor innocuously called them, could be measured on the Crackphone. Brain cracks were recorded visually like earthquakes on a seismograph. Like whoppers on a lie detector. Though grisly, the Crackphone was another brilliant piece of engineering on Hugh's part.

As for the brain cracks, today's cryonicists have left it to tomorrow's doctors to deal with them. Medical technology will one day advance to the point where that's no problem to fix, they say.

An Alcorian's head, once wired with the microphones, was balanced on top of a BumbleBee tuna can and placed upside down into the LR-40 cooling machine. The top of the LR-40 was sealed with duct tape, the microphone wires trailing out from it.

For every Alcor member I knew of except two—A-1949 and his CryoStar roommate—the heads were moved in this way straight from the cephalic isolation box into the LR-40 for the great cool-down to −321 degrees. The final destination was the dewar, but normally after three days in the LR-40, the heads were deposited into Neuro Cans and then moved into the Neuro Vault. Those dewars were sacred, Alcor's fragile Promised Land. As Charles had told me during my initial tour, they didn't open up the dewars until they had to. Heads were stored in the Neuro Vault, underneath packets of DNA samples and decades-old cat heads, dog heads, and monkey brains, until a dewar absolutely had to be opened—basically until the Neuro Vault was so full of heads they couldn't possibly fit another one into it.

When a dewar finally had to be opened, staff at Alcor made a day of it. They pushed the dewar out from the steel-reinforced security wall, then wheeled it out of the Patient Care Bay and into the adjoining Cool-Down Bay. As Charles had told me during my initial tour, there was a removable skylight in the Cool-Down Bay and a crane on the roof to haul bodies into the dewars.

It would have been a lot better for all concerned if the entire cryo-suspension process had been carried out by trained professionals. Alcor's surgical team mainly consisted of volunteers who were there to party, and Jerry Lemler's family members who were there to pick up bonus checks. The retired surgeon, Jose Kanshepolsky, came in, performed the decapitation, grabbed his check, and got the heck out. He didn't hang around to see what happened next.

Even this description makes the procedure sound a whole lot more organized than it really was. As I said, it was really just one big mess.

———————

Dr. Munson's cryo-suspension became an all-night affair. I walked out of the OR at seven a.m. for a quick breather and saw James Sikes walking toward me with an empty twenty-liter bucket. That bucket, I knew, had been full of Dr. Munson's blood, fecal waste, and other body fluids, as well as fifteen or so liters of the toxic cryo-preservant chemicals. I knew Alcor had no proper laboratory sinks and no emergency eyewash stations. This was a safety issue I had already brought up to Charles, one more example of Alcor's being what I called a thirty-year-old start-up. I asked James where he had disposed of the hazardous chemicals and body fluids.

"I just dumped it down the bathroom sink," he said.

"What?"

"Yeah. Sometimes I flush it down the toilet," he said.

Most of Alcor's patients were sick, many with cancer or infected with AIDS. That diseased blood was just being poured down the drain, together with the toxic chemicals? This was clearly a biohazard! My God, I wondered if Scottsdale reclaimed its water like other desert cities?

"You can't do that!" I was appalled. "You can't just flush contaminated blood and dangerous chemicals into the local water system!"

"Well," he said, "sometimes I dump that stuff into the shrubs and flower beds out back."

He walked on by me. I was beside myself.

———————

Later that morning, while Dr. Munson was lying in two pieces on his way to his second life cycle, I found Charles in his office. We were all beat from a long, stressful night's work.

I related to Charles what James Sikes had told me. I told him that I was positive the City of Scottsdale, the EPA (Environmental Protection Agency), and OSHA (the Occupational Safety and Health Administration) would not appreciate Alcor's practice of disposing of biohazardous waste and toxic chemicals out the back door, into the sewers, or into the shrubs and flower beds.

"Charles," I said, "you really need to address this."

None of this came as a surprise to Charles and he said, "You're absolutely right, Larry. We need to clean up our act. I'll talk to Jerry about it next chance I get. Thanks for bringing this to me. I'll take care of it."

I got home, exhausted, around nine a.m. The raw-hamburger and stale-blood stink coming off of me from the Alcor cryo-preservant chemicals was nearly making me wretch. Outside our second-floor apartment I stripped down to my underwear and dropped my scrubs by the door. My truck would stink like rancid meat for days. From that day on I started keeping multiple pairs of scrubs at Alcor.

As soon as she heard the door, Beverly rose from her coffee at the kitchen table to give me a hug, all smiles, but then stopped short.

"Hey, how was your—why are you wearing your—oh my God!" She covered her mouth. "What is that smell?"

NINE

SUSPENSION 2:
REMEMBER THE ALAMO

I didn't have long to wait until the next cryo-suspension came along. It occurred only one week later, on Saturday, March 1, 2003. Jerry Lemler had sent me to Los Angeles to visit some sick Alcor members as research for the Patient Assessment death list he had asked me to compile early in my tenure. I was there interviewing ill and aging Alcor members, asking them questions, surreptitiously jotting down notes on how soon I thought they'd be cashing in their chips.

A Los Angeles Alcor member happened to be sick and in the hospital, so that evening I met up with a hardcore Alcorian by the name of David Hayes. We sat in the hospital waiting room for two or three hours in case the Alcor member died.

Then Lemler received a phone call from a friend of another Los Angeles Alcorian: member A-1025. This eighty-eight-year-old man had been lying on the floor of his home for two days before his friend found him—alive but in bad shape. Paramedics responded to the home and immediately transported A-1025 to the California Hospital Medical Center in downtown L.A., where he died shortly thereafter. At approximately eleven p.m. Pacific time, Hayes and I got the call from Jerry Lemler. We had a member down. We needed to assemble the Los Angeles team immediately and get a U-Haul full of emergency response gear down to the California Hospital. It was a fortunate coincidence, he said, that I was already in L.A.

Almost halfway to the California Hospital, I received another phone call from Lemler. There was a problem with the paperwork and the hospital was balking about releasing the body to Alcor. Normally, bodies are released to the next of kin or to a mortuary service. Lemler told me to find the patient and try to begin the washout procedure, and meanwhile he'd get ahold of Klockgether.

I explained to Jerry that doctors and nurses get a bit upset when people come into their hospital and start injecting people, dead or alive, with drugs. It would be wise to wait until Klockgether signed for the body, I told him.

"Oh, right," Lemler said. "Damn, I wish Charles were here." And he hung up.

Bobby June met up with us in his jet-black Mercedes-Benz. June, Hayes, and I parked on a side street behind the hospital, then we all hopped in June's black Benz to wait. I was in the backseat. Like thieves in the night, like the body snatchers we were, we waited outside the downtown Los Angeles California Hospital Medical Center for Joe Klockgether, the mortician, to work his magic and get us the body of Alcor's newest futurenaut.

Bored, Bobby June started showing me his tattoos. I liked him but he was definitely what I would call a hard-core cryonicist. He showed me his A-number tattooed on his chest. More than that, Bobby told me he actually had Alcor's phone number and the first stages of suspension protocol tattooed on his body as well. "Ice my body, inject heparin," etc.

"Bobby," I asked, "what if we change suspension protocol? What if we go with something beside heparin?"

His jaw dropped. "What? Could they do that?"

While June and I were having this absurd conversation, Hayes began drawing up the first medications we would be injecting into A-1025.

Right then an LAPD squad car came down the street, cruising right toward us. There we were, three guys in downtown L.A. in the middle of the night, sitting in a black Mercedes with dark tinted windows, one guy holding his shirt up and another guy drawing up drugs into syringes. My silver paramedic badge had gotten me out of a lot of traffic tickets, but I didn't think it was going to help me this time.

That's it, I thought, *we're going to jail*. It didn't seem like saying, "No, Officer, really, we're cryonicists," would get us out of this tight spot.

Hayes noticed the cop car just as it was passing us and froze, his hands suspended in midair, the hypodermic needle twinkling in the night. For some reason the cops drove right by us. I thought for sure they were going to stop, but the tinted windows must have prevented them from peering inside. Either that or the cops in L.A. are just as jaded as you hear.

After an hour of playing drug lords, we got the okay from Lemler. Klockgether had done his duty. June pulled his Benz into the ER parking lot and I followed in the U-Haul (after noticing that our U-Haul had gotten tagged by a graffiti artist while we were waiting in June's Benz).

I've worked at some busy hospitals but I've never seen anything like the spectacle of Saturday night at the California Hospital Medical Center ER. There were so many people waiting to be seen that they were spilling out into the parking lot. All hospital ER personnel are overworked but these guys must have been dead on their feet by the end of their shifts. I mentioned this to David Hayes as I got out of the U-Haul.

"Good," David said. "It'll be easier to get the patient out."

Klockgether handed the body off to us in the hospital parking lot. We got A-1025 loaded into the U-Haul truck around midnight, packed him with bags of ice, and sped off toward Rancho Cucamonga.

We arrived at CCR at 4:40 a.m. There, we began the process of flushing out the patient's blood and infusing him with the cryo-preservant solution. I assisted Steve Harris in the procedure and this time there were no problems with the femoral artery. Afterward, we placed A-1025 into a body bag with 150 pounds of ice packed around his body to keep him cold. He was ready for final transport to Alcor by seven a.m.

The suspension equipment inside the U-Haul needed to stay in California with the L.A. response team, so Mike Lee, a part-time CCR employee, had been dispatched earlier to pick up a minivan from Alamo Rent A Car in Rancho Cucamonga.

I was going to fly back to Phoenix to help prepare the OR. As I was leaving CCR for the airport, I told everyone how tired I was. I had been up for twenty-four hours straight. Steve Harris reached into the pocket of his lab coat, pulled out a handful of pills, and said, "Here, take some of these. They'll keep you wide awake."

The man was a walking pharmacy.

"No thanks," I told him.

When I landed in Scottsdale, I learned that Jerry had been unable to reach the surgeon Jose Kanshepolsky. Instead, A-1025 would have to be decapitated by a local veterinarian. Still, Jerry had waited too long to call her and she hadn't even arrived at Alcor yet.

Then I was told there was a mix-up back in Rancho Cucamonga. Jerry had neglected to instruct the L.A. team to procure a transit permit from Klockgether. David Hayes realized at the last minute that they needed one to move the body to Alcor. With A-1025 in the back, Mike Lee drove the Alamo minivan an hour in what amounted to the wrong direction to get to the Klockgether mortuary in Orange County, California. But when he finally arrived there, everyone was gone.

Continuing this tragicomedy of errors, Steve Harris next realized there was no death certificate. He called the California Hospital Medical Center in the hopes of convincing the ER physician to sign a death certificate, only to hear that the ER doctor had already gone home.

Mike Lee sat outside the Klockgether mortuary with A-1025's body warming in the Orange County morning sun for three more hours while Steve Harris worked out the death certificate situation.

Although we had had him prepared by seven a.m., A-1025 did not leave Southern California until after eleven a.m. It was a disaster, completely avoidable if Jerry Lemler had had any clue how to manage the transport process, or anything else.

In the March 10 Alcor News Bulletin, Charles gave a brief description of A-1025's cryo-suspension. It was a heck of a lot different than the scathing memo he later circulated around Alcor criticizing Jerry Lemler's performance and calling for his resignation. In the public bulletin, Charles only wrote:

"The patient was delayed overnight by mortuary paperwork problems."

I found out later that Alcor sometimes publicly blamed these colossal screw-ups on hospital staff and car rental companies.

Mike Lee finally pulled up to Alcor's back door at 5:33 p.m. A-1025 had been in the back of the Alamo minivan for ten and a half hours.

I came out the back door and helped wheel the patient into Alcor's OR. I asked Jerry Searcy where James Sikes was.

"I don't know where Sikes is, goddamn it," he said.

I went out back again and found James Sikes standing by the Alamo vehicle, shaking his head. When I asked what was wrong, he pointed to the back of the minivan.

"Look," he said.

I almost gagged.

The floor of the vehicle was covered in human blood, hair, bile, urine, fecal waste, and God knows what other bodily fluids, all mixed into a nauseating soup. During the six-and-a-half-hour trip from Southern California to Scottsdale, Arizona (*after* sitting in the Orange County sun for four hours), somewhere in the middle of the Sonora Desert in the middle of the day, the ice had begun to melt. Every fluid inside A-1025 had seeped out every opening in his body. And then the body bag had leaked.

Now there was a thick puddle of yellow, red, and brown pestilence soaking into the minivan's upholstery, the carpets, everything. I thought I had seen it all as a paramedic. I was wrong. This was beyond revolting.

"James," I said, "you need to clean that up right away and then notify Charles Platt."

He nodded. There was nothing else I could do at the time. I had to go back inside to assist in the OR.

The next morning, when I asked Charles about the Alamo minivan, he acted as if he did not know what I was talking about. I found James Sikes and asked what he had done with the minivan. He shrugged his shoulders.

"I hosed it out."

"That's all?" I said. "Where is it now?"

"I don't know," he said. "I guess someone returned it."

I had to turn away. If I stood there one second longer, I would have punched him in the face. I walked straight into Mathew Sullivan's office, but he wasn't there. I knew where he kept the case files of recent Alcor suspensions. I opened up the cabinet, leafed through, and sure enough, there was the A-1025 file. I pulled it.

I walked straight to the dusty Xerox copier by the dusty fax machine behind Dick Clair's dusty Emmy Award and made a copy of the Alamo Rent A Car receipt. I got the vehicle identification number, everything. This was one of those minivans a guy might rent for himself and his kids to travel cross-country and it had been merely hosed out after it had been steeped in blood, bile, and feces, not to mention large amounts of toxic chemicals. If someone were to pull back the rear panels or swab the carpets, I'm pretty sure they'd find A-1025's DNA, or much worse.

It's no reflection on the folks at Alamo Rent A Car, but think about this one the next time the kids are playing in the back of a rented minivan as you're truckin' cross-country to Grandma's for Thanksgiving.

I returned the file to Mathew's cabinet. Without realizing what I was doing, or having planned it, I had just gathered my first piece of damning evidence on Alcor.

TEN

AN ADRENALINE JUNKIE, THE CULT AT VENTUREVILLE, AND SUSPENSION 3: THE HAMMER AND CHISEL

Three days later I watched Hugh Hixon transfer A-1025's head from the LR-40 cooling device into a Neuro Can to prepare it for permanent storage. When Hugh lifted the head out, I was shocked by the drawn, leathery appearance of the face. Drained of water, the skin had shrunk and stretched, especially around the mouth. A-1025's face was pulled into a gruesome, permanent grin, revealing a full set of teeth.

"Looks like he's having a good time in there," Hugh said.

To complete the ghoulish picture, someone had put a strip of duct tape over the old man's eyes. I never found out why.

Hugh bobbed the head up and down as if he were operating a puppet and mimicked the man's voice like a ventriloquist: "See you in a hundred years, Sonny!"

I was congratulated on all sides for my performance at work thus far, especially during the two suspension procedures. Michael Riskin reminded me that if I ever wanted to become an Alcor member, he'd have the company pay everything for me, even the insurance. Hugh visited me in my office, thanked me for my help, and also encouraged me to join up. I knew it would alleviate a lot of tension around the office. I also knew it was a surefire way to learn more about the bizarre and increasingly dubious world in which I was working.

Many people have asked me why I stayed at Alcor when it was so creepy and then, later, when it became so frightening, as it eventually did. Ultimately, I felt obliged to stay in order to gather evidence. There were some unbelievable things going on there, to say the least. Who would believe what I had seen if I had no proof, no real evidence? To understand why I stayed on at Alcor during those first few months, though, before things had gotten really weird, I think you need to understand a little about why I became a paramedic in the first place.

I have always been an adrenaline junkie.

I grew up outside Albuquerque, New Mexico. There's mostly outdoor stuff for a teenager to do there. I used to mountain climb, rappel down cliffs, hang glide. It's practically the unofficial hot-air balloon capital of the world.

We'd shoot guns—handguns, rifles, shotguns. I'm part good ol' boy, I don't deny it.

I've been on motorcycles my whole life. I got my first minibike when I was nine years old, a little 50cc job my dad bought for my brother and me. We had that for about a year and then, seeing how we hadn't broken our necks on it, my dad bought us a bigger Honda trail bike. I don't think my dad ever realized how fast the engine on that Honda dirt bike could carry us. I was ten years old, ripping around the desert on, basically, a full-blown motorcycle.

Up by the Sandia Mountains, outside Albuquerque, when it rains you get a lot of washes where flash floods carve out mini Grand Canyons in the soft earth. We used to jump over those. They could be thirty or forty feet deep and ten feet wide. Doing that was sort of dumb, I admit, but we had fun at it.

I had friends with dune buggies. Rail cars, we called them. We'd go fly-ing up hills, over sand dunes, trying to flip our cars on purpose. I used to love that. We were fifteen or sixteen.

I've been launched over the handlebars of a wide variety of motorcy-cles. I've gone headfirst into barbed-wire fences. I've been in two acci-dents on the street riding a motorcycle. Both times someone pulled out right in front of me real fast and I didn't have time to stop. These things happen when you ride motorcycles. I know I'll never stop riding, though. It's too much of a thrill. This is a trait I share with most paramedics. I have had more than a few good friends who were paramedics die in high-speed motorcycle accidents. That's the type of person drawn to emer-gency medicine.

When I was a boy, I found a dead person.

It happened in the little town of Belen, New Mexico, south of Albu-querque. At the time, my dad worked for the telephone company. He was also a professional musician. He taught himself to play music by ear, and then he taught himself to read music. My father is an extremely talented man. He can play the piano like you can't believe. In fact, he can pick up just about any instrument and play it.

My dad worked for a record producer by the name of Norman Petty, who produced every big act in that part of the country back then. My dad was a session pianist. Dad played with Johnny Cash, Buddy Holly, Waylon Jennings, Johnny Horton—just about everyone who came through that area in those days.

As a result of his love and talent for music, my dad wasn't home much. He would work all day for the telephone company, then gig all night.

He played a lot of nightclubs, country clubs, piano bars, and such. He didn't make much money at it; my dad played because he loved it. I al-ways respected him for that. It was tough on my mom. We lived in a poor area, in a mobile home. But I've always admired my father because he fol-lowed his passion.

I had friends but I also hung out by myself a lot as a kid. Behind the trailer where we lived was a huge irrigation canal. I would climb around down there and play or maybe catch crawfish. The canal was more like a river than anything else. It had a swift current that swept by real fast. My mom would freak out about me going down there, saying a boy could drown down there. I blew that off for years, but it turned out she was right.

One Saturday I went down to play by the water by myself. Years earlier, some local farmers had laid down long planks of wood in order to cross the wide canal. A couple poles were driven into the canal bed like columns, supporting and connecting the planks. I used to play around that slender bridge, running back and forth across it because it was narrow enough to give me a thrill. There was a real danger of falling the eight or ten feet down into the rushing water below, but this never stopped me.

On this particular Saturday morning there was a dead body down there beneath the bridge. It seemed to be a small boy, caught on one of those columns. His little body was bent around it like a horseshoe. He was pretty well dead, no doubt about that, face-up and bloated.

I found out that way up the waterway there was a school for mentally challenged kids in Los Lunas, New Mexico. This boy had snuck out of school and fell in the canal up there. He was swept clear down twenty miles of the waterway.

I stayed there by myself a bit and investigated the scene. I wasn't creeped out or scared. On the contrary, I found his dead body interesting. I wasn't poking at it with a stick or anything, just looking at it real close. After a while, though, the way his little body was bent around the bridge pole made me uncomfortable. I felt guilty of something, or maybe I thought what I was doing was disrespectful.

So I went and told my mom. Man, she got the whole police department out there. They hauled a big ol' construction crane out there to lift the boy out.

My mom tried to keep me inside so I wouldn't go back down there and see the kid all dead and puffy and, with my delicate eight-year-old sensibilities and all, get scarred for life. Hey, I told her, I was the one who had found him in the first place! But she was dead set against me going down there to see them pull him out.

So I snuck out to watch.

From a real early age, then, I was exposed to dead people. I wasn't grossed out by it, but I wasn't drawn to death in a macabre sense either. It just intrigued me.

Several years later, my parents got divorced and my mother, brother, and I moved to Albuquerque. No more trailer park, but it was a poor area again, a pretty rough neighborhood. There were always big Harley-Davidsons around as far back as I can remember. I had a friend, Ike, whose mom was single and she used to date a lot. Bikers mostly. You'd hear them rumbling through the neighborhood, picking up Ike's mom, dropping her off.

Our house was a stone's throw from a major interstate, the I-40. It must have been a particularly dangerous stretch of the freeway, because there were lots of car crashes. Horrible accidents. I could hear them from my house.

We'd be sitting at home, watching TV, and you'd hear a big SCREEEEEEE—CRASH! I'd be off, tearing for the highway to check it out, my mom calling after me, telling me not to go. There was a chain-link fence stretching along the side of the highway. I'd race up to it, stick my fingers through the holes. I was always the first one at the scene and I saw some pretty hairy stuff.

I'd look at the accident scenes for a little while, then run over to Ike's house.

"Hey, Ike, c'mon! There's another accident!"

If he was home, Ike'd join me and we'd go back and gawk a bit more.

Ike's full name was Ivan Dickmeyer. With a name like that, Ike grew up a fighter. He ended up protecting me a lot when we got a little older. Ike became a biker, but back then, he was just a big kid no one wanted to mess with. Tough as hell. We'd run back to the accident and Ike would look for a while but then he'd have to turn away. Even he'd get squeamish looking at these crash scenes. I'd be fascinated, though.

"Hey, Ike, look, you can see that guy's arm just about completely severed at the shoulder!"

Then the paramedics would arrive. That was the best part. They'd roar up, a hundred miles an hour, lights blazing, sirens screaming. They'd jump out of their truck and get straight to work—saving lives. They were heroes. In the middle of the yelling and crying and blood and arms and eyeballs and cops and everything, the paramedics were in control.

I never cracked a book but did well in school. It just bored me. My dad had a genius IQ, while I've been tested two points below genius. Dad never let me live that down. A near-miss genius, he called me. That's me, a Southwestern trailer-park, danger-loving, gore-watching, gun-shooting, bike-riding redneck, two points shy of genius.

When it came to education and a career, my dad would say, "Beans or steak, Larry? You want beans or steak? If you don't want to go to school, you'll be eating beans your whole life. But if you want to eat steak, you need to go to school and work hard. So what'll it be, Larry? Beans or steak?"

I was a working paramedic by the time I was nineteen. Another one of my dad's sayings was, "Larry, the only job where you get to start at the top is digging ditches." So while my old high school buddies were still smoking weed and spotlight-hunting jackrabbits in their daddies' trucks, I was busting my hump working sixteen-hour shifts—and I loved it.

In those days, funeral homes still ran the paramedic services in smaller communities like mine. We had two teams but only one ambulance. We'd work shifts like firefighters, sleeping upstairs in the funeral home during downtime. When we got a call and the first team was already out in the ambulance, we'd jump in the old sixties Cadillac hearse. Can you imagine somebody lying on the side of the road, bleeding, and here come a couple guys tearing up at a hundred miles an hour in a hearse? I mean, what kind of message does that send?

Paramedicine is a steady living but you're not going to retire to a vineyard in the south of France or anything. I guess I ended up somewhere in the middle, Dad, somewhere between beans and steak. Paramedicine provided me with a meat loaf–type of lifestyle and that's always been just fine with me.

What I loved most, though, was the sense of responsibility and control. Someone's got to be in that position barking orders and keeping people alive. What a rush to be that person.

I worked in an environment of complete chaos. People didn't wait for me to get out of the ambulance. They'd charge at me while I was pulling up. In a glance I had to surmise who was and who wasn't in immediate danger of losing his or her life. People were screaming at me to help their loved ones, running back and forth from their bleeding father to me. Bystanders were in shock from what they'd witnessed. Was it a crime scene? Was a gunman still around? Were my partner and I in danger?

People might be screaming, crying, throwing up, pointing at their own limbs on the ground. Maybe someone went through a windshield and was sprawled out on the road. Maybe someone else was trapped in a car, screaming in pain. There was never enough of me and my partner to go around. I had to make quick judgments. Who did we treat first? Could that choice determine who lived and who died today? Yes, it sure could.

I've trained hundreds of paramedics and written chapters in emergency medicine textbooks. On the street, I always felt like I was contributing. I was doing something for other people, something not everyone could do, and I was good at it.

So I guess I could say I spent my life either putting myself in danger or helping other people out of it. After all those experiences, whatever it was I spent my time doing, whatever job I took, I knew it had to be damn exciting to keep my interest.

I didn't know what I was getting into by taking the job at Alcor, but I suspected there would hardly be any dull moments. I knew it was going to be an eccentric place to work; that was part of the draw. But Alcor seemed like it would be a good mixture of science and excitement. It turned out I overestimated the science and underestimated the excitement.

A few days after the cryo-suspension of Alcor member A-1025, Charles and I took another drive. This time it was to a resort called the Creekside Lodge out near Mayer, Arizona. I had been asked to hold training classes, instructing Alcor volunteers in emergency medicine procedures.

As I drove I again told Charles the story of the Alamo minivan and re-iterated my concerns about what seemed to be more and more environ-mental and safety problems at Alcor. Alcor still needed eyewash stations. It needed to contract with a biohazard waste removal company. It was ridiculous to even hear myself saying something so obvious, but I re-minded Charles that James Sikes had to stop dumping toxic chemicals and human blood into the shrubs and local water system!

Geez, it finally hit me, *that's why those shrubs out there look so sick and scraggly.*

Charles made me feel like he was on my side. He again promised he would take care of it.

"Charles, are things usually so disorganized during cryo-suspensions?" I asked.

"Larry," Charles said, "hopefully you saw a big difference between how things went when I was in charge of Dr. Munson's suspension, and then how things went when Jerry Lemler was in charge of A-1025's suspension."

Charles was right. The word circulating around the office was that Jerry had botched the suspension of A-1025 so badly that A-1025's chances for reanimation in the future were greatly reduced as a result. That was quite an accusation. In their eyes, because of his ineptitude, Jerry had endan-gered the man's resurrection and second life, the whole reason for Alcor's existence in the first place.

Charles told me he was compiling a list of Jerry's bad decisions during the A-1025 suspension. It would be the next missile in his endless e-mail campaign against Jerry Lemler and would later culminate in a twenty-seven-page petition he circulated around Alcor calling for Lemler's resig-nation. As I drove, Charles presented his opinions to me very convincingly, basically summarizing what he would later put into that petition.

Charles said that Jerry had called the veterinarian so late that she ar-rived forty minutes *after* the much-delayed body—which itself arrived over six hours late. Still, incredibly, the OR had not been properly prepped and Jerry had the wrong sequence of procedures planned. Incredulous that Lemler was so ignorant of the proper order of things, the veterinarian asked why Jerry didn't want her to start with the cannulation (inserting the tubes that delivered Alcor's cryo-preservant chemicals). Of course, she was right. At least another half hour was wasted. Now Jerry had to set up for the insertion of the cannulas or tubes, and the blood-draining procedure. He had not even prepped the surgical trays.

Hugh Hixon believed that due to the long delays, clotting had occurred and the perfusion (delivery of chemicals into the bloodstream) was not as successful as in other cases. By Alcor's own standards, A-1025 had less of a shot at a second life cycle than the average Alcorian.

Furthermore, Charles complained, Jerry had hired his daughter to function as the OR scribe, yet she took no notes at all. Then Jerry awarded her a $500 bonus and gave himself an extra $700 for good measure.

Worst of all, Jerry had been caught on video camera giving reassurances that all the long delays were not significant to the patient's suspension or chances of eventual reanimation. This flew in the face of everything cryonicists believed about the need for speed. Charles claimed that Jerry was just trying to save face. In his petition, Charles spelled out that Jerry's real goal as Alcor CEO was to "find a place in history. . . . to look good on a grand scale. . . . He wants the 'big picture,' not day-to-day tasks which may seem trivial and demeaning compared with his ambition."

Still, Charles left all of these legitimate complaints out of the case summary he published in the public Alcor News Bulletin. The only time he mentioned Jerry was to thank him for filling in during his own absence.

The majority of Alcor members, I knew, lived in Southern California. Although there were a few paramedics in Florida paid to be on call as a response team, Los Angeles had the only real experienced Alcor emergency response team. Even then, that team was composed of a ray-gun maker, a musician, and a college kid. And then there was Jerry Lemler back at the ranch, coordinating it all, or not, as I had seen.

Scottsdale, we have a problem . . .

If members died outside Southern California or greater Phoenix, the best Alcor could do was put the remains on a plane and fly them to Alcor. There weren't many mortuaries around the country like Klockgether's that would allow cryonicists to pump corpses full of hazardous chemicals in their basements. That's why Alcor encouraged its members to pay them up front for the rental of a private plane. Well, who could afford that? The other option was to move to Scottsdale.

"Charles," I said, driving us through the Arizona desert, "after watching Jerry in action, I wouldn't be surprised if more Alcorians didn't beg to move into Hugh and Mike's little secret bedroom to be close to the dewars."

"Well, of course it's best to freeze a patient at the exact moment of death," Charles said. "Or," he added ominously, "before."

Charles told me about a court case involving an Alcor member by the name of Thomas Donaldson who was suffering from cancer and wanted Alcor's creepy board member and ex-president, Carlos Mondragon, to euthanize him with Alcor's crash team in the room so as to begin his suspension at the exact moment of his death. Donaldson wanted to have his body suspended "premortem," before the cancer destroyed his brain. He called it elective cryo-preservation. Mondragon was all for it. They went through a lengthy court battle in Santa Barbara, ultimately suing the California attorney general. Finally, a California judge voted Donaldson down. The judge didn't want to open the door on assisted suicides. (I read somewhere that there was a similar case portrayed on an episode of *L.A. Law*, though I didn't know which came first, Donaldson's case or the TV episode.) Alcor members stormed the Internet posting sites, up in arms.

What Charles didn't mention, and which I learned later on my own, was that Donaldson's cancer went into remission. Years later he was still up and around, speaking at Alcor meetings (in fact, I believe his court case happened in 1990 and he was ultimately suspended in 2006, which means he lived sixteen more years). This made me wonder if any Alcorians would admit that had Mr. Donaldson been euthanized when he wanted to be put down, he'd have missed a whole lot of living.

Charles was being very candid with me inside my truck and I appreciated that. Somehow those long desert drives loosened his tongue. I decided to share a few of my own misgivings about Alcor's procedures in return.

"Charles," I said, "I'm a little unclear about Alcor's suspension procedures in terms of the blood-brain barrier."

"What do you mean?" he asked.

"The blood-brain barrier is like a microscopic net in your head that protects your central nervous system. It lets in oxygen molecules but blocks out anything dangerous before it can come into contact with your brain.

The molecular structure of Alcor's chemical solution is too big to cross the blood-brain barrier. It gets strained out like spaghetti."

Charles was silent.

"Charles," I continued, "what this means is the secret formula Alcor claims is the key to preserving its members' brains cannot even come in contact with the brain. Or, if it does, it can only do so by ripping the blood-brain barrier to shreds."

"But what about the new vitrification formula they're working on," Charles said, "where they're flash-freezing organs into something akin to glass?"

"First of all," I said, "their vitrification technique is, to say the least, in the experimental phase. Second, it's terribly toxic. It's like pouring gasoline into a brain. They use the old standby argument that doctors of the future will be able to fix that but I don't know. And, it still has to shred the blood-brain barrier to get through to the brain."

"What about the pictures of perfectly preserved rabbit kidneys Greg Fahy and Saul Kent are always publishing as proof the vitrification formula works?"

"Charles, I'm not denying that Greg Fahy is making progress cryopreserving rabbit kidneys," I said. "But you have to understand that, even if you forget about the blood-brain barrier for a minute, the brain is a unique organ in that it is not vascular at all. Kidneys and other organs are porous. The vitrification solution can flow into them and distribute evenly. The brain is another story altogether."

I paused, wondering how far I should take my doubts with Charles.

"Charles," I continued, "have you heard the quote from that famous cryobiologist that reanimating a person suspended at Alcor would be like turning hamburger back into a cow?"

"Sure, I've heard that," Charles said.

"And you've heard the thing about defrosted strawberries and how that's what your brain is like on cryonics?"

"Of course."

"Well, what do you think of all that?"

Charles sighed. "Larry, it comes down to this. I know the science isn't there yet. I'm no fool. I'm going to die. But I have a choice. If I'm cremated or buried, there's absolutely no chance for a second life. But if I'm frozen at Alcor, there is always the hope that future science can reverse the freezing damage, and then reverse death. Given those choices, I choose cryo-suspension. If it doesn't work, what have I lost?"

"But what about people like Riskin who are always telling sick, dying people that they're going to have another life?" I said. "What about Lemler telling people on tours that if they sign up they will live forever?"

"Larry, I've known them both for a long time. Michael Riskin is only concerned with two things in this life cycle: his own cryo-suspension, and Alcor's finances—and he's probably only passionate about Alcor's finances because his own suspension and storage depend on it. As for Lemler, I think Jerry Lemler has always been drawn to the romantic side of cryonics more than the scientific. He probably sees himself coming back a hundred years from now and honored as one of the first cryonics pioneers—and then spending the ensuing centuries skipping through daisy fields, signing autographs, plagiarizing speeches, and writing bad poetry. I'm not saying Jerry is a fraud or that he's malevolent, he's just inept. But that ineptness is starting to endanger the second life cycles of Alcor's members. That's what I'm trying to avoid.

"As for me, Larry, maybe cryonics will work, maybe it won't. Maybe nanotechnology will save us when the time comes, maybe not. We'll see. Given the other options of cremation or burial, cryonics is the only choice with a possible future. And it's very exciting to think of seeing that future, isn't it, Larry?" Charles peered at me. "Isn't that what you said in your television interview? That you were obsessed with seeing the world several hundred years from now?"

"Yeah, Charles. That's what I said."

David Pizer was an intimidating bear of a man with a thick build, scraggly hair, and a full beard. If he hadn't amassed a personal fortune of ten million dollars with his Creekside Lodge resort and other endeavors, Pizer probably could've made a killing as a professional wrestler. Captain Cryo.

The Creekside Lodge was off Arizona Route 69, in the township of Mayer, outside Prescott, Arizona. Prescott was a pretty little city known for its hiking trails and Old West history. The area was greener and hillier than the surrounding desert.

Pizer was one of those prominent Alcorians who believed some sort of Armageddon was coming. Pizer, however, was actively preparing for it, building a survivalist community of cryonicists that was remote and secluded, yet only an hour and a half away from Alcor's dewars.

From what I gathered that weekend, Pizer's Creekside Lodge was one part survivalist camp, one part religious cult compound, and one part travel motel. When the place wasn't closed down for an Alcor training session or cryonics soiree, families rented cabins by the night. Since the full name of the place was the "Creekside Preserve," some Alcorians punned on the double meaning of the word and called it "The Preserve" (using the word as it pertained to a natural habitat, and also as it related to cryonic cold storage).

Pizer and his followers, though, referred to the compound as Ventureville, which was in itself pretty creepy. Pizer lived there with his wife and John Grigg, his most dedicated disciple. Grigg was the manager of the Creekside Lodge, but his main function, as far as I could tell, was to worship the ground Pizer walked on.

On his Web site, Pizer referred to himself as "El Patron." Charles told me he had started out as a car upholstery salesman or something. After spending a weekend there, though, I believed David Pizer was basically a cult leader.

Pizer had formed his own religion, originally called the Church of Venturism, then renamed the Society for Venturism (though it remained, on the books, a religion). Mike Perry was a big pal of Pizer's and an ordained minister in the church. He provided wedding services. This was no joke. I don't think I would have opted to be married by a man who had removed his own testicles with a razor and then intentionally severed the nerves to his penis. Father Mike wasn't someone I'd send my confused teenage son to for counseling.

Pizer's followers called themselves Venturists. I had met a few of them at that Alcorian meeting in the Barnes & Noble in Santa Monica, California. Back then they had struck me as very intense and focused young men. Whereas some other Alcorians enjoyed the sci-fi, flying-car mystique of cryonics, the Venturists took it much more seriously.

Spending time with them on their turf, so to speak, I realized that they considered themselves frontiersmen. More than just the outdoors types, they were survivalists. I saw cases upon cases of canned food and water stored around Ventureville, and vast amounts of medical supplies.

My official role at Ventureville for that weekend was to train Venturists and some other fanatical Alcor members in emergency medicine procedures as they pertained to cryonic suspension. Pizer had a lot of medical equipment stockpiled at Ventureville and nobody seemed to know what to do with it.

Cryonicists came from all over the United States and as far away as England to attend my seminars. They wanted me to show them how to intubate a patient—that is, how to put a tube in someone's throat to ventilate them. I wasn't sure why they needed to know that. I asked Charles why they would want to intubate someone who had already finished his or her first life cycle. Charles couldn't figure it out either.

I taught them how to use blood pumps and other equipment used during cryonic suspension operations. I showed them how to make injections and perform femoral cutdowns. I demonstrated how to perform CPR or, rather, CPS. Our poor Resusci Annie was probably the only CPR practice dummy in history whose students didn't want it/her to pull through. Those Venturists were interested in learning how to get a dying person's blood pumping just enough to circulate cryo-protectant chemicals—not enough to get the patient breathing again.

During my weekend stay, at night, the Venturists gathered around a fire pit—after sharing dinner in a large common dining room—and talked in antigovernment slurs about federal law enforcement and how President Bush was too soft on crime. American society was breaking down, they said. Some explained to me that they felt fortunate to have found David Pizer, the great man who would lead them into a new civilization after this one inevitably fell into ruins. Several Venturists spoke to me in clear terms of preparing for a "holocaust." In truth, they men feared me. They struck me as malcontents looking for something to belong to, loners looking for a father figure and, God help them, they thought they'd found it in David Pizer.

The Venturists had a Web site that I came across later. In their "Bylaws" section, one of the "primary objectives and purposes" they listed was "To furnish a friendly, supportive community for persons who wish to act rationally to bring about the abolition of death and the establishment of a free society of immortals."

Elsewhere, in their Web site's "About Us" section, they wrote that they advocated respect and love for others, yet they were "willing to defend others against danger. We must be ready to put our lives on the line if necessary (as in the case, for example, of a physical threat to a cryonics patient)."

In conversation, they explained their beliefs to me a little more aggressively. Venturism is essentially the pursuit of physical immortality, they told me around that fire pit. Since science and medicine could not guarantee physical immortality yet, the Venturists turned to cryonics to suspend them until medical technology caught up. To them, cryonic suspension was the means by which they would live long enough—that is, forever—to bring about the advanced society that their leader, Pizer, had envisioned. In my experience, Alcorians were often arrogant, believing themselves to be the smart ones. Talking to these young men, though, it seemed that while many Alcor members hoped for a second life after cryosuspension, these Venturists expected it. Out of all humanity, they believed they were the few who deserved immortality, that it was their due. They were the chosen.

Jerry Lemler always seemed to be seeking followers but was never charismatic enough to draw them. Pizer was another story. Frankly, it terrifies me still to think what that man seemed capable of. Pizer was one of the Alcorian leaders, Charles had told me, originally arrested during the Dora Kent homicide investigation.

David Pizer pioneered a cryonics trust fund in which he was leaving his money to his future self. If it worked out, with interest, he'd have billions of dollars waiting for him when he reanimated and he'd be, according to what he told the *Wall Street Journal*, "the richest man in the world." Other cryonicists worth hundreds of millions of dollars followed his cue.

What would David Pizer do with all that money? "I'd like to come back and buy a big spaceship and travel to other planets," Pizer told another newspaper. "Who knows, if you could live for thousands of years, maybe you could even get out of this galaxy."

———————————

Being on Pizer's property gave me the creeps. There was a real quaint, rustic, log-cabin feel to the place but at the same time there were the stores of food, water, and medical supplies that pointed to some darker preparedness. When I mentioned the cases of food and water, Charles raised his eyebrows and said, "Have you seen the weapons?"

These were the hardest-core true believers of the entire hard-core cryonicist bunch. After seeing them fawn over their El Patron, I believe that to say they worshiped Pizer would not be an exaggeration. And with what I would call a raging messiah complex, Pizer happily encouraged it. Pizer carried himself like the father of a large family. His word was law. He spoke with an air of infallibility and the Venturists hung on his every word. When I dealt personally with the Branch Davidians in Waco, I saw people under the control of a charismatic leader, ready to kill or die for him. I saw that same look in the eyes of the Venturists.

Like many other cryonicist leaders, Pizer dabbled in writing science fiction. He had self-published a novel about a man diagnosed with a terminal illness who was cryonically preserved and then reanimated in the twenty-second century. Charles told me that, sometimes, Pizer sat his followers down around the fire and read his short stories to them. It made me think that if only these zealous cryonics leaders had achieved commercial success as writers, maybe they would have laid off the dark obsessions, the way Hitler might never have caused so much horrendous damage to humanity if he had found early success as a painter.

In my estimation, after having seen both places firsthand, Ventureville was another Waco waiting to happen. The only difference between David

Pizer and David Koresh was that Pizer claimed his religion was based on science. Underneath it all, though, it felt to me like his main objective was simply to have militant, dedicated followers hanging on his every word and command.

And then there was Pizer's personal fortune. He could fund virtually anything his mind cooked up. Imagine what David Koresh could have done with a $10 million bankroll.

When that weekend training session finished, I was relieved to get the hell out of Ventureville.

A few weeks after returning from David Pizer's compound, I witnessed my third cryonic suspension. An eighty-two-year-old female member, Alcor number A-1234, was found dead in a Hollywood-area nursing home on Saturday morning, March 22, 2003. She had died sometime overnight. Paramedics were called, and due to the span of time that had passed before the patient was found, no attempts were made to resuscitate her. At 8:15 a.m. Alcor time, Jerry Lemler received a phone call from a nurse at the facility. This time, fortunately for A-1234, Lemler was able to reach Charles Platt immediately. Charles directed Lemler to assemble the surgical team in Scottsdale, then called the volunteer team in L.A.

Charles dispatched Bobby June to rent a U-Haul truck. With great candor, Charles subsequently wrote in the Alcor newsletter case summary that Bobby June was "not entirely happy to be woken since he had been up partying for most of the night." Next, Charles called Todd Huffman. Todd was heading out of Los Angeles with a college buddy on the way to do some snowboarding. Todd turned around and sped home to grab a meds kit. Charles also reached Peter Voss, who left home to fetch the standby equipment. The volunteers were to meet up at the nursing facility.

Meanwhile, in accordance with the instructions etched on the dead woman's Alcor ID bracelet and at Charles's request, an employee at the nursing facility injected A-1234 with heparin and administered chest compressions to circulate the drugs.

There was no signed consent form from A-1234's next of kin, so Charles called Joe Klockgether, Alcor's mortician. Klockgether placed a call to the nursing home and convinced the staff to release the body.

The team converged on the nursing home and pushed more drugs into A-1234's body. Over the phone, I explained to Todd Huffman how to place the prone body into the Trendelenburg position, with the feet higher than the head, in order to distend the jugular veins and start an IV. I was getting pretty good at phoning in emergency medical procedures.

Charles Platt consulted with Steve Harris at CCR. Because of time already lost in this case, they agreed it would be wise to have the volunteers bring the patient straight to Scottsdale instead of stopping at CCR for the initial blood washout.

Charles proved infinitely more organized than Lemler had been. Bobby June had some difficulty finding a truck to rent in Los Angeles on a Saturday with no advance notice, but he finally did. Todd Huffman and Peter Voss drove the body to Scottsdale, and A-1234's transport from Los Angeles came off without a hitch.

I waited outside the back door of Alcor with Jerry Lemler, his daughter Jessica, her husband, James Sikes, and a few others. Alcor's Chevy Suburban was in the rear parking lot.

Again, there was a party atmosphere, cause for celebration. It was Super Bowl Sunday all over again.

When the U-Haul arrived, I jumped in back to help carry the body inside. I was nonplussed to see that the elderly woman was wearing a Walkman and headphones. She must have died that way. It was disrespectful that whoever packed her in the body bag had left those things on her.

In the photo section of this book there is a picture of me in the back of the U-Haul, unzipping A-1234's body bag. I had been a paramedic for twenty-five years. Take a look at the expression on my face. That's how bad the body smelled after traveling through the desert in an unventilated, uncooled U-Haul truck.

This time I stayed close to the operating room. I was sickened at the method used by Jose, Alcor's retired surgeon, to decapitate the elderly woman. He used a common hammer and chisel and went at her like she was a diseased tree stump he wanted removed from his backyard. He bashed his way through her neck bone, hacked through her spinal cord, and finally wrenched off her head. By the time it was over, what was left looked truly awful. Then I watched them drill a hole into the woman's neck bone to insert the handle Alcor used to carry heads around, upside down. Bits of neck bone flew around the OR.

One time as a rookie paramedic I ran a call out to a remote stretch of New Mexico desert. A young couple had heard a shotgun blast from the double-wide down the road.

I found the body out in the backyard. Sure enough, there was evidence of a shotgun blast around much of his throat, but the head was completely missing. I called my senior partner over and showed him the body.

"I've seen this before," he said. "See those marks there and there?" My partner pointed to some jagged wounds on the neck. "Those are teeth marks."

It took a moment for it to sink in. The guy had blown his head half off with the shotgun. Then some hungry coyotes had come and finished the job.

What those coyotes did to that man's neck was a damn sight prettier than what Alcor's surgeon had done to the body of the elderly woman now known as A-1234.

Young Todd Huffman remained in the OR throughout, assisting. Once again, there was a crowd of nonessential Alcorians in the OR, gawking and posing around the body. This time I took pictures of my own.

After the decapitation was complete, I walked outside for a breath of air and found Mathew Sullivan arguing with the local mortician, Steve Rude. There was a pile of trash on the ground near Rude's truck. From what Rude was yelling, I learned that James Sikes had treated A-1234's body bag like his personal OR trash can. He was trying to have it all cremated along with the elderly woman's headless body.

"You can't cremate a person with all this crap!" Rude was shouting, pointing down at the garbage he had removed from the body bag. "What are you thinking?" Rude fumed. "It's goddamn disrespectful!"

Along with the poor woman's torn clothes were mounds of bloody gauze, paper wrappers, the Walkman and headphones, the razor James Sikes had used to shave the poor woman's head, and most of her hair.

I returned inside. Soon after, I spotted James Sikes coming in the back door carrying the familiar large white plastic container. When he saw me, he stiffened. He passed me in the narrow hallway without a word, without meeting my eyes. I saw that the bucket was empty. I walked straight down the hall and opened the back door. There was a fresh wet stain and some white residue leading from the back door down to the storm drain in the middle of the parking lot.

I couldn't imagine any other possibility: As I had requested, Sikes didn't dump the biowaste and hazardous chemicals down the toilet or into the sink that day. Instead, he dumped them down the City of Scottsdale storm drain behind the building. I thought of my first day at Alcor and remembered seeing that same chalky white residue outside the back door, leading to the drain.

What were these people thinking?

ELEVEN

ALCORIAN A-2032

The days following the third suspension were increasingly nerve-racking. I read more on the Internet about the suspicious death of Saul Kent's mother, Dora, and read comments on cryonicists' online bulletin boards that were smug and arrogant, labeling the Riverside authorities a "merry troupe" of "Keystone Coroners." They gloated over the fact that after it became clear that formal charges couldn't be brought against Mike Darwin, Carlos Mondragon, David Pizer, Hugh Hixon, Mike Perry, et al., Alcor had sued the coroner's office and won settlements totaling $120,000.

My conscience was a steady pinprick on the back of my neck. My complaints about the dumping of toxic chemicals and disease-ridden blood had fallen on deaf ears at Alcor. I had also visited what I considered to be the "cult" at Ventureville, witnessed three brutal cryo-suspensions, and heard Charles's stories about the suspicious death of Dora Kent. It seemed incredible, but I now suspected that premeditated criminal acts had been perpetrated by Alcor officers, board members, and other high-ranking members. I also suspected that people at Alcor were determined to cover up all of this. I still had more to learn but as an outsider, it was going to be tough for me. People at Alcor just didn't trust me enough.

So at the end of March 2003 I marched into Jennifer Chapman's office and said, "Jennifer, I've been thinking about it a lot. I want to fill out the paperwork and do whatever I have to in order to become an Alcor member."

It was the first and last time I ever saw Jennifer smile.

"Really? Oh, Larry, that's great!"

Magically, the paperwork appeared in front of me. That girl really loved her job—she just about hopped over her desk to sit next to me and go through the documents page by page. Sign here, notarize there, here's the phone number for Rudy Hoffman, the Alcorian insurance agent who would get the life insurance policy going, and so on.

"We waive the membership fees for employees but you'll have to pay the insurance premiums," she told me.

But I'd be damned if I was going to pay a dollar of my own for this. I went to my office area and called Michael Riskin.

"Michael, I've decided to join Alcor as a member. I've signed up for cryo-preservation."

"Larry, that's outstanding!" Riskin said over the phone. He was truly happy for me. "Congratulations! I'm so pleased!"

"Thanks, Michael," I said. "So I wanted to talk to you about that promise you made me, about Alcor making my insurance payments for me."

He stayed true to his word and didn't protest. Alcor would pay for my insurance premiums and I wouldn't have to spend a dime for my membership.

It made me wonder, though, what sort of conflict of interest this was. My company was paying my life insurance premiums and it was the beneficiary. Was that ethical? *Here, Larry, drink this.* What if somebody wanted me dead, somebody who would benefit from that?

Yet I knew this was the only way that I would ever be welcomed into their inner circle. It would take three months for my membership to become active, but the knowledge that I had begun the process would be good enough in the minds of my fellow employees. My fellow Alcorians.

––––––––––––––

Good news traveled fast. Within an hour, Jerry Lemler came to me with a huge smile on his face.

"Larry!" he said. "Congratulations! Welcome aboard!"

"Thanks, Jerry," I said. "I've been thinking about it for a while. I just want to do the right thing."

"Follow me."

Lemler led me out of my open office area and down the hallway, stopping by a door next to his own office. Alcor's facility was pretty big inside, and there were rooms in the complex that I still didn't know about. I had never paid much attention to this particular door. Jerry pulled out a huge set of keys and winked at me as he unlocked the door. We stepped inside a large office.

"Welcome to your new office, Larry." Jerry beamed. "Right next to mine."

Membership had its privileges. No more open-area, ex-marketing-division full of supply boxes for me. The walls of my new office were lined with filing cabinets.

Jerry swept his arm toward the cabinets like he was Vanna White revealing a brand-new car I had just won on *Wheel of Fortune*. He was so pleased. "Larry, these are files of Alcor's members. Many are duplicates of files stored elsewhere around the building. I want you to read through them when you can."

"You got it, Jerry."

I went back to my old office area and started packing my things. For the first time ever, Joe Hovey sought me out.

Joe pumped my hand up and down. "Alcor changed my life, Larry. I'm so happy for you."

"Thanks, Joe."

Then Hugh Hixon and Mathew Sullivan came by. Hugh actually smiled at me.

Every single person at Alcor congratulated me that day. It wasn't as if they threw a surprise party and gave me a cake in the shape of a head or anything, but each of them came and shook my hand. I asked Mathew Sullivan if I could choose my own A-number.

"Sorry, we have a system for that. But why, what number do you want?" he said.

"A-5150," I said.

Hugh started laughing.

Mathew didn't get it. "Why is that funny?"

"Because 5150 is the emergency code number for an involuntary seventy-two-hour psychiatric hold," I said. "When you're bringing a crazy person into a hospital and want them to know you've got a loon on your hands, you radio in that it's a '5150.'"

Mathew laughed that shrill, staccato laugh of his. No dice, though. Once my application had gone through the proper channels, I was to be A-2032.

Mathew said, "Larry, I want you to feel free to enter my office whenever you want. All the Alcor member case files are in there and I think the more you know about them all, the better you can be prepared for assisting suspensions in the future."

"Thanks, Mathew," I said. "I'll take advantage of that."

Later that day, when Mike Perry actually looked me in the eye and gave me a little nod as he passed me in the hall, I knew I was on my way into the inner circle. Honestly, it was like switching on a light. The change had been immediate.

That day after work I went straight to a lawyer and added the following clause to my will:

III. ADDITIONAL DIRECTIVE

It is my wish that all previous arrangements made with the Alcor Foundation of Scottsdale, Arizona, become null and void upon the signing of this document for reasons that I do not wish to make public. And furthermore that my wife Beverly S. Johnson shall become the beneficiary of my life insurance that was purchased for the purpose of my Cryopreservation with Alcor. I wish either burial or cremation. I hereby authorize my Executor to make all final decisions regarding my remains.

Then I went home to Beverly and told her what I had done. I gave her a copy of my updated will and said, "For God's sake, if I'm killed on my Harley or something, don't let Alcor get ahold of me!"

I didn't tell Beverly, but I was literally having nightmares about ending up on Alcor's white mortician's table with masked figures approaching me, syringes in their hands, ready to start my cryo-suspension while I was still alive. It was as if I were channeling Dora Kent, reliving the experience she seemed to have endured at the hands of Mike Darwin. Now if I died in the streets of Scottsdale and Beverly somehow wasn't around to be notified, I would probably be brought straight to Alcor and decapitated. The thought chilled me.

I could see something in Bev's eyes, like I had passed a turning point. She was looking at me the same way I looked at Mike Perry when he didn't see me: *He's lost it, he's a kook,* she seemed to be thinking. Now Beverly had to deal with this madness too.

Everyone who worked at Alcor had a hobby, something to pass the downtime on the job. Jessica Sikes had her computer games. Charles obsessed over his anti–Jerry Lemler memos. Hugh Hixon had his Internet porn. My hobby became investigating Alcor.

I took Jerry and Mathew up on their offers and started reading through all the files that I now had access to.

Among other things, I learned that Alcor had a poor track record when it came to human resources. About a month before my job interview at Alcor, Jerry Lemler had written the following for the Alcor News Bulletin, under the heading "Recent Employee Changes at Alcor":

> Karla Steen, who was active in the public relations department, has left the organization.
>
> Steve Rude, a mortician and former perfusionist, is now an independent contractor but is continuing to provide services to Alcor on that basis.
>
> Tom Brown, a mortician who had participated in two standbys and hoped to sell cryonics through mortuaries nationwide, has left the organization.
>
> Dave Shipman, who had been Director of Suspension Services and then moved to part-time status after he resigned from that position, has left the organization.

What Jerry didn't mention was that, in Charles's words, two of those four ex-employees had "left Alcor under controversial circumstances and subsequently initiated an expensive dispute." The third was fired for failing a drug test. And I had recently seen the fourth, Steve Rude, blow his top when James Sikes tried to have him cremate Alcor's OR garbage along with the headless body of A-1234.

Between what I found in Mathew's file cabinet and what I could piece together from conversations I had around the office, David Shipman and Karla Steen had had a fling together. It sounded to me like they were fired for having sex. Karla, I was told, was a very attractive woman. Evidently, Jerry Lemler's wife, Paula, disagreed with her manner of dress and lifestyle and around the office took to calling her a slut.

Charles and Joe Hovey each told me that Karla had sued for harassment and discrimination, while David sued for wrongful termination. Personally, I never found proof of these lawsuits, and maybe the ex-employees had only threatened the suits, but according to my colleagues, each settled out of court with Alcor, to their advantage, shortly before trial.

Tom Brown was an ex-mortician Alcor hired to do arterial cutdowns during cryonic suspensions. Like Klockgether, he made bank off Alcor. Alcor had hired him on full-time for a while, until he failed a drug test. Jerry Lemler announced around the office, and then in a public board meeting, that Tom Brown had tested positive for marijuana and so he'd fired him. This struck me as pretty ironic when I thought about Jerry getting busted in Tennessee for, as Charles had put it, selling uppers to housewives.

I've had paramedics under me fail drug tests. You take them into your office, tell them you have to let them go, and explain the reason. This is Human Resources 101. You don't mention it to anyone else. You don't publicly flog them for it. If you do, you're asking for trouble for invasion of privacy and defamation. In my opinion, Tom Brown might have had grounds for a lawsuit against Jerry Lemler and Alcor.

I had already sat in on a few job interviews conducted by Charles Platt. They were a disaster. He asked all kinds of inappropriate, personal questions.

One interview I had witnessed was for a young man to do maintenance work. His girlfriend accompanied him on the interview. They were typical goth kids—black clothes, dyed black hair, facial piercings. During the interview Charles asked the kid how old he was. That's about as wrong as it gets in an interview and could open the door to an age discrimination complaint, if not a lawsuit. Then Charles asked point-blank if they thought cryonics was "too weird." The kid said that all his life he had been treated as an outsider, an outcast. That's what drew him to Alcor, he said. His girlfriend nodded in agreement. Charles told them that he would fit in fine at Alcor.

In other interviews I attended, Charles asked about people's religion, then asked if they thought cryonics was bizarre. Basically, Charles did everything that an interviewer was not supposed to do.

There was another personnel fiasco involving a public relations guy named Bill Haworth. From memos, conversations, and Alcor's newsletters, I learned that Jerry Lemler had convinced Alcor's board to pay Haworth a retainer of $10,000 a month for promotional services. Haworth claimed to have big media connections and made a lot of grand promises. He said he was going to make Alcor a household name. Jerry bought it all and retained Haworth, then began running around telling everyone at Alcor they were going to get thousands of people to sign up because of Haworth's efforts.

But apparently the only notable thing Bill Haworth ever really did for Alcor was endanger the patients in the dewars.

According to memos from Charles and talks I had with Jerry, Haworth thought the dewars would look good in a bowling-pin configuration for a photograph he claimed was going to be in some big national magazine, so he ordered them to be pulled away from the walls. But one of the dewars held the reserve of liquid nitrogen and fed it to the others through a delicate piping system. Even when members had died and been suspended, no one at Alcor moved the dewars around until it was absolutely necessary. Nevertheless, Haworth had them muscled around for his picture and Charles Platt absolutely freaked out, saying that he'd endangered the lives of the patients inside for a photo shoot!

Haworth put the suspended Alcorians at risk and took his picture, the national magazine story never happened, and he was let go—but only after Alcor had paid him a small fortune.

There was one human resources problem I was able to help with while I worked for Alcor. Charles Platt had Jerry Lemler put Todd Huffman on staff. I liked Todd very much but could see there was a problem with his transition at Alcor.

Todd was given the title "Laboratory Assistant." Charles told Hugh that Todd was there to help him. But Charles told me that he had Todd hired so he would one day be able to replace Hugh. Charles and Hugh were always at each other's throats and Charles would have ousted Hugh if he could have. For that matter, Charles would have ousted just about everyone there if he could have.

Mathew once told me that not everyone was happy with Charles working at Alcor. When the board of directors took a vote to hire him in the first place it was a close call, Mathew said. Charles could have gone to work for CI [the Cryonics Institute] or SA [Suspended Animation]—these were the two other, much smaller cryonics organizations in the United States besides Alcor—but Charles was such a troublemaker, Mathew said, the board figured it was "better having Charles inside pissing out rather than outside pissing in."

This time, Charles was pissing on Hugh Hixon. Hugh's job security was ensured due to the fact that he never wrote anything down. No one but him knew how to fix the machines he had jury-rigged together. No one knew the chemical makeup of half his formulas. He didn't put them down on paper; they were all stored in his head. As long as things stayed that way Charles could never get rid of him.

When Todd started at Alcor full-time, Hugh wouldn't even talk to him. He actually made a point of ignoring him.

Charles asked me to speak to Hugh, to convince him to work with Todd and train him.

I was surprised. "Me?" I asked.

Charles said, "Larry, out of everyone at Alcor, you have the best relationship with Hugh. He relates to you. He doesn't chat with anyone else the way he does with you."

I thought it would only benefit the company to have Todd around helping Hugh, so I agreed. First, I appealed to Hugh's pride. Like every other person at Alcor, he had great regard for himself and believed that he was a genius. In Hugh's case, it happened to be true.

"Hugh," I said, "you run everything around here. If it weren't for you, not a single Alcor member would receive a successful cryonic suspension. They'd all get fouled up."

Hugh studied me over the top of his glasses, quietly. The buttering-up wasn't working.

"So what about when you get suspended?" I asked.

"Er . . . what?"

"Hugh, when you deanimate, who's going to suspend you? Who's going to know how to mix the formulas? Or run the machines? God forbid one of the machines malfunctions. Who's going to fix it? Jerry?" Hugh's eyes widened at that one. He knew the machines malfunctioned every single time there was a suspension and he was the only one who could improvise their repair. He was the one and only MacGyver of the immortals.

I leaned in for the kill. "Hugh, who will oversee *your* cryo-suspension?"

After that, Todd had to run around following Hugh with a notebook. Hugh wouldn't shut up, telling him everything he knew.

Reading over the member files in Mathew's office, I began to appreciate what type of people joined Alcor.

There were the science fiction fans and space exploration aficionados, like some of the folks I had met at the Barnes & Noble in Santa Monica. Unless someone cracked the speed of light and developed hyperspace travel—not a likely prospect—how else could they hope to travel the vast distances between stars? Instead, most star travel buffs' biggest hopes lay with the development of ultracold biostasis that would permit them to travel for many light-years within a single lifetime. Cryonic suspension and suspended animation were close cousins—the only difference being that cryonics hoped to preserve the dead body for reanimation in the future, and suspended animation was intended to indefinitely preserve people while they were still alive. Thus, some people interested in space exploration kept an eye on the "advancements" at Alcor and CCR.

I think my own true interests in cryonics fell somewhere close to this. I was honestly fascinated by the prospect of seeing the future. My forebears crossed the United States during the Depression, heading west from Missouri. Real *Grapes of Wrath*–type stuff, loading up all their possessions and crossing the dust bowl, some dying on the way, others making it to the Southwest to prospect for gold. I think my interest in cryonics stemmed from the possibility of seeing the unseeable and experiencing whatever adventure I could find along the way.

The huge letter "A" in the Alcor logo was modeled after the Starfleet insignia from *Star Trek*. I didn't notice it until I found myself staring at an Alcor polo shirt with the little logo on the left breast—right where a *Star Trek: The Next Generation* crew member would press to communicate with the ship and ask to be beamed up.

The lobster pot–type Neuro Cans Alcor used for cephalon storage were numbered nearly the same way Federation starships were in the *Star Trek* franchise. Alcorian heads awaited reanimation inside cans marked, for example, NC-23. Captain Kirk's original USS *Enterprise* was designated NCC-1701.

Many of Alcor's pamphlets were printed in *Star Trek*'s blocky, sideways-slanted typeface. It wasn't just similar, it was exactly the same font. I found a recruiting article titled "Make It So," a direct rip-off of one of the most famous *Star Trek: The Next Generation* lines. One article referred to *Star Trek* eleven times in three pages. Alcor must have figured some science fiction fans were lonely and insecure enough to be attracted by all this. It wasn't a surprise that Alcor aggressively targeted sci-fi fans, but it was unsavory.

I also found records of countless donation campaigns. Alcor hit up its members relentlessly, asking for money over and over again. Because of Alcor's nonprofit status, members were reminded that their donations could be written off as deductions from their taxes. I saw receipts for donations of $20,000 and $50,000 at a pop from Alcor's wealthier members.

Researching old Alcor member files, I found that Dick Clair still helped finance Alcor from his dewar by leaving them half his ongoing royalties from sitcoms he had created, including *Mama's Family* and *The Facts of Life*. Sadly, I also found that Clair had had a real hard time at the end of his first life cycle, suffering from AIDS. I read an article in *People* magazine stating that a few days before he died, Dick had had second thoughts about leaving everything to Alcor and amended his will in order to leave half of his estate to his family members, including some needy nieces and nephews. (*The Facts of Life* brought in $800,000 per year by itself.) He also changed the executor of his will from Saul Kent to his friend and writing partner of twenty-seven years. Alcor spent six figures contesting the revision for six months but eventually gave in and accepted the new will when it looked like it would go to court. It sure was distasteful to read about the Alcorians fighting Dick's will in order to keep all of his money for their company and away from his family.

Timothy Leary, I learned, had signed up for cryonic suspension with Alcor and then switched to another cryonics organization called CryoCare. He backed out of his cryonics agreement a few weeks before his death, though, telling the press that he didn't want to "wake up in fifty years surrounded by humorless men with clipboards," referring to the cryonicists he had met. Charles Platt was working with CryoCare at the time and wrote a case summary. In it, Charles said he and his colleagues were working the case without pay because Leary was so famous that his involvement would benefit all of cryonics. The cryonicists Leary had the most interaction with—apparently the types he didn't want to share eternity with—were Charles, Steve Harris, and Mike Darwin.

Although Lemler also proudly invoked the names Peter Sellers and Walt Disney on tours, neither one seems to have signed up for cryonic suspension with Alcor's predecessors. Both men had entertained the idea—reportedly, Peter Sellers even invited cryonicists to his office to talk about the details—but in both cases their PR people talked them out of it. As I mentioned earlier, I didn't find anything in writing on Michael Jackson, though that was Jerry Lemler's favorite name to drop when speaking of people who had made contact with Alcor and inquired about membership.

Then, as I read the current member files from Mathew's office, I found that Alcor's current membership consisted mainly of sick people. AIDS patients, cancer victims, people diagnosed with brain tumors—basically, people who had gotten a raw deal in this life and were desperately grasping for the hope of a second one. These were the people I overheard Jerry Lemler talking to on tours, telling them they would be guaranteed a second life if they signed up with Alcor.

I took a close look at Alcor's marketing literature. On the inside cover of every *Cryonics* magazine published by Alcor was a statement titled, "What *is* cryotransport?" It read:

> In principle, this is no different from bringing a seriously ill person out of the jungle and to a modern hospital. . . . As human knowledge and medical technology continue to expand, people who today are considered hopeless will be easily restored to health.

"Easily restored to health"? That last statement didn't seem to portray the tremendously improbable chance that more realistic cryonicists like Charles Platt were willing to take by freezing their dead bodies. It sounded a lot more like Alcor selling false hope to the "hopeless."

It also seemed to me that they actively targeted the terminally ill by inserting the names of specific diseases right into their definitions of cryonics. On the very first page of the Alcor Web site, I found:

> Cryonics, simply stated, is the rapid cooling of a person's body, usually in liquid nitrogen, in order to preserve the tissue, cellular and molecular structure in the hopes that future advancements in science and technology will be developed to allow Alcor the scientific means to repair the ravages of diseases like cancer, Alzheimer's, Parkinson's, the effects of aging; thereby potentially restoring the individual back to good health.

To me, it felt like a scare tactic. I investigated the archives on the Alcor Web site. There were many flowery lures to imagined immortality:

> Cryonics may seem like a radical idea, but really it's just another way of giving people what they are already trying to get, and what they have wanted for thousands of years: a longer, healthier life.

Imagine the possibility of having more time as much as you need to do all the things you've always wanted to do. Imagine the chance of being reunited with the people you care about, in a future of exciting possibilities. Imagine the reassurance of knowing that you may be freed from the limitations of a twentieth-century lifespan.

The Alcor Foundation is *your* ambulance to that future of advanced medicine.

Knowing what I knew, it read like propaganda. I thought of the horrendously bumbled cryo-suspensions I had witnessed—Alcor members decomposing during botched transports, baking for hours in the desert sun, brain cells dying by the billions, people bleeding out inside rented minivans. I thought of the "thawed strawberries" argument, the line about turning hamburger back into a cow, the blood-brain barrier, and how Alcorians like president and CEO Jerry Lemler looked at the work CCR was doing on rabbit kidneys and, despite all this, then told people in no uncertain terms that Alcor's highly toxic vitrification process would work on the human brain. To me, Alcor's hard sell was starting to sound like hucksters pitching expensive snake oil to the terminally ill.

On the back of those *Cryonics* magazines was an advertisement placed by Saul Kent's Life Extension Foundation, exhorting people to become members. The ad claimed that people who mailed a check to Saul would be sent inside information on groundbreaking medical techniques for a variety of illnesses, information that was otherwise unavailable.

Bullet points claimed that once signed up, members would be made privy to "unique medical information," including:

- The missing link in **depression** therapy overlooked by psychiatrists
- A cholesterol-lowering drug that stops **cancer cells** from dividing

They were aggressively targeting the sick and dying, promising lifesaving information that would allow members to either miraculously cure what ailed them now, or be cryo-transported to a time when their diseases would be defeated. To me, Saul Kent and Alcor were like the worst of televangelists, preying on the depressed and dying.

———————

Once in a great while I'd have to field membership calls when Jennifer Chapman was out of the office. I answered the phone one time and found myself trying to help a very distressed man who was asking about an emergency membership. His wife was near death. They had taken the tour a few months earlier and had been considering joining but it was now or never. I could hear that the man was terribly upset about his wife. I put him on hold and ran into Jerry Lemler's office.

"Jerry, you need to talk to this guy. He's requesting emergency membership for his wife. She's close to deanimating."

Jerry's expression fell. "I don't know, Larry," Jerry said. "We're not supposed to take on any more deathbed conversions. We've had too many lawsuits from family members. What's this guy's name?"

When I told him, Jerry's face lit right up.

"I remember him. He's Asian. Asians always have big families. And they have money." It took a split second for Jerry to make the decision. "All right, Larry, go back and make him an offer. Tell him we'll grant his wife emergency membership if he signs up the entire family right now and pays for them all in advance."

"What?"

"That would mean a lot of money for us. I don't think he'll say no," Jerry said.

"Jerry," I said, "I can't do that."

Jerry frowned, disappointed.

"All right, Larry. Transfer the call to me."

———————

I continued to read up on Alcor and leaf through individual case reports. Alcor tried to document their cryo-suspensions very carefully. They believed doctors of the future would refer to these surgical logs, photos, and videotapes before reanimating the patients.

Althea Flynt, the wife of *Hustler* publisher and media mogul Larry Flynt, had signed up for cryo-suspension. However, after her death in 1987, a posting on CryoNet from Mike Darwin explained, "She was not cryopreserved because she was autopsied with subsequent refusal of the ME [medical examiner] to release her brain."

Even if the medical examiner had released Althea's brain to Alcor, autopsies are unavoidably disastrous to the cryo-preservation process. The brain is often sliced up, and days might pass before Alcor could take possession of the body and begin the cooling process.

When I asked Charles about Larry Flynt, he told me Mr. Flynt had also been signed up for suspension until he found out the physical realities of the suspension process. According to Charles, Mr. Flynt backed out, calling Alcor's procedures "gruesome." This didn't stop Jerry Lemler from naming Mr. Flynt as one more celebrity Alcor member when he gave tours of the facility.

Larry Flynt did seem sympathetic to cryonics, though. He published an article written by hard-core cryonicist and Extropian Max More. On the fightaging.org Web site, More posted:

> In case anyone is looking for an excuse to pick up a copy of Larry Flynt's *Hustler* magazine, note that the March 2006 issue (now available) features my cover article, "How to Live Forever." Flip past the lovely Victoria to p.43 and you'll find it. Have fun.

I found that, due to the chronic disorganization at Alcor, they had a habit of changing their emergency phone numbers and then not telling their members. Imagine a true believer calling the emergency number to report his or her mother's sudden deanimation, knowing every passing minute will diminish her chances for everlasting life, and then hearing, "The number you have reached has been disconnected. If you feel you have reached this message in error, please hang up and try your call again. . . ."

Maybe Bobby June, who told me he had the Alcor phone number inked on his body, should have kept his tattoo artist on speed dial.

I came across information regarding something Alcor called the Time-Ship. Plans were under way to build a humungous "Cryotorium" facility. Several articles were written about it, including interviews with various Alcorian bigwigs involved, that described it as being from six to sixteen acres large, and big enough to store ten thousand to fifty thousand cryonauts. It was compared to an Egyptian pyramid, only much bigger. The project was spearheaded by Saul Kent and another wealthy cryonicist, Bill Faloon, Kent's friend and fellow director of the Life Extension Foundation. They had hired a very gung-ho architect to draw up plans and were considering a location in Florida, not far from Disney World. It was to be a lavish cryonicist paradise.

Typically, there was much Alcorian bickering over the TimeShip. One cryonicist posted his opinion on CryoNet that since it would be built close to Orlando and Disney World, it was "plainly obvious that they want it to be a 'cryo-theme park.'" He went on to write, "If they want to make this truly a 'timeship,' they better situate it away from dense metropolitan areas that may be possible nuclear targets," and that Orlando was "more than likely to take a nuke hit."

David Pizer posted an online complaint also arguing against Florida as the site of the TimeShip, claiming, bizarrely, that when Fidel Castro died in Cuba there might be "political unrest" in the Sunshine State, implying that the TimeShip would be endangered. Pizer also questioned why Alcor would consider moving its home base from Arizona, which was considered very cryonics-friendly. Alcorians hoped Arizona would become the first state to legalize euthanasia. "For those of you with a short memory," Pizer wrote, "when Alcor was in California the bureaucrats there were trying to shut Alcor and cryonics down. When Alcor moved to Scottsdale, Arizona, the mayor of Scottsdale invited Alcor's president to his office and personally welcomed cryonics." More so, in Pizer's estimation, Arizona might even "be the first state to allow pre-death suspensions."

Always at the center of any controversy, Charles chimed in. He distributed memos and e-mails, posting his opinion on the cryonics Internet bulletin boards, saying the whole thing was too showy and would perpetuate the public perception that cryonics was only for the wealthy. Charles mocked what seemed to be the Disney World-esque, cryo-themed amusement attractions planned inside the TimeShip, such as a mirrored promenade filled with liquid nitrogen vapor to give visitors an inkling of what it would be like to be frozen. Plus, Charles complained, why spend so much money on it when Alcor's freezing procedures were so sketchy? Why not invest that money in perfecting the vitrification process?

I found references to a separate, underground storage facility—a salt mine Alcor owned outside Hutchinson, Kansas—where the company encouraged its members to send their most prized possessions, the things they wanted to have with them in the future. It was the kind of thing weapons manufacturers did. They would buy an abandoned salt mine in the middle of nowhere and store sensitive materials and documents inside it. Because of its remote location and the fact it reached deep underground, it was supposed to be impervious to natural disasters, plagues, even nuclear war. Alcor had bought its salt mine in the hope that it would remain unmolested for hundreds or thousands of years, until members could be thawed out and reanimated.

When I became a member, Alcor gave me what was called a Memory Box. Alcorians put their birth certificates, teddy bears, family photographs, whatever they wanted, into their Memory Box and then it was shipped off to the salt mine, to be retrieved upon reanimation. I never took advantage of my Alcor Memory Box but some members did.

As I continued flipping through Mathew's files, I wondered what else Alcor had stored deep underground in its salt mine outside Hutchinson, Kansas. Then, there inside Mathew's filing cabinet, I saw a folder labeled "Ted Williams."

TWELVE ————————————————————

"THAT GUY WHO WAS FROZEN"

Show me a hero and I will write you a tragedy.
—F. SCOTT FITZGERALD

I walked into a bookstore in the Los Angeles area in early 2004 and asked for the new Ted Williams biography by Leigh Montville.

The clerk's name tag read "Chuck." Chuck looked about twenty-five years old. "Ted Williams? Oh, you mean that guy who was frozen?"

To Chuck, that's who Ted Williams was. That's what he had become in the national consciousness. What a shame.

Jerry Lemler told a Miami newspaper that before Ted Williams, "We weren't showing up on anyone's radar screens. I want to take this whole concept, and Alcor, down Main Street U.S.A., and move it away from the computer geek, 148-IQ, single hacker. They're not our future." Through Ted Williams, Jerry said, Alcor had "raised the public's consciousness about cryonics."

And yet, to this day Alcor's leaders have done their best to avoid even publicly admitting they have Ted Williams's remains. If they did so, they would have to address a variety of questions pertaining to how they came to take possession of his body. Alcor also dreads the public's learning the details of Ted Williams's cryo suspension. But in assembling this narrative, I've been able to discover and piece together the details of Ted's surgery and subsequent freezing inside Alcor. They seem to have been especially gruesome, barbaric, and utterly botched—even by Alcor's minimal standards.

That is not what Ted Williams should be remembered for.

Throughout his life, Ted Williams dedicated himself to the pursuit of perfection. Sportswriters marveled at what they called Ted Williams's "natural" swing. Some attributed his batting prowess to his unusually acute eyesight. Ted Williams himself attributed it to hard work. According to Ted, his swing became "perfect" through trial and error. It became "natural" through hard work and repetition.

John Updike called Ted Williams "the classic ballplayer." Joe DiMaggio called him "the best hitter I ever saw."

To be accurate, Ted Williams was no saint. His cussing, like his hitting, was legendary. He was a star from the time he was seventeen, and aspects of his personality just never matured. Why would they have had to? He was Ted Williams, "The Kid," "The Splendid Splinter." He was a veritable rock star. Cops who pulled him over for speeding drove away with an autograph. Still, no fan of adulation, he raged against photographers and journalists and tried to keep his personal life out of the public eye. He could take or (mostly) leave the public's affection.

In terms of baseball accomplishments, Ted Williams is largely remembered for being the last major league player to finish a season with a batting average of .400 or better. No one has achieved that since Ted did it, in 1941. On the final day of that season, the Red Sox had a doubleheader scheduled against the Philadelphia Athletics, and not even in friendly Fenway Park, but in Philadelphia's Shibe Park. Ted went 4 for 4 in Game One, finishing the first contest with his average already at .404. His manager, Joe Cronin, had earlier given him the option of safeguarding his mark, and not hitting in the second game if his average was above .400 after the first. According to reports, Ted said, "No, I'm going to play. If I'm going to be a .400 hitter, I'm not going to slip in through the back door, and I'm not going to do it sitting on the bench."

Ted went 2 for 4 in Game Two, raising his batting average again, and finishing the season at .406. He didn't slip through the back door. He smashed through the front door.

If you add the number of hits he had (185) to the number of times he was walked (145), when Ted Williams went to the plate in 1941, he was more likely to get on base than not. Ted's .406 season is still considered a nearly superhuman achievement.

The following year, at the height of his career, Ted Williams left baseball and enlisted to serve in World War II. He became a Marine. Because of his natural athleticism, quick reflexes, and remarkable eyesight, he was trained to be a fighter pilot. According to Johnny Pesky, another Red Sox player who trained as a fighter pilot (though he wasn't accepted into the same advanced training program as his teammate), Ted set Marine flight-student gunnery records. Ted Williams broke records for "hits" with the Marines, just as he had with the Red Sox. When he completed his advanced flight training, Ted chose to remain at the Pensacola, Florida, Naval Air Station for a time as a flight instructor in order to get as much shooting practice under his belt as possible before engaging in war. When the war ended, Ted was in Pearl Harbor, awaiting assignment to the China fleet.

Ted returned to baseball in 1946. However, when the call came again eight years later to serve his country in Korea, Ted Williams answered. At the end of World War II, Ted had been promised by the commandant of the Marine Corps that he would never be called on to serve another day in active duty if he allowed the Marines to use his name for publicity. Ted agreed. Still, he was called up for Korea. Some say it was a mistake, others say the Marines needed qualified pilots like Ted. Ted himself once said that the Marines did it for the publicity. Ted grumbled about it, but he went. He was invited to sit out the war safely on a service baseball team but refused and chose instead to fly jets in combat.

Ted's plane was hit by enemy fire during his third combat mission over Korea. As he opened his wheel doors to land, his plane caught fire. He hit the runway at 200 miles an hour, slid 5,000 feet (or 6,000 or 9,000 feet, depending on the account), and scrambled out of his burning plane. A Jeep raced up to him moments after he escaped the blazing wreck. A colonel jumped out, handed Ted Williams a piece of paper—and asked for an autograph.

Looking on, with a bit of gallows humor, the base chaplain flung his arms out wide like a baseball umpire and yelled, "Safe!" Indeed, Ted had safely slid into home base.

In all, Ted flew thirty-nine combat missions in Korea and was the wingman—and friend—to future astronaut and senator John Glenn, who has said, "Ted only batted .406 for the Red Sox. He batted a thousand for the Marine Corps and the United States."

No other Hall of Fame baseball player saw military service in two wars. As one description in the book *Ted Williams at War* recounts: "There aren't too many athletes who are truly heroes. Ted Williams was one such athlete. Imagine Alex Rodriguez or Barry Bonds flying dive-bombing missions in close air support of troops on the ground, taking anti-aircraft fire as they pulled out of dives as low as 500 feet. Imagine the records Williams might have set had he not devoted nearly five full seasons to serving his country."

John Glenn has echoed that thought: "I was well aware of Ted Williams, of course, and his records in baseball. Who knows what those records might have been if he hadn't had two hitches in the Marine Corps?"

Ted Williams earned more than a dozen military medals, including three Air Medals, the Republic of Korea Presidential Unit Citation, a Navy Unit Commendation, Korean Service Medals, top gunnery honors, wingman honors, and a place in the U.S. Marine Corps Sports Hall of Fame.

John Glenn has also said, "There's nobody, I swear, there's nobody that served in the Marine Corps that is any more proud of having been a Marine than Ted Williams. . . . He was out there to do the job and he did it. He did a helluva good job."

After returning to baseball from his second war, Ted fell into a batting slump, hitting under .300. When his contract came up for renegotiation, he demanded a change. When the Red Sox offered him the same salary, he refused. He told them he wanted a 25 percent pay cut, saying he didn't deserve his old salary. Such was Ted Williams's integrity. Can you imagine any professional sports figure making that demand today?

By the time he retired from baseball in 1960, Ted Williams had accrued a tremendous list of accomplishments. He was Rookie of the Year in 1939, voted American League MVP twice, won baseball's Triple Crown twice, and played in seventeen All-Star Games. He was named 1957 Associated Press Athlete of the Year and 1951–1960 Player of the Decade. The Ted Williams Museum in St. Petersburg, Florida, was the first of its kind built while the athlete was still alive, and his number, 9, was the first in Red Sox history to be retired. He was the first retired player to put forth the idea that players from the Negro League should be considered for membership in the Baseball Hall of Fame. Ted did so in his own Hall of Fame acceptance speech.

Ted Williams proved to me and generations of Americans that with perseverance and dedication, you can accomplish anything you set your mind to. In California, there's a highway named after him. In Boston, they've named tunnels, desserts, and children after him.

In 1991, Ted was awarded the Presidential Medal of Freedom, the nation's highest civilian honor, the equivalent of the military Medal of Honor.

One sportswriter summed it up with, "When Ted Williams died America lost one of her greatest heroes. Without Ted and the rugged code of honor he lived by, baseball is a lesser sport."

But Ted Williams was so much more than a baseball hero. He was a war hero, a national hero. And now—after a lifetime of bravery, excellence, and service to his country—because of his son's warped mind and the publicity-mongering fanatics at Alcor, Ted Williams had become late-night comedy fodder, a dumb head joke. He was known to a new generation of Americans, to people like Chuck in the bookstore, only as "that guy who was frozen."

In contrast to his stellar service as a fighter pilot and a ballplayer, by most accounts, Ted wasn't much of a father. When each of his three children were born—Bobby-Jo, John Henry, and Claudia—he was literally gone, out fishing.

He didn't have much patience for his children. He was very demanding and treated them no less harshly than he treated adults. Claudia, the youngest child, moved to Europe after college, reportedly to escape the shadow of her father's celebrity and brash personality. She later sided with John Henry in all contests regarding Ted's estate and last wishes. Many people think Claudia was afraid of John Henry, the sibling responsible for sending their father's remains to Alcor. When John Henry was at odds with Claudia, he limited her visiting privileges with their father. One time he sued Claudia over a bunch of Ted Williams autographed baseball bats. Another time John Henry took a baseball bat and, in a rage, smashed the windows of her car. Regarding his other daughter, Ted Williams once spoke to a reporter of "my little girl, Bobby-Jo. You should see her. An iddy-biddy little thing, pretty and sweet, just as sweet as she can be. . . . Is she smart! She can do anything, that iddy biddy little thing . . . the most important thing in my life is my little girl."

That same Ted Williams would deliver blank checks to friends who were sick in the hospital, offering to pay whatever it took to make them well again. He threw himself into his Jimmy Fund charity work. He would stay up all night in a hospital, holding the hand of a dying little boy.

––––––––––––

Meantime, John Henry could have been the stuff of doctoral studies in abnormal psychology. Let's just say he had issues.

During his high school years at the Vermont Academy prep school, John Henry was caught robbing an arcade game on school property. In his senior year, John Henry doused a dead cat with a flammable liquid, placed a lit match to it, and then ended up in a burn ward himself.

Even John Henry's Vermont Academy admissions director was surprised that John Henry got into Bates College. Ted Williams had made a call on his son's behalf.

John Henry didn't make the baseball team at Bates. He didn't do much better in his studies and lasted only one year there.

Next came the University of Maine at Orono. The baseball coach there, John Winkin, was an old friend of Ted's who had spent fifteen years working at the Ted Williams Camp. Still, John Henry did not come close to making the team. Coach Winkin said of John Henry, "You had to watch him like a hawk. . . . I thought he was a sneaky guy."

Ted, who had always regretted his own lack of a college education and was very big on his children getting degrees, cried at John Henry's college graduation ceremony. What Ted didn't realize was that John Henry didn't really graduate at that ceremony. The folder John Henry accepted onstage was missing the diploma. John Henry later lied to his father, saying there must have been some mix-up. In truth, John Henry was missing a credit. To make it up, he enrolled in a course at a local college but never attended the class. For the final exam, he bought a mini walkie-talkie system and had a friend sit outside in a car with the textbook, feeding him answers. That's how John Henry finally "earned" his college degree.

An observer would never have known it from the parade of Porsches and beauty queens, but John Henry Williams failed spectacularly at every business venture he tried. He was a reverse King Midas—everything he touched turned to crap.

John Henry financed a poster print featuring three great Boston athletes: Ted Williams, Larry Bird, and Bobby Orr. He took out a very expensive full-page ad in the *Boston Globe* that included an incorrect toll-free number. He didn't sell a single poster from the ad.

He opened a "Ted Williams Store" in Boston—hidden behind a pillar in a deserted corner of the third floor of an upscale mall. It failed miserably.

John Henry even failed at an Internet porn business. That has to be hard to do.

Still, he squandered his father's money freely. One of Ted's nurses and longtime friends, Frank Brothers, said, "I'd never seen anyone spend money like him who wasn't a drug dealer." Frank once picked up one of Ted's credit card statements and saw that John Henry had spent $38,000 in a single month on pure fluff. One time he spent $15,000 on a camera lens. Even while spending his father's money, Frank said, John Henry would tell his father he was coming by for dinner and then stand Ted up nineteen out of twenty times.

John Henry finally realized he could make his fortune off the one thing he could control that did have value—his father's celebrity.

John Henry moved into his father's house in December 1994. Soon Ted's friends started complaining that Ted wasn't returning their calls. John Henry wasn't giving his father their messages. Then John Henry had the phone number changed and didn't tell Ted's friends. He started controlling every facet of his father's life. By 1996 he had convinced Ted Williams to sign over power of attorney to him.

Sports memorabilia is a big business. John Henry worked his father like a dog, even when he was ill, then claimed the activity was like therapy or some kind of exercise. He created the pretense that this was good for his father, and he was doing him a favor. Sometimes Ted would end a marathon autographing session by screaming at his son and throwing the pen against a wall. Ted Williams once said to his close friend John Sullivan, "I'm eighty-whatever and I'm still fucking working."

In the sports memorabilia world, Ted Williams's is considered one of the most commonly forged signatures in circulation, and those "authenticated" by John Henry are among the most suspect. Incredibly, John Henry actually used to boast that he could forge his father's signature perfectly. One time he signed his father's name in front of a Massachusetts sports memorabilia dealer and then laughed, saying there was no way to tell it wasn't the real thing.

Then John Henry had the nerve to accuse this same dealer of selling fake Ted Williams autographs. He told the man he needed to throw them all away and buy new, authentic ones from John Henry. The owner told John Henry to get the hell out—Ted Williams had held an autograph session in the man's store just four weeks earlier.

"I would bet my life that there are autographs that he has authenticated and sold that he signed himself," this dealer later said of John Henry.

John Henry walked into another sports memorabilia store and told the owner his Ted Williams signature items were all fakes. He could tell by the penmanship, John Henry claimed, that they were forgeries. The owner said that could very well be true—he had bought them all off John Henry three months earlier.

Ted Williams autographed pictures sold for $300. John Henry bought a BMW 700 series. Ted Williams autographed bats sold for $700. John Henry

The Alcor facility, where I worked from late January through mid-August, 2003. From the front, it looked like just another small business.

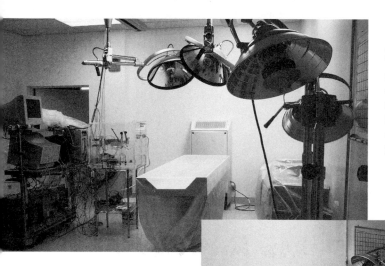

Alcor's operating room. They used a mortician's table rather than a standard operating table. The raised sides acted as "blood dams" for containing the blood during the decapitation procedure.

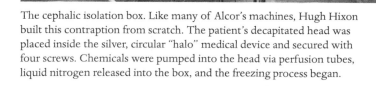

The cephalic isolation box. Like many of Alcor's machines, Hugh Hixon built this contraption from scratch. The patient's decapitated head was placed inside the silver, circular "halo" medical device and secured with four screws. Chemicals were pumped into the head via perfusion tubes, liquid nitrogen released into the box, and the freezing process began.

The Crackphone. Another of Hugh Hixon's inventions, this computer rig was connected to microphones drilled into the head to measure brain cracks during freezing. Alcorian brains always cracked during cool-down, without exception, and most Alcorians simply said doctors of the future would fix them. These "acoustic events," as Alcor called them, registered onscreen like earthquakes on a seismograph.

Patient Care Bay with dewars and Neuro Vault (second container from right). The tall dewars housed either four whole body "patients" or a combination of bodies and heads. While I was there, the Neuro Vault held several heads, pieces of brains from a few Alcorians who suffered severe head trauma, patient DNA samples, cat and dog heads, and a monkey brain.

This was the storm drain behind Alcor, just outside the back door. Notice the white residue. My suspicions were ultimately confirmed that Alcor was dumping toxic chemicals and AIDS and cancer-contaminated blood out back, into the city's sewer system.

Mathew Sullivan—the Alcor employee who joked about sending Ted Williams's body back to his daughter COD in a frosted cardboard box unless they paid up—posed with the Neuro Can lid he prepared for Williams's head. Mathew was so proud of it and asked me to take this picture.

Close-up of Neuro Can lid with Ted Williams's name plate. Alcor refused to publicly admit that they had taken possession of, decapitated, and stored Williams's head and body.

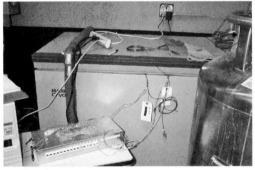

The CryoStar with Ted Williams's head tag trailing out (he is known at Alcor as member A-1949). It troubled me that Alcor's officers kept Williams's head inside the chronically malfunctioning CryoStar, stuck half-way through the freezing process, but then Charles Platt told me the terrible truth—they needed it somewhere easily accessible so they could grab it and run in case they came under court order to return it to his family for the cremation Williams had requested in his will.

LR-40 with A-1949's head in it. Liquid nitrogen vents and escapes from inside—that's why there's frost accumulated on the LR-40. After about 12 months in the CryoStar, once the Alcor officers felt comfortable that no one was coming to take Ted Williams's head from them, they finally transferred it to the LR-40 cooling tank to bring it down to the "normal" cold storage temperature. I was present for the transfer. Employees, volunteers, and other Alcorians crowded the room, hoping to get a glimpse of the famous head.

Ted Williams's daughter, Bobby-Jo, fought to get her father's remains released from Alcor, so he could have the cremation he requested in his will. Special thanks to Frank Sullivan for permission to use this photo.

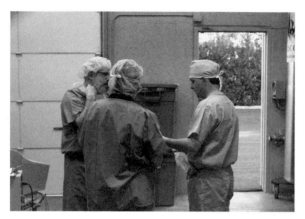

Alcor President Jerry Lemler (on the left) and I (right) awaited a patient's imminent arrival, near Alcor's back door. That's Paula Lemler with her back to us.

Hugh Hixon prepared equipment for surgery, gathering the tubing that would connect the big bottle of perfusate (Alcor's secret chemical formula) to the roller pumps (blood pumps) to the body.

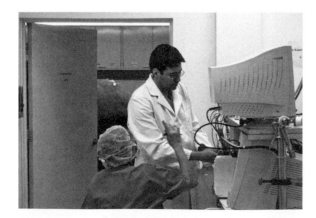

Mathew Sullivan prepared the computers for the operation. That's Paula Lemler again, with her back to the camera.

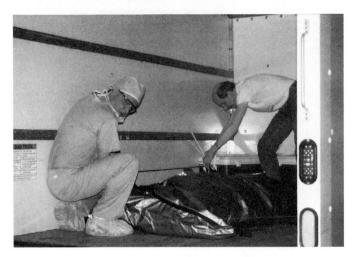

Arrival of patient in U-Haul truck. Even after twenty-five years as a paramedic, I was repulsed by the condition of this body, after it had been driven through the desert in a truck with no refrigeration. In this picture you can see me turning my head away in disgust from the smell.

James Sikes (right) and I (left) transferred the patient from the back door to the operating room. Mike Perry looked on.

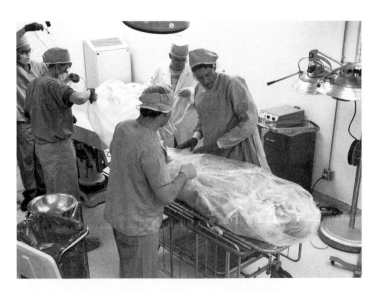

Alcor's operating team unwrapped the body, preparing for the decapitation surgery.

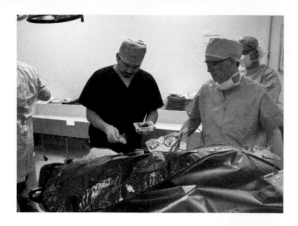

James Sikes (left) shaved the patient's head as I (right) watched. Later, as I discuss in this book, Sikes put the poor woman's hair, clothes, Walkman, and bloody towels all into her body bag, treating it like his own personal OR garbage bin. The mortician who came to take the headless body to be cremated objected vehemently, calling it disrespectful.

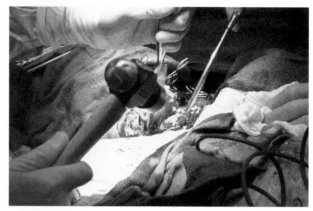

Cephalic removal. Alcor's hired surgeon smashed through the patient's neck and spine with a hammer and chisel to remove the head. It looked like the surgeon was hacking at a tree stump. This was nothing like any traditional surgery I had ever witnessed before. In fact, it was appalling.

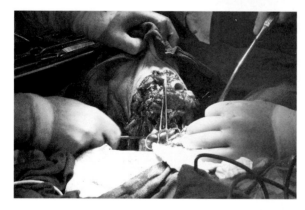

Preparing the head for final detachment.

Cephalic separation. If this looks gruesome, I assure you, it was much worse in person.

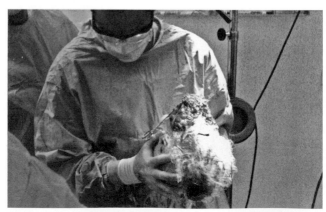

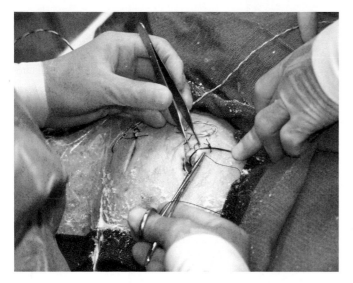

After the burr holes were drilled into the head, microphones were slid in until they rested on the brain. Wires from the microphones were secured to the head, and then connected to the Crackphone computer rig to measure the inevitable brain cracking during freezing. Alcor then stapled the wires to the head to make sure they stayed in place.

The head went into the cephalic isolation box. More chemicals were perfused into the head and liquid nitrogen was pumped into the box to begin cooling.

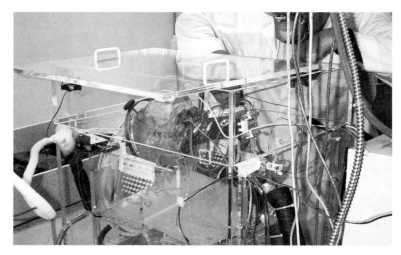

The Alcorian was now ready to be frozen.

After a hook was drilled into the neck bone for easier carrying, the head was placed inside the Neuro Can, which was lined with a pillow case.

This head had been frozen down to -321 degrees Fahrenheit in the LR-40 and was next taken out for permanent cold storage. Notice the tuna can stuck to the bottom, the pedestal on top of which the Alcorian will await reanimation in the future.

Me in the Patient Care Bay—I refer to this picture in the book. Mike Perry discovered me in the Patient Care Bay after midnight, taking pictures, and took this for me, thinking I wanted a souvenir photo of myself in front of the dewars. Notice the look on my face—I was in shock, fearing I had been caught red-handed gathering evidence against Alcor.

Please note that none of the surgery pictures in this section are of Ted Williams.

bought a '78 Porsche. Ted Williams autographed jerseys sold for $1,000. John Henry bought a condo for himself and his girlfriend in a trendy development within comfortable driving distance of his father's house.

George Carter was another of Ted's live-in nurses. He started working for Ted in the summer of 1994 and stayed by his side for eight years. George was an ex-Marine who came to love his friend. He lived with Ted Williams twenty-four hours a day—he fed him, bathed him, did everything. He saw it all, heard it all, and he absolutely hated John Henry. George Carter regretted not telling Ted exactly what he thought of John Henry. But, he says, Ted sacrificed for his son and wanted very much for John Henry to be a success.

Another of Ted's dedicated nurses, Jack Gard, complained to John Henry once about a box of photos, bats, and balls that John Henry had mailed to his father to sign while Ted was on vacation. As a result, John Henry fired Jack.

These live-in nurses came and went, hired and fired under John Henry's cold eye. All of them became close friends of Ted's, but not one of them held fond memories of John Henry.

John Henry became so upset whenever his father signed things for friends without charging them that he installed video surveillance cameras in the house to make sure Ted wasn't doing any signings he hadn't authorized.

The family became a laughingstock when John Henry made a public announcement that he would marry his Miss Massachusetts girlfriend on 9/9/99. He was making a spectacle of the supposedly lucky number 9, the number Ted wore on his Red Sox uniform for nineteen seasons. Although John Henry never actually married the woman, these were the sort of plans John Henry routinely concocted—trying to capitalize on his father's celebrity by publicizing his own wedding date as four number 9s.

When Ted Williams was recovering from a pacemaker operation in 2000 and was given a fifty-fifty chance of survival, John Henry had instructions inserted into his medical charts that no IVs were to be put into Ted's right arm. Nothing was to interfere with his father's ability to sign autographs.

After Ted had a stroke in 1994, John Henry instructed a hospital nurse to tape his father's hands open so he could still hold a pen and sign his name. While Ted was convalescing, the only physical therapy John Henry would approve for his father involved restoring strength and mobility to his right arm and hand.

People who sign a lot of autographs often warm up, practicing their signature on scratch paper before picking up the eight-by-tens and posters and whatnot. Ted's nurses reported that these little scraps of paper were all over the house.

Ted's caregivers also believed that John Henry was getting his dad to sign documents he didn't even understand, or worse. Family friend John Sullivan recalled the time he was visiting Ted and a bank officer came in with some contracts for Ted to sign. Ted asked Sullivan to read them for him, and Sullivan was astonished to see that the contracts were blank. He told this to Ted, who promptly refused to sign them. John Henry then came into the room and an argument ensued. John Henry was caught trying to trick his father into signing blank bank documents, the details and amounts of which John Henry was apparently going to fill in later.

The biggest fiasco of John Henry's career of pimping his father happened at the 1999 Major League Baseball All-Star Game.

During the game, to celebrate the last season of the millennium, Major League Baseball presented an "All-Century Team," a gathering on the field of the top living players in the history of the sport. Willie Mays was there. Hank Aaron and Cal Ripken were there. Heck, even Kevin Costner was there, aka Crash Davis, the fictional slugger in the movie *Bull Durham*. By all accounts, it was one of the most amazing nights in baseball history and Ted Williams had been asked to throw out the first pitch. It was a tremendous privilege, singling out Ted among the most celebrated players in the game's history. To make the honor even greater for Ted, the game was to be played at Fenway Park, home of the Boston Red Sox, Ted's team.

John Henry couldn't resist the promotional opportunity.

Despite the money he was making off his father's memorabilia, John Henry's run of failed businesses was coming to a head. His most recent and largest gamble was a company called Hitter.net. It was to be an Internet service provider, part of the dot-com boom of the late '90s.

What happened that night was an embarrassment to Ted Williams and all of baseball. All those world-famous athletes, the greatest living baseball players of the century, were of course wearing their team uniforms and caps. John Henry, however, dressed up his father, the guest of honor, in a hitter.net shirt and a hitter.net cap. John Henry tried to turn Ted Williams into a bumper sticker for yet one more of his failed businesses.

It's a testament to Ted's love for his son that he wore that shirt and cap. It's also a testament to John Henry's greed and obsessive need for control that he had his dad wear them in the first place. It was big news in the sports world, where for purists, it tainted a great event in baseball history.

Not long after John Henry's disgraceful All-Star Game promotion, a close friend of Ted's spoke to him about a loan John Henry had taken from this man. John Henry had borrowed half a million dollars from this friend of Ted's back in 1991 and had agreed to repay it within four years. Now, eight or nine years later, not even half of the debt had been repaid. Ted Williams didn't know about the loan until his friend finally complained to him, saying the money was for his children and he wasn't a wealthy man. Both men were by then in their eighties. He pleaded, when would John Henry pay him back?

John Henry declared bankruptcy the next day. Hitter.net had $12.8 million in bad debt. Ted Williams was so upset that he broke out in shingles in the following days. He decided to sell off his investment properties to pay back his friend, only to discover that John Henry had already lost or mortgaged them to finance the now-bankrupt Internet company.

Ted Williams was broke.

His health had been poor, but now it began declining at an accelerating rate. Ted's nurses figured this was the beginning of the end.

Many people who knew the Williams family through the years believed that John Henry, apart from being eager to cash in on his father, was attempting to exercise control over his once controlling father. Others felt John Henry wanted to do something, anything, to make his father proud. Perhaps John Henry looked forward to the day he would be resurrected next to Ted Williams and could hear his father say, "John Henry, goddamn it, you finally did something right."

It was definitely John Henry who came up with the idea of freezing Ted Williams. His sister Bobby-Jo Ferrell claims he also planned to preserve Ted's DNA for future sale and profit. She says John Henry was going to sell Ted's DNA to the highest bidder, to people who wanted to clone him.

"There are lots of people who would pay big bucks to have little Ted Williams running around," she has quoted him having said.

When John Henry first told Bobby-Jo he wanted to freeze their father, she said, "No way, that's not what Dad wants!"

John Henry first toured Alcor in June 2001. Jerry Lemler knew what a marketing coup he was onto and threw a party for John Henry at his home. This was very unusual.

The Alcor employees who met John Henry at Lemler's party later described him to me as "odd," with "the personality of a wet mop." That made me chuckle—you know somebody's in trouble when the folks at Alcor think he's strange.

Lemler continued courting John Henry aggressively. After the tour and private party, Lemler wrote a letter to John Henry. Underneath his favorite closing, "Sooner AND Later, Jerry Lemler," Jerry wrote a long postscript that included:

> I'm not certain of the magnitude of a full pre-mortem disclosure of your dad's becoming an Alcor member would generate, though I do believe it would be huge. In nearly three decades of providing biostasis services, we've had a few so-call[ed] "heavy hitters" look us over, but we've never had a .400 hitter as a member. It's a genuine first for us!
>
> Stated bluntly, the Williams name can be expected to provide Alcor with a fund-raising and membership enhancing leverage wedge it has never possessed.

Jerry seemed to be pitching John Henry on the idea that the publicity surrounding his father's suspension at Alcor would be good for both of their enterprises. Maybe Jerry was trying to induce visions in John Henry's fertile imagination of promotional paydays unlike any he'd generated while his father was alive. After all, he seemed to suggest, wouldn't all this notoriety be likely to drive up the value of all the autographed memorabilia?

Along with the boost in publicity for Alcor, Jerry was also hoping for a big cash contribution from John Henry. It just shows how little he knew about John Henry's hapless entrepreneurial skills. In the same letter, Jerry presented John Henry with a "wish list" of improvements Alcor could make in the event of a cash gift from the Williams family. Jerry really seemed gullible enough to believe he was going to get a donation out of John Henry, above and beyond Alcor's normal fees.

Nine months after Ted Williams's body disappeared into Alcor, and soon after I read all the information in his file in Mathew's office, I asked Jerry Lemler if he would still make the same decision in regards to taking Ted Williams's body, given all of the fallout Alcor had endured over it.

Jerry told me that the week after Ted Williams arrived at the Alcor facility, Alcor's Web site exploded from 5,000 to 600,000 hits per day.

"Would I do it again?" Jerry grinned. "Absolutely!"

Ted Williams's cryonic suspension occurred half a year before I started working at Alcor, so to be clear, my account here is not a firsthand report. What follows is the result of my conversations with the Alcorians who were in the room and performed the procedures, the files I have read, and the discussions I've had with other people involved, including members of Ted's family. It is a terrible story of degradation and mutilation, all the worse if you believe, as I do, that Ted Williams never, ever wanted cryonic suspension for himself.

In the early-morning hours of July 5, 2002, paramedics arrived at the Florida home of Ted Williams. They rushed him to the Citrus County Memorial Hospital emergency room in Crystal River, Florida, in cardiac arrest. Not long after, Ted Williams was declared dead, at 8:49 a.m. In a letter to his attorney, and then in his will, Ted Williams had left directions for

December 19, 1991

Robert E. McWalter, Esquire
Sherburne, Powers & Needham
One Beacon Street
Boston, Massachusetts 02108

Dear Bob:

    This letter is to confirm our discussions over the years
relating to my desires for funeral and burial arrangements. I
feel strongly about what I want and do not want, and I hope you
will make my wishes known to Louise and my family at the time of
my death.

    It is my wish that no funeral or memorial service of any kind
be held and that my remains be cremated as soon as possible after
my death. I want you to see that my ashes are sprinkled at sea
off the coast of Florida where the water is very deep.
Naturally, I understand that others may want to have some sort of
memorial service, but I do not want it sponsored by my family or
you, my friend and professional advisor.

    From time to time as we talk, I will give you further
details, but for the moment I want to document my present
thinking.

                    Sincerely,

                    Theodore S. Williams
                    Theodore S. Williams

Ted Williams's letter to his attorney requesting cremation.

his body to be cremated and his ashes "sprinkled at sea off the coast of
Florida where the water is very deep." Ted Williams never changed this request; on the day he died, this was how his will read. His son, however, had
a will of his own.

———————————

John Henry took the call on his cell phone while at baseball practice in
Fort Myers, Florida. Although John Henry was by all accounts a third-rate
player, his father's name had helped land him a spot with a Red Sox minor
league team. Once he learned of his father's death, John Henry hung up
and immediately called Jerry Lemler at Alcor.

    Even though John Henry visited Alcor in 2001, there had never been
any paperwork signed—not by Ted Williams nor yet by John Henry. As
mentioned earlier with regard to the Asian family that Jerry wanted to

Last Will and Testament

of

Theodore S. Williams

I, THEODORE S. WILLIAMS, a resident of Citrus County, Florida, do hereby make, publish and declare this instrument to be my Last Will and Testament, hereby revoking any and all Wills and Codicils I formerly may have made.

ARTICLE 1 - CREMATION/FUNERAL

1.1 Cremation. I direct that my remains be cremated and my ashes sprinkled at sea off the coast of Florida where the water is very deep.

1.2 No Funeral. It is my wish and direction that no funeral or memorial service of any kind be held for me and that neither my family nor my friends sponsor any such service for me.

ARTICLE 2 - PAYMENT OF DEBTS, TAXES AND EXPENSES OF ADMINISTRATION

I direct that all estate, inheritance, succession and other death taxes of any nature, other than generation skipping transfer taxes, which may be levied or assessed by reason of my death by the laws of any State or of the United States with respect to property passing under this Will or any other property (exclusive of any tax imposed as a result of Section 2041 or Section 2044 of the Code, or a corresponding provision of State law) shall be considered a cost of administration of my estate, and that such taxes, together with all debts and expenses of administration of my estate, shall be paid out of my residuary estate. Provided, however, any excess retirement accumulations in qualified employer plans and individual retirement plans shall bear the increase in estate tax imposed by Section 4980A of the Internal Revenue Code.

In the event my residuary estate lacks sufficient liquidity to pay such debts, expenses, taxes and other charges properly chargeable to my residuary estate, I authorize my Personal Representative to request such amounts from the Trustee of the TED WILLIAMS TRUST OF JULY 1985 as amended and restated on ____December __ _____, 1996, as the same may be amended from time to time before my death, as my Personal Representative deems advisable for the payment in whole or in part of such debts, expenses, taxes and charges (whether due with respect to the trust property or otherwise). Such debts and expenses, however, are not to be a charge against any portion of my property or my trust property constitutionally or otherwise exempt from debt by the laws of the State of Florida. There shall be no right of reimbursement

1

Ted Williams's will. Note Article 1.1—Cremation.

sign up as the mother was dying, it is Alcor's stated policy to avoid cases that are deemed last-minute, because the company had had too many legal problems accepting deathbed patients. However, Alcor seemed all too willing to make exceptions, and this was one of those special cases.

So Jerry Lemler jumped at the opportunity to get a celebrity of Ted Williams's stature inside Alcor. He made frenzied phone calls to muster up a team that could get to Ted's body swiftly, overlooking the fact that there was no signed Alcor membership paperwork, and no signed Cryonic Suspension Agreement.

Next, John Henry called the attending doctor and had him sign the death certificate, then called the local funeral home, which was located very near the hospital. The funeral director, mistakenly thinking he was helping fulfill Ted's last wishes, agreed to allow Alcor's representatives to use his mortuary's vehicle and basement for the transport and initial suspension procedures. This was in a remote stretch of the Florida peninsula, Cajun country, where township populations often measured in the dozens. The small-town funeral director had absolutely no idea what the cryonicists had in mind when he agreed to this.

The Alcorians converged, injected Ted Williams's body with chemicals, packed 150 pounds of ice into the Ziegler case (an insulated, water-tight shipping container used by funeral homes) that Ted's body was being transported in, and performed chest compressions to circulate the anticoagulants. Their work on Ted's body began without any authorization whatsoever. The funeral director witnessed these events and was "horrified." Meanwhile, at 11:29 a.m., the last two pages of Alcor's consent documentation were faxed to John Henry. These were signature pages only, containing no details of the agreement. After the injections of anticoagulants, the body was rushed on ice to a private airport in Ocala, Florida.

John Henry met Alcor's representative, David Hayes, on the tarmac next to the National Jets air ambulance that was to whisk the body away to Scottsdale. David Hayes was the Alcorian I had worked with during the suspension of A-1025, the one involving the Alamo minivan. John Henry finally attended to the Alcor paperwork there on the runway and signed for his father on both documents, identifying himself as "Son" and writing "POA," for power of attorney. John Henry marked the time as 2:44 p.m. The space reserved for Ted's own signature was blank.

e) Social, political, and ethical objections to Neurosuspension or to the technology required to revive Neurosuspension patients may result in problems which could delay or prevent my revival.

f) Neurosuspension patients may be stored with Whole Body Suspension patients in order to achieve maximum economic benefit, and, as a consequence, have less protection than is currently offered against fire, earthquake, terrorism, and natural disaster.

16) If I have selected the Whole Body Suspension Option, I understand and accept the following:

a) I may receive less secure protection against fire, earthquake, terrorism, and natural disaster than Neurosuspension patients due to economic and logistic limitations currently imposed upon Alcor.

b) I may be subjected to more injury from the suspension process as a result of longer perfusion and cooling times, although no quantification of such injury has been established.

c) Due to the increased costs and logistic difficulties associated with Whole Body Suspension, I may not remain in suspension under adverse political, economic, and/or social conditions outside the control of Alcor.

d) Due to the need to repair/rejuvenate the entire body, it may require more resources to effect revival of Whole Body Suspension patients or it may cost more, resulting in delays that could delay or prevent my revival.

17) With full understanding of these conditions, I consent to cryonic suspension and attempted revival.

SIGNATURE OF PATIENT

YOUR SIGNATURE BELOW CONFIRMS YOUR ACKNOWLEDGMENT THAT:

1. You have read, understood, and consented to all of the foregoing provisions of this CONSENT FOR CRYONIC SUSPENSION

2. You are fully aware of and accept the risks and limitations explained in this document.

3. These proposed research procedure(s) have been satisfactorily explained to you by the officers, representatives, and/or other personnel of Alcor.

4. You declare that the arrangement described herein, in conjunction with the Cryonic Suspension Agreement and the Authorization of Anatomical Donation, constitutes your last wish as to the disposition of your human remains after legal death.

5. You hereby give your authorization and consent.

Signature of Member _____

_7_ \ _5_ \ 20 _0 2_
Month   Day   Year

_2:44_   (a.m./p.m.)
Time

John Henry Williams

Responsible person if Member is
unable to sign or is an unemancipated
minor or otherwise incompetent.

Son / POA
Relationship or Authority

Consent for Cryonic Suspension, March 2002

Page 6 of 7

Ted Williams's unsigned Alcor Suspension Agreement. Note "POA" under John Henry's signature.

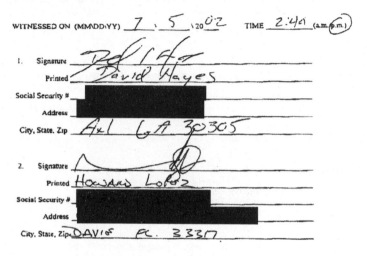

WITNESSES

Two (2) witnesses are required to sign in the presence of each other and the Member. At the time of signing, witnesses must not be relatives of the Member, health care providers of any kind, or officers, directors, or agents of Alcor.

YOUR SIGNATURE AS WITNESS CONFIRMS YOUR ACKNOWLEDGEMENT THAT:

1. The Member has represented to you that he/she understands and agrees to the purposes and terms of this document.

2. The Member has declared to you that cryonic suspension is his/her last wish as to the disposition of his/her body and person after legal death.

WITNESSED ON (MMDDYY) _7_ , _5_ , 20 _02_   TIME _2:40_ (a.m./p.m.)

1.   Signature _____

       Printed   David Hayes

Social Security # _____

       Address _____

City, State, Zip   Axl GA 30305

2.   Signature _____

       Printed   Howard Lopez

Social Security # _____

       Address _____

City, State, Zip Davis FL 33317

The Witness Page from Ted Williams's Alcor Suspension Agreement. Note "Witnesses" clause, top, and David Hayes's signature, bottom.

However, according to Florida law, John Henry's authority as Ted Williams's power of attorney expired the moment his father was pronounced dead, six hours earlier. John Henry was not remotely within his legal rights to pose as POA for Ted Williams on these documents.

There on the steamy Florida airstrip, as the body was being loaded into the private plane, David Hayes took the sheets of paper from John Henry and signed his name as "Witness." The text at the top of the page Hayes signed reads, "At the time of signing, witnesses must not be relatives of the member, healthcare providers of any kind, or officers, directors, or agents of Alcor."

In the rush to grab its heavy hitter, Alcor broke its own rules. It was a gross conflict of interest. By Alcor's own standards, as a contracted Alcor representative, David Hayes invalidated the cryonics suspension agreement by signing it.

Even so, at that moment, Ted Williams had become Alcor member A-1949.

David Hayes hopped into the plane and continued working the body in the air.

———————

As the body was unloaded from a U-Haul truck and wheeled across the Scottsdale, Arizona, parking lot, cryonicists with cameras swarmed from Alcor's back doors, laughing, joking, and snapping souvenir pictures. It was as if Ted Williams had at last lost his lifelong battle with the paparazzi.

Inside, the OR was being prepped.

Bright lights shone down onto the hard white plastic mortician's table. Wires and tubes sprouted from the cephalic isolation box. Blood-pumping machines hummed expectantly and computers beeped with electro-cardiogram-type readouts. Hundreds of pounds of ice waited in large coolers. Scalpels lay by the head of the operating table, alongside a bone saw, hammer, and chisel.

The nonessential bystanders spilled into the room, following the gurney, flashing more pictures and chatting merrily. Ted Williams's mutilation was standing room only. Even more spectators than usual crowded the OR, celebrating, having a good laugh that the media and relatives of Ted, other than John Henry, were chasing their tails, trying to figure out where Ted's body was that night.

Because of Ted's celebrity, the Alcor volunteers were in a photographic frenzy. Many brought in family members to pose around his dead body. Charles Platt was so upset with the unprofessional behavior of Alcor's officers and volunteers in the case of A-1949 that he later distributed the following internal memo to Alcor board members and employees.

> Security in the operating room during this case was grossly negligent. . . . Many people photographed the subsequent surgical procedure. None of them signed any nondisclosure form. None of them

agreed that Alcor would own the pictures. We do not know what happened to all these people with their cameras and photographs. None of the videos of this case is in the possession of Alcor (with the possible exception of the reference video shot from the upper corner of the room), and most of the photographs (possibly all of them) have been stored outside of Alcor.

Alcor employees bustled about, preparing A-1949 for surgery. Charles Platt's girlfriend, Erico, sat in a corner scribbling notes in the surgery log. English was not her first language. Her notes looked like a child's, full of misspellings and crossed-out words.

Two men entered the OR dressed as surgeons, though neither was. Hugh Hixon, while a brilliant mechanical engineer, was no doctor. His counterpart, Mike Darwin, was a dialysis machine technician.

Although Darwin hadn't officially worked at Alcor for ten years, he was called in especially for the Ted Williams suspension. Darwin was the one who had written the online postings I had read before joining Alcor about killing dogs and exploiting people's weaknesses. And as Charles had let slip to me in the car, Darwin was the one the Riverside County coroner's investigators believed responsible for prematurely ending Dora Kent's life with an injection in order to hurry up her cryonic suspension. The ringer that Alcor called in out of retirement for Ted Williams's surgery was the man who had been arrested for leading the team that killed Saul Kent's mother.

The buzz of the nonessentials' chatter intensified. The body was ready. The knives were standing by. The moment had come. Mike Darwin approached the body, lifted a scalpel, and began the process of removing Ted Williams's head from Ted Williams's body.

———————

Meanwhile, family friends were calling Ted's house, trying to find out what was happening. They had heard rumors of Ted's death and were following the troubling reports on television that the body had disappeared. Former president George H. W. Bush called Ted's home hoping to give his condolences to the family. Ted's friend John Glenn called three times.

The sports media, aware of John Henry's long history of exploiting his father, started speculating, expecting the worst—a pay-per-view funeral perhaps or Ted's last change of clothes being auctioned on eBay. But even the most imaginative Williams-watchers could not have conceived the journey that Ted's cadaver had traveled, or the procedure and treatment that his body was enduring.

———————

Ted Williams's suspension was plagued with extraordinary confusion and incompetence.

From the OR log, kept by Erico:

20:50   Mike [Darwin] needs carving knif!

20:52   They are trying to open up some part on the front neck (looks like his throte) and stuffing some gauze. . . .

21:07   They had some trouble on the sucksion. They got a bad sucker! We need a new tubing.

21:08   Hugh said pressure is gettin down for some reason. Drainage wasn't over from the right jugular.

21:13   Mike has to cut something, but the knif looks like it's not working well. He murmured "We need electric carving knif . . ."

21:16   Flow rate got down in last half of a minute, Brian [noted]. Mike started using a little saw.

The OR log also tells that "one of the tubes was too stiff . . . we are not getting any cryo-protectant in venous . . . pump was making some funny noise . . . pressure dropped to zero in the last 60 seconds . . . they got an error into air fluent . . . one of the tubes is not getting any fluid." Plagued with bad suction and randomly fluctuating blood pumps, OR "Team Leader" Mike Darwin and his amateur surgeon counterpart, Hugh Hixon, stuffed gauze into their patient's throat to absorb the excessive flow of blood. Drainage and suction ebbed and flowed with the faulty equipment.

The decapitation progressed too slowly for Darwin. Frustrated with the knife he was using to sever A-1949's spine, Darwin joked about needing an electric carving knife, then reached for a bone saw. Next to the saw, on the surgical tray, was a Sears Craftsman carpenter's hammer and chisel—ironically, from the very store that Ted had represented for more than twenty-five years as spokesman.

Mike Darwin began sawing through Ted Williams's neck.

David Hayes, the Alcor technician who had taken possession of the body in Florida from John Henry, wandered into the room to see how things were going.

Incredulous, Hayes blurted out, "Wait! This is a full-body suspension!"

Hayes delivered the news that John Henry Williams had signed his father up that morning to be frozen in one piece, not a "neuro-suspension." They weren't supposed to decapitate him. Even for Alcor's amateur surgical team, this was an unfathomable blunder.

Darwin looked down at the bloody mess that used to be Ted Williams's neck. The head was literally hanging by a thread.

The bloodied surgical team waited in the OR, halted in their tracks, while Jerry Lemler placed frantic calls to John Henry Williams. Alcor had nearly finished the decapitation procedure on Ted Williams. Now the Alcor leaders had to convince John Henry that his father really should be decapitated. To my knowledge, and for obvious reasons, none of this was recorded in the OR log.

Hopping from foot to foot in the OR, Lemler had difficulty reaching John Henry. Frustrated, he rushed out Alcor's back door with his cell phone, alone.

Several minutes later, Jerry Lemler returned smiling. He said everything was okay. He had spoken to John Henry and convinced him to have his father converted to a neuro, though Alcor would be storing the body as well. Lemler claimed he had caught John Henry at a restaurant. Not the ideal dinner conversation. In the coming weeks, the Alcor rumor mill took off with this one. No one had actually overheard the conversation. Did Lemler fake it? It was nearly midnight for John Henry in Florida. That's awfully late to be eating dinner. To my knowledge,

John Henry never denied or confirmed speaking with Jerry Lemler that night.

Darwin and Hixon got back to the matter at hand. As the hours ticked by, more problems arose.

Alcor's equipment malfunctioned. As was often the case, the blood pumps randomly sped up and slowed down of their own accord. When the pumps worked too aggressively, they pushed the blood and chemical mixture through Ted's head and body too forcefully. The veins and vessels in the head were not made to take such a beating. Liquids pumped through the head at these pressures can rupture the blood vessels. The blood and chemicals would then spill throughout the cranium and pool there. When frozen, this pooled liquid could expand and burst through the skull.

Alternately, the faulty pumps sometimes stopped working without warning. Pressure dropped to zero, causing no perfusion (delivery of chemicals into the bloodstream) at all. People in the OR just happened to notice that the pumps had stopped, though no one knew how long they'd been down. As a result, Ted's blood pooled and congealed. Again, upon freezing, the head could burst like a soda can under pressure.

At one point the bumbling neurosurgeon hobbyist Mike Darwin actually "shut down some tube accidentally and the pressure got suddenly high up," followed by pressure falling and rising—again. Once more, the pressure dropped, and the blood stagnated.

In what had to be the most spectacular display of ineptitude, the perfusion tubes were accidentally knocked out and Ted's blood poured out onto the floor. It was a gruesome travesty illustrated in detail by the shocking OR log.

Darwin was not even a board-certified perfusionist, never mind a surgeon. The only medical training he had ever had was as a dialysis machine technician. Alcor's retired surgeon, Jose, was listed on the front page of the OR log as "Surgeon," yet the only mention of Jose in Erico's notes is that he was called in once when Darwin had a problem—and regarding that one instance, Erico wrote, "it seemed to me Jose didn't complete his job." Reading the OR log notes, it was Darwin who obviously performed the surgery, assisted by Hugh Hixon, who also had no medical training or certification for this type of procedure. It wasn't Jose who called out for a carving knife on two occasions, it was Darwin. Erico's notes are full of other references to Darwin sawing, cutting, and complaining. So the question is: Why was Jose listed as the surgeon on the front page of the OR log? Was it to mislead the family or anyone else reading the OR log into thinking, at a glance, that qualified medical personnel had performed the surgery?

After Darwin was finally able to completely saw through Ted's neck, an "enormous amount of arterial leakage" was noted in the log, including blood draining from A-1949's left pupil, indicating the washout had failed. There was obviously a great deal of blood left in the head, blood that would most likely burst during freezing. This was exactly what Alcor always hoped to avoid, the reason the ghastly surgery was performed in the first place. By Alcor's own standards, the suspension of Ted Williams was a failure before he left the operating table. The horror show had been all for naught.

The humiliation, however, continued. Alcorian volunteers continued snapping pictures. Ted's bloody, headless body became like a celebrity cardboard cutout at the beach—"Take your picture with Ted!" After they had had their fun, Ted's headless body was placed upside down in a steel pod, which in turn was placed inside a dewar with several other "dewar-mates" to be cooled to –321 degrees.

A hole for the carrying hook was drilled into the neck bone in A-1949's severed head.

Normally, the freshly decapitated cephalons were placed in the LR-40 head-freezing device for the safest possible cooling down to −321 degrees. Then they were deposited upside down into the Neuro Can lobster pots and temporarily stored in the Neuro Vault until they could be permanently placed inside a dewar. Instead of putting A-1949's head in the LR-40, though, Alcor placed it in the CryoStar experimental cooling machine. By Alcor's own bizarre standards, this was highly irregular.

Cryoprotection Data Collection Sheet B

Date Sheet Page Number **2**   Name of Scribe **ERICO**   Date **07/05/02**

Patient Name **T. Williams**   Case Number **A-1949**

Patient Weight _____   Total Rinse Soln Vol _____   Total B2c Conc Vol _____

Time	CPA Concentrations				Pressures			Reservoirs		Arterial flow rate (PUMP)
	Jugular Conc LEFT	Jugular Conc RIGHT	Arterial CPA Conc	~~Burr Hole CPA Conc venous~~	P.1 Arterial pressure	Filter ~~back~~ pressure	~~Intra-Cranial pressure~~ RAMP	Concentrate level	Effluent level	
22:40	9.49	23.02	23.14	-36.14	53.88	9	16		600	36 / 260
22:45	14.24	21.25	30.78	-36.14	48.41	10	16		500	26 / 260
22:50	17.54	21.07	35.97	-36.13	73.15	12	16	1040	600	40 / 326
22:55	10.28	20.47	32.57	-36.11	49.38	10	16	1010	600	34 / 280
23:00	11.71	21.47	36.15	-36.11	52.19	13	16	920	650	26 / 260
23:05	12.64	21.43	40.35	-36.13	49.34	12.5	17	800	650	29 / 240
23:10	19.96	20.91	42.62	-36.12	49.38	13	18	720	650	28 / 225
23:15	23.17	38.69	48.51	-36.19	51.88	13	18	620	630	26 / 210
23:20	25.25	40.37	49.32	-36.14	90.36	19	0	600	600	10 / 78
23:25	30.06	42.64	42.90	-36.16	50.61	13	6	570	600	12 / 90
23:30	31.84	42.89	44.31	-36.13	30.49	9	6	550	560	12 / 90
23:35	33.74	34.00	46.36	-36.17	69.24	17	8	520		10 / 78
23:40	33.63	41.08	47.54	-36.11	45-93	16				
23:45	36.96	41.31	47.46	-36.13	64.06	24	9	440	300	15 / 120
23:50	32.89		48.68	-36.10	68.04	28	14	380	200	14 / 110
23:55	18.59	37.88	46.70	-36.13	52.27	24	16	340	200	10 / 78
24:00	30.68	35.41	54.12	-36.01	37.09	25	16	240	300	10 / 78
0:05	32.65	39.11	62.98	-36.08	34.65	25	14	120	400	10 / 78
0:10	32.08	38.35	61.60	-36.12	-10.18	2	9	80	250	10 / 78
0:15	33.10	38.69	61.84	-36.14	59.67	5	10	40	200	29 / 200
0:20	36.10	37.65	48.47	-36.10	83.11	5	0	almost zero	200	12 / 90
0:25	45.63	51.71	46.29	-36.12	56.65	5	30	2000	200	18 / 150
0:30	41.51	50.20	73.44	-36.14	73.95	5	20	1800	100	18 / 150
0:35	45.40	50.25	72.03	-36.09	80.31					
0:40	51.79	57.19	74.83	-36.14	69.79	5	30	1420	2400	14 / 110
0:45	55.30	60.78	85.53	-36.08	75.68	5	30	1230	400	10 / 110

Alcor's OR Data Sheet for Ted Williams. Note "Patient Name" and "Case Number."

20:40 Mike put about 1.5 mm (catheter?) to the left

20:44 Mike is trying to do something on the right.

20:46 Right jugular is not schloerosed.
Because of scarring in the carade, he could put about 2mm.

20:50 Mike needs curving knif! (Cunyon?)

20:52 Mike is trying to seal up (the tubes?)
They are trying to open up some part on the front neck (looks lik
20:?? his throte) and stuffing some gauze.

20:58 Approximate lightation (?)
Mike is trying to stuff more gauze on the right side.
Need another sucksion tape

21:07 They had some trouble on the sucksion. They got a bad
sucker! We need a new tubing. → sucksion start sto
working after they got a new one.

21:08 They are getting lots of dranage. Mike said.
Hugh said so pressure is gettin down far some reaso
The right jugular Dranage wasn't from the right jugular

21:13 22mm pressure (arterial) over 150 cc (flow late)
Mike has to cut something, but the knif sea looks
like it's not working well. He mm murmured "we nee
electric curving knif..."

21:16 Flow rate got down in last half of a minute, Brian
Mike started using a little saw.

21:17 The head was completely detouched.
Hugh was muttering "everything is not okay yet"
responding Mike's question.
Mike said this guy looks like he has an incomplet ci
(cy

21:24 Mike said, lots of drainage coming out from everywhere
but not from jugular. Lots of. enormous amount of
arterial leakage. Blood fluid coming out from the
left pupil.

21:30 14 gage didn't work. They are inserting 12 gage.

21:34 pressure dropped to zero in the last 60 seconds. (Bria
They got an error into air fluent.

21:36 Brian noted the pressure got zero again

Alcor's OR log notes for Ted Williams (1 of 3).

Cryoprotection Data Collection Sheet B

Name of Surgeon _José_   Perfusionist _____

CPA Ramp Tech _____   Team Leader _Mike Darwin_

Neuro/Whole body _N + W_   Ramp Start ~~22:02~~
22:02
Ramp Stop 23:17

23:22
(turning the RAMP
Generater back on)

Notes and Observations

21:38 They moved the head into a small plastic container and attached the head to the metal stabilizer

21:40 Brian noted the reservoirs is going to overflow.
Hugh came back from the head section and told Brian how to fix it.

21:41 Mike was complaining about something about Hugh.

21:48 Mike asked Brian to keep the pressure ~~at~~ 40.

21:50 Brian asked Hugh's help about flow. Brian ~~asked Hugh~~ pointed out that we should recycle the reservoirs instead of just dumping it into a cylinder.

21:58 Mike said, still lots of drainage from everywhere.
(Everyone kept

21:56 MHP-2 → B1 (changed the reservoirs by Hugh)

21:59 Mike said, "we are loosing fluid now."

:03 RAMP is on 15 (by Hugh)

2:04 no sign of clotting, Mike said.
They are adjusting the leveler (should be the same level as the head) ← Mathew was adjusting.
no venous on the right jugular, Mike said
one of tubes was too stiff. Mike was trying to re-put a tube into the right side hole (canyon?)

2:18 Mike has done his first critical cryoprotectant part.

2:20 Brian said, we are not getting any cryoprotectant ~~tube~~ in venous.
Mike back to the head.

25 Mike said, right is getting any, but the left looks it has lots of fluid.
Mike called José. Jose came back in.
(It seemed to me that Jose didn't complete his job.)

:27 Brian said, "the ~~rig~~ left side is getting a reasonable reading."
Mike responded, "You'll probably get good reading on the right side soon."

:31 Brain is down to about 2 cm, Mike noticed.

:33 Green & white tube coming out from the surgery table and lots of blood flowed out on the ~~the~~ floor, which means blood from the rest of his body).

2:34 Mike started helping samples (Joe's job). I noticed Filte back pressure gets

:36 The reservoirs suddenly started getting low, very low.   while they tried same
Called Hugh. (Pump was making some funny noise for a little while)

2:41 Mike noticed one of the tubes is not getting any fluid.
Hugh fixed tube congestion.

2:47 Mike thinks they need a new ~~red~~ reflectometer.
The right reflectometer had air.
The right carotid is short. ~~too~~ Trying to re-tie the canylar(?)

22:53 No air is coming out from the left side as well, Brian noted.

23:00 The left jugular reading again, Brian noted.

Alcor's OR log notes for Ted Williams [2 of 3]. Note "Name of Surgeon" and "Team Leader."

23:00 They are still trying to stop some leakage from the head.
("The line is not long enough. that's the problem from the ~~be~~ begin
that's why we are loosing lots of fluid. They are too short and too
stiff," Mike muttered)

They replaced the rightside ~~vert~~ ~~verti-set~~ vertébi.

23:13 5mm down from the scalp (Brain)
(Dave Shumaker checked it with a flash light)

plateu concentrate percent. 48-50%

23:17 Brian turned off RAMP

23:21 Mike shut down some tube accidentally, and the pressure got
suddenly high up. (to 90)

the part of the flowrate was incorrect, because bypass line was of
They closed it now, so the RAMP is on now as of 23:23.
(Brian described)

23:27 PO surface was ~~filled~~ free of blood. The brain is now
plain white. Dave noted

23:31 The pressure started dropping again about 20%.
(arteral)

23:36 6 cc of florecent green (?) in.
~~(They were two~~ (they were startled by a-symetry of t wash

23:40 They raise the arterial pressure up to 70
by Mike's order.

23:43 Mike crump the right calited.

23:46 Mike pinched the left side.

23:49 Mike opened up the left side.
(We are getting better flow on the right side,
Brian noted. ~~~~
(There might have been miscaliblation of the set
That's Brian's guess. He was discussing it w/Mathew;

23:50 Mike pulled out left calited ~~canter~~ canular.

23:56 Green fluid is leaking from the ~~~~ connecter.
We need to do some thing about the filter, Mike said

0:01 Arterial pump stopped by Brian

0:02 The pump is on.
(Replaced the cable ~~tip~~ tie on the hexox)
Mathew is ~~~~ preparing to add a ~~first~~ sacond thermocaple to
the arterial input.

Alcor's OR log notes for Ted Williams (3 of 3).

The story of Ted Williams's remains quickly became a media sensation. Daughter Bobby-Jo battled it out with son John Henry in court and in the press, arguing over the final resting place of their father. Bobby-Jo wanted her father's last wishes honored. She vehemently believed Alcor had taken possession of her father's remains illegally and demanded that Alcor release the body so it could be cremated, according to her father's will. The Alcor staff kept stalling, never admitting that they even had Ted Williams's body. Meanwhile, Ted's brain was cracking inside the faulty CryoStar, registering on Alcor's Crackphone like earthquakes on a seismograph.

During the following weeks and months, the CryoStar was plagued with problems. Damning memos rocketed around among the Alcor staff, reporting the machine's malfunctions.

During one Alcor meeting I attended, Charles Platt told everyone in the room that he was concerned about uncontrolled random temperature swings in the CryoStar that may have exacerbated the risk of fracturing.

Still nothing was done about it.

On Monday, May 12, 2003, ten months after A-1949's head was placed in the CryoStar, Mathew Sullivan distributed a memo:

> We are having some problems with the CryoStar, and the temp has warmed up to −128C. According to Mike Perry, we had the same problem yesterday evening around 6pm.

Again, nothing was done to rectify the problem. Even Rick Potvin, the Alcorian who hosts the online cryonics bulletin boards, knew the story.

> In trying to figure out what I can say and not say—which I suppose is going to be par for the course if I continue to write about cryonics—I concluded that it's okay to talk about what a piece of junk the Cryostar is.

Rick also wrote that he had heard Hugh Hixon admit that the CryoStar was in danger of failing. Potvin surmised, "So the moral of the story is don't get your head caught in a fluctuating temperature Cryostar freezer."

Charles later confided in me that Alcor received the CryoStar as a gift from CCR and had never even tested it. Hugh had told me that it was never intended to be used for storing human heads. Now it was randomly fluctuating up and down by 10 degrees. In the world of cold-temperature storage, these were huge numbers. In fact, even if Alcor's CryoStar was performing optimally, it froze down to only −125 degrees Celsius (−193 Fahrenheit). This was well shy of the −196 degrees Celsius (−321 Fahrenheit) Alcor considered the optimal temperature for head storage.

Charles reported in an Alcor News Bulletin with surprising candor that

> a technician visited Alcor and noted that the ambient temperature in the [CryoStar's] operating environment should not exceed 80 degrees Fahrenheit. Exceptionally hot Phoenix summer weather had driven the temperature above 80 degrees in our patient care bay, even with Alcor's industrial-strength air conditioning running constantly.

Because of Alcor's inability to keep the surrounding room any cooler than 80 degrees Fahrenheit, the failing CryoStar was being even further taxed. It seems incomprehensible but a company that charged its members over $100,000 each for cold storage somehow failed to keep the heat of the Arizona desert out of its cold-storage room.

If it weren't so tragic, it would have been a joke, although a bad one. The officers at Alcor were keeping their most famous member indefinitely stuck two-thirds of the way through the freezing process, suffering crack after crack inside an experimental freezer they knew was malfunctioning, inside a room they couldn't keep any cooler than 80 degrees Fahrenheit.

Why would they have let this continue to occur?

THIRTEEN

"PAY UP OR DIE"

I was staying later and later at work, poring over Mathew Sullivan's files. I stopped feeling like a conscientious employee doing my homework and began to feel like some sort of amateur undercover agent gathering evidence.

I found Ted Williams's membership documents and saw with my own eyes that Alcor did not have Ted Williams's signature anywhere, on anything. I found myself in agreement with what Ted's daughter Bobby-Jo Ferrell had been saying since her father's death and the public controversy that swirled around the handling of his body began in 2002—Ted Williams never wanted cryonic suspension for himself.

For someone to voluntarily take the zillion-to-one chance of reanimation and unfortunately suffer the indignities of a bungled cryo-suspension is one thing. It's quite another thing, and much worse, for a son to sign over his father's body against the stated will of that parent, and against the pleadings of his sister. As if that weren't utterly objectionable, then consider that in this instance the cryonics company had proceeded without regard for even its own stated policy about what constituted valid signatures on its cryonics suspension agreement, seemingly for no better reason than to acquire a "celebrity" patient—a coup that, as Jerry Lemler had gushed in his 2001 letter to John Henry, "would be huge" for Alcor.

Charles and I took another drive to Los Angeles to check up on an ailing Alcor member. What Charles shared with me on the way back to

Scottsdale was more frightening than the story of Mike Perry slicing off his own testicles, more despicable than the desecration Ted Williams's body was suffering, more frightening than the cult at Ventureville. It would become a turning point for me.

Charles told me about an incident that happened in North Hollywood, California, in 1992. An Alcor member, a prominent gay rights activist named John Dentinger, was suffering from AIDS and near death. Mike Darwin, Hugh Hixon, and some other Alcorians arrived at Mr. Dentinger's home to sit the death watch, ready to start the cryo-suspension as soon as the man expired.

However, the Alcor member evidently wasn't dying quickly enough for Mike Darwin's tastes, Charles said, so Darwin gave him an injection that made the man stop breathing.

"What?"

Charles saw my reaction and seemed to realize he had perhaps told me too much. It was just like our Dora Kent conversation, though this time Charles had come straight out and unequivocally accused Darwin of prematurely ending Dentinger's life. I asked for more details but Charles clammed right up. He ended by saying only that Darwin was a loose cannon and, though he had done much for the advancement of cryonics, Alcor was better off without him around anymore.

This was by far the darkest secret I had heard yet: I was actually being told that Mike Darwin, Alcor's ex-president, had euthanized an Alcorian by lethal injection. I had seen how the Alcor officers and employees, engaged in their CryoWars, traded information, giggled over their secrets, and used whatever was at their disposal to discredit and manipulate each other. Charles couldn't be the only one privy to this, I thought.

I knew I had to do something. These people had given me every reason to believe that they were fanatics and that they were dangerous. But who would believe me?

———————

Saturday, May 10, 2003, became another day I will never forget. Alcor had a monthly board meeting scheduled for this weekend day.

One order of business on the agenda was a written request for membership from a hopeful Alcorian prospect. In its paperwork, Alcor claimed to be selective, and I had read online posts where cryonicists maintained that only a portion of those who applied to Alcor were granted membership, as if it were Mensa or an Ivy League college. Honestly, though, anyone who paid up front was pretty much accepted. In fact, during my time at Alcor, I heard of only one person who was turned down for membership. That was the case we discussed at this board meeting.

Michael Riskin objected to this request for membership because the man was big in the news at the time. His name and face were all over the newspapers and television.

"We need to learn our lesson from the recent scandal involving Alcor's celebrity member," Riskin said. "Alcor has been in the spotlight more than enough lately." Since this was a board meeting open to the public, Riskin avoided using Ted Williams's name.

Jerry Lemler took an opposing view. As far as Jerry was concerned, any publicity was good publicity and Alcor should jump at the chance of grabbing another celebrity.

The prospective member in question was Kenneth Kimes.

Kenneth and his mother, Sante, were infamous criminals. Even before their arrest for killing a woman named Irene Silverman, the Kimeses were pursued by authorities for years of criminality. Silverman had converted her Manhattan home into a bed-and-breakfast for visitors to New York, when Kenneth, impersonating a well-off tourist, paid $6,000 cash for a room rental and soon after introduced his mother, Sante, as his business assistant. The evidence that they'd murdered Silverman was so overwhelming that at the last moment of his trial, Kenneth admitted to his guilt in order to avoid the death penalty. Then he ratted on his mother.

Sante was also accused of a long list of other crimes including shoplifting, theft, and keeping slaves. In the latter instance, she allegedly brought girls up from Mexico and imprisoned them in her home, burning them, branding them, and making them sleep in a closet. This was all discovered when one of the poor girls escaped and was found running down the street, screaming.

Before landing a wealthy husband, Sante had worked as a prostitute in Los Angeles and Palm Springs. She carried on an incestuous relationship with Kenneth. Simply put, the woman was a horror.

Sante was implicated in other murders, including that of a man who had committed real estate fraud with her. In another scandal, her family lawyer disappeared while on vacation with Sante in Costa Rica soon after admitting he had committed arson on Sante's behalf. He was never seen again. Sante had another son, Kent, who was Kenneth's half-brother. Kent published a book about the family, *Son of a Grifter,* which was made into a TV movie.

Ultimately, Kenneth Kimes was sentenced to 125 years to life in prison. Sante received a similar sentence.

Kenneth Kimes's letter to Alcor was read out loud at the meeting. I thought it was actually very well written and intelligent. Kimes seemed very serious about the hope of future reanimation. He claimed he saw cryonics as a way to get a second shot at life. He wrote that he'd been raised as a criminal by his mother and wanted the opportunity to live another, better life.

Jerry Lemler commented that in the future, doctors might be able to cure Kimes of his criminal tendencies. But Riskin didn't want anything to do with him. He said the media would tear Alcor apart if it accepted Kenneth Kimes as a member.

I didn't know if Kimes could legally even leave his body to Alcor while serving a life sentence. Maybe after serving fifty years he would deanimate, be suspended, and eventually be reanimated to serve out the remaining seventy-five years of his full sentence.

What struck me as most unsettling was that no one in the room was mentioning Kimes's crimes. No one said, "He's a murderer; we shouldn't grant him membership." They didn't even seem to wonder whether the money to pay Alcor would come from his swindles and crimes. They were only debating whether he was too much in the public eye, with Riskin saying, "We don't need the scrutiny right now."

Riskin and several others were acting especially haughty. They acted as if they really believed it was in their power to grant or deny everlasting life. It was like they were sitting atop Mount Olympus, pompously deciding the fates of the mortals below, bestowing immortality only on those they deemed worthy. It was the first time I had seen this level of arrogance and, frankly, delusion. Inside me, distaste turned to disgust. But then things got even worse.

The next item up for discussion concerned a few Alcor members who were late on their payments. Joe Hovey read off the names and the amounts of money owed.

Michael Riskin, evidently still high on playing God, responded, "Joe, tell them they need to pay right away or we will be revoking their status as Alcor members. If they don't pay up, we will have no choice but to take them off the list for cryo-suspension. Tell them we won't be responding when they deanimate. That ought to speed things up." Riskin was indignant and pissed off, like he was taking it personally.

Others around the table agreed. I know every business, including Alcor, needs money to stay afloat. However, all the company literature I read claimed how benevolent the company was, how it wanted to share the gift of a second life with its members. Officially, it was a nonprofit organization. Now the CFO was trying to collect money from his fellow Alcorians by telling them they would not be put into cryostasis if they didn't pay up. Joe Hovey took notes. Charles Platt looked on like it was business as usual. Even the Alcor members in the peanut gallery were nodding their smug approval.

I looked at Jerry Lemler. Between his salary and his annual expense budget his employment package came to over $100,000 a year, and he was still billing Alcor for $400 sushi lunches for him and his friends beyond all that. He was handing out $500 and $1,000 bonuses to his daughter, wife, even his son-in-law. Now he was standing by Michael Riskin, ready to deny people a shot at what he believed was a second life because they were late on their payments. If these people really believed in what they were doing, how could they act this way?

Then Joe Hovey brought up the late payment for A-1949. Still, no one used the names Ted Williams or John Henry Williams. It was just "A-1949 and his son."

Joe Hovey told the committee that A-1949's son still owed $111,000 for his father's suspension. The debt had been past due now for more than nine

ALCOR LIFE EXTENSION FOUNDATION
SINCE 1972
"Celebrating Life through Science"

7895 E. Acoma Dr. #110 •Scottsdale, AZ 85260-6916 • Ph (480) 905-1906 • Fax (480) 922-9027
Membership Information (877) GO-ALCOR • Email: info@alcor.org • Website: http://www.alcor.org

John-Henry Williams
2448 North Essex Avenue
Hernando, FL 34442

Friday, January 24, 2003

Dear Mr. Williams,

As you will agree, during the extended time period in which your family was working towards a settlement of the issues raised by Barbara Joyce, Alcor maintained a respectful distance from the proceedings. Now that the agreement has been reached, (and we are all, of course, relieved by the results), it is time for us to complete our contractual obligations.

Accordingly, I have enclosed an invoice for the remainder of the outstanding monies owed by you for your father's cryosuspension procedure and long-term storage. Our accepted charges total $136,000.00, and we acknowledge receipt of your partial payment (made last year) of $25,000.00. Please remit to Alcor at your earliest convenience the sum of $111,000.00.

Thank you, Mr. Williams, for your timely attention to this matter, and for your confidence in the Alcor Foundation.

Sooner AND Later,

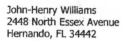

Jerry B. Lemler, MD
President/ CEO
Alcor Life Extension Foundation

A letter from Jerry Lemler to John Henry Williams, requesting $111,000 past due for Ted Williams's cryonic suspension.

months. Jerry Lemler had repeatedly contacted the son to no avail. Above is one such letter, written four months previous to this board meeting.

John Henry wasn't even returning Lemler's calls. Hovey mentioned that the son had a history of failed businesses. The fact was, John Henry Williams owed money to lots of people and businesses. Alcor would just have to get in line, and its leaders knew it. I wondered if Alcor's senior people could now admit that—even from a financial perspective—maybe taking on this suspension hadn't been such a winner, after all.

ALCOR LIFE EXTENSION FOUNDATION

7895 E. Acoma Dr. #110 •Scottsdale, AZ 85260-6916 • Ph (480) 905-1906 • Fax (480) 922-9027
Membership Information (877) GO-ALCOR • Email: info@alcor.org • Website: http://www.alcor.org
Alcor's Mission: The Preservation of Individual Lives

January 24, 2003

Mr. John Henry Williams
2448 North Essex Avenue
Hernando, FL 34442

Dear Mr. Williams:

Please pay the following balance in full for suspension member A-1949.

Whole Body suspension 7-5-2002	$120,000
Air ambulance (National Jets) 7-5-2002	16,000
Amount paid (ck.#0351, 7-30-2002)	-25,000
Balance due	$111,000

Sincerely,

Jerry Lemler, MD
President/CEO

Lemler enclosed this bill with the letter on the opposite page.

Riskin stood up. "Enough is enough," Riskin said. "You need to tell A-1949's family the time has come to pay up or die."

Others around the table nodded. Riskin was working himself up, pacing the room. And this wasn't even one of Alcor's secret board meetings.

"You tell them that if they don't come up with our $111,000, we will be taking A-1949's body out of stasis and trashing it. They need to understand. It's pay up or die. Pay up or die." Strutting about like a rooster, Riskin kept ranting: "Pay up or die! Pay up or die!"

This was the ultimate threat. From Alcor's strange perspective, to take this lonely man out of stasis would have been to kill it. I knew my coworkers were arrogant. I knew they got off on the power they wielded over the suspended members in their care. This, however, was unprecedented in what I knew about Alcor. As I watched Riskin swagger around the room, telling Hovey to demand money from Ted Williams's kids by threatening their father with eternal death, I realized they were willing to cash in on what they believed was their godlike power. And if their demands were not met, they were ready to unplug and, in Riskin's own words, trash the body. In their own parlance, they were ready to destroy Ted Williams's body over his son's debt.

"Pay up or die, pay up or die!"

After that meeting I went to Best Buy and bought a digital voice recorder.

What Alcor was willing to do to Ted Williams and his family was despicable. But it was what Charles had told me about John Dentinger—and Dora Kent—that pushed me over the edge. Riskin and the others were willing to "kill" Ted Williams's body in the cryonics sense of the word. But if what Charles had told me was true, Mike Darwin had killed Dora Kent and John Dentinger in the real sense of the word—as in, with a lethal injection. And there had to be other Alcorians who knew about it and were keeping quiet to everyone outside the inner circle—Alcorians I was going to work with every day. I just couldn't get it off my mind. I didn't know where this was going to take me, but I knew I had to act.

I waited in bed quietly that night until I heard Beverly sleeping. Then I walked into our bathroom and closed the door.

I put the digital recorder in my pocket.

"Hello, hello. Test, test, one, two."

I dug it out, played it back. No good. It was unintelligible. I knew I had a little Radio Shack microphone that I once used with a microcassette recorder. I found the mic and plugged it into the recorder.

"Test, test."

Success. I put on a shirt and did a full test. You'd think a veteran paramedic would use something smarter than duct tape to attach a microphone to his own chest, but the mic worked perfectly.

Wincing as I ripped out little tufts of chest hair, I felt awfully foolish—but mostly I was scared. I knew now there would be no turning back. I wondered about what I was doing but realized I really had no choice. Finding out the truth about Alcor had become the most important thing in my life.

FOURTEEN

HI, MY NAME'S LARRY AND I'M A WHISTLE-BLOWER

The next day, Sunday, I got in my pickup, drove to a secluded spot, and called Charles Platt on my cell phone. I didn't want Beverly overhearing the conversation or learning what I was up to. I was nervous as hell. With the truck windows rolled up, I held the digital recorder up to the phone and asked Charles about the threat made at the Alcor board meeting to thaw and trash Ted Williams's body. I didn't want to overpower Charles's voice on the recorder, so I found myself nearly whispering, then pushing the machine hard against the phone as Charles spoke. Honestly, it was the nerves that had me whispering, too. I don't know why but I felt like I had to keep my voice down, like I was afraid of being caught. I know it didn't make sense. I was shaking too.

Below is a transcript of the recording, the first taped interview I made during my covert investigation of Alcor.

> LARRY JOHNSON: Well, it was brought up in the board meeting . . . ,
> Charles, that I guess John Henry owes Alcor like $111,000. How does
> Alcor plan to recover that?
> CHARLES PLATT: Well, we're gonna sue him.
> LARRY JOHNSON: Well, somebody on the board mentioned converting Ted
> to a neuro, just keeping his head. What are they going to do with the
> body?

CHARLES PLATT: That's the threat. It just means basically throwing the body away. I mean, that's not what we would ever normally do but it's a, it's a bargaining chip.

Alcor had never even come close to publicly admitting that it had Ted Williams's body, and now I had Charles on tape implicitly admitting that the company would use the threat of "throwing the body away" as "a bargaining chip" to demand money from Ted's family.

Success!

Being "undercover" like this was making me feel a bit dizzy. I felt my adrenaline really starting to kick in.

I knew Ted Williams was in two pieces inside Alcor but I wanted to record Charles saying so. I pressed on and asked about the CryoStar.

CHARLES PLATT: Yeah, well, the reason we don't talk about it too much is because Ted Williams is in there.

LARRY JOHNSON: Really.

CHARLES PLATT: Yeah, um . . .

LARRY JOHNSON: Okay, now I'm confused. I thought Ted Williams was a whole-body, that he was in one of those dewars. So you're telling me that his head is actually in the CryoStar?

CHARLES PLATT: (Pause) He is half-and-half. The other half is in a dewar. I don't know which one, but the head is in the CryoStar.

It made me wish I had bugged my truck when Charles had told me about Dora Kent and John Dentinger. It made me wish I had recorded Riskin shouting "Pay up or die!" around the Alcor board meeting the previous day. If only I had been recording these people for the past few months! I'd just have to intensify my efforts from this point forward. What else would I be able record them admitting to?

I needed to make sure the recordings would be my property, that I could share them with people and that they would, if necessary, be admissible in a court of law. I was not going to do all this for nothing, or put myself in legal jeopardy.

With a little Internet research I found out there were one-party and two-party states in terms of recorded conversations. Fortunately, I learned that Arizona was a one-party state.

In a one-party state, if you record a conversation and you are part of that conversation, that recording is yours to do with as you will, even if the other party doesn't know he or she is being recorded. It is your property. In a two-party state, both parties need to know they are being recorded. Hoping to be completely sure, though, I called a private investigator. It was either that or a lawyer, I figured, and a PI would probably have more experience with this type of thing than some attorney I found in the yellow pages.

"Is it legal to record a conversation in the state of Arizona?" I asked the private detective after giving him a fake name and blocking my caller ID.

"Are you part of the conversation?" he replied.

"Yes," I said.

"Then yes, it's legal. We're big on personal freedoms here in Arizona. Why do you ask? Is there something you need a private investigator for?"

"I think my wife's cheating on me," I said, "and I want to confront her."

"You'd be surprised at how often I hear that," he said.

Even in a two-party state, I learned, if you hear evidence of a possible crime and investigate it yourself, you can legally record subsequent conversations in order to make a record of it.

It seemed I was covered any way I looked at it.

———————

The next day, buoyed by my initial success with Charles, and heartened by the fact that I was finally taking matters into my own hands, I taped the mic to my chest, ran the cable under my shirt into the recorder in my front pants pocket, took a deep breath, hit the REC button, left my office, and approached Mathew Sullivan. It had been nerve-racking as hell to sit in my truck and interview Charles Platt over the phone. But this was infinitely worse, to stand inside the Patient Care Bay, the heart of Alcor, secretly recording Alcor's "Director of Suspension Readiness." I kept both my hands in my pockets, shaking. I greeted Mathew, made some small talk, then aimed the conversation toward the threat of trashing Ted Williams's body. Mathew always struck me as an extremely paranoid person, so I needed to be delicate. I told him I had already discussed it all with Charles the day before. Most people around Alcor were so paranoid they said "TW" instead of "Ted Williams" even when talking among themselves at work.

> LARRY JOHNSON: So now I'm a little bit more clear now, because I know during the meeting they were talking about, you know, money that TW's family still owes and all that and [you] made the comment of just converting him to a neuro only and I'm thinking, okay, his whole body is in one of those and they're going to take him out . . .

I motioned to one of the dewars.

> MATHEW SULLIVAN: We've been very overwhelmed and hush-hush about TW. . . . Even if we did talk about TW we probably wouldn't talk—we wouldn't mention the fact that he's in two different places.
> LARRY JOHNSON: Yeah, that wouldn't be good.
> MATHEW SULLIVAN: It's a PR thing. So, but, yeah, I think I was one of the first ones to mention that early on that if he doesn't pay . . . I threatened to get rid of this part . . .
> LARRY JOHNSON: I mean, what would you do with that?

I tried to say "Ted's body" with my inflection.

> MATHEW SULLIVAN: I suggested that we should send it back C.O.D. or something, a frosted cardboard box or something shows up on his front doorstep. . . . Send it back to his daughter Bobby-Jo.

Astonishingly, Mathew finished this last statement with a hearty laugh. I continued probing

LARRY JOHNSON: So, I mean, realistically . . .

MATHEW SULLIVAN: What we'd end up doing is, he'd be cremated if we
    did do that. I don't know that the board would have the guts to do it.
    You know, I would if he wasn't paying.

My nerves were really getting the better of me and I figured that was
enough. I was having a hard time maintaining eye contact with Mathew.
I made some excuse and got out of there.

I marched down the hall and straight into the small bathroom located
off Alcor's front lobby. Somehow I felt better being close to the outside
door. I locked the bathroom door behind me and sat down on the toilet
seat lid. The recorder had a tiny speaker on it. I held it up to my ear and
hit play, both hands still shaking. I fingered the volume down so that it
was extremely low and no one outside could possibly overhear. It turned
my stomach to hear myself yukking it up with Mathew over his joke of
sending Ted Williams's decomposing body back to his daughter in a cardboard box. I was going to have to develop some acting skills, real quick.

The recording was hard to hear. I strained to listen but still I could
barely make out what Mathew was saying. I knew I would have to get better at this. I also knew I needed help.

I was on edge the rest of the day. I sat at my desk, avoiding my colleagues for hours, but I forced myself to stay until my normal quitting
time, then drove straight home.

I wasn't ready to tell Beverly what I was doing. We ate dinner and
watched some TV. I kept quiet, planning my next move, waiting for Beverly to get sleepy. When she was finally ready for bed, I told her I had some
work to do on the computer.

Online, I researched journalists who had seemed sympathetic to Bobby-
Jo Ferrell and the rest of the Williams family who were fighting to get
Ted's body released from Alcor. There was no lack of sportswriters who
were on the side of Bobby-Jo and her cousins. I decided on one of them,
a writer who prefers to remain anonymous in this book, and had a man
named Sam Rhodes make contact.

Rhodes e-mailed the writer: "What if I knew someone inside Alcor
who was upset with what was going on in there in regard to Ted Williams,

and in regard to the other horrors repeatedly perpetrated there? And what if I said this guy inside Alcor wanted to let the world know exactly what was going on in there?"

The e-mail reply came back almost immediately! "If what you say is true and you are in contact with an insider like you say you are, the person you need to speak to is John Heer, the attorney fighting to get Ted Williams the cremation he requested in his will."

Sam Rhodes passed this on to me. Of course, it didn't take long. Rhodes was me—a fake name I had decided to use for times when it didn't seem wise or safe to use my own name.

I wasn't exactly trained in whistle-blowing but I had figured it would be prudent to create an alias. I needed to feel people out before telling them who I was. Sam Rhodes used the computers at Kinko's so that Larry Johnson's computer IP address wouldn't pop up anywhere. Maybe I was a bit paranoid, but not without plenty of justification. I believed it wouldn't have taken much money or smarts to do some Internet tracking that could have led to me. There were a lot of wealthy Alcorians who could have paid for this, and then there were others, like Mike Perry, who had PhDs in computer science. Better to be safe than sorry, I concluded.

The next day, I called John Heer, the young Cleveland attorney the sportswriter had referred me to. John was representing Bobby-Jo Ferrell, Ted Williams's elder daughter, in the fight to have her father's remains released from Alcor. Even though Alcor wouldn't publicly admit to having Ted's body, the company—as well as John Henry and his sister Claudia—claimed they had proof of Ted's own intentions for cryonic suspension but they refused to release any of those documents to Bobby-Jo or John Heer. I knew differently; I knew the truth.

Someone at John Heer's law firm connected me to his office.

"Mr. Heer, my name is Larry Johnson. I work at Alcor. I know you are representing Bobby-Jo Williams and I, I wanted to tell you that I have seen the Ted Williams suspension documents and membership agreement and—you and Bobby-Jo are right—his signature isn't on any of them. I started bugging myself at work. I recorded an Alcor officer joking about thawing out Ted's body and mailing it back to Bobby-Jo in a cardboard box, unless John Henry pays Alcor the money he owes them."

I knew I was taking a chance, exposing myself like this.

The line was quiet for so long, I thought we had lost our telephone connection. Or worse, maybe John Heer wasn't who I thought he was. *Shit.*

"Mr. Heer? Are you there?"

Then I finally heard, "Man, where were you a year ago?"

––––––––––––

John and I talked at least once a day from then on. We became fast friends, though as of the completion of this book, we've still never met face-to-face.

John Heer's wife at the time, Liz, had been good friends for years with Bobby-Jo and her husband, Mark Ferrell, from their different interests in the music business. Years ago, Mark and Bobby-Jo wrote a real nice song about Ted Williams and Liz sang the vocals when they recorded it.

When Bobby-Jo realized she was going to have to engage in a bitter and, in ways, surreal fight with John Henry over their father's body, she also realized she would need an attorney. She mentioned it on the phone to Liz, who said, "Hey, you should talk to my husband, John."

Bobby-Jo knew she could trust John. When he heard what had happened to her and her father and how they had been mistreated by John Henry and Alcor, John didn't hesitate—he said he'd take the case.

Up to this point, John's background had been in environmental law. He's one of those lawyers with a good heart, willing to fight the good fight. A rare breed, I know, but John Heer is proof they exist. You can see it in his television interviews. The week after Ted Williams died, John was on TV a lot, speaking on behalf of Bobby-Jo, claiming that Alcor did not have any paperwork with Ted's signature on it and that their possession of his body was in direct contradiction to Ted's will. That's why he wished I had been around "a year ago," to provide him with the truth back when John Henry was lying to the media.

I don't think John ever imagined, when he started his career in environmental law, that he'd end up on CNN, ESPN, Phil Donahue, and Court

TV talking about such a scandalous, high-profile case. He had never pursued that kind of publicity as an attorney. John came across on TV as reserved and a bit nervous, but real honest and earnest—those are the best words to describe him. He looked young, every bit the boy next door.

Like me, John Heer was a Ted Williams fan. He wanted Ted to rest in peace the way Ted had wanted, according to the instructions left in his will. John received payment from Bobby-Jo for the first two months he worked on the case. When she started running out of money, he continued working for free and even to this day he hasn't stopped. Since August 2002, John has spent hundreds, maybe thousands of hours of his own time fighting for Ted and hasn't made a dime doing it.

I started living two lives: Alcor employee by day, whistle-blower by night. I bought a special microphone attachment to use with a telephone. I also started keeping a 9mm Beretta in my truck.

My manner of dress changed. I had previously worn my shirts tucked in at work, nice and neat. Now, all of a sudden, I was wearing big, loose shirts, always untucked. I hoped Mike and Hugh figured I was following in their slovenly ways. Of course, I was wearing my shirttails out to hide the digital voice recorder. It didn't fit in my pants pocket very well and created a pretty suspicious-looking bulge, so I started hooking it on my belt, in its little leather case. It all took some getting used to, especially the fear I felt that my shirt might hike up and accidentally reveal the recording device.

I developed the nervous tick of running my hand over the bottom of my shirt, just to make sure everything was okay down there.

At first, I'd hit the record button as I entered work and let it rip, recording hours and hours at a stretch. Then I'd sit up all night at home listening back to it, after Beverly had gone to sleep. I didn't get much sleep. Most of those early recordings were useless; there were long pauses, the sounds of me walking down the hall and initiating conversations with my coworkers, conversations that went nowhere because I was too scared to ask the more provocative, even dangerous questions. There were long hours of inane conversations, Charles complaining about Hugh, Hugh complaining about Mathew, Mathew complaining about Charles. So after a few days I got more efficient—and more daring. When no one was looking, I would hit REC outside an office and then go engage a coworker in conversation.

That got frustrating too, because I missed recording some very incriminating impromptu discussions. I developed another new habit. Now I kept my right hand in my pants pocket most of the time. From that spot, through practice, I got good at reaching up under my shirt with my thumb and hitting the REC button by feel. I felt most comfortable with Charles, so I targeted him the most often. I wanted to document how Alcor was keeping Ted Williams's head inside the CryoStar even though the company knew it was malfunctioning. I also wanted to get someone on record admitting that TW's head had cracked even worse than the average Alcorian's due to his bungled, amateurish cryo-suspension. During those early days of recordings, I managed to get Charles on tape with the following:

> LARRY JOHNSON: Well, one of the tasks that came up, you know in the board meeting before last, was the issue with the CryoStar and stuff. Has all that been taken care of?
>
> CHARLES PLATT: . . . The deal we had with Twenty-First Century [aka CCR] is we're not actually supposed to use that to put any human heads in it because they never really had time to test it very much.
>
> LARRY JOHNSON: Right.
>
> CHARLES PLATT: We're supposed to be doing some testing on it. . . .
>
> LARRY JOHNSON: . . . Okay, so is there an ongoing issue right now with the CryoStar, the way it's functioning now, or has that all been fixed?
>
> CHARLES PLATT: Oh, that part. I was just leading around to the fact that the board basically wanted to wait until June 14 to see if we could move the patients [Ted Williams and his roommate] out of the CryoStar and into the new thing. Well, of course we can't because it's not ready yet.
>
> LARRY JOHNSON: Yeah.

CHARLES PLATT: So meanwhile the CryoStar is still misbehaving and . . .

LARRY JOHNSON: You know, Hugh told me the other day that, you know, with TW being in there?

CHARLES PLATT: Mm-hmm.

LARRY JOHNSON: Said that I guess a couple months ago in April that there was a pretty good-sized crack in Ted's head.

CHARLES PLATT: That's correct.

LARRY JOHNSON: Yeah. I mean, is that anything that could've been avoided, or? . . .

CHARLES PLATT: I don't know. It's very hard to know with Hugh whether he's made a mistake or not 'cause he never admits it.

LARRY JOHNSON: Yeah.

CHARLES PLATT: So possibly, but I mean, whatever has happened has happened. . . . The CryoStar is not what I would regard as a reliable piece of equipment.

––––––––––

There was another conversation I had with Charles regarding the CryoStar that I was unable to record, though I wish I had. I cornered him and asked flat out why Ted Williams's head had been kept in the CryoStar for almost a year, especially when the CryoStar was known to be malfunctioning. It didn't make any sense and I demanded a full explanation.

At first, Charles said that they had wanted to keep monitoring Ted's head on the Crackphone because of all the difficulty they'd had with his operation. This was possible only if the head stayed in the CryoStar.

"Charles," I said, "I know all that. But there's got to be another reason."

Somehow, I think, Charles could sense I wasn't going to stop asking until I had the truth.

"Larry," Charles said, "we want Ted's head in a place where we have easy access to it in case we have to relocate it."

Ted's daughter Bobby-Jo had made quite a stir about getting her father's remains released from Alcor. Although she herself had run out of money and been forced to drop the legal dispute with her siblings in December

2002, sportswriters, fans, and other Ted Williams relatives were far from ready to throw in the towel. Charles, and the other company officers, had to have realized that Alcor's legal claim to Ted's remains was still dubious and the ultimate outcome uncertain.

"You can't just reach into a dewar and grab a head to go," Charles continued. Those dewars were locked up too tightly. Charles said that if Alcor fell under court order to give up the remains, it was prepared to rush Ted's head out of the building and stash it. I knew Charles wasn't exaggerating. Alcor had been down this legal road before. As Charles had already told me, Mike Darwin, Hugh Hixon, Mike Perry, Carlos Mondragon, David Pizer, and other Alcor officers had for a time been under suspicion—and were actually arrested—during the investigation into Dora Kent's death. The Riverside, California, authorities had been forced to drop the investigation when after they mistakenly failed to confiscate Dora's head during their first visit to Alcor, it promptly disappeared.

As with Dora, it looked like Alcor wasn't going to give up Ted Williams's head without a fight.

―――――――――――

In those days, I'd rush home from work, tell Beverly I had some work to do on the computer, download my digital audio files, obsess over them into the night with my headphones on (I told Bev I was listening to Stevie Ray Vaughan), wait for Beverly to fall asleep, and then call John Heer. Some I mailed to him on CD, some I e-mailed. Sometimes I'd rush home and talk to John on my lunch breaks, sitting in my own furry, animal-print bathroom, hiding from my own wife, whispering into the phone:

"Guess what I saw today, John?!"

"Guess what Charles told me just now, John?!"

And yet, anxious not to miss anything, I continued to record hours and hours of useless discussions. That Alcor bathroom off the front lobby became my whistle-blowing office. I'd be sitting in there fiddling with the recorder, erasing conversations that went nowhere, and then somebody would knock on the door.

"Larry? You still in there?"

"Just a minute!" I'd scramble to get out of there and leave the bathroom with a sheepish grin, like I was embarrassed for having stayed in there so long, the recorder safely hidden under my shirttail.

I became better and better as a sound engineer, working within the limitations of my recording rig. That first recorded conversation with Mathew Sullivan, about trashing Ted Williams's body, had occurred in the Patient Care Bay. That's where the huge steel dewars were. Voices spread thin and echoed around like crazy in there, so that recording of Mathew was hard to understand. A few other conversations I also attempted to record in there were complete failures. As a result I started cornering people in their offices and striking up conversations. I learned how close I needed to get to them for adequate sound quality. When I had to, I would lean toward people inside certain rooms as I spoke with them. I worried that these were wary, insecure people, some of them paranoid social misfits to begin with, so it was a balancing act to get close enough to record them properly without freaking them out because of my proximity.

Here, Mathew, talk into this flower.

I started getting bolder, leading my witnesses. I would remind my coworkers of discussions we had in the past, hoping they would reiterate what I hadn't yet gotten on tape.

"Jerry, didn't you say yesterday inside the Patient Care Bay that . . ."

"I know we shouldn't be talking about this, Hugh, but I wanted to ask you some more details about . . ."

"Oh, sorry, Charles, I know we're supposed to refer to Ted Williams as 'A-1949'—no names, right, ha-ha, just in case someone's listening, right, ha-ha, but . . ."

Listening back later to some of those recordings, I was amazed that no one knew what I was doing. Honestly, I have to say it was thrilling, it gave me a buzz. When Beverly had commented that going to work at Alcor might just be another type of adrenaline rush for me, she had had no idea how right she was. But this was a whole new type of rush for me—now I was always afraid. What if they caught me? What would they do to me?

———————

Beverly was no fool. I was getting jumpy and keeping to myself. I was "working" on the computer until three or four a.m. every day. Then, twice, after waking up at dawn and finding me still sitting at my computer with my headphones on, she tapped me on the shoulder and I just about had a heart attack. She knew something was up. Normally, we shared everything. I didn't feel right shutting her out, so after my first two weeks of bugging my colleagues, I came home from work one day and admitted to her what I was doing. I told her about Ted Williams. I told her I knew Alcor was dumping toxic chemicals and diseased blood behind the building. I told her I had heard rumors that Alcor officers had prematurely ended the lives of at least two members.

"Bev, I'm sorry, but I don't think anyone will believe me without proof," I said.

Her expression grew very serious. At first I thought she was going to tell me either I was nuts or that it sounded too dangerous. After thinking for a minute, though, Beverly said, "They can't get away with that, Larry. Someone's got to stand up to these people. I don't like that it has to be you, but . . . I'm proud of you."

Man, that was great to hear!

Beverly frowned and asked, "Can I hear one of the recordings?"

"Sure!"

So now I would rush home from work every day and Bev would be waiting for me at the kitchen table with coffee, ready to join me in listening to that day's recordings. She shared my frustration at the long, boring conversations and gasped with me at the darker, more serious revelations. I was already used to a lot of bizarre things being status quo at Alcor. Bev would remind me of how shocking all this was to an outsider. Her presence was a great comfort and made me feel less isolated.

"Their brains actually crack when they're frozen?" Bev would ask.

"Always," I'd say.

"What do they say about that?"

"They leave it up to doctors of the future to fix," I'd say.

"Huh. Why do they put heads on top of tuna cans again?" she'd ask.

"So that they don't fall over and stick to the bottom of the freezers," I'd say.

"My God," Bev would say.

Like me, she was fascinated and scared at the same time.

Beverly's blessing was about all that came easy, though. I started feeling vulnerable, even away from work. I didn't tell Bev in so many words, but I was awfully scared. I was on my own. I wasn't a cop, I had no training, and I didn't have any backup. Even though Beverly was supportive at this point, it was impossible for me not to withdraw into my own little paranoid world at times.

I had become obsessed with gathering information from Alcor. I'd seen evidence that they were dumping toxic chemicals and AIDS-ridden blood out the back door. I'd heard them proclaim their devotion to the "immortal lives" of those under their care and then joke about mailing one of their bodies in a cardboard box to his kids as a "bargaining chip." I'd seen how they had lied about Ted Williams's tragic story. And I'd been told that Alcor company officers had euthanized people. I saw that they had gone, and would continue going, to great lengths to protect these secrets. As far as I was concerned, they simply couldn't get away with all this.

I didn't want Bev to know I was so scared. So every single day I went to work bugging my paranoid colleagues while pretending to be one of the guys, then came home to my wife and pretended like I wasn't scared out of my wits. As a result, I was constantly on edge. It took a big toll on me.

Recording was only half of it. At the same time, I also began copying incriminating documents. Again, I did my best to make sure that whatever I uncovered would be admissible in a court of law, if it ever came to that.

Because of my background as a paramedic, emergency medical flight director, and ambulance company clinical director, Jerry Lemler wanted me to write articles for periodicals and paramedicine magazines. He wanted to spark an interest in cryonics among paramedics and nurses. Jerry always jumped on any chance to see his own words in print, but he often came under fire from Charles for his lack of technical knowledge. So Jerry wanted me to handle any technical or medical writing. It's ironic if you think about it. Here was the president of the company, a medical doctor, yet he was asking me to write and publish medical articles under my own name.

When he first made this request, I told Jerry I'd do it but I was concerned about asking around for information, and the fears this might arouse. Even though my membership was in the works and my coworkers were opening up to me, I was not yet inside the innermost of Alcor's circles. That could take years. If I went around asking questions and borrowing documents and taking pictures and all, they'd think I was up to something and just clam up. Jerry understood the dilemma.

I told him I wanted a letter from him that I could show the other Alcorians, granting me his permission to gather information for the purposes of publication. That way everyone around Alcor wouldn't look at me with suspicion when I asked them questions or wanted to copy files.

Jerry told me to write something up. He was too busy to do it himself but would read it over and sign it.

Jerry was famous around Alcor for never doing any typing himself. As I understood it, that was the reason his wife had been hired, even though she wasn't really around all that much. I was told early on by Charles that if I ever wanted Jerry to sign anything, I'd have to type it up myself, put in on his desk, and leave nothing for him to do but sign it. If he liked it, he'd sign it. If he didn't, he'd tell you what changes to make and then have you retype it.

I typed up the letter real quick and brought it straight to Jerry. I told him I was happy to change anything he wanted. He read it over, told me it looked great, and then signed it.

I had forgotten to use Jerry's favorite signature, "Sooner AND Later," but Jerry didn't object.

After Jerry signed that letter, I got out of there and went to my office next door. I just stood there, looking at his signature, all proud of myself. That letter granted me the permission of the Alcor president to gather whatever information I wanted "for the purpose of publication." A pretty broad mandate, huh?

ALCOR LIFE EXTENSION FOUNDATION
7895 E. Acoma Dr. #110, Scottsdale, AZ 85260-6916
(480) 905-1906 or (877) 462-5267 (877-GO ALCOR) • Fax (480) 922-9027 • www.alcor.org

Alcor's Mission: The Preservation of Individual Lives

May 16, 2003

Larry Johnson has the permission of Alcor Foundation to utilize various
photographs or documentation for the purpose of publication.

Jerry Lemler, MD
President/CEO
Alcor Foundation

"Permission to Publish" letter from Alcor's president and CEO, Jerry Lemler.

I had not gone to Alcor with the intention of exposing it. I went there
to earn a living. I wanted a research job close to my dad. I knew the people
there were weird and I figured it'd be an interesting place to work but I
never thought I'd witness what I had seen and heard. I never thought I'd
be forced to document the horrors I discovered, but now I was deep in it.
The letter signed by Jerry Lemler was definitely going to help me get at
the truth.

I had been hanging out at work later and later, striking up conversations with Hugh and Mathew and others, recording a lot. Now I had authorization to photocopy documents for the express purpose of
publication. I rose to the challenge.

Alcor was so disorganized I don't think any one person knew where all
the files were. There was no structured storage system. Things were
spread out all over the place. All I could do was sift through everything in
the hopes of finding something. There were filing cabinets everywhere—
in my old office area, in my new office, in Charles's closet office, in Jerry's
office, in Mathew's office—as well as in numerous locked drawers in Jennifer Chapman's desk. I found duplicates of many documents stored in

various locations throughout the facility. The filing cabinets in my new office were stuffed with a variety of materials, ranging from paperwork on the suspended members inside the dewars to old legal documents dating back to Alcor's Riverside, California, days. These I could peruse at my leisure. Many of the more secret documents, I discovered, were inside Mathew Sullivan's office.

I had been given permission to read through all the files I wanted, but it would have looked bad to get caught leafing through, for example, Mathew's Ted Williams files. I began to stay even later and later at work, waiting until Mathew went home for the day. Then I'd sneak into his office and search through his file cabinets.

One thing really bothered me about Mathew Sullivan's office: the bulletin board on the wall behind his desk. He had clipped a slew of cartoons out of different newspapers and tacked them up. They were all about Ted Williams's cryonic suspension: "Tedcicle" jokes, bits about Ted's DNA being traded for baseball cards, John Henry carrying an ice chest to Father's Day at Fenway Park, and drawings of Ted's talking head under glass with ice dripping from his nose. Mathew displayed them like trophies, thumbing his nose at the world—proud to have Ted Williams's body on the premises yet afraid to admit it.

Several times Mathew was still in the building when I thought he had gone home. After a few uncomfortable confrontations with Mathew entering his office to find me up to my elbows in his cabinet drawers, I decided to step up my James Bond routine. I started leaving work around five in the afternoon and then returning late at night.

There were two cameras outside Alcor pointing down at the area in front of the building. I had noticed them on my first day of work, as well as the four-quadrant video monitor and video recording machine in Charles's office. I had to take all these into consideration.

Next to Alcor's front door was another door made of clear glass. This door led straight into my old ex–marketing department office area. They gave me the key right after I started working there. Jerry Lemler smoked the occasional cigar during work, right outside that clear door. I started joining him. Then I started going out there by myself, taking little breaks out front. Because of the desert landscaping, there was loose gravel covering much of the front yard rather than grass. I'd stand outside, smoking a cigar, and casually sweep my foot in a little arc, tracing shapes in the gravel, making little mounds on the sidewalk, just passing the time.

Then I'd make up some excuse for walking into Charles's office and steal glances at the monitor. I was checking for blind spots between the outside cameras. *Whoa, my little gravel mound there is well inside the view of the right camera . . . so that camera sees about three feet farther to the right than I thought . . . the other mound is not onscreen at all, though . . . where's the outside edge of the left camera, then? . . . Is that another mound there? Hard to say . . . hard to see my piles of gravel . . .*

So I started using Styrofoam cups. They stood out better. I'd crouch down like I was resting my legs, sipping some coffee, la-di-da, and then oops, I'd leave my cup there on the ground, after having put some gravel in it to make sure it didn't blow away. Then it was back into Charles's office to keep checking the blind spots.

I successfully mapped and memorized the front of the property so that I could enter the building at night without being caught on camera, flattening myself and inching along a portion of the exterior wall, then zigzagging to the clear door through my pathway of blind spots.

That clear door was a godsend to my whistle-blowing investigation— if I had had to enter Alcor's main door, I would have set off the buzzer and been caught by the front lobby security camera.

So I'd sneak in the clear door, go straight to Charles's office, and switch off the video recorder to avoid getting caught on the other interior cameras. If someone reviewed those tapes and saw the time codes starting and stopping, they'd know something was going on, but I was willing to take the chance. There was still the camera in the Patient Care Bay that fed directly to the video monitor in Mike and Hugh's secret bedroom. I did my best to avoid that one but I still got caught walking past it several times.

After turning off the video recorder in Charles's office I would make for my office to establish my cover, before going on the prowl. I would turn my computer on and sit there until I was satisfied Mike and Hugh weren't up and about. I was awfully paranoid. Sometimes I would sit in my office, jumping at every sound, for over an hour.

On one side of my new office was Jerry Lemler's office. On the other side of me was Mike and Hugh's bedroom. My office shared a wall with their makeshift apartment. I tried awfully hard to be quiet when I was in there after-hours. This was extremely stressful for me. Mike and Hugh rarely left Alcor's facility, and Perry absolutely haunted the place. It was his domain—he didn't sneak up on you so much as simply materialize, suddenly visible out of the corner of your eye.

If Mike or Hugh did find me in my office, I was just catching up on some work. That happened quite a few times. There were many wasted trips. I'd be sitting there around midnight, making believe I was working, finally get up from my desk to start a night of photocopying and suddenly Mike Perry was there in the shadow of the doorway, staring at me. I'd say hello, make believe I was stretching my back, sit back down, putter around on the computer for another half-hour, and then go home, dejected and anxious.

One time I was sneaking around the Patient Care Bay at midnight, taking pictures, when Mike Perry caught me. I nearly jumped a mile when I heard his thin, monotone voice.

"What are you doing, Larry?"

"Mike! Um, uh, hi."

"Oh, I see. I know what you're doing," he said. "Give me the camera, Larry."

"Mike, let me explain."

"Stand there. If you let me, I can get the dewars in the picture too," Mike said.

He thought I was taking souvenir pictures. It somehow impressed Mike that I wanted to photograph the Patient Care Bay. He was happy to help and actually told me it would be a compliment if I let him take my picture in there.

As Mike aimed the camera at me, I couldn't smile. I was too shook-up. That picture is in this book. I'm leaning up against one of the dewars. You can see the shock in my face.

I continued digging during the month of June, recording like a madman. I was now six or seven weeks into my investigative activities. There were three issues I was researching. The first was the environmental infractions that I believed Alcor employees had committed. I was busy gathering proof of them but in the meantime I wouldn't have been able to stand by if I knew there were more dumping incidents. Fortunately, there were no more cryonic suspensions during the remainder of my time at Alcor, so there were no further opportunities for James Sikes to dump toxic chemicals and diseased blood into the shrubs and the Scottsdale sewer system. On June 18, 2003, I wrote a memo detailing my concerns and what I believed to be Alcor's current environmental infractions. I sent it to Jerry Lemler, hoping he would do something about it.

The second area I was investigating was Alcor's seemingly unlawful possession and mutilation of Ted Williams's body.

It was the third area, though, the suspicious deaths of Dora Kent and John Dentinger, that I really wanted proof of. These were the most serious and heinous and thus the most difficult to ask about without raising suspicion. I was working my way up Alcor's ladder of wrongdoings, asking people about Ted Williams to warm them up to the idea of sharing their darker secrets with me.

Unfortunately, I was also neglecting my relationship with Beverly more and more. She didn't make a fuss, but I was spending all of my time either at work digging through files or poring over documents and recordings at home, late into the night, alone. The deeper I got, the less I shared with her. She no longer sat down at the kitchen table to listen to the recordings with me. She'd ask once in a while but I started keeping them from her. I didn't want to scare her more than necessary. Quietly, Beverly and I were growing apart.

As the days and weeks passed, I began spinning conversations at Alcor more and more aggressively toward the Dora Kent and John Dentinger incidents. I was still the new guy, so I had to be careful and tactful. This meant it was all taking lots of time. Due to my own fear of being caught and my inexperience as a whistle-blower, I missed recording some very incriminating, impromptu revelations and yet on the other hand I still deleted hour after hour of useless conversations every night. I was sleeping less and less, and becoming more and more obsessed with finding the truth.

I hit the record button and approached Hugh Hixon in his office. I struck up a conversation about Alcor's cryo-suspension procedures, just rehashing things I already knew. I figured this was a back door into discussing the rumors that Mike Darwin and others had injected people with barbiturates and paralytics to make them die more quickly.

As always, Hugh was happy to talk shop with me. He was off and running, blabbing about injections, chest compressions, and blood pumps. Hugh was looking up over the top of his glasses, as usual, but I noticed he wasn't looking me in the eye. I followed his gaze down. There in the middle of my sternum was a tentlike protrusion sticking straight out from under my shirt about an inch and a half. The microphone had come untaped and was poking out from under my shirt, aiming straight at Hugh!

I started sweating. Hugh kept talking. *Doesn't he see that?* There was no way to fix the thing without calling more attention to it. Pretty soon, I couldn't take it.

"Hugh, listen, I forgot, I need to make a phone call. I'll be right back."

I twisted out of my chair and raced out of there. I nearly screamed as Mike Perry came slinking around a corner of the hallway followed by Jennifer Chapman. I raised my hand with a little wave, trying to hide the bulge in my shirt. I rushed into my office, shut the door, and started ripping that mic off. Immediately, someone knocked on my door.

I was in the middle of stuffing the microphone into my desk when Jennifer Chapman stuck her head into my office.

"Larry, I just saw you in the hallway."

"Yeah, um . . ."

"I have to tell you something."

"What?"

"Congratulations, A-2032."

"Huh?"

"Your paperwork has gone through. You're officially one of us now."

Alcor members were issued a necklace and a silver bracelet. Their A-number was engraved on each, and the bracelet also listed the initial suspension protocol for hospital staff, as well as Alcor's toll-free phone number—at least whichever one the company was using at that moment. Alcor members were expected to wear their bracelets 24/7.

The only time I wore my bracelet was while I was actually at the Alcor facility. Whenever I left to go to lunch or go home at the end of the day, I took the bracelet off and hid it beneath the carpet I had pulled up under the passenger seat of my truck, hoping to God no one would find it if I was ever involved in an auto accident. The last thing I wanted was to end up on that white table. I was still having a recurring nightmare of being strapped down to that white mortician's table in Alcor's OR, with Mike Darwin approaching me, needle in hand.

Charles Platt announced in the June 18 Alcor News Bulletin that he had stepped down as Alcor's COO and was transferring his duties to me.

In the July 1 Alcor News Bulletin, Jerry Lemler wrote:

New Chief Operating Officer

With the resignation of Charles Platt, the vacancy in the Chief Operating Officer's position has been filled by former Director of Clinical Services Larry Johnson. Though Larry has been with the organization but a short period of time, he has demonstrated a remarkable ability to absorb much of the knowledge he needs (specifically with respect to cryonics), that when coupled with his outstanding paramedic and management of paramedic skills should bode well for him in his new position. Charles Platt, likewise, has groomed Larry to take his place, and I know will be of continuing assistance to him in his new role. I hope all of you will support Larry in his new capacity and wish him well, as we all do here in Scottsdale.

Although I was already being referred to as the chief operating officer around Alcor, the board of directors needed to vote on it for the title to become official. During the next board meeting, Jerry Lemler proposed that they put my promotion to a vote. A few people around the table exchanged glances. An Alcor board member and ex-president by the name of Steve Bridge was participating in the meeting via telephone. He spoke up, voicing the unspoken discomfort several others in attendance were apparently also feeling.

"Jerry, I object to Larry becoming Alcor's chief operating officer," Bridge said over the speaker. "He's not a cryonicist." Bridge didn't know that my Alcor membership application had been officially approved. "Larry isn't an Alcor member," he said, "and I don't think he should be our COO."

Several others around the table nodded. Jerry grew uncomfortable and, wanting to avoid a confrontation, suggested we postpone the vote until the next meeting.

I kept my cool but boy was I pissed!

Jerry moved on to the next item on the agenda, Alcor's worsening financial situation. Alcor was floundering, Michael Riskin said, so he proposed a policy where each employee would "voluntarily" donate 10 percent of his or her salary back to Alcor. I couldn't believe it. He wanted to implement a mandatory tithe, like it was the Middle Ages and Alcor was the Vatican.

I spoke up.

"You've got to be kidding! Listen, I am not going to 'voluntarily' donate a portion of my salary so my wife and I can eat dinner at Jack in the Box every night while Jerry Lemler continues to treat his friends to $400 sushi lunches outside his expense account on Alcor's dime!"

Silence.

"Well, uh," Jerry said, "yes, why don't we postpone that vote also until the, um, next board meeting. We can discuss it amongst ourselves until then and take it up next time. Is there, uh, anything else?"

Charles knew I was upset. As soon as the meeting broke up, trying to avoid a confrontation with me, he made straight for his car and left for his home in northern Arizona. I caught him on his cell phone.

"Charles, what the hell was all that about?"

"I'm sorry, Larry," Charles said, "let me talk to Steve Bridge. He doesn't know you're an Alcor member yet. I'll straighten it out."

"Charles, it shouldn't matter if I'm a member or not! That was blatant discrimination, not wanting to promote me because I'm not a member of the club. And you know what else, it sounded pretty damn cultish! What's next, are they going to ask me to drink some grape Kool-Aid or something? And what about that tithe? This place is sounding more and more like a religious cult every minute! Charles, I'm performing the duties of chief operating officer already, and never mind the fact I was supposed to have already gotten a raise for that, now they want to take money out of my pocket and give it back to Alcor like it's the Mormon church or something!"

Charles turned around and drove back to Alcor to calm me down, but the damage was done.

John Heer began calling just to check up on me. He sensed my tension and was growing more and more concerned that my investigation was becoming unhealthy for me. John was a tremendous help and a great friend. He was as supportive as he could be. Still, he was only a voice on the phone. Ultimately, I was alone and vulnerable.

When I was a paramedic, I was selective about what I would tell Beverly.

"How was your day, honey?"

Oh, well, you know, about an hour ago I arrived at the scene of a drunk-driving accident to find a hysterical seventeen-year-old mother clutching her dead baby to her chest. The baby's brains were splattered all across the girl's dress. I think the dress used to be blue. See these scratches? That's from her nails as I tried to pull the pieces of dead baby from her arms. How was your day?

I just didn't share the horrors I'd seen. Now it felt even worse to tell her about my days, and I became more and more secretive. Beverly saw the obsession growing in me. Finally she told me I was becoming as fanatical as the people at Alcor, that I was becoming a "whistle-blowing junkie." She said I was taking it too far. In return, I began seeing Beverly as a liability. I feared that Alcor could somehow use her against me if the company found out what I was doing.

Beverly decided to get a job. The extra money would be nice but mostly I think Beverly wanted some human contact. She was lonely. Maybe she just wanted to spend some time away from me, as well. I couldn't blame her.

And now, whenever I rode my Harley, I did so by myself. No more weekend rides in the desert with my wife, no more picnics by the lake. Now I rode to be alone, to organize my investigation and plan the next day's recordings. Beverly and I had never gone out much with other people but now we lost any semblance of a social life.

Beverly and I became little more than roommates. When she wasn't working, she was spending more and more time in the bedroom, alone. I would come home from Alcor, download the files onto my computer, put my headphones on, and quietly obsess into the night. My dinner would be in the oven. Beverly would eat in bed, alone, and then fall asleep watching TV. I slept mostly at my desk and only for a few hours in the early morning. I had been averaging two or three hours' sleep every night for eight weeks. There was so much to do—recordings to listen to, files to send off to John Heer. And there were the nightmares. I would wake up, frightened, shower, and go straight back to Alcor.

And still I didn't feel like I had enough to show for it.

July 5, 2003, approached, the first anniversary of Ted Williams's death. It drove me. I was more than focused, I was fixated. I was pushing harder and harder, sleep deprived, spiraling.

But finally, I struck gold.

FIFTEEN

"HE KILLED HER"

On July 3, 2003, I was at my wit's end. My investigation was threatening to break up my marriage and drive me mad. I had developed yet one more nervous tick. Now I had a habit of bending my head down and running my fingers through my hair. I was looking to see if the mic was sticking out again—even when I wasn't at work, even when I wasn't recording.

The long Fourth of July weekend was here and I resented it. I resented the idea of three torturous days at home, unable to think about anything except finding out the truth about Alcor. I dreaded being away from the office. Now it was two days until the first anniversary of Ted Williams's death. When would it end? I needed to take matters into my own hands and force the situation.

I wired myself up and marched into Joe Hovey's office. He was one of the longest-serving Alcorians and seemed to know the entire history of the place. He also knew that people around the office were plotting and planning to oust him. Maybe these shifting sands would make him eager to have a friendly conversation with me.

I started off by telling Joe that Charles had mentioned Mike Darwin and the John Dentinger incident to me. I led him to believe I knew more than I actually did. Still, Joe wasn't exactly keen at first to volunteer information about homicide.

So I changed tack and hoped to steer the conversation back to the subject of the suspicious deaths in a roundabout way. I asked Joe about Keith Henson, a former Alcor board member. Joe had spoken highly of Henson to me in the past and I figured this might loosen him up. I already knew that Keith Henson had been arrested in 2000 by the Riverside County sheriff's office for making terrorist threats against the Church of Scientology. Ultimately he was convicted on a charge of "interfering with a religion," but instead of appearing for sentencing he fled to Canada and sought political asylum, which I guess is where he was when I was at Alcor.

I knew that Joe Hovey approved of Keith Henson's hate campaign against Scientology. I had heard Joe in the past refer to the group as "the scum of the earth."

I had also heard talk around the office and read a few online articles claiming that Henson's first wife, in divorce documents, had accused him of the hideous act of child molestation with two of his own daughters, though she subsequently declined to testify against him. Everyone at Alcor felt that Henson had gotten away with this crime. Regardless—and this made me extremely uncomfortable—he was considered a hero by most Alcorians, including Joe Hovey, for his battles with Scientology. I got Joe talking about Henson to break the ice. This is the conversation that followed, transcribed from my recording:

> JOE HOVEY: He [Keith Henson] was a great help during the Dora Kent affair when the county coroner in Riverside County, in California, really wanted to shut us down, wanted to destroy us completely. . . .
> LARRY JOHNSON: . . . Now is that the one that Charles was telling me about that, um, the one that, um, that Mike Darwin helped along with . . .
> JOE HOVEY: Yeah.
> LARRY JOHNSON: . . . with potassium chloride . . .
> JOE HOVEY: No . . .
> LARRY JOHNSON: Or was that a different one?
> JOE HOVEY: Oh, geez, did he tell you about that?
> LARRY JOHNSON: Yeah.

JOE HOVEY: Oh, that was later. That was one of the main reasons why
we . . .

LARRY JOHNSON: Before Dora?

JOE HOVEY: It was after Dora.

LARRY JOHNSON: After Dora?

JOE HOVEY: Yeah.

LARRY JOHNSON: So what did he do? Did he just . . .

JOE HOVEY: He killed her.

He said it, just like that. He was completely casual about it. It made my skin crawl. But to Joe, it was no big deal.

LARRY JOHNSON: Really?

JOE HOVEY: Oh, no no, not, uh, not Dora Kent.

LARRY JOHNSON: The other lady?

JOE HOVEY: Yeah, it wasn't a lady, it was a guy. . . . I forget his name. It
was in L.A. and it was in, I think it was in '92, late '92, something like
that. I can't remember his name.

I believe Hovey had been speaking about Dora Kent, but then he realized I was asking about John Dentinger. He was thinking about one suspicious death while I was asking about another. How many were there?

LARRY JOHNSON: Well, see, Charles had told me that, um, I guess he [Dar-
win] gave him a loading dose of potassium chloride and he said what
was the kicker to it was, I guess, was that Jerry Leaf, when he died,
had a note or something in a safety deposit box saying . . .

JOE HOVEY: Oh yes.

LARRY JOHNSON: Mike Darwin's . . .

JOE HOVEY: Yeah.

LARRY JOHNSON: . . . you know, committed a homicide . . .

JOE HOVEY: Yeah.

LARRY JOHNSON: . . . or something really bad.

JOE HOVEY: Yeah. He, oh man, this could take all day . . .

LARRY JOHNSON: Why would Mike Darwin do such a thing? I mean, he just got overzealous or . . .

JOE HOVEY: Yeah. Exactly. Mike is a loose cannon from the word go. He is a person who thinks his own needs, requirements will take precedence over all other institutions and all other individuals no matter what. At the same time, there's no question he's brilliant; he's very charismatic, he was president of Alcor, uh, he was very articulate, a great speaker, very effective presence on television.

To me, it sounded like Joe was describing David Koresh or Jim Jones.

LARRY JOHNSON: He just didn't have much patience when it came to waiting for somebody to die.

JOE HOVEY: Exactly. And other things as well. . . . Charles was the last guy trying to save him for being involved in cryonics somewhere.

LARRY JOHNSON: Yeah.

JOE HOVEY: And finally just Charles gave up on him. He just . . .

LARRY JOHNSON: Yeah, that's what Charles was telling me. He just said that, uh, you know, that he had done that and apparently he said it upset Steve Harris enough to where he wanted I guess potassium chloride pulled out of the . . .

JOE HOVEY: Yeah.

LARRY JOHNSON: I don't know if it was potassium chloride or vecuronium, one of the two.

JOE HOVEY: I don't know.

LARRY JOHNSON: That's exactly what Charles told me. He just said that he just, uh, was very impatient. He actually did it I guess in front of a hospice nurse or something.

JOE HOVEY: Uh, well, if you're talking about Dora Kent, I don't know.

LARRY JOHNSON: No, he said it was somebody . . .

JOE HOVEY: Now the other person was, uh, he did do it in front of, I don't know if it was a hospice nurse there or not, I don't think so, but I know it was another one of our members who was there who was engaged in the suspension. It was Tanya Jones.

LARRY JOHNSON: Oh.

JOE HOVEY: And he did it in front of her. And he asked her, "Do you want to help me in this?" And she looked at him, she says, "No, I can't do that." And he says, "Okay, I understand, I'll take care of it."

LARRY JOHNSON: She was smart. Yeah.

JOE HOVEY: Well, yeah. But that's when we decided—Alcor decided this guy's just too dangerous to have around.

LARRY JOHNSON: Yeah, that's, I mean, that's Dr. Kevorkian stuff.

JOE HOVEY: You know, look, morally I've no objection to doing that sort of thing. I think Dr. Kevorkian is a great man, but we live in a real world. We just can't do stuff like that. That would absolutely destroy us. That could kill us.

LARRY JOHNSON: Yeah.

JOE HOVEY: We're pretty secure in all this stuff because even though a lot of people nowadays know about it, nobody can really prove anything and if it came down to a court issue, you know, who's gonna say anything? Who's gonna admit to anything?

LARRY JOHNSON: Yeah.

JOE HOVEY: And it's deniable.

Deniable? Not for long, Joe.

As the conversation continued, we spoke even more about Mike Darwin. He was last known to be somewhere close to where Charles lived, between Ash Fork and Flagstaff up in northern Arizona, pumping gas at a desert service station.

Joe said that although Darwin was brilliant, he had become too embarrassing and politically problematic to keep around. So this was the reason Joe gave for Darwin getting pushed out of Alcor—not because other company officers were upset that he had taken it upon himself to kill off Alcor members before their time, but because of company politics. Joe lifted his chin in the self-important way most Alcorians did and spoke of the CryoWars, saying that there had been "warfare between different factions within Alcor" for control of the company. Darwin had been a political liability for the opposing factions—one led by Saul Kent, the other by Carlos Mondragon. Neither camp could afford to have Darwin around with all his explosive secrets. He was drummed out before he could become an embarrassment to them all.

So Carlos Mondragon and Saul Kent were among the others who knew about Darwin prematurely ending Alcor members' lives?

Joe spoke further, about cryonicists being "mountain men" and "libertarians," "hard-core" pioneers, marching into the future. They had to be strong enough to put up with "so much crap." Keith Henson could do that, Joe gushed. Then Joe repeated his opinion that the Church of Scientology was the scum of the earth and spoke proudly about Keith Henson defying them.

We spoke a little more about the Dora Kent scandal. Joe referred to the Riverside authorities as "Keystone Cops," gloated over the "stupid-ass coroner," and finally said, incredibly, regarding the Dora Kent homicide investigation: "We were lucky."

Joe was glowing, talking about the glory days of cryonics. At one point his mouth stretched into that creepy plastic smile of his and he said, "This whole thing would make a wonderful extended soap opera."

I remember that Fourth of July with great regret. Beverly and I barbecued some steaks and my dad came over after his wife, Mary Jane, fell asleep early. I was completely on edge. Bev and my dad talked while I was pretty much silent the entire time. My dad asked me what was wrong. "Nothing" was all I'd say. After dinner they sat down to watch fireworks on TV. I sat down at my computer, alone, with my headphones on, listening to Joe Hovey say, "He killed her," over and over. The next thing I knew, my dad had gone home and Beverly was already asleep. In my obsession, I was blind to how terribly wrong it was of me to ignore and alienate the people who loved me. All I could think about was getting back to Alcor and recording more and more.

I started carrying my gun on me at work.

I walked in there the following Monday with the recorder hidden under my shirttail and my 9mm Beretta tucked deep into the back of my pants.

Anxious as I was, I constantly feared the gun or the recorder would go clattering onto the floor. However, I felt like I needed them both.

I approached Hugh Hixon, seeking corroboration regarding John Dentinger's suspicious death. I had learned a sort of whistle-blowing lesson from my recent recording of Joe Hovey: get these guys talking about something they're comfortable with, then ease into the darker issues. Hugh loved talking about Alcor's procedures, so I started off by getting him to talk about the vecuronium and other dangerous drugs stored all around Alcor.

> HUGH HIXON: Our biggest problem [during the first stages of cryo-
>   suspension] . . . was you get into the question of somebody reviving. . . .
> LARRY JOHNSON: Oh, okay.
> HUGH HIXON: So we used a two-prong approach. A very long time ago
>   we used bars of potassium chloride, now we use . . .
> LARRY JOHNSON: Was that just to pretty much to stifle the cardiac, um, the
>   chances of coming back?
> HUGH HIXON: It was to kill them . . .

Oh my God.

> LARRY JOHNSON: Yeah, pretty much.
> HUGH HIXON: . . . to put them down and make sure they stayed that way
>   rather than, "Hey, he's awake, get him back on the pump, guys!"
> LARRY JOHNSON: Oh, okay, I'm with ya. Yeah, I remember . . .
> HUGH HIXON: We did not want anyone waking up and causing problems.

That was what Hugh called saving a person's life. That was what, as a paramedic, I had done for twenty-five years before coming to this place.

> LARRY JOHNSON: Yeah, Joe was telling me the other day, about an incident
>   involving Mike Darwin where I guess he kinda helped somebody
>   along a little bit.
> HUGH HIXON: Yeah.
> LARRY JOHNSON: What, who was the patient? Was it . . . It had to happen a
>   long time ago.

HUGH HIXON: You'll excuse me if I don't name names.

LARRY JOHNSON: That's okay.

HUGH HIXON: We had a guy, in fact I was in charge of the fucking transport.

LARRY JOHNSON: Figures.

HUGH HIXON: Anyway, his name escapes. . . . Couldn't set up in the guy's living room 'cause we couldn't get it [Alcor's MALSS cart—an operating table on wheels] past the fucking doorway without knocking down a wall, [laughter] so what we did was, we had this garage up the street and, and you know it was well ventilated, you could look up and see the sky through the roof. We . . . put plastic drop cloths and lightweight wood and a little bit of twine and we built ourselves a little operating suite in the garage. And anyway this guy didn't need hydrating and he was unconscious. And it got a little too close a little too fast, so we pumped another liter or so of IV solution in him and brought him back from that edge.

Hugh seemed to be saying that they had kept Dentinger alive temporarily because they weren't prepared yet for his suspension.

HUGH HIXON: (continuing) And we got set up there. When things started looking real tight, we got him downstairs. We had to carry him. I forget which end I had. I think he was on my back. Got him onto a gurney, took him up the street to the garage, and got him tucked in. And we waited. And we waited quite a while. He was not very far away from dying . . .

LARRY JOHNSON: So did Mike just get impatient and? . . .

HUGH HIXON: He got . . . well, it's a little hard to determine what the hell Mike's reasons were. You know, there's real reasons, then there's reasons he gave . . . plus there were other considerations too. Traffic was a problem.

So, in part, Mike Darwin wanted to kill John Dentinger in order to avoid traffic.

LARRY JOHNSON: Yeah. So was it in California, L.A. or something?

HUGH HIXON: Could have been.

Hugh continued being coy, not wanting to name names.

LARRY JOHNSON: Okay.

HUGH HIXON: . . . Anyway so, um, Mike asked Tanya Jones for some
Metubine iodide [one brand name of metocurine iodide, a neuro-
muscular blocking agent used to induce skeletal muscle
relaxation] . . .

She didn't know what it was for and a couple other people did notice and Mike gave it [injected it], and after about another seven or
eight minutes he [John Dentinger] quit breathing, which was entirely
to be expected.

I took this to mean that, along with Hugh, there were "a couple other
people" present at the time who "did notice" exactly what Darwin was
doing. I wondered who they had been.

LARRY JOHNSON: Oh, was it a paralytic like vecuronium or something like
that?

HUGH HIXON: Yeah, that's the one we use. You can't get Metubine anymore. . . . And, uh, anyway so the guy quit breathing. Now he wasn't
very far from quitting breathing but . . .

LARRY JOHNSON: Yeah.

HUGH HIXON: We don't like that kind of thing. . . . Mike Darwin's philosophy is situational consequentialism, which is to say if he can get
away with it, he'll try it.

LARRY JOHNSON: Yeah. He seems like an interesting person. I mean, I've
never met him but I've heard a lot of stories.

HUGH HIXON: He's very smart but he has a tendency to leave chaos in his
wake. He's just totally disruptive.

LARRY JOHNSON: Well, I know Charles was telling me a story the other
day about him and about that incident and he said, I guess, the other

guy, Jerry Leaf, I guess, apparently left a note or something about it when he passed away.

Charles had indeed told me about this during our drive back from Saul Kent's house, and I had recently recorded Joe Hovey talking about Leaf's note. I had also heard that Jerry Leaf was the Alcor officer who had experimented on Saul's dog, Dixie.

> HUGH HIXON: That was actually something separate. Wait a minute . . . was that . . .

Now I could tell that Hugh was trying to remember which premature death Jerry Leaf had written about in his note. He was trying to straighten out the confusion among several different homicides!

> LARRY JOHNSON: Well, Charles was telling me apparently . . .
> HUGH HIXON: Jerry was gone by that time. Jerry had been suspended by that time.
> LARRY JOHNSON: By the time . . .
> HUGH HIXON: . . . so this case was not the issue.
> LARRY JOHNSON: Oh, okay.
> HUGH HIXON: It was an earlier one which . . .
> LARRY JOHNSON: So it was after Jerry had died. So Jerry [Leaf] was referring to a totally different, different deal.
> HUGH HIXON: Yeah.

This was incredible! How many suspicious deaths had there been?!

> LARRY JOHNSON: It happened I guess way after the Dora Kent thing then, right—that was, when you were telling me the story the other day . . .
> HUGH HIXON: Dora Kent was in '86, '87; this was in about . . . must've been '93 . . .
> LARRY JOHNSON: Around '93?
> HUGH HIXON: Yeah. Anyway, so this is particularly annoying since Mike Darwin was always vociferous about our people not being left in the

room with patients alone and here he is, he pulls the exact fucking
stunt and then he tells me about it, which leaves me with really no re-
course but to . . .

Larry Johnson: So what did you say? How'd you . . .

Hugh Hixon: I told Carlos Mondragon, who was the president at the
time. And that is one of the other reasons that Mike Darwin quit
working for us.

Hugh spoke next about Mike Darwin being unstable and about him
"curling up in a ball" during the Dora Kent scandal. Then Hugh came
back around to the death of John Dentinger:

Hugh Hixon: Anyway, so that's what, uh . . . It wasn't anything that
wasn't gonna happen but . . . we did beat the traffic.

Larry Johnson: Yeah.

Hugh Hixon: But it was . . . very irritating. I had noticed what was going
on but I didn't realize what he'd asked her for was vecuronium.

Hugh was saying that he had seen Darwin make the injection but he
hadn't known what drug was in the syringe until Darwin told him.

Larry Johnson: Oh, he asked for vec or the other . . .

Hugh Hixon: Excuse me, Metubine.

Larry Johnson: Metubine. Yeah . . . Yeah, for some reason I was thinking, you know because, what even got me thinking about it was
Charles had told me this story awhile back . . .

Hugh Hixon: You will find . . .

Larry Johnson: . . . and I found some drugs on an old drug list that just
was kind of wild and that kind of raised . . .

Hugh Hixon: Well, Mike didn't use potassium chloride, he used
Metubine.

Larry Johnson: Metubine . . .

Hugh Hixon: The reason we used Metubine, ah, it was part of a—he actually had thought this out, talked around about it. Hicker can't keep
his mouth shut, he did it because it was part of our protocol, and

what it does, it would prevent shivering and while we're busy with cooldown, on life support . . .

LARRY JOHNSON: Yeah.

Improbably enough, Hugh was telling me that they gave the member Metubine because they didn't want him shivering while he was being frozen alive.

> HUGH HIXON: So there's perfectly good reason to use it and it is impossible to tell whether it was administered before or after because the two events were pretty damn close.
>
> LARRY JOHNSON: Close, yeah, so it's hard to detect.
>
> HUGH HIXON: Well it isn't hard to detect but you cannot tell when it was administered.

So the real reason Darwin specifically used Metubine iodide was that even with an autopsy, experts could not tell if it had been administered before or after clinical death. Darwin had "thought this out" beforehand and even "talked around about it." It was completely premeditated. Unbelievable.

> LARRY JOHNSON: So I guess what's her name . . . what is her name, um, Tanya Jones. So she was there, but she just wasn't comfortable there, didn't really . . .
>
> HUGH HIXON: Well, she, she was doing what Mike asked her to.
>
> LARRY JOHNSON: I think if I'd have been her I'd have . . .
>
> HUGH HIXON: Mike was doing what he damn well pleased.
>
> LARRY JOHNSON: If I had been her, I think I would've left the room.
>
> HUGH HIXON: Mike was one of the surgeons and I was the other. We did the cutdown, the bypass cutdown right there [in the garage] and washout and I don't remember how the hell it went. . . . Took us ninety minutes to get in 'cause Darwin was trying to play surgeon and not do any damage, so we were, we got tangled down here [Hugh indicated his groin area, where the femoral artery is]. I didn't know as

much as I do now about the situation there. This is before we started getting better on our surgery, so anyway . . .

Our conversation continued for another ten minutes or so about the surgery, the drugs they used, and the letter Jerry Leaf allegedly left in the safety-deposit box describing Darwin making the lethal injection that ended Dora Kent's life.

I sort of tuned out, though. As soon as Hugh said they used potassium chloride "to kill them . . . to put them down and make sure they stayed that way," it became harder and harder for me to stay in the room. But then when he said, "We did not want anyone waking up and causing problems," I knew I had to stifle my revulsion and keep digging, trying to get him to be even more specific about the case of John Dentinger. And he had obliged.

Hugh had come right out and said Darwin gave Dentinger the injection that ended his life. Apparently, Hugh had been present during the entire incident and even told me there were a couple other people in the room who "did know about it." At the moment he witnessed the injection, Hugh didn't know exactly what was in the syringe until Darwin told him later that it was Metubine.

Hugh had also said that Darwin didn't want any Alcorians left alone with patients but then "he pulls the exact fucking stunt," which seemed to mean either killing members like this was something they had had experience with in the past or that it was something other Alcorians were willing to do.

It was all very scary and shocking to listen to, especially the casual way that Hugh spoke about it. Joe Hovey had been just as casual when he had said a few days earlier, "He killed her." Killing off Alcor members was nothing new to these guys. Joe had preferred talking about Keith Henson, and Hugh had preferred chatting about the drugs. To Joe and Hugh, the apparent homicides were trivial, mentioned only in passing.

Like his colleagues, Hugh wanted me on his side in the CryoWars. I believed he was telling me the truth, at least as well as he remembered it. He had nothing to gain by lying to me about all this, so many years after the fact. Darwin wasn't around anymore; it wasn't as if Hugh would gain some advantage by setting me against Darwin. No, in my opinion, Hugh had let his guard down and simply took me deeper and deeper into his confidence in the course of this conversation. By tending to Hugh's health problems early in my tenure at Alcor, I believe I had gained his trust. We had had frequent discussions about Alcor's procedures. During all those talks I only ever found Hugh to be straightforward with me. This time it felt the same way.

———————

I left work early that day. Beverly was surprised to see me. I couldn't tell her what I had heard. I was afraid of the effect this information would have on her, so I evaded her questions and basically kept quiet. I couldn't even look her in the eye. Hell, I think I was in shock, but my silence was one more brick in the wall I was building between us.

Bev shook her head at me. "Look at you. You're a wreck. Is this worth it? Larry, what do you think they'll do to you if they find out what you're doing?" she asked.

"Bev," I said, "I can't stop now."

She went into the bedroom and shut the door.

I did tell John Heer. He was floored.

"That's it, Larry," John said over the phone. "We have what we need."

But I wasn't convinced I should leave yet. I wanted more. I didn't realize then that this is a typical pattern for people who go undercover—in law enforcement and other settings, the covert operator often refuses to shut down his investigation. Sometimes an agent will even go rogue and refuse to come in from the cold. There was a lot about living this undercover life that I didn't know then.

John Heer told me he needed to contact the Los Angeles police. As an officer of the court, he explained, it was his duty to alert the police when he was made privy to evidence of a serious crime. The recordings I had seemed to implicate Alcor officials in the North Hollywood death of John Dentinger.

"You have to get out of there," John said. "The police may come knocking on Alcor's door. It wouldn't be safe for you. Plus, they could find you out at any time, Larry. Look what they're capable of."

Bev had said just about the same thing to me. They were both right. The problem was, I was taking it all personally. I felt duped; I was outraged over what they had done, what they were still doing. I knew how adept they were at lying, at covering up. I wanted more proof of the suspicious deaths, the environmental infractions I was sure they had committed, and Alcor's illicit actions in regard to Ted Williams. Plus, I had heard rumors of even more cases of euthanasia, ones that I hadn't been able to document yet. I wanted these people to be held accountable for everything they had done.

John had no choice but to contact the LAPD, so I threw my investigation into high gear, knowing the end was near.

I set up a meeting a few days later with Jerry Lemler and Charles Platt to address my OSHA concerns. Charles arrived early and accompanied me to Jerry's office. That caught me off guard and I was unable to record the meeting. Maybe it was for the best. They were looking at me the whole time and I was too nervous to try and hit the record button. For the first time, Charles read the memo I had sent Jerry several weeks earlier. He absolutely blew his lid. Charles screamed and ordered me to destroy the printed document and wipe the file off my computer's hard drive.

That night, alone, I plugged in my telephone mic adapter and called Jerry Lemler. I wanted to get him on tape reiterating what had transpired during that day's meeting.

JERRY LEMLER: Hello?

LARRY JOHNSON: Hey, Jerry, this is Larry.

JERRY LEMLER: Hey, Larry.

LARRY JOHNSON: Hey, uh, sorry to bother you at home. I got back as quick as I could from lunch and wanted to chat with you real quick and Paula said you had already gone home.

JERRY LEMLER: Yeah.

LARRY JOHNSON: You have a couple minutes?

ALCOR LIFE EXTENSION FOUNDATION
7895 E. Acoma Dr. #110, Scottsdale, AZ 85260-6916
(480) 905-1906 or (877) 462-5267 (877-GO ALCOR) • Fax (480) 922-9027 • www.alcor.org

Alcor's Mission: The Preservation of Individual Lives

Date: June 18, 2003

To: Jerry Lemler, CEO

From: Larry Johnson, Director of Clinical Services

Ref: Potential OSHA and Other Regulatory Violations

This is to reference past conversations with Charles Platt, COO, concerning potential OSHA and other regulatory violations. There are a fair number of issues that should be addressed regarding laboratory safety as well as the potential risks involving exposure to body fluids and blood born pathogens. These issues could be violations of federal and Arizona laws, including occupational safety and health laws and environmental regulations.

As it stands today there really are no guidelines that employees at Alcor can follow regarding lab safety. There is currently no Personal Protective Equipment (PPE) readily available in the lab area. My greatest concern regarding the lab is that there is no access to an emergency eye wash station, which is an OSHA requirement for laboratories. See generally 29 C.F.R. Part 1910.

An incident occurred during the last suspension that resulted in the dumping of waste water on the ground behind the Alcor facility that contained human blood. I have mentioned in the past to Mr. Platt, that such disposal of biohazardous medical waste is a violation of federal and Arizona law and cannot be allowed to continue. See Ariz. Admin. Code Sections R18-13-1401 through R18-13-1420.

I would like to suggest that Alcor actively seek advisement on applicable OSHA rules and other environmental regulations that pertain to clinical laboratories, as well as provide in-service training for those actively involved in patient care who are at risk of body fluid exposure.

Please come see me, should you have any question regarding these issues. I am more than willing to help Alcor comply with OSHA and EPA regulations.

My OSHA memo to Alcor's President and CEO, Jerry Lemler.

JERRY LEMLER: Yeah, sure.

LARRY JOHNSON: Hey, I just wanted to tell you, you know earlier when we had our talk with Charles about the OSHA thing, I didn't mean to, like, set him off or anything. You know, regarding that memo that I gave you.

JERRY LEMLER: Oh, okay, I didn't even know a thing about it. I didn't know whether he knew about it or not.

LARRY JOHNSON: Yeah, yeah, he did, but I think he kind of in a way took offense to it when he told you to, you know, to shred the document and for me to get rid of it off my hard drive.

JERRY LEMLER: Right.

LARRY JOHNSON: You know, I just wanted to say that I didn't really mean to . . . I didn't think it would make him angry like that.

JERRY LEMLER: No, I wouldn't have expected that either, quite frankly.

LARRY JOHNSON: Yeah, so it just kind of surprised me 'cause I was just wanting basically just to kind of call your attention to it.

JERRY LEMLER: Sure.

LARRY JOHNSON: You know, the conversations Charles and I had, you know, he told me it was common practice that they . . .

JERRY LEMLER: Right.

LARRY JOHNSON: . . . you know, dump human waste behind the building.

JERRY LEMLER: Well, maybe I shouldn't have brought it up in the context in what I did. I was just trying to clear the deck of as many unfinished items as I possibly could.

LARRY JOHNSON: Yeah, yeah.

JERRY LEMLER: Yeah.

LARRY JOHNSON: So I'm gonna try to come up with some suggestions to Charles about, you know, dumping blood and all that other in our backyard.

JERRY LEMLER: Okay.

LARRY JOHNSON: I just, I just didn't know that . . . 'cause the incident was kinda common practice, I didn't know—I had only seen that one time.

JERRY LEMLER: Right.

LARRY JOHNSON: Anyways, I just wanted to tell you that wasn't my intention.

JERRY LEMLER: Okay, sure, I understand and I appreciate you clearing that up for me.

I hung up with Jerry and immediately called Charles.

LARRY JOHNSON: . . . Earlier when we had the meeting with Dr. Lemler and he showed you that memo I wrote about the OOI LA stuff, I didn't mean for that to upset you.

CHARLES PLATT: No, it only upset me in that it was written down.

LARRY JOHNSON: Yeah. I went ahead and did, you know, as you requested.

CHARLES PLATT: Okay.

LARRY JOHNSON: I wiped it off my hard drive and I guess Jerry shredded it. But I, uh, it was just an issue that I, you know, wanted to talk to Jerry about because you and I had talked about it in the past and I just wanted to make sure that he knew that, you know, eventually we have to do something 'cause we can't, you know, dump human waste in the backyard.

CHARLES PLATT: I know. No, every time it happens it makes me very nervous because you know there could be some *National Enquirer* photographer with infrared film or something. Who the hell knows?

LARRY JOHNSON: Yeah. Yeah, it's just one of those things that, um . . .

CHARLES PLATT: It should be, it should be, it should be better. I . . . I don't know what the correct procedure would be. Whether you can filter or what.

LARRY JOHNSON: Well, I'm just familiar with the systems that hospitals use, utilizing containment tanks that are buried in the ground.

CHARLES PLATT: Right.

LARRY JOHNSON: And then they contract with a service every once in a while to come pump that stuff out.

CHARLES PLATT: I guess we could have a containment tank which is just not buried in the ground.

LARRY JOHNSON: Yeah. So I don't know as far as human waste and stuff, you know, dumping it in the back, it's just a matter of time before . . .

CHARLES PLATT: Yeah, I agree.

LARRY JOHNSON: . . . somebody sees that. . . . Okay, well, I just wanted to make sure that you were okay. I didn't want to upset you or anything over it. It wasn't my intention.

CHARLES PLATT: No, it didn't bother me.

It didn't bother Charles that they were illegally dumping tainted blood and dangerous chemicals. But it did bother him that they might get caught, that I had written it down, and that there might be "some *National Enquirer* photographer with infrared film" back there.

A week or so later, I watched Hugh Hixon transfer Ted Williams's head out of the CryoStar. Alcor had been unsuccessful, as expected, in getting another dime out of John Henry Williams, but the company officers finally felt secure that no one was going to come to try to take Ted's head away from them.

There was a crowd of people in the room, all of us craning our necks to see. The air conditioning inside the facility was malfunctioning again—another problem Alcor dealt with by simply ignoring it—and it was a typical desert summer day. It was damn hot in there. It took Hugh a few minutes to remove the padlock and heavy security chain that was wrapped around the CryoStar, safeguarding Ted's head. Hugh had already set the tuna can at the bottom of the LR-40. They didn't want the head outside the freezers too long, so Hugh donned insulated gloves, lifted Ted Williams's head out of the CryoStar by its neck handle, and ran across the room dodging audience members like Emmitt Smith running for a touchdown. I never saw him move so fast. The onlookers jostled each other for a better view but Hugh moved too quickly for anyone to get a good look at Ted's head. As Hugh lowered the head into the LR-40 and onto the BumbleBee tuna can, another Alcorian was already opening up the valve on the liquid nitrogen tank that fed the LR-40. It was a very quick transfer, taking less than a minute.

Jerry Searcy rushed into the room just as they were wrapping the LR-40's lid in silver duct tape and said, "I missed it? Goddamn it, why didn't anybody wake me up?"

Heads were usually kept in the LR-40 for three days as they gradually cooled down to −321 degrees Fahrenheit. During Ted Williams's cooldown, Hugh Hixon distributed an e-mail to the Alcor board members and staff reporting that "A-1949 has had nine cracking events in the first 35 hours of cool-down." Later, he wrote that A-1949's head suffered a total of sixteen cracks during the cooling process.

At the end of several days of cooling, I watched Hugh Hixon and Mike Perry transfer A-1949 from the LR-40 into the Neuro Vault. The transfer was not announced to Alcor's volunteers, so this time there was no big crowd of gawkers.

While Mike Perry was fiddling with the Crackphone, Mathew Sullivan came into the Patient Care Bay, all smiles, carrying the Neuro Can he had prepared in Alcor's metal shop. This was the lobster pot–type vessel Ted's head would be permanently stored in. Mathew had stenciled "A-1949" and "NC58" on the side. Inside, the silver can was lined with a nice, soft pillowcase. The lid sported a red plaque Mathew had engraved in white letters:

> Theodore Samuel Williams
> First Life Cycle
> 30 Aug. 1918 to 5 Jul. 2002
> A-1949
> S-1000000943

Mathew was so proud of the Neuro Can he asked me to take his picture with it as his own personal souvenir. That picture is in the photo section of this book. Then Mathew left the room to take care of some other preparations.

Hugh put on his insulated gloves, picked up a five-foot-long wooden pole with a hook at the end of it, and approached the LR-40 like an ice fisherman. He snagged A-1949 by the neck handle and lifted. I knew very well the identity of A-1949 but as Hugh hauled the upside-down head up through the white fog of the LR-40, the disembodied face set in that awful, frozen scream looked nothing like any picture of Ted Williams I had ever seen.

I'd encountered a lot of dreadful things in my days as a paramedic. I've dealt with decapitated heads at accident scenes. I've seen more than my share of faces twisted in the final agonizing moments of death. At Alcor, I had already witnessed three monstrous cryo-suspensions. Still, the frozen look of horror on Ted Williams's face was one of the most disturbing things I had ever seen. There was a tube coming out of his nose, a temperature probe. My childhood hero had become a pupilless, grimacing, upside-down bust mounted on top of a little round BumbleBee tuna-can pedestal.

Hugh grabbed the head by the handle and shook it vigorously to dislodge the tuna can but it was, of course, frozen on. Things tend to stick together at −321 degrees Fahrenheit, like hamburger patties in your freezer, times about a thousand.

Hugh lifted his leg and executed a few off-balance kicks, his foot whiffing two feet below the head. Then he grabbed a monkey wrench, heaved a mighty swing, missed the tuna can completely, and smacked the head dead center. Tiny pieces of frozen head sprayed around the room. I couldn't believe what I was seeing. Hugh Hixon was treating Ted Williams's head like some kind of grotesque piñata. Hugh immediately swung again and this time connected squarely with the can. Crack! The tuna can took off like a line drive, ricocheting around the room. Little gray chunks of Ted's head flew off, peppering the walls, skittering across the floor, and sliding under the machinery.

I was speechless.

Mathew Sullivan poked his head into the room, took one look around, and cracked, "Wow, talk about dandruff!" His rat-a-tat cackle echoed down the hallway.

Mike Perry's cat appeared, sniffing the air.

Meanwhile, Alcor's attorneys were trading memos back and forth from Arizona to Florida, discussing strategy for suing John Henry and the Williams estate for the outstanding $111,000 owed to Alcor.

To me, for Alcor to bungle a cryonic suspension so horrifically, subsequently treat the patient's body so disrespectfully, and then have the gall to sue for the outstanding suspension fees took serious nerve. Worse than that, in the last line of a memo dated July 11, 2003, one attorney wrote: "If you feel there are no options, then it may be appropriate to consider advising John Henry and his sister [Claudia] that it is our intention to terminate the suspension pursuant to the terms of the agreement, which, if necessary, would bring this whole matter to a conclusion."

Even the attorneys wanted to threaten the Williams family, saying that Alcor would unfreeze Ted Williams's body if the balance was not paid.

———————

The last meaningful conversation I recorded at Alcor was with Mathew Sullivan. I had heard that some samples of Ted Williams's DNA were missing. I called him on the phone:

> LARRY JOHNSON: Hey, it came to me, a question. I'm here at the house. I wanna try to relax a little bit before I go to the doctor's office.
>
> MATHEW SULLIVAN: Sure.
>
> LARRY JOHNSON: Have you checked with Hugh yet, regarding those missing samples of Ted Williams's?
>
> MATHEW SULLIVAN: Oh, yeah, I talked to him about that, uh, actually, A-1949 . . .
>
> LARRY JOHNSON: Oh yeah, that's right; "A-1949," don't mention no names.
>
> MATHEW SULLIVAN: Yeah, I did talk to him about that. He couldn't give me an answer.
>
> LARRY JOHNSON: Oh, okay, because when we were sitting there in the meeting I was thinking because he kinda putters around a lot back there, I don't know if he physically moves samples or not.
>
> MATHEW SULLIVAN: No, no, that's not something—you know, I've known Hugh for, geez, over eight years now, and Hugh has his issues but he wouldn't open up a can just to move things around.
>
> LARRY JOHNSON: Oh, okay.
>
> MATHEW SULLIVAN: So he has his weak points but . . .
>
> LARRY JOHNSON: But he wouldn't do anything like that.
>
> MATHEW SULLIVAN: Not on this particular issue, I would say no.
>
> LARRY JOHNSON: So how many are actually missing, do you know?
>
> MATHEW SULLIVAN: Well, see, that's part of the part that is confusing because, well, let's see here, I'm actually going through the paperwork now because I'm trying to get ready to do consolidation of transfers and stuff . . .

Later:

> MATHEW SULLIVAN: . . . based on the numbers that they were working
> with, there is a number missing: 164 . . . and 176.
> LARRY JOHNSON: So there's two samples missing?
> MATHEW SULLIVAN: No, there's more than that. What I'm saying is poten-
> tially of these two, those could have actually been taken before or dur-
> ing the suspension.

These blood/DNA samples were all drawn during the suspension procedure, so by "taken" Mathew did not seem to mean collected, but rather
"taken away by someone."

Later:

> LARRY JOHNSON: Those are all 1949's?
> MATHEW SULLIVAN: Yeah, 1949's . . .

Later:

> MATHEW SULLIVAN: I have no knowledge of what happened to those sam-
> ples . . . It looks like, based on the numbers I see, there's what, two,
> three, four, five, six, seven—eight samples.
> LARRY JOHNSON: Eight that are missing.
> MATHEW SULLIVAN: Yeah.
> LARRY JOHNSON: Okay.
> MATHEW SULLIVAN: Now if there is a digit higher—you know, it goes up
> to 182 based on the number system, there could be a 183 floating
> around, I don't know.
> LARRY JOHNSON: Yeah, that's true.

Later:

> MATHEW SULLIVAN: You know, I don't know what the deal is. They're just
> effluent samples, you know, arterial and venous fluids so—of course,

you know there could be, there's obviously other markers in there and even DNA, so I don't . . .

Here, I believe Mathew was saying that he didn't think Alcor had failed A-1949 or his family because there were surely enough redundant DNA samples should they ever be needed.

> MATHEW SULLIVAN: . . . you know . . . I just don't know what happened to them.
>
> LARRY JOHNSON: Okay.
>
> MATHEW SULLIVAN: Hugh did joke a little bit and say maybe they're out on eBay or something like that and then my response was, I said, well, actually Jessica and James did joke about doing something like that.

I thought back to a conversation I had had where James Sikes told me he had bought the Boston Red Sox license plate on eBay and then put it on the Alcor van to thumb his nose at the media. In all honesty, I wouldn't be surprised if Ted's DNA had been put up for sale. After all, according to Bobby-Jo Ferrell, that had been part of John Henry's plan all along, to sell off their father's DNA to the highest bidder.

Beverly and I were now continually snapping at each other. She saw the changes that had come over me and knew there was something I wasn't telling her. I had been sleep deprived and paranoid for nearly three months, ever since I had started wearing the wire. Now I looked worse than ever. In a moment of personal clarity, probably unusual for me during those few months, I realized just how much I had been asking of her during my whole homegrown investigation. It was taking a huge toll on me, but what about her? I hated keeping anything from her and she deserved to know. Hell, it was a wonder she had stuck by me so far. So I told her what I had recorded regarding the suspicious deaths; I told her both Joe Hovey and

Hugh Hixon had admitted to me that Alcor officers had prematurely ended the lives of at least two Alcor members.

I'll never forget the look in her eyes, or the way she spoke her next words.

"Larry, that's it. We need to leave. Now."

SIXTEEN

"FOR YOUR CRIMES AGAINST CRYONICS YOU WILL DIE"

Back in high school I had a very good friend named Greg Davidson. He taught me how to hang glide when I was sixteen years old. I kept that a secret from my mother.

To the east of Albuquerque are the Sandia Mountains, one of the city's signature features. Among all the peaks, there's one narrow point that sticks straight up, only about eight feet wide. Locals call it Devil's Thumb. I watched Greg land on and take off from it many times. It terrified and thrilled me at the same time. I needed to know what it felt like to do that.

I circled that little peak, looking down at it, summoning my courage. Then I took a deep breath, swooped down to about five feet directly over Devil's Thumb, and then pushed out on the control bar. The hang glider lost momentum, tilted back, flared upward, and then stalled. Gravity took over and I dropped like a stone. I bent my legs, ready for the shock, and, luckily, landed dead center on the peak. It was more like a controlled crash than anything and took great aim—but then it took even better balance. A hang glider gets real heavy and unwieldy when it's out of the air—if I had stumbled backward, even just a few feet, I would have fallen off the edge and bounced all the way down the mountain. People died every year trying to land on Devil's Thumb.

Landing on that peak was a frightening and exhilarating experience. The pinnacle of terror, though, was not landing on that small circle of rock. It was standing there, struggling for balance, knowing that within seconds I would have to take off from that spot again, before a strong wind came and pushed me over, backward. And there was only one way to do it. I'd have to inch over to the edge, jump, fall like a brick, and trust that my glider would catch air before I crashed onto the rocks below.

Jump, Larry. You can do it. Jump. Don't look down. Swallow, buck up, and jump. And fall, and fall—and hope to catch air.

Was it courage or stupidity? I'm still not sure. I think it was stupid to put myself on that peak in the first place. Skill and luck kept me balancing there. The courageous part was jumping off. Terrifying, but once I was there it had to be done.

Now I was balanced on a similarly precarious peak at Alcor. Getting myself to that point had been an adrenaline-pumping feat comparable to any I'd ever experienced. Keeping myself balanced had begun as an exciting challenge but quickly degenerated into a nearly impossible task with personal sacrifices and nerve-racking close calls along the way.

Now, I knew the Alcorians would come after me once they found out what I'd been doing. Some of them were filthy rich. Some were crazy. All of them would consider me a traitor. I always knew it would come to this. The time had come for me to swallow hard, buck up, jump—and hope to catch enough air to carry me away from the place.

I lost touch with my hang gliding sensei, Greg Davidson, after we left high school. A few years later I heard he had been killed in a hang gliding accident.

Jump, Larry. Jump.

————————

Soon after I told Beverly about the recordings I had made regarding the suspicious deaths, John Heer told me I needed to take a trip to California in a few weeks to speak with the LAPD. He had already arranged the meeting for me. The police would begin a homicide investigation into John Dentinger's death, John told me.

I agreed to continue helping in any way I could.

John also told me that the information I had gathered regarding Ted Williams would be invaluable in the efforts to get Ted's remains out of Alcor. "It is a gift," John said, "that you can give to Ted and his family."

So toward the end of July, I contacted a writer from *Sports Illustrated* by the name of Tom Verducci. He was very interested in what I had to say. I explained to him that it was my desire to expose Alcor quickly through the national media in the hope that their various misdeeds would then be fully investigated. I worked with Verducci for several days on the story. Though I had been faking it at Alcor for months, living a double life, this really put my acting skills to the test. It was extremely stressful to go to Alcor every day as if I were one of them, then work into the wee hours on a news story that would uncover the despicable ways they had desecrated Ted Williams's body. Honestly, it was terrifying.

Contrary to rumors later spread by cryonicists, I was never paid a dime for the *SI* story. I could have gone to a tabloid and gotten paid a lot of money for a story like that. That was never my intention. I wanted to see a story published in a respectable magazine. *Sports Illustrated*'s editorial and legal departments were sure to fact-check and double-check every possible detail of the story. Verducci and his colleagues took weeks on the reporting and the checking, which made the double game I was playing all the harder to sustain.

In early August, the time came for me to meet with the LAPD. Beverly accompanied me on the drive because it was also to be a scouting trip for us, searching for a hiding place, somewhere to run to once the story broke. Even though I had opened up to Beverly about the homicide recordings, things were still very strained between us. Though she believed I was doing the right thing, she had never chosen to be married to a whistle-blower, especially one revealing the homicidal tendencies of wealthy cultlike fanatics. As much of a wreck as I was, Beverly was suffering even more than I. Not a day went by that I didn't regret putting her in that situation. We made the five-and-a-half-hour drive mostly in silence.

I took Bev straight to some friends of ours who lived on a very private and secure property in Glendale, California, between Los Angeles and Pasadena (ironically, Glendale is the birthplace of cryonics, the same city where Bob Nelson "froze the first man," Dr. Bedford). It was the safest option Bev and I could think of at the time. We explained the situation to our friends. I'll never forget the looks on their faces—like they couldn't believe what I was doing. But they saw how scared Beverly was, and they knew we were about to leave our jobs, our only sources of income. Our friends bravely offered to put us up for as long as we needed the sanctuary.

I left Bev at our friends' place and then, as directed, I drove to the big police station in downtown Los Angeles.

I pulled the car into the parking lot and a man in a sport jacket immediately approached me, walking quickly. I was constantly paranoid about getting found out and Alcorians coming to harm me, so this guy set my radar right off. He was in his mid-fifties, with a medium build. He was already on top of me when I closed the car door behind me.

"Are you Larry Johnson?" he asked.

"Who are you?" I asked. I was 100 percent ready to fight this guy to the death.

He reached out and I swear, I was so jumpy in those days, I'm lucky I didn't just kick this guy in the groin for all I was worth. I looked down at his outstretched hand; his sport jacket flapped open, and I saw a holstered gun.

"Nice to meet you. I'm Detective Brian Carr."

Oh, thank God. But damn, how did he know who I was? This guy must be a friggin' supercop.

We shook hands and, breathing a sigh of relief, I followed Detective Carr inside.

The huge police station was decades old. We went upstairs to the homicide division and it was like something right out of a movie or an old episode of *Dragnet*. There were dozens of rickety desks all in one huge open room. Stacks of paper were piled everywhere. Detective Carr led me to a desk in the middle of the room and introduced his partner, Detective John Garcia. Garcia was younger than Carr, maybe in his mid-thirties. He was dressed in a white button-down shirt and slacks.

"We'll use this room over here," Carr said.

We walked toward a door and I noticed a small black-and-white picture on the wall. It was a shot of Charles Manson in handcuffs being taken into this exact homicide division room, with uniformed cops all around him.

I stopped to look at it. Carr said, "Yeah, this is the station where Manson was arrested."

"Actually," said Garcia as he opened the door, "this is the interrogation room they questioned him in."

That did not exactly set my mind at ease. Inside were a few chairs and a small table. We all sat down. The room was small and suffocating. The two detectives were very respectful and professional, but I could tell they'd seen it all. I could easily imagine them coming across as very gruff when they wanted to be. That and the dingy interrogation room made me glad I wasn't a criminal.

We spent about an hour in that room. Carr and Garcia were very inquisitive about Alcor. They had both heard about the Ted Williams / Alcor scandal in the news. I showed them a picture of John Dentinger's decapitated body and related the story of Mike Darwin euthanizing him in a North Hollywood garage. I also briefly described Dora Kent's suspicious death and cryonic suspension, to illustrate how Alcor had a history with this type of thing. Carr and Garcia seemed very interested and asked lots of questions.

I gave them a CD with the two greatest hits of my secret recordings, the one with Joe Hovey saying, "He killed her," and the one with Hugh Hixon telling me about the drugs they used to "put people down and make sure they stayed that way." There was no CD player in the room but both detectives said they would listen to the recordings very soon.

"Thanks for coming forward, Mr. Johnson," Carr said. "We're going to look into this."

I'd come into contact with dozens of homicide detectives in my years as a paramedic. I knew they were all overworked. But I left the downtown Los Angeles police station feeling hopeful. Maybe Detectives Carr and Garcia would really get to the bottom of the John Dentinger case.

Beverly and I returned to Scottsdale on August 6. I tried to make her feel better by telling her the cops were on the case, but again we mostly drove in silence.

Several days later Verducci called to tell me *SI* was going to contact Alcor officials within the week and invite their comment for the article.

"Are you ready to leave Scottsdale?" he asked.

It was happening so quickly. We were far from ready. We had an entire two-bedroom apartment to pack. I knew it had to happen, though.

MONDAY, AUGUST 11, 2003, 1:00 P.M.

Beverly and I were in the living room, packing, rushing to get out of town, when suddenly there came a thunderous banging on our door. Beverly screamed.

The banging was so intense, the molding was breaking off from the wall—they were literally bashing their way in. I ran to the bedroom. I felt like I was in a movie, running in slow motion. It was both surreal and terrifying—was this really happening? I was praying they wouldn't smash their way in during the few moments I was away from Beverly. I grabbed my gun from under the bed and rushed back to the room. I raised the weapon and inched toward the door. Beverly fell to the floor, her hands over her ears, and started screaming again. I put my eye to the peephole but the door was vibrating too violently to see out. Shouts came from the other side.

"Johnson, you motherfucking traitor! We'll get you, you son of a bitch! We'll kill you!"

Panicked shouts came from my neighbors. Suddenly the banging stopped. Silence. Then footsteps ran down the outside stairs. I rushed to the window and saw a man jump into a waiting car. I recognized him. It was Mathew Sullivan. The car tore away.

Beverly was on the floor, sobbing.

Sports Illustrated had called Alcor.

Beverly and I knew *SI* would be calling Alcor at any time, and we knew we were dealing with fanatics, but we just weren't prepared for this.

We were terrified. I convinced Bev that it was safer to hole up rather than risk fleeing at this point. God knows what was waiting for us outside.

We stacked every moveable piece of furniture against the door and barricaded ourselves inside our apartment.

Charles Platt left me a very disturbing voice message. He was crying, completely distraught. "I'm very upset that you would hurt me this way! I want to know why you hurt me. Why did you do it, Larry? Please call me. Just tell me why!" When I played the message for Beverly, her puffy eyes went wide.

"That man is out of his mind," she said.

The harassing phone calls began immediately. The phone would ring, I'd pick it up, and there would be silence. I'd hang up and it would happen again immediately. And then again and again.

Those geniuses at Alcor didn't have the common sense to block their caller ID. The incoming number that came up on our phone display was Alcor's main line.

TUESDAY, AUGUST 12, 2003

Before dawn, with Beverly asleep, I tucked my gun into the back of my pants and snuck out of the apartment to send Alcor my letter of resignation via certified mail, along with my company cell phone. I didn't want them having anything to hang over my head. Returning from the post office, I considered our options. Alcor was withholding my last paycheck and now I was without a job. Bev and I didn't have any savings. Things were looking dim.

One thing I kept brooding over was what I had gotten Beverly into. It was one thing for me to expose myself to danger, but it was unfair and wrong to have put another person, my devoted wife, in lethal jeopardy.

WEDNESDAY, AUGUST 13, 2003

I didn't know where to turn. I knew I was in for a long lawsuit and I knew, financially, I was heavily outgunned by Alcor—a real David and Goliath situation. In the heat of the moment, I made a huge mistake.

A few days earlier, in between packing our belongings and stewing in anxiety, I had started a Web site called freeted.com. Now, on Wednesday morning, I posted some pictures on my Web site and charged visitors a fee for viewing them. Some of them were shots of an Alcor patient taken during cryonic suspension. The photos were completely anonymous but very graphic. Out of the extreme stress of uncovering the hideous acts of Alcor's officers—and being in fear for my life—I sank to Alcor's level. I also gave them an avenue to attack me ("Johnson's just trying to make a buck off all this"), which they immediately jumped at. The photographs were on my Web site only a few hours before I came to my senses and took them down, but I'll regret posting those pictures for the rest of my life.

Alcor held an emergency press conference. Carlos Mondragon had rushed down to Scottsdale from his home in Oregon. Just like in the Dora Kent affair, he became Alcor's spokesman. Mondragon immediately set about bad-mouthing me to the press, calling me a disgruntled employee, a liar, and a thief.

He denied every allegation I made. He said Alcor had not committed any environmental infractions. He said he could neither confirm nor deny that Ted Williams was inside Alcor, but if he were, he surely had not suffered any indignities or mistreatment. He said Alcor never stored patients' DNA, so how could any be missing?

Off camera, Mondragon gave my home address to the press. A caravan of media vans invaded the parking lot of our apartment building. A mini-forest of satellite dishes sprang up outside my window. Beverly and I stayed inside and did not open the door.

John Heer's phone started ringing, as he had agreed to screen the press calls and interview requests—at least the ones that didn't come straight to my home phone. There were certain media people John felt we could trust, folks he thought wouldn't try to put their own spin on the story.

We had offers from Connie Chung, Larry King, HBO, Showtime, ESPN, and all the major networks. It seemed like every newspaper in the country had called John—the *New York Times,* the *Boston Globe, USA Today,* etc. We got calls from reporters as far away as Russia and Japan. There were lots of invitations from radio stations to do on-air interviews, and I

did a few of those without having to leave home. I gave one live radio interview over the phone for a station out of Florida, figuring there would
be lots of folks from Ted Williams's neck of the woods who wanted to
know what was really going on with Ted's remains.

John and I agreed it would be too dangerous for me to be on TV. With
a thousand or so cryonicists floating around the country, never mind the
threatening fanatics down the street at Alcor, we feared that my life would
be in danger.

When the nine o'clock news came on local TV, the lead story was a five-
minute report centering on yours truly. Bev and I watched it in shock. It
was surreal. It was the first time I heard myself referred to as a whistle-
blower. It felt very odd. The phone started ringing even before the TV report ended. Along with the harassing silent calls from Alcor, I was getting
more calls from the press straight to my home phone.

Then, Charles sent me an e-mail saying I should contact him immediately: "I am probably the only person whom it is safe for you to talk to at
Alcor right now," he wrote. I didn't like the sound of that.

FRIDAY, AUGUST 15, 2003

Newspaper makes for crummy toilet paper.

Beverly and I were out of all the essentials, including food. The phone
calls hadn't stopped. In fact, they continued even in the middle of the
night. Beverly was withdrawn. We hardly spoke at all. She spent hours sitting on the floor, rocking back and forth, stealing glances at the door, flick-
ing through the news stories about us on television. My hands were sore
from clutching my gun like a maniac, day and night.

We had been locked inside for five days. We needed supplies. I waited
until it was very late, tucked my gun into the back of my pants, and snuck
out. I was completely on edge. If so much as a cat had meowed at me
right then I probably would've shot it six times on instinct. I avoided my
truck. I was probably halfway nuts, remembering that Hugh Hixon was an

explosives expert, imagining they could've wired my truck to blow up. Avoiding the streetlights, I walked to a nearby twenty-four-hour convenience store and loaded a basket with canned soup, frozen dinners, and toilet paper. By the cash register were the magazines. I picked up a copy of *Sports Illustrated*. The top banner on the cover had a picture of Ted Williams and read: "WHAT REALLY HAPPENED TO TED WILLIAMS: He lived a life unquestioned in its greatness . . . in death, Williams is shrouded in unthinkable controversy . . ."

The clerk nodded toward the magazine.

"That Ted Williams thing," he said. "It happened right here in Scottsdale."

"Yeah, I know," I said.

"Those people froze his head. Can you believe it? That guy who spoke out against 'em must have some pretty big balls."

"Either that or he's really stupid," I said.

During the next few days, Alcor continued to bad-mouth me. Mondragon was now claiming I made up all these lies about Alcor because I was unhappy with my salary. Truth is, they had been paying me pretty much the same salary I had made as a paramedic, and I had accepted that when I took the job seven months earlier. Then he said I had absconded with company property. On television and in newspapers, including the *New York Times,* Carlos Mondragon accused me of stealing what he claimed was "over $1,000 worth of electronic equipment" from Alcor. This included my cell phone and pager. Man, did that upset me. It was a baldfaced lie. I had already returned those things to Alcor. In fact, Mondragon accused me of stealing these things *even though Alcor had already signed for them upon their return.*

Because I was in hiding, I hadn't been able to defend myself to the press, apart from those few radio interviews over the phone. It was really getting to me, though, hearing lie after lie coming from Alcor. I figured the whole nation must be thinking I was a crank or a thief, so I decided to give a TV interview. I was extremely nervous about getting in the open but I just had to tell my side of the story.

The harassing phone calls from Alcor had stopped. Beverly hadn't been outside for a week, and I had made only those two quick trips. The shades had been drawn down over the windows the whole time. It was just possible Alcor thought we had already fled Scottsdale.

With such a grisly story, and Ted Williams being one of the most famous athletes of all time, there was no shortage of television stations and news programs that wanted me on camera. Given their reputation, John Heer and I decided to go with CNN. The CNN guy on the phone told me there was a Phoenix TV station associated with CNN where I could go for the interview.

"There can't be any indication that I'm in Phoenix," I insisted. "You don't know these people. I don't want anyone to know where I am at all."

"Mr. Johnson, we understand. Believe me, we have a lot of experience with these kinds of things. We'll shadow you out, we'll keep the location a secret, no 'Live from Phoenix' text or anything on the screen. Leave it to us."

Once more I left my apartment, nervous as hell, looking over my shoulder, and I drove to the address he'd given me. It was a small television studio in downtown Phoenix, just like he said. I walked in the back door, as planned, and they were ready for me. The cameras were all set up facing a chair with one of those fake backgrounds behind it. And do you know what that background was? A skyline of Phoenix. All the landmark buildings and Camelback Mountain to boot. I found the lady in charge.

"What's that?" I said, pointing to the skyline.

"That's our background," she said.

"You're going to have to change that," I said.

"Why?"

"Lady, there's a real safety issue here. There are a few people who'd love to know exactly where I am right now. The people at CNN told me you were going to shadow me out and keep my whereabouts a secret. It's kind of dumb to tell me you'll keep my location a secret and then videotape me with the Phoenix skyline behind me, isn't it?"

"Uh, I suppose you're right," she said.

"So will you change the background?"

"Well," she said, "we're not really a big station. Let me see what I can do."

A couple minutes later she was hanging a thin white sheet over the Phoenix skyline. Let's just say that now my confidence was shaken *and* stirred.

I was afraid for my life by being there in the first place and they had set up a backdrop of the Phoenix skyline—only now there was the silhouette of the Phoenix skyline showing through a white sheet. The interview hadn't even begun yet, and they were already making life-threatening mistakes. This was being stupid in a no-stupid zone. I wasn't going to wait around to find out how else they might put Bev's life and mine in jeopardy.

I walked past her on my way out the back door.

"Where are you going?" she asked.

Without slowing down, I said, "Why don't you just type my home address into your system so you can flash it underneath me while we're on the air."

I didn't look back to see her reaction.

I don't mean to bad-mouth CNN. It was only the incompetence of the local TV station—mixed with my own paranoia—that wrecked the interview. Soon after, John Heer and I had a bunch of conversations with Bill Redeker of ABC News and eventually I agreed to appear on *Good Morning America*.

I told Bill about my experience in the Phoenix television studio. He was very kind and assured me they wouldn't make a mistake like that. He flew to Phoenix two days later. They set up cameras in a small conference room in a local hotel and Bill Redeker interviewed me live on TV for *Good Morning America*. I sat there, in the dark, answering Bill's questions. They kept my face in shadow, limiting my exposure to cryonicists across the country who might want to do me harm. I was very nervous but I also knew I was doing the right thing.

TUESDAY, AUGUST 19, 2003, 12:15 A.M.

Beverly and I were sitting on the floor of our living room, packing the last of our belongings, when suddenly someone started banging on our door again, pounding the hell out of it. A voice started screaming, "JOHNSON, YOU MOTHERFUCKER, WE'LL KILL YOU! YOU TOO, BEVERLY! FOR YOUR CRIMES AGAINST CRYONICS, YOU WILL DIE!"

I jumped up. I was still carrying my 9mm on me inside the apartment. I aimed my Beretta at the door, shaking in its hinges, and screamed, "If you come through that door I'll put a goddamn bullet in your head!" This was the ultimate threat for any cryonicist whose number one purpose in this life was keeping his brains intact for freezing. And I meant it. Little pieces of molding were flying off the door frame.

"Larry, get back!!" Beverly cried. "They might have a gun!"

Whoever was outside was twisting and bashing the doorknob, trying to break it off. Beverly was screaming, in hysterics. I honestly believed I was going to have to kill someone to protect my wife and myself.

Just like before, shouts stabbed out from the neighboring apartments. The banging stopped. Footsteps ran down the stairs. I stood there, my Beretta trembling as I tried to keep it aimed at the door. I heard a car squeal out of our parking lot. Beverly was still on the floor, now sobbing uncontrollably.

I knelt down next to her. My voice wavered as I tried to soothe her. "Bev? Honey? They're gone. It's okay, it's all right."

She recoiled from my outstretched hand, hugged her knees tightly, and started rocking back and forth, crying. She kept repeating, "Why, why, why?"

What have I done?

SEVENTEEN

ON THE RUN

Someone at Alcor posted my picture on CryoNet.org, along with my Scottsdale address. It was an open invitation to every cryonicist on the planet to come after me. Beverly and I were terrified to leave the apartment but we also knew we'd be safer in the long run if we left town. We couldn't stay indoors forever. Finally, we snuck out late one night.

Of the more than 620 Alcor members signed up for cryo-suspension at the time, approximately 70 percent of them lived in Southern California. So on the run and in fear for our lives, where did we go? Glendale, just outside Los Angeles.

You could say it was reverse psychology, that the safest hiding place would be the most obvious one. You could say L.A. was such a big city it was easy to get lost in the crowds. But the truth was Beverly and I felt alone and vulnerable. Alcor was withholding my last paycheck. We didn't know what else to do but turn to our friends in Glendale. I loaded my Harley onto the the flatbed of my pickup, and Bev followed in her car. Thankfully, we got out of Scottsdale without incident. I don't think we drove less than ninety miles an hour the entire way.

The property in Glendale was situated on a small hill on top of a larger hill—we felt better, taking the high ground. The roads were narrow and secluded. Drivers had to pull over to let oncoming cars go by. I would see anyone coming long before they got to me. The little guest house Beverly and I were in was behind a number of obstacles. There was a tall fence and a big wrought iron gate with several sturdy padlocks they'd have to climb over, break through, or shoot off to get to us.

Both my parents knew about my problems with Alcor. My dad was especially supportive. He offered to monitor the newspapers for me. He called me whenever my name was in the news, then clipped the articles and mailed them to me. I still have a stack of them.

Not long before I left Alcor I had told Dad what was happening at Alcor, that things were getting dangerous for me there and I was going to have to leave. He was 100 percent behind me. When the *Sports Illustrated* article was published, he read it and assured me I had done the right thing. He told me he was proud of me. I was forty-something years old when my dad said that and it sure made me feel good. You never outgrow that, I guess.

After the *Sports Illustrated* article came out, my dad reminded me of the story he liked to tell about the day I was born, in 1960. It was in a little town called Grants, New Mexico, close to an Indian reservation. My dad was in the waiting room. The doctor came out in his surgical gown and my dad says he knew right away he had a son. The doctor's scrubs were wet up on the chest. When the doctor had slapped my behind to make me cry, I raised my little pecker and peed all over him.

My dad remembers, "I knew it the day you were born. When you peed all over that doctor after he slapped you, I knew you weren't going to take any crap off of anybody."

Underneath his good humor, however, my dad was concerned. And I was afraid for his safety, too. Alcor knew where he lived. Above all, though, my dad believed in doing the right thing.

A big part of my taking the job at Alcor had been the opportunity to live close to Dad. Now our chance to finally spend quality time together was over. We each regretted that. I had just started to really get to know him for the first time in my life and suddenly I had to flee town, on the run from fanatics. I didn't think I'd ever be able to drive anywhere near Phoenix and even visit him again without being afraid for my life. What a huge disappointment.

My mother, who was living in Las Vegas, was even more frightened than my father. She worried about me, told me "those Alcor people" all sounded dangerous and that I should be even more careful. I didn't want her to worry, so I chose not to tell her everything.

Then there was Beverly's family. How can you tell your mother-in-law that you're endangering the life of her daughter by coming forward as a corporate whistle-blower and exposing the apparent homicides committed by fringe-science lunatics who'd stop at nothing to safeguard their own immortality? It sounded crazy. What is worth that risk? That's a struggle I continue to deal with every day.

Weeks passed, the worst of my life. I was never more than arm's length away from a gun. I had been obsessing over Mathew Sullivan and whoever else had been pounding on our door. I was prepared to do whatever I had to in order to protect Beverly and myself. I would rather be judged by twelve than carried by six.

I had become the hot topic in online postings on cryonics chat groups. I was dubbed "Cryonics Enemy #1." Cryonicists posted disturbing messages about me, accusing me of some sort of "attempted murder." I read them all.

```
X-Message-Number: 22349
From: "Omnedon" <Omnedon@          .com>
Subject: The seemingly disgruntled Larry Johnson
Date: Wed, 13 Aug 2003 22:34:22 -0400

I would think at this point, this Larry Johnson person would be hard
pressed
to find anyone that would succumb to any motivation to suspend him in
the
event of untimely demise.  Am I unfairly biased in this?

Whatever problem this guy has, he apparently has no problem risking the
potential futures of the current patients, and prospective patients.
Logically (not legally) it could be argued that this is tantamount to
attempted murder or some flavor thereof.
```

One of many disturbing Alcorian Internet postings against me.

Still fearing for my safety, I continued turning down invitations from Larry King, Barbara Walters, and many other interviewers.

There is an actual oath some Alcorians take to protect the lives of their defenseless, suspended comrades. Joe Hovey had told me about it on several occasions. To the faithful, the heads and bodies inside Alcor's dewars

This is a very scary article
August 15 2003 at 7:16 PM

Response to I wrote the whole timeline!

---

http://www.floridatoday.com/!NEWSROOM/indexkerasotis.htm

Make no mistake about it, my fellow cryonicists: this columnist, Larry Johnson, and the people allied with him, are trying to kill us. When we are declared legally dead, these people want to make sure we stay that way.

Another Alcorian hate posting against me.

---

were still alive. Since they believed I was trying to shut the place down—which wasn't even true—they considered me guilty of attempted murder. To them, I might as well have been holding a gun to the heads of people in hospital beds. And then, for the less altruistic and perhaps more deranged among them, I was guilty of trying to destroy *their own* afterlife, their heaven, their immortality. Many of them believed in it with cultlike ferocity. It seemed like something a guy could get killed over.

I didn't think any Alcor employee would have the guts to come after me. There were, however, over six hundred card-carrying Alcor members out there I had never met. In my experience the people who signed up for cryonic suspension were not the stablest specimens of humanity, not exactly happy-go-lucky types who'd be apt to just let perceived assaults slide. In fact, many were severely depressed and zealously dedicated to cryonics, to the point of fanaticism.

And then there was David Pizer and his cult at Ventureville, who stated on their own Web site: "We must be ready to put our lives on the line if necessary (as in the case, for example, of a physical threat to a cryonics patient)." They really seemed capable of anything.

The real threat though, it struck me, was from hired assailants. I had seen this as a paramedic. It wouldn't have cost much to hire a killer. This was greater Los Angeles, where crackheads downtown would take a gun and an address in exchange for a few baggies of rock. Spend a few years driving an ambulance in North Vegas working with junkie overdose victims and gangbangers, then tell me there aren't some scary characters out there who will ice a stranger for a few days' fix.

I e-mailed Rudy Hoffman and canceled my Alcor life insurance. "Greetings Rudy, by now you know I've left Alcor . . ." That's all I needed—true poetic injustice—to be offed by Alcorians and then they'd try to collect on the insurance policy. After that, I envisioned them also collecting my body. Can you imagine if they did suspend my body and then it somehow turned out cryonics actually worked?

Imagine how darkly my name would figure in the cryonicists' future. To the true believers, Larry Johnson would have the same ring as Judas Iscariot or Benedict Arnold. It would be a curse, something kids would call their little brothers, hoping to make them cry.

What if Mike Perry and Mike Darwin et al. were revived and in charge and decided to wake up ol' Larry? What would be in store for me? Perhaps an immortality of torture. Perry would slice off my scrotum with a razor. Darwin would conduct science experiments on me. Jerry Lemler would make me listen to his poetry.

Finally, after weeks of cowering and fearing for my life, I woke one day to realize that despite some scary moments—like the two times those fanatics had banged on our apartment door and threatened our lives—Bev and I were still alive and kicking. I'd been down too long. Now I was angry and though I wasn't about to start going on TV a lot or hanging out much in public places, I was determined to finally stand up for myself and start fighting back.

So when Alcor sued me, I found one of the hottest litigators in the Southwest and sued them right back. My lawyer was one scary-looking dude, a real attack dog. His picture on the Internet seemed to say, "Come on, I dare you to mess with me, go ahead!"

He and his associates did a lot of work under RICO, the federal law designed to battle racketeering and organized crime. If they were not afraid of taking on the mob, I figured, they would be okay squaring off against Alcor.

Carol, one of the associates, told me that Sid Horwitz, one of Alcor's attorneys, had filed a motion to keep me quiet, a gag order.

"Carol," I said, "you call Sid and tell him to stick that gag order up his ass."

Carol laughed. She said I must have spent some time in Texas because I tell it like it is.

I instructed her to find whatever legal term they had for that anatomical improbability and employ it as aggressively as possible.

Among other things, I was accused of breaking corporate confidentiality, though I had never signed a confidentiality agreement or a nondisclosure at Alcor. They said I was disclosing company secrets, like details about their secret chemical cocktails the rest of the cryonics world was supposedly jealous of. The truth was, whatever I had revealed about their "secret formulas" and techniques *was already posted on their Web site or widely distributed in their own newsletters.* Alcor's claim was ridiculous. In order to break confidentiality, my attorney told me, there has to be confidentiality in the first place.

Basically, Alcor was trying to save face by suing me. The one thing I hadn't returned to them immediately was a laptop. When Alcor had bought that laptop for me, I told Jerry Lemler I wanted to use it for personal as well as Alcor business. If I ever left Alcor, I told Jerry, he could deduct its cost out of my final paycheck. He had agreed.

Alcor made a big stink about getting it back. My lawyers and I figured what they really wanted was the hard drive. They probably thought I had been writing and e-mailing John Heer from that laptop. Maybe they hoped I had downloaded my recorded digital audio files onto it.

Even when you delete files off your computer, shadow copies may survive on the hard drive. A computer expert can often come up with those files, partially or fully. Alcor was full to the brim with computer experts, including Mike Perry with a doctorate in computer science. Alcor officials must have figured if they could get their hands on that laptop, they might be able to reconstruct my files and thus learn how to oppose me. They knew I had been bugging myself but they didn't know exactly what they had said on my recordings. That's why they wanted the laptop back so badly.

My lawyers and I did eventually give it back to Alcor. What Alcor didn't know was that I had swapped hard drives long before we were ever involved in civil lawsuits. The laptop wasn't even formatted. I would've loved to see them turn it on, all excited to do surgery on it, then see a single MS-DOS "C://" prompt blinking at them. Not even an operating system on it. Not even Windows 95.

Once they realized the hard drive had been switched, they sent the laptop back to my attorney. Then they claimed they had been withholding my last paycheck all along as payment for it. That last paycheck would have bought four of those laptops and to this day I still haven't seen a dime of it.

When Alcor returned the laptop to Carol's office, she called me again, this time to ask what she should do with it.

"Carol," I said, "I'd like you to call Sid Horwitz. See if he's still got any room up his ass next to the gag order for that laptop."

I was, however, afraid to start working again. Beverly and I didn't want to give out my social security number. We had been real careful about using credit cards. There were no utility bills in our name, no rental agreements or hotel receipts. Saul Kent, David Pizer, or another wealthy hard-core Alcorian could have easily hired a private investigator to find that kind of paper trail and sniff us out. In fact, I figured someone probably already had. It may sound paranoid, but in my heart I knew they were looking for us.

I kept a close eye on the media, obsessing over any news I found regarding Alcor or me. On September 29, 2003, about six weeks into our seclusion in Glendale, a story broke in the Scottsdale papers that Los Angeles homicide detectives were investigating Alcor's involvement in the death of John Dentinger. Things were heating up on that front.

Without leaving that guest house in Glendale, I did more telephone interviews for radio programs. I also spoke with a few newspaper journalists. Alcor continued bad-mouthing me and although I didn't want to go back on camera and definitely didn't want to clue them in as to my whereabouts,

I did want to continue presenting my side of the story whenever possible in whatever forums I could.

Meanwhile, Alcorians were still posting hate messages to and about me on their online bulletin boards. Some of these were very troubling and made me think the people writing them were, to put it lightly, not mentally stable.

```
X-Message-Number: 22633
References: <20031003090003.55265.qmail@rho.pair.com>
Date: Fri, 3 Oct 2003 17:49:26 +0200 (CEST)
Subject: LJ goes to Hell!
From: "D. den Otter" <otter2@███████████>

From: http://www.4degreez.com/misc/dante-inferno-information.html

Level 9 - Cocytus

This is the deepest level of hell, where the fallen angel Satan himself
resides. His wings flap eternally, producing chilling cold winds that
freeze the thick ice found in Cocytus. The three faces of Satan, black,
red, and yellow, can be seen with mouths gushing bloody foam and eyes
forever weeping, as they chew on the three traitors, Judas, Brutus, and
Cassius. This place is furthest removed from the source of all light
and
warmth. Sinners here are frozen deep in the ice, faces out, eyes and
mouths frozen shut. Traitors against God, country, family, benefactors
[and employers, especially Alcor!] lament their sins in this frigid pit
of
despair.
---

Ah, the "frigid pit of despair"...the perfect punishment for crimes
against cryonics. LJ, B*bby-Jo W*lliams F*rrell, R*ymond C*rillio;
Hell's
gaping maw awaits ye!
```

Another disturbing post against "LJ."

It wasn't "hell's gaping maw" I was afraid of—it was the fanatical cryonicists taking the time to write posts like this that worried me.

Thankfully, some non-cryonicists had used the Internet to comment on the situation as well. A loyal fan of Ted Williams launched a Web site called saveted.net. This fan contacted me via e-mail and told me I should check out the postings on his site. They included:

> This whole issue is so pathetic. I'm sure that every Williams fan is outraged!! Will his poor soul ever rest in peace?? I can only pray.
> —10/07/03 JPL

This lab should have never been permitted to operate. The name of the game is the same old thing, M-O-N-E-Y.

—10/01/03 EN

A tragedy like no other. Bring Ted home and give him and his first born peace. It will never be over for her as long as her father's wishes are ignored. One day Ted's other offspring will have to face their maker. I wonder if they're ready for that. I think not!!

—09/08/03 PF

As long as he remains frozen his great accomplishments are diminished.

—08/16/03 CJ

I believe Ted Williams should be buried (treated), as he wished. And his son should be charged with a crime along with his cronies, this is fraud.

—08/13/03 GH

It's a complete travesty what they have done to "The Splendid Splinter." Mr. Williams deserves so much more than the freak show he is getting. My condolences not only on his passing but also on his treatment after his remarkable life.

—08/12/03 TA

I am a family member, and I have to say there is nothing in my knowledge of Ted Williams to lead me to believe this is what he wanted after death. A terrible insult to a great man's life and memory.

—03/10/03 Family Member

Since there was so much negative news concerning this matter, we would really like to know if an investigation is in progress, and if so, what is the result? Thanks for your response.

—03/03/03 MM

Let's honor Ted Williams's wishes in his legal will for him to be cremated. This will has been ignored by his son and the courts.

—02/26/03 MS

I agree that this is a disgraceful end to a life that was so positive. With baseball being only one element of this true American hero's life.

—02/22/03 GB

Hello, I am writing to you regarding the website you have established for Ted Williams. While I do not know you personally . . . I would like to take a moment to thank you from the bottom of my heart, on behalf of my entire family. This is truly an injustice, not only by law, but by his personal wishes, which were known and stated to all of us. Retrieving his body from Alcor is all we could ever want to see happen at this point. . . .

We would love nothing more than to see justice brought to Ted Williams, not just the American hero, but also the man that he was to our family. I just wanted to express my appreciation to you and let you know that I am definitely going to file both an inquiry and a complaint form, and I thank you for keeping this story alive.

—02/21/03 SM

Those sentiments helped me a great deal. Scared as I was for Beverly's and my own safety, and after reading so many hateful and threatening postings about me, it was very encouraging to hear Ted's fans and family members thanking us for what we were doing. It inspired me to use the time I had on my hands, hiding out in Glendale, to organize the materials I had, listen again to my secret recordings, and further investigate the legal questions surrounding Alcor's possession of Ted Williams's remains.

EIGHTEEN

TED'S LAST WISH

Had Alcor been willing to break its own rules to get its hands on Ted Williams's body? It had taken three months for my application paperwork to go through before I was granted full membership, and I had been the acting COO of the company. How long had the waiting period been before Ted was granted membership? There was none. It was approved immediately—and he never even applied for membership himself. As far as Alcor was concerned, Ted Williams became A-1949 the minute his son signed the paperwork on the tarmac at the Florida airport, illegally representing himself under "power of attorney"—and then, by Alcor's own standards, the contract was invalidated by David Hayes, an Alcor representative, signing as "witness."

Right before I fled Alcor I had called the Florida paramedic who made a few bucks on the side working for Alcor during Florida suspensions and training sessions. He was not an Alcor member. After John Henry had toured Alcor and was feted at Jerry Lemler's house in 2001, John Henry never finished the paperwork but Alcor wanted it all in ink. So this paramedic was sent to Ted's house in Florida to get Ted's signature.

> LARRY JOHNSON: I was gonna ask you a couple questions when you and I last talked, not about the Howard stuff, but about the Ted Williams stuff we had talked about.
>
> FLORIDA PARAMEDIC: Mm-hmm.

LARRY JOHNSON: You, when you went out there, to see him, was that long before, you know, when he actually passed away? Was it several months or was it just right before it happened?

FLORIDA PARAMEDIC: It was several months before, it was probably like almost, almost a year.

LARRY JOHNSON: And Alcor just kinda sent you out there just basically to obtain his permission?

FLORIDA PARAMEDIC: . . . We never even got in to see him. We heard him, but we never saw him.

LARRY JOHNSON: So you never saw Ted.

FLORIDA PARAMEDIC: No.

LARRY JOHNSON: Yeah, so I mean, and I remember you telling me that when you were talking to his son, he just really didn't talk to you, he just kept putting you off and stuff.

FLORIDA PARAMEDIC: Yeah, that's all he was doing.

LARRY JOHNSON: Yeah, that's weird. I'm just kinda curious because I was reading some stuff on it the other day here. . . . So was he [Ted] just hollering from a back room?

FLORIDA PARAMEDIC: Yeah, that's all he was doing. You know, and I mean he was, you know, disoriented, so . . . I know before, Jerry had kinda asked me if there was, like, something that we may want to bring up, but, or whatever, you know . . . did he say anything or whatever, I'm like, actually no, it did more harm because the guy was not with it.

The purpose of the paramedic's visit had been to get Ted Williams's signature on the Alcor paperwork. Now the paramedic was telling me that Ted Williams had been disoriented and that John Henry had refused even to tell Ted who was at the door. Even from John Henry's warped perspective, the trip did more harm than good because there was absolutely no way the paramedic was going to get Ted's permission to have his body taken to Alcor after he died. *John Henry was keeping the very fact that he was communicating with Alcor at all a secret from his father.*

LARRY JOHNSON: Yeah, so he was pretty much out of it . . .

FLORIDA PARAMEDIC: Oh yeah.

LARRY JOHNSON: . . . and John Henry is running the show.

FLORIDA PARAMEDIC: Oh yeah.

LARRY JOHNSON: And he never came straight out and told you exactly what he wanted, he just pretty much ran around the house.

FLORIDA PARAMEDIC: Yup, that was it.

LARRY JOHNSON: That's weird.

FLORIDA PARAMEDIC: So, you know, when . . . John just kept on, you know, putting things off, putting things off. You know . . . He wanted something, and then he didn't, then didn't know what he wanted. You know, he had his friend who works for one of the county EMS there to come in too. . . . You know, he was just, it was one of those weird things.

LARRY JOHNSON: Yeah. You know, I'm just asking 'cause I was reading a bunch of stuff 'cause, you know, the anniversary of his death is coming up and we've already got the media pounding on the doors . . .

FLORIDA PARAMEDIC: Oh brother.

LARRY JOHNSON: . . . so, you know, if anything like that should occur down there, just plead ignorance.

FLORIDA PARAMEDIC: Yeah, yeah, "I know nothing!"

With his inflection he was imitating Sergeant Schultz from the TV show *Hogan's Heroes.*

LARRY JOHNSON: Yeah, "I know nothing." So, I don't know, it's just weird, it's a weird ordeal. I was thinking about that after you and I talked.

FLORIDA PARAMEDIC: Yeah.

So I knew that the Florida paramedic returned without a signature from Ted or John Henry. The two things he felt he knew for sure were (1) John Henry gave him the runaround, and (2) John Henry wouldn't let his father know that the people at the door were Alcor representatives. John Henry was keeping both sides in the dark—he wasn't signing anything for Alcor himself, and he wasn't even telling his father that he had been communicating with Alcor at all. That is a far cry from having his father's permission to freeze him, against his written will.

Before I had contacted John Heer, for six months after Ted's death—between July 2002 and December 2002—he and Bobby-Jo had mainly been disputing Ted's last wishes with John Henry, Claudia, and Albert Cassidy (the executor of Ted's will, who was on John Henry's side), not Alcor. Then Bobby-Jo ran out of money and was forced to give up the fight. Six months passed. Then, when I contacted John in May 2003—and during the next three months as I bugged myself at Alcor—John learned through me how Alcor had botched Ted's suspension, how he had been mistakenly decapitated, how amateurish Alcor's surgical practices were in general, and how apparently unethical Alcor's practices were in terms of the environment and animal experimentation, etc. And, of course, John learned of the suspicious deaths of Dora Kent and John Dentinger. Now, John realized, Bobby-Jo had settled the Florida probate litigation after being misled about what really happened with her father and Alcor. Perhaps these revelations could help get Ted's body released from Alcor and cremated as per his will if John could get the full truth from Alcor directly. John has always been very clear that he and Bobby-Jo simply wanted Ted's will followed. There was never anything personal going on. He was never crusading against Alcor.

In terms of the law, Alcor operated under the Uniform Anatomical Gift Act (UAGA). This legislation was passed to regulate organ donors and standardize how people may leave their body to science for research or organ harvesting. The intentions of cryonicists are pretty far from those of organ donors or future medical school cadavers. I think that Alcor manipulated the system and intentionally let itself fall between the cracks.

The UAGA requires that donors sign a Document of Gift (DOG) to prove their intentions for donating their bodies. In January of 2004, on behalf of Bobby-Jo, John Heer asked Alcor to present Ted Williams's DOG. Bobby-Jo had agreed not to object to the disposition of her father's remains anymore, but now she and John Heer were able to confront Alcor itself and pursue the real truth. I believe I've seen every document at Alcor regarding Ted's case, and I never saw his signature on a single piece of paper, certainly no Document of Gift.

Alcor's response was that since Bobby-Jo had settled the Florida probate litigation, she did not qualify as an "interested person" under the UAGA and they were not obliged to honor her request. John Heer told me he feared going down in history as the man who failed to get Ted Williams out of Alcor. It got to the point where I tried to be encouraging to John, a real role reversal from the days when he had called me, just to be reassuring, while I was "undercover" at Alcor. I told him it wasn't over. Like doctors, attorneys have to be real careful not to get too emotionally attached to cases. John for sure went over the line on this one.

I dug into my research even deeper, obsessing over legal documents, trying to help free Ted.

I researched current Arizona state rules regarding the disposition of human remains. Under "SECTION 8, ARTICLE 11. PRESERVATION, TRANSPORTATION, AND DISPOSITION OF HUMAN REMAINS" in the Administrative Code of Arizona's Department of Health Services I found:

> 2. Bodies in vaults
>
> a. A body kept in a private or public vault, including a receiving vault, longer than 15 days shall be placed in an airtight casket or other container. This provision does not apply to bodies kept in mausoleums or other places of final disposition where aeration or dehydration processes are used.
>
> b. A body kept in a receiving vault longer than 30 days shall be regarded as interred. At such time as it is further buried, cremated or removed, a disinterment permit shall be obtained.

Technically, it seemed to me that Alcor was violating state code in storing bodies in the dewars. Several paragraphs lower, another section read:

> B. When being removed, disinterred remains shall be deposited in a casket, or other container, so constructed so as to prevent any seepage of fluids or escape of gases or offensive odors. . . . The casket or container shall not be opened for viewing of remains, except in cases involving medical or legal investigations.

I had watched Alcor transfer heads, including Ted Williams's. There was definitely an "escape of gases."

One night I read the 2002 Arizona Uniform Anatomical Gift Act thoroughly and saw:

> On request of an interested person, on or after the donor's death,
> the person in possession shall allow the interested person to examine
> or copy the document of gift—Ariz. Rev. Stat. Section 36–847(B).

I called John Heer, actually woke him up in the middle of the night, and quoted him the passage. We had a new angle to help free Ted.

Bobby-Jo wasn't the only family member, the only "interested person," outraged over the condition of Ted's remains. A new challenge was brought against Alcor by John Heer, representing not only Bobby-Jo but now Ted's nephews John Theodore (Ted) Williams and Samuel Stuart Williams as well.

John continued requesting that Alcor present Ted Williams's Document of Gift through January and February 2004. In March, Alcor basically told John to get lost, so, on behalf of Bobby-Jo and the nephews, John initiated litigation against Alcor in Arizona.

Al Cassidy in turn sued Bobby-Jo and her husband Mark for breach of the 2002 settlement. Bobby-Jo dropped out of the Arizona lawsuit. John Heer continued the suit, though, claiming that the nephews had a right to see the DOG but Alcor was not presenting it. John won and after several court orders in August and October 2004, Alcor produced documents that it claimed constitute the DOG in December 2004.

True to form, Alcor had dodged and balked for months. When it finally released something, it was more Alcor paperwork signed by John Henry and Claudia. John Heer told me that what they sent him was a disorganized jumbled mess of papers. It must have been extremely frustrating for John. Even under court order Alcor was unable to produce anything with Ted's signature on it other than a poor copy of the oil-stained note that I'll describe later in this chapter. Unfortunately, no one had the money to pursue it any further. Regarding this point in time, John has said, "we knew Alcor didn't have Ted's signature anywhere, but we didn't have the money to fight."

Alcor's strategy of stalling and outspending just kept working. It was terribly frustrating for the people who wanted to see Ted's last wishes fulfilled.

The statutes of the UAGA differ by state. Alcor, the destination of the anatomical gift, was in Arizona. John Heer used the Arizona statutes, requesting that Alcor present its Document of Gift to Ted's nephews, who were obviously "interested persons." This was a perfectly valid approach on John's part.

However, a case could be made to look at it all in terms of the Florida statutes. Ted Williams died in Florida. That's where John Henry and Claudia lived at the time they made their "gift," and that's where Alcor took possession of the body.

In Florida, there was a statute in the Anatomical Gift Act reading:

STATE OF FLORIDA 2002 STATUTES
SECTION 765.512
(4) If the donee has actual notice of contrary indications by the decedent or, in the case of a spouse making the gift, an objection of an adult son or daughter or actual notice that a gift by a member of a class is opposed by a member of the same or a prior class, the donee shall not accept the gift.

Alcor had "actual notice" of Ted's contrary indications. According to the above statute, in that case Alcor could not accept the donation.

In fact, Ted's daughter Bobby-Jo had vehemently objected on the very day of her father's death. She sent an e-mail to Jennifer Chapman at Alcor several hours after her father died:

——Original Message——
From: [Bobby-Jo's e-mail address]
Sent: Friday, July 05, 2002 1:25 PM
To: [Jennifer Chapman's Alcor e-mail address]
Subject: Ted Williams

My name is Barbara Joyce Williams Ferrell, the daughter of Ted Williams. It has come to my attention that you and your organization may be in route to Citrus County Florida, to pick up my Father's body. I am letting you know now, "DO NOT go any further—I am opposed to this procedure and you are 'On Notice' at this time." John Henry Williams is not taking care of my Father's last wishes. This was never my Father's wishes, ever!

Barbara Joyce Williams Ferrell

No wiggle room there.

———————

During the legal battle against Bobby-Jo, one attorney representing John Henry and the Williams estate, Eric Abel, went from sleeping with Claudia Williams to living with Claudia Williams to eventually marrying her. Obviously, this was not illegal, but it did prompt the question of whether there might be some conflict of interest in that relationship. Albert Cassidy, executor of the Williams estate, claimed he once had a conversation with Ted in which Ted said he wanted to be cryo-suspended. Cassidy said he intended to uphold that request. Cassidy represented the estate, and thus represented John Henry's interests.

During my research I ran across a very similar court case from Santa Barbara, California, regarding a woman named Cynthia Pilgeram, the only person I know of who was ever pulled out of cryonic suspension. Cynthia had toured the Alcor facility in Riverside with her husband, Laurence, but she decided not to sign up. When she died, Laurence, a gung-ho cryonicist, had Alcor suspend her anyway. They performed her suspension surgery and placed her entire body in cold storage.

Cynthia's sister and some other relatives sued to have Cynthia's body removed from Alcor because they knew Cynthia didn't want cryonic suspension for herself. In her will, Cynthia left "testamentary directions for a 'Christian burial.'"

Laurence claimed Cynthia had revoked the will and instructed him to have her suspended. However, there was no Document of Gift specifically signed by Cynthia. The California Health and Safety Code Section 7150.5 dictates that the Document of Gift must be signed by the donor, or by representatives in the donor's presence. Laurence Pilgeram lost the case, appealed, and lost on appeal. The judge's final ruling was: "The will, as well as the other evidence credited by the trial court, demonstrate that Cynthia's directions for a 'Christian burial' must be honored." Her body was removed from Alcor and she was given the Christian burial she had requested in her will.

The Pilgeram situation was almost exactly the same as the Ted Williams case. What was the difference? Why did Alcor fight so hard to keep Ted but not Cynthia, dodging and stalling every court order it received? Cynthia Pilgeram was not famous. She didn't drive traffic to the Alcor Web site up from 5,000 to 600,000 hits per day in less than a week. She wasn't a heavy hitter.

The only document ever publicly produced to "prove" Ted Williams wanted to be cryo-suspended upon his death was a now infamous oil-stained scrap of paper brought forth by John Henry several weeks after Ted's death. It was allegedly signed by John Henry, Claudia, and Ted Williams on November 2, 2000, while Ted was in the hospital for pacemaker surgery.

Close friends of Ted's and sportswriters alike have accused John Henry of pocketing one of the autograph warm-up scraps of paper that littered Ted Williams's house, and writing the bit about biostasis long after Ted had practiced his autograph on it. Then, this theory goes, he persuaded Claudia—dubbed "Frandia" by the unsympathetic sports press—to

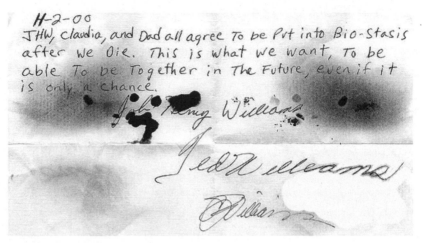

H-2-00

JHW, Claudia, and Dad all agree To be Put into Bio-Stasis after we Die. This is what we want, To be able To be Together in The Future, even if it is only a chance.

John Henry Williams

Ted Williams

Williams

John Henry Williams's "oil-stained note."

countersign it. Is this type of deception beyond John Henry? John Henry lied to his father about receiving his college diploma. He robbed a soda machine and set a cat on fire as a youth. He cheated on his final exam to "earn" his last college credit. And most damning of all, Ted's friend John Sullivan witnessed an occasion when a bank officer, at John Henry's behest, actually tried to get Ted to sign blank contracts.

Whenever Ted signed his name for an autograph, he signed "Ted Williams." Whenever he signed his name to a legal document, like his will, and like the separate letter he sent to his attorney requesting cremation, he signed "Theodore S. Williams." He was consistent on this throughout his life. I've done homework on this point. I've seen a number of legal papers Ted signed and I have never seen "Ted Williams" on any of them. This gives further weight to the idea that John Henry grabbed a stray scrap of "autograph warm-up" paper and wrote the rest later, without Ted ever knowing.

Opposite: Ted's signature on a legal document (top), and the signature on the oil-stained note (bottom).

John Henry claimed that the note was covered in oil supposedly because he had left it in the trunk of his car. I find it odd that he would treat

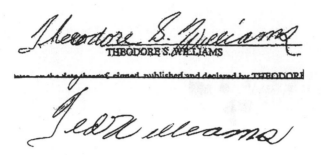

Ted Williams's signature comparison.

this note so carelessly when it was the only ostensible proof he could muster attesting to his father's wish for cryonic immortality.

If all that is not enough to throw suspicion on the oil-stained note, John Henry actually boasted, even to sports memorabilia dealers, that he could forge his father's signature perfectly—and then, laughing, proved it by signing a very convincing "Ted Williams" right in front of them. The value of Ted Williams's autographed memorabilia has suffered because it is common knowledge that many fakes exist—bats, balls, and jerseys signed by John Henry, not Ted.

Given all this, it is all the more shocking and ludicrous that Alcor officials had the gall to trot out that oil-stained note as part of the document package they claimed constituted Ted Williams's Document of Gift.

———

Frank Brothers was a caretaker of Ted's for years. He is a registered nurse and, like Ted, an ex-Marine. By all accounts, they became like family to each other. Frank was present when John Henry spoke with Ted about cryonics back in 2001.

Frank was making breakfast for Ted and John Henry: "[John Henry] brought up to his dad, about, you know, when you die, 'how about we'll freeze your body in cryogenics' [in quoting John Henry, Frank appeared the common mistake of confusing cryonics with cryogenics]. And Ted told him, he said, 'Are you crazy?' He said, 'Well, Dad, we don't have to do your whole body. We can just cut your head off and do your head.' He said, 'What are you, nuts?' You know, Ted was adamant about it. He didn't want to be frozen."

That's the version Frank Brothers provided in a CNN interview. More bluntly, according to what Frank told me personally, Ted's actual words were, "John Henry, you're out of your fucking mind! Fuck you!"

When Ted had been faced with the idea of open-heart surgery to install a pacemaker, he was given a fifty-fifty chance of survival. His response was, "You know what? I've had a hell of a life. I have no regrets. If I have to die on an operating table, so be it." Frank Brothers was in the room with Ted Williams and his doctor, and that is a direct quote.

Is this the attitude of a person planning on cryonic suspension? You don't hear many cryonicists talking about dying on an operating table. Other friends say that near the end, Ted spoke fondly, longingly of the idea of suicide. Is that the attitude of someone who wants to prolong his life? Sounds like someone ready to check out, not someone pursuing immortality.

Frank Brothers swears Claudia Williams did not hear of her father's hospitalization for the pacemaker surgery until November 4, 2000. This was two days after she allegedly visited him in the hospital and she supposedly signed the oil-stained note with Ted and her brother. George Carter, an eight-year employee of Ted's also working at Ted's house at the time, agreed with Frank's account. Claudia called them both on November 4 or 5 to yell at them for not alerting her that her father was in the hospital, saying she had just found out. Frank Brothers felt so strongly about this that he recorded a sworn statement.

How could Claudia have signed that note in the hospital on November 2 when she didn't even know her father was in the hospital until November 4 or 5? George Carter has written a similar sworn statement corroborating Frank Brothers's claims. These men have nothing to gain by coming forward like this—except to help their friend, Ted Williams, receive the cremation he wanted for himself. Unless both of these men are lying, there's no way Claudia could have countersigned that note in the hospital on November 2.

To whom it may concern,

On October 31st, 2000, I was one of Ted Williams personal assistants. Around about 10 or 11 o'clock that night, I experienced a problem with Ted Williams who had not slept for two days. Neither had I. He was experiencing chain stroke breathing, which is associated with congenital heart failure. At that time I called George Carter to come to Ted's house and assist me with him. When George arrived, he called John Henry, Ted's so, to advise him that Ted needed to go to the hospital. By the time we left the house, it was early morning hours of November 1st. George Carter and I drove Ted in his personal vehicle to the hospital. John Henry, Ted's son, followed us in his personal vehicle. Once we got to the emergency room, Ted was admitted in the hospital. John Henry advised George and I to get a room in the motel across the street. I registered us in the motel. After registering, I went to the hospital to discuss with George our working hours. At that time, I witnessed George Carter directly ask John Henry if he should contact his sister about their father being in the hospital. John Henry replied "No, I will take care of it." So, at the time I went to the hotel to get a few hours sleep. I returned at 9 a.m. of the morning of November 1st to relieve George. From that time on, I was with Ted in the hospital from 6 a.m. to 6 p.m.. George was with him from 6 p.m. to 6 a.m..

Then on or around, November 4th or 5th, Claudia Williams called George on our business cell phone. She accused George of not being her friend because she just now found out that her father was in the hospital, on the 4th or 5th of November. My question is then, how could Claudia have signed that piece of paper on November 2nd?

Sincerely,
Francis M. Brothers

STATE OF FLORIDA
COUNTY OF OSCEOLA

The foregoing instrument was acknowledged before me the 14, day of July, 2003 by Frank Brothers. He is personally known to me and did not take an oath.

TAMMY R. BASS
Notary Public, State of Florida
My comm. expires June 16, 2005
No. DD 033705

Notary

Frank Brothers's statement regarding the oil-stained note.

Furthermore, a nurse who was present at Shands Hospital when Ted underwent his pacemaker surgery on November 2, 2000, received a surprise phone call from John Henry on July 10, 2002, five days after his father's death—exactly when the media storm was howling its fiercest, with friends of Ted's coming forward on television and in newspaper interviews, calling the whole thing crazy, saying cryonic suspension was not what Ted wanted for himself. The nurse started offering her condolences but, she said, John Henry brushed them away. Over the phone, John Henry asked the nurse what date his father had had his pacemaker surgery and heart catheterization. He was referring to the November 2, 2000, surgery that allegedly inspired Ted, John Henry, and Claudia to sign the supposedly not-yet-oil-stained note. Yet, according to that nurse, *John Henry was not even in the hospital on November 2, 2000.* Other nurses at the hospital agree— John Henry did not visit his father that day. So how could John Henry, Claudia, and Ted Williams have signed the note that day, in the hospital, as John Henry had claimed?

The nurse, who was disinterested with regard to the Ted Williams scandal, remembered the date in question clearly. She had nothing to win or lose. Within days of that July 2002 phone call, John Henry was entering into mediation with Bobby-Jo. Now was exactly the time he would have to provide proof that Ted Williams wanted cryonic suspension for himself. It seems to me that John Henry was asking the nurse about the November 2000 hospital dates to correctly back-date the oil-stained paper.

John Heer presented the Florida state attorney's office with all of the above information, including the sworn statements from Frank Brothers and George Carter. To date, though, that office has not contacted either of them. Nor has it ever called the hospital nurses or investigated if Claudia was indeed in the hospital that day. This is puzzling and disappointing.

When I listen again to the numerous stories from CNN and reread the papers from early July 2002, I realize that just about every expert interviewed said they believed Alcor would have to release Ted's body "soon."

In one CNN interview, Lisa Bloom of Court TV pointed out that normally in disputes like this, the person cut out of the will was the one who'd argue to get something from the estate. In this case, amazingly, Bobby-Jo was disinherited entirely in her father's will, and yet she was the one arguing that the will be enforced.

Lisa Bloom continued: "Every state is going to look at the written will above an oral statement [Albert Cassidy's claim]. Many states won't even look at an oral statement but apparently Florida is going to have to take a look at the oral statements that were allegedly made. But . . . the whole purpose of having wills is so that we can speak from the grave as to what our wishes are. If Ted Williams did indeed change his mind, I wonder why his attorneys didn't suggest that he have a codicil or an amendment to the will to memorialize, in writing, his change of mind."

For some reason, the Florida state attorney's office put more weight on Cassidy's recollection of his alleged conversation with Ted than Ted's signed will itself. And it never investigated all the information John Heer sent. It might have been a case of the Florida state attorney's office not having the manpower to follow through with the investigation. I don't know. In my opinion, John provided them with strong evidence that Claudia had engaged in fraud against the court and all they said was that they were not going to pursue criminal charges. John Heer and I couldn't understand this decision. It seemed like they never even looked at any of the evidence John sent them. For some reason, they dragged their feet and never followed through on their own demands for Alcor to produce documents with Ted's signature on them.

From a more personal standpoint, if Ted had really sought cryonic suspension, why did he never sign Alcor's membership papers or the suspension agreement? John Henry's oil-stained note is dated November 2, 2000. Ted died on July 5, 2002. Cryonic suspension is not a choice made lightly. Surely twenty months was enough time for Ted to sign the Alcor paperwork. He was specific in his will regarding cremation. He was famous for being hardheaded and detail-oriented in everything he did. If Ted Williams was truly looking for immortality, wouldn't he have made damn sure to sign the paperwork?

In their rush to deny every allegation I made against them before I fled Scottsdale, Alcor made an incredible and very telling mistake. In response to my revealing to the media that Alcor had lost eight samples of Ted Williams's DNA, Alcor published the following in its August 13 News Bulletin:

Finally we must emphasize, contrary to news reports, that Alcor has never collected "DNA samples" from its cryopatients. Obviously Alcor has no need to collect "DNA samples," since a neuropatient already contains billions of DNA molecules.

Likewise, the *New York Times* reported: "Regarding Johnson's claim of missing DNA samples, Mondragon said none are collected or stored. 'We don't need to do that,' he said."

But then less than four months later, in another News Bulletin, Alcor published this:

> Alcor does, however, encourage its members to deposit a DNA sample in its dewars, and we even went so far as to send out sample kits to all our members some years back. . . . There are hundreds of those samples logged and stored in our vaults.

Amazing. First they denied it, then they admitted it. In my experience, this was indicative of how Alcor dealt with the press. They were likely to tell the media one thing, then tell their members another.

It could have been that things were so disorganized at Alcor that one corporate officer wasn't aware of the falsehoods another had concocted for the press. Or maybe it was further proof that the people in charge there were not playing with full decks. To me, knowing them and their messiah complexes, it seemed more like they were simply so arrogant that they couldn't be bothered to keep their own lies straight.

––––––––––––

As for the treatment of Ted's body inside Alcor, I'm not the only one who would call it mutilation. After the *Sports Illustrated* article was published, Phil Riske of the *Arizona Capitol Times* interviewed Rudy Thomas, director of the Arizona Board of Funeral Directors and Embalmers:

> If the *Sports Illustrated* report about Alcor's treatment of Mr. Williams's remains is true, said Mr. Thomas, the facility is guilty of mutilation. Arizona law prohibits mutilation of a body. Among sev-

eral allegations made by Larry Johnson, a former Alcor employee, are that Alcor severed Mr. Williams's head, drilled holes in it and fractured the skull, the magazine reported. "That to me is mutilation, if it happened," Mr. Thomas said.

I remember hearing somewhere that if the mothers of American servicemen had spent one night in the trenches of Vietnam, the war would've ended the next day. I say if other interested people—lawmakers, children of Alcor members, Mr. Thomas, and other state officials—had witnessed the three gruesome Alcor suspensions I had, I believe they would fight awfully hard to regulate cryonics. Actually, I would bet my beloved Harley Fat Boy that the average person, if they saw what I saw, would spend considerable energy trying to have Alcor regulated right out of business. And if Ted Williams fans and other members of Red Sox Nation had stood in the Alcor operating room during Ted's grotesquely bungled suspension, I shudder to think what they would have done to Mike Darwin, Hugh Hixon, and everyone else associated with Alcor at the time.

Many people have made the case that, given his war record, Ted should be unfrozen and buried in Arlington National Cemetery. That would be about as far away from Alcor's dewars as I can imagine.

Although that would be appropriate, given Ted's war service, I'd rather see Ted cremated, as he requested in his will, and his ashes sprinkled at sea, off the coast of Florida, where the water is very deep. I want to see Ted's last wish fulfilled. He deserves it.

NINETEEN

"WE WILL GET YOU
YOU WILL PAY"

After three months of hiding out in Glendale full-time, Beverly insisted on getting a job. It made me uncomfortable, but we did need the income. Plus, I was no picnic to be stuck with 24/7—paranoid, jumpy, carrying my gun into the bathroom, memorizing every news story that mentioned me or Alcor or Ted Williams. The people who were supporting us were a godsend, but they weren't exactly well-off, either. I hated the fact Beverly was working and I was not, but we needed her contribution. I wanted Beverly exposed as little as possible, so I drove her to and from work, constantly looking over my shoulder. I'd rush home, circle the block to make sure no one was following me, then lock myself in and spend the day pacing that little place like a caged animal. The lawsuits were crawling along at a glacial pace. I bugged John Heer, calling him often. I also called my Phoenix attorneys and spent hour after hour online, researching case law and cruising cryonics postings, reading and obsessing over the threats and slanderous accusations against me. I was going stir crazy.

Honestly, I had some moments of regret, remembering some individual kindnesses Charles had shown me, or remembering the way Hugh Hixon had opened up to me. I felt like I was betraying them somehow. Then I'd think back to more telling moments between us, like the time Hugh had cracked an atrocious joke to me in the Patient Care Bay.

As he was working, Hugh nonchalantly asked me to make a note about installing ovens into the Patient Care Bay.

"Why would we need ovens?" I asked Hugh.

"In case any Jews deanimate!" Hugh laughed real hard at that. That joke was in such bad taste, I was completely stunned.

In mid-December 2003 my paranoia was confirmed. In the mail, I received a typewritten note with no return address:

we know where you are johnson we will get you you will pay drop your campaign against cryonics!!!!!!!!!!!!!!!!!!!!!!!!!!!!

Larry Johnson
▬▬▬▬▬▬▬▬
Glendale, CA 91205

Threat Letter #1

According to the postmark, the letter was sent from Long Beach, California, on December 16, 2003. Long Beach was less than an hour's drive away from Glendale. That's where Bobby June, the response team member with Alcor's 800 number tattooed on his chest, lived. I personally knew three other hard-core Alcorians who also lived in Long Beach.

I thought I had been paranoid before but now it was severe. They knew my mailing address, and they could come for me at any time. Worse, now I was putting not only Beverly at risk, but the people we were staying with as well.

How did they know where I was?

They had to be watching me.

———————————

It was a tough decision but I kept that threat from Beverly. Financially and mentally, we just weren't capable of moving cities again. Beverly had suffered so much already. Just when she had finished decorating our pretty Scottsdale apartment and made it feel safe for herself, because of my whistle-blowing activities, those fanatics from Alcor had started banging on the door and threatening our lives. So much for providing Beverly with the stable home that meant so much to her, and that she deserved. I felt terrible about this. Going back to work in Glendale had brought a shred of normalcy back to Beverly's life. I didn't want to drag her back down into that pit of constant panic. But with that threat, a whole new level of fear came crashing down on me alone.

I took long rides on my Harley but they didn't afford me the peace they once did. I found myself looking over my shoulder to see if I was being followed. I rode by John Dentinger's old house in North Hollywood. I saw the garage where Mike Darwin had, according to Hugh Hixon's eyewitness account, given Dentinger the injection that killed him.

It was disturbing, thinking of what had happened in there. Did the neighbors know what had occurred in that garage? What about the house's new tenants? Was there a bicycle hanging on the wall, children playing on the cement floor where John Dentinger's AIDS-contaminated blood had once pooled?

I was freaking myself out and spending way too much time alone. In an effort to get out some, I started hanging out at a biker bar I found up in the Santa Monica Mountains.

Many of my friends, especially my wife's friends, always found it funny that I had so many biker pals. I love Harley-Davidsons but I sure don't look the type, if you subscribe to the biker stereotype.

The bar was called the Rockstore, up on Mulholland Highway in the hills separating Los Angeles from the San Fernando Valley. There were some colorful characters in the Rockstore but mostly the people there were just real nice. I've always felt comfortable around motorcycle enthusiasts and Harley riders. At that point in my life, after receiving a threat from some Alcorian fanatic and constantly feeling like I was being hunted, I found the company of bikers comforting. Plus, I couldn't have found an environment more opposite to Alcor than a biker bar. If any Alcorians came looking for me in there, they would stick out like a—well, like a cryonicist in a biker bar. Heck, they stuck out in a crowd full of normals, let alone among bikers. Can you imagine Mike Perry pedaling up on his Schwinn, hunchbacking up to the bar, and asking for a veggie-mix milkshake, please?

Many of my conversations with John Heer in those days were on my cell phone while I was up there at the Rockstore. I'd get a call from John and step outside for some privacy.

"What's that, Larry? They mailed you a note that said what? I can't hear you."

"Sorry, John, hold on a minute, there's a V-Twin Softail going by. Hang on . . ."

I got close with a couple regulars. One man in particular I became friends with was called Moose. Two hundred and fifty pounds, big, long ZZ Top–looking salt-and-pepper beard, nearly bald head wrapped in a bandanna, sunglasses with rose-colored lenses. You know those leather vests? He had the largest one they made and it still didn't go all the way around him. Like a lot of bikers, Moose was a Vietnam vet, and that had, in his own words, screwed him up a little. Real nice guy, though. So the Rockstore was the only place in LA where I could relax—but only to a point.

I continued driving Beverly to and from work every day. We were living like fugitives and I couldn't help but feel it was all my fault. Even though she didn't know about the recent threat letter, the stress on her was still heavy. In certain moments she would remind me that we were living like refugees. When would things get better? When would it stop? I couldn't answer. I also couldn't blame her one bit.

Then, several days after the first threatening letter, another one arrived.

Consider yourself dead not even cryonics will you

You are a murderer and a trader your death will be slow

FUCK YOU

Threat Letter #2.

"Not even cryonics will . . . you."

"Save" was the only word I could imagine they had mistakenly left out. That and the misspelling of the word "traitor" gave me pause. It's not like these people were dumb. Quite the contrary. They must have been furious, or worse, when they typed this.

This time they had come right out and threatened to kill me. It was a very difficult decision but I didn't tell Beverly about this letter either.

But why would anyone go to these lengths unless they believed I had information that would be seriously damaging to them? What if they really were coming after me to kill me? Didn't Beverly have a right to know?

I began sleeping with my gun, under the mattress, under my head. Again, I didn't tell Beverly.

In January 2004, a few weeks after the second threat letter, I read a press release about a book called *Mothermelters*. I had set up Internet news alerts to notify me of articles with keywords like "Alcor," "cryonics," and "Ted Williams" in them. That's how I became aware of Detective Alan Kunzman and his book.

Turns out, I wasn't the only one Alcor had stalked. Kunzman was the senior county coroner investigator in Riverside, California, a veteran police detective assigned to the coroner's office, mainly to investigate suspicious deaths. He was the detective who had investigated Dora Kent's suspicious death when Mike Darwin, Mike Perry, Hugh Hixon, David Pizer, and Carlos Mondragon had been arrested. This was back in 1987, when Alcor was located in Riverside. After this scandal Alcor left California and moved to Scottsdale, Charles had told me.

From what I read in the press release, Alan seemed to believe 100 percent that they had killed Dora Kent, that they had committed homicide and gotten away with it. He was so incensed that he self-published *Mothermelters* about the experience. Sounds familiar, huh? Alan took the name of his book from a letter he received from anonymous Alcorians after his investigation fell apart (see next page).

I dug up Alan's contact information online.

When I first called Alan he was real suspicious of me. He had the paranoid thing going too. I couldn't blame him for that. I could've been anyone claiming to be Larry Johnson. I could've been Carlos Mondragon's hired goon sniffing out information.

"I've been in law enforcement my whole adult life," Alan later told me. "When I got the call from someone claiming to be the former COO of Alcor, the first thing I thought was, 'What is the true nature of this call?'"

Mr. Dan Cupido
Chief Deputy Coroner
Riverside Coroner's Office
Riverside, California

Dear Mr. Cupido:

In order for cryonics to work, persons who are frozen must remain in that state until technology can repair them and restore them to life. A single incident of thawing, even after perhaps a hundred years of loving and secure care, means eternal death. Therefore, it is important that any potential aggressors against patients in cryonic suspension be deterred. To that end, the following applies to you, Mr. Carrillo, Mr. Bogan, Mr. Kunzman, and others where appropriate. Some years from now, after the one hundred and sixteen or so actionable items against you have worked through the courts and been settled against you (and your careers and reputations ruined), the Coroner's Office abolished and replaced with a Medical Examiner System, and justice has been served you for your murderous thuggery, a dossier will be created that will document your misdeeds. Wherever you go, this dossier will follow you for the rest of your life. It will be sent to your neighbors, your employers, any customers you serve, your local community leaders (including, but not limited to all local political offices, law enforcement agencies, attorneys, civic and social organizations, church leaders, prominent businesspersons, etc.), any insurance company foolish enough to ever consider bonding you again, all the major local media outlets, and basically everyone you come into contact with on a regular basis. Eventually, this may stop when it is no longer needed: when cryonics and suspended animation are perfected and accepted, and you take your rightful place in the history books alongside slave owners, the Luddites, those who opposed anesthesia and the germ theory, etc.

In the meantime, have a nice life, mothermelter.

cc: Riverside Press Enterprise
    San Bernardino Sun
    Riverside Police Department
    Alcor Life Extension Foundation
    Riverside District Attorney's Office
    Los Angeles Times
    Orange County Register
    Raymond L. Carrillo
    Scott D. Hill
    Stephanie A. Albright
    Rick A. Bogan
    James C. Camp
    Alan E. Kunzman
    Kenneth P. Nugent
    Rowe (Mickey) Worthington
    Riverside County Board of Supervisors

"Mothermelter" letter.

Despite Alan's concerns, we soon met for a long talk on the UCLA campus. Alan was there promoting his book at the L.A. Times Festival of Books. It took only a few minutes for us to trust each other.

Alan was quite a presence, big, strong, and powerful-looking. Like the LAPD detectives I had met, Alan fit another cop stereotype with his intimidating bearing, thick mustache, and cut-to-the-chase attitude.

Alan had been a cop since the 1980s. In fact he'd been the police chief of three different departments. After all those years, Alan said, his investigation of Alcor was the first and only time in his career he was truly frightened for his family. The more I spoke with Alan, the more I realized we really had a lot in common.

Alan told me that when he was investigating the Dora Kent case, he had been stalked by Carlos Mondragon. Alan had been working late one night at the coroner's police office, got up to walk to the john, and saw Carlos Mondragon's gaunt, sinister face in a window, watching, waiting. Alan served two tours in Vietnam and had gone through walls fighting with criminals. Still, even he got creeped out by Carlos Mondragon.

At the same moment Mondragon was eyeing Alan, he said, Alcorians were calling his wife at home and just breathing into the phone without speaking, listening to her ask who was calling. The poor woman grew more and more frightened. This was the exact same thing they would do to harass me and Beverly fifteen years later. Alan's wife was so scared he had to rush home from the office and search his yard, gun drawn.

"I became concerned about my wife and family's well-being," Alan told me. "When your wife starts getting phone calls at home, you get concerned. These people were willing to step outside the bounds of what a normal crook was willing to do. Initially we thought we were investigating a very introverted group of people and now my wife is getting threatening phone calls at home."

Alcor was trying to scare Alan into ending his investigation of Dora Kent's death.

"It's an organization that needs to be looked into by every law enforcement agency there is," Alan told me.

Dora Kent's suspicious death was one of the most persistent mysteries I had encountered at Alcor. Through Alan's book, the conversations I've had with him, the many talks I've had with Alcor employees, and my own research, I've put together what I believe to be the true story.

On the day her son, Saul, moved her out of the Carewest nursing home in Riverside, California, Dora Kent was having "one of her better days," nurses have said. Though suffering a long decline from degenerative illnesses including Alzheimer's, Dora had conversed a little that morning, recalling her past and knowing full well where she was. She was not at all in an "imminent death situation," a doctor would later affirm. This was December 9, 1987.

Saul Kent showed up with a sallow-looking young man. The nurse thought it was odd that both were dressed in white medical coats, though surely neither was a doctor. She felt like they were playing a part, trying to look official and medical. Worse, they arrived in an ambulance with the name "McCormack" painted on the side. The ambulance pulled up to the front door of the nursing home. This was highly unusual. First of all, the McCormack ambulance company didn't cover Riverside. More important to the nursing staff, though, all the ambulance drivers knew patient pick-up and drop-off happened in the rear of the building. Elderly residents didn't like seeing ambulances pull up to the front door of their nursing home—for them, not the most reassuring scene.

A few days earlier, a doctor named Steve Harris had briefly appeared at the nursing home, saying he needed to examine Dora. The charge nurse believed he stayed such a short time he could not even have given Dora a basic physical exam. This single visit allowed Harris to later list himself as Dora's attending physician on the death certificate. Evidently, the whole thing had been carefully planned. Fifteen years later, I met Harris at CCR as he inflicted a cruel experiment on an unfortunate dog. Clearly Harris had been lending his varied medical talents to Saul Kent's projects for a very long time.

According to Detective Kunzman, the charge nurse reminded Saul Kent that his mother needed around-the-clock care. Saul assured her that he was taking her home, where there was a full-time nurse and constant monitoring. He told the charge nurse that Dora would be in good hands and have the best medical care available.

In truth, this particular nurse had never liked Saul Kent. She always thought he visited his mother on a "prescription label schedule," putting in just enough time to appear proper. On the day Saul Kent took Dora from the nursing home, the nurse felt that he and his anemic-looking partner were really only going through the motions of caring for Dora. She felt that the man taking his mother out of her doctor's care was cold and emotionless. She didn't want to release Dora to Saul, so she called Dora's physician of record. He was taken by surprise. Over the phone, he asked Saul if there was a problem. Saul said no, he just wanted to take his mother home. He reiterated to the doctor that Dora would have the best of care, including a full-time nurse, oxygen, and all necessary monitoring equipment. Dr. Steve Harris would attend to her, Saul said, and provide her with all the medicine she needed.

The nurse didn't like it. The doctor didn't like it. But there was nothing they could do. Saul Kent was Dora's legal guardian. If he said he was taking her "home" to care for her, there was nothing they could do to stop him.

According to Alan Kunzman, though, Saul Kent had lied. The ambulance drove Dora straight to the Alcor facility.

In his book, Alan wrote, "Once Dora was wheeled inside she was immediately taken off all medication, and was pumped full of incredibly high levels of barbiturates. During the last forty-eight hours of her life she was subjected to a cold-blooded exercise, and monitored with no more compassion than a lab rat. There was no scientific or moral validity to the lethal experiment which was done simply because the people in whose hands Dora had fallen were without conscience. Dora Kent, a tired old woman with failing health died without ever knowing what had happened to her."

Saul Kent and Mike Darwin next showed up at the county coroner's office, trying to get someone to sign Dora's death certificate. This was unheard of. A deputy coroner was supposed to be sent to the scene of a death, then provide a death certificate to the mortuary, which in turn filed the completed death certificate.

For someone to have his mother's death certificate in hand was not only extremely unusual, it was dangerous. If somebody had his mother's death certificate, he could kill her himself, fill in the blanks, then have it signed and filed away. It was precisely what the system was created to try to avoid.

Another investigator, Rick Bogan, was talking to Saul and Mike Darwin just after they entered the coroner's office and Alan happened to overhear. There were some awfully fishy things concerning the death certificate that these two had shown up with. Alan stepped in and joined in the conversation.

First, they tried to pass Alcor off as a residence when, in fact, Alan knew that area of Riverside was zoned as an industrial park. Yes, Hugh Hixon and Mike Perry were at the time living in a Volkswagen bus behind Alcor, but they were doing so illegally. To avoid suspicion, Alan believed, Saul Kent and Mike Darwin were trying to fool the coroner's office, trying to make it look like Dora had died at a residence.

Worse, Steve Harris was not in the room when he declared Dora legally dead. He did it over the phone. Again, it seemed like the whole sequence of events had been carefully choreographed. It was completely illegal, Alan said, but this way Mike Darwin, Saul Kent, and the others could begin Dora's cryo-suspension at their discretion and on their own schedule—never mind the fact that on the day they came and took her, she was having "one of her better days" and had been chatting with nurses, telling them stories from her past.

I have never been able to understand why, at minimum, Steve Harris hadn't lost his medical license over this clear violation of procedure and medical ethics.

That Saul Kent and Mike Darwin had shown up at the coroner's office and tried to get someone there to sign Dora's death certificate sent up a bright enough red flag for Alan to visit Alcor's facility and begin to investigate.

Mike Darwin gave Alan a tour of Alcor during his first visit there. One of the first things Darwin told Alan was that he planned to "deanimate" himself when the time came on his own terms, not death's terms, in order to have the best possible chances for reanimation. To Alan, this was another red flag. Anyone wanting that for himself might be willing to do the same to others.

Darwin told Alan that Dora's head and hands had been detached from her body and they were cooling, as per Alcor's protocol. The rest of her body was to be cremated. Darwin showed Alan a plywood box wrapped in plastic that contained Dora's headless body, covered with crushed ice. Alan's radar began to ping: "This wasn't a hospital," Alan told me later. "It wasn't even officially a research facility." The only reason Alan could imagine for Alcor cutting off a person's hands was to avoid body identification.

I had found an online account written by Mike Perry in 1992, improbably titled "Our Finest Hours: Notes on the Dora Kent Crisis," stored on the Alcor Web site archives. In it, Perry claimed that they had removed Dora's hands to experiment on them with a new chemical perfusion formula. It made me shudder, imagining Saul Kent ordering his mother's hands cut off for the purpose of experimentation.

As Alan tells it, during his initial visit, Darwin also showed him Alcor's Dora Kent file. Inside was the paperwork that documented Dora's death and decapitation surgery. One document had the word "DEANIMATED" emblazoned across the top in inch-high red letters, which sounded awfully suspicious to Alan. He flipped through the pages and found listed the barbiturate cocktail that Darwin had given to Dora. Alan was incredulous—they were documenting their own crimes. Continuing Darwin's peculiar tendency to incriminate himself and Alcor, he also admitted they had a videotape of Dora's cryo-suspension procedure. Alan knew he would have to get a search warrant and come back to seize the files and videotape.

Darwin talked at length about Alcor's cryonic procedures. Alan immediately felt as if Darwin was trying to impress him. Alan just continued to listen, thinking Darwin was on his way toward deeply incriminating himself with his boasts.

Proudly, Darwin continued showing Alan around, giving him the tour of Alcor. In Alcor's garage Alan saw the very ambulance that Saul had brought to the nursing home to ferry his mother in, the one that read "McCormack" on the side. It was Alcor's own vehicle, though, bought years earlier from the McCormack ambulance company and never repainted. Saul and the others had apparently used it so it would appear as if Dora were being transported by a legitimate ambulance company. Had they faked this too, purposely creating a mistaken impression in the nursing home staff? Alan's cop radar pinged again.

Darwin told Alan that he performed the postmortem operations on Alcor members himself, along with his fellow Alcorian Jerry Leaf. Yet another red flag shot up for Alan. They had no training or certification for that, but Darwin was practically bragging about it.

"They had this godlike demeanor," Alan told me. "They absolutely loved to talk about themselves. That was their way of trying to impress on you how much smarter they were than you. They could all throw out medical terms to make them seem more intelligent and knowledgeable than you. I had been around medicine. I had been a corpsman in the Navy. I was in the first graduating class of paramedics in Riverside. A lot of the times when they would utilize a particular word, it would have some meaning but they pretty much used it just to show you they knew the word. I played dumb. I had to stop myself from turning around and gagging. I kept thinking to myself, 'You gotta be kidding me!'"

During Alan's initial visit to Alcor, Darwin told him, "There is an incredible amount of envy and outright jealousy in the cryonics world. . . . Believe me I'm not overstating things when I say that it is very secret. There are cryonic organizations worldwide that would love to get their hands on my formula." Darwin alternately called cryonics a science and then a belief. Alan got the feeling there was something very "cultlike" going on. Boy, did I know that feeling.

Alan considered Mike Darwin a "hustler." I noticed that in conversation Alan never actually referred to him as Darwin. He called him Federowicz, not even giving lip service to what he regarded as the man's ridiculous self-aggrandizement in taking the Darwin name. He called him a "snake-oil salesman."

From my conversations around Alcor, I believe even other Alcorians agreed with this assessment of Darwin. Cryonics was a means to an end for Darwin, the same way a religious cult would be. He wanted disciples who hung on his words and ultimately believed in him. Cryonics, Hare Krishna, anything would do. Alan and I believed that like David Pizer, Mike Darwin had a messiah complex and was a David Koresh wannabe.

"He projects himself as a believer but I don't think he is," Alan said. "I don't think he has any faith in God. He doesn't care what happens to his own body. I think his 'philosophy' is to get money from people for lopping off their heads."

This was pretty close to what Hugh Hixon had told me when he described Darwin's personal philosophy as "situational consequentialism"— he would do whatever he thought he could get away with, and completely without conscience.

Alan also met Jerry Leaf on that first visit. Mike Darwin's surgical partner and an ex–Green Beret, Jerry Leaf was the Alcorian bigwig Hugh Hixon and Joe Hovey had told me about, the one who apparently had left a note in a safety-deposit box accusing Mike Darwin of killing Dora Kent by giving her a lethal injection. Whenever anyone at Alcor had mentioned Leaf to me, they talked about him like he was a god. They described him as brilliant and fearless. Alan's perception of Jerry Leaf was that he was the most apocalyptic, survivalist-minded of the then-active Alcorians.

"I was able to convince them that I had to take Dora Kent's head to get it x-rayed," Alan told me, to be sure it wasn't murder, that there were no hatchet wounds or bullet holes. "I told them I was going to treat it respectfully, that they could come along and oversee it all, that they could make sure we weren't going to do anything to it that would be a problem for them, and then we'd give it back. It was all set up. They agreed. I had already called for transportation.

"So the transport team arrived and I was telling them where the body was and then lo and behold here comes Ray Carrillo." Carrillo was Alan's boss, the county coroner. "He had never, ever shown up on the scene before. He had no idea what we had. I still to this day do not know how he found out about this or why he showed up. Our transportation team took possession of Dora Kent's body. However, Carrillo told them to leave the head and hands at Alcor. We weren't taking them. I couldn't believe it. To this day I have no idea why he left Dora Kent's head and hands at Alcor.

"The government code section we operated under, 27491, gave us tremendous authority when it came to investigating a dead body," Alan told me. "If, for instance, I'm on the scene of a car accident or explosion and there are body parts around, on the street, in a yard, whatever, it's my responsibility and duty to recover and remove all of those body parts, and then identify them. Same case here. I had hands that had been removed, a head that had been removed, and a body that had no identifiers, no tattoos, no scars that I could see. I needed the head and hands to identify Dora Kent. To this day, I cannot say with 100 percent certainty that the body we took from Alcor was Dora Kent's."

Unable to confiscate the head and hands, though by now wanting to investigate Dora's death more thoroughly, Alan asked Mike Darwin to bring the Dora Kent file to his office the next day. Darwin did so and, as Alan suspected might be the case, it was much thinner. Pages that Alan had seen

inside the file folder at Alcor were now missing, including the incriminating document with "DEANIMATED" written on the top. And Darwin did
not hand over the videotape. Now it really looked to Alan like Alcor had
something to hide.

Alan had Dora Kent's headless body put on the fast track for an autopsy, and with the suspicious omissions in the materials Darwin had
brought him, he was able to obtain a search warrant for the purpose of
going back to Alcor and seizing Dora's head and hands, as well as the missing documents.

Alan then returned with several other investigators and the search warrant, and was told by the people at Alcor that Dora Kent's head and hands
were gone. There were a handful of Alcorians present. Every one of them
refused to comment on where Dora's head or hands were.

Another investigator pointed out a huge amount of medical equipment
on the premises with UCLA stickers. This also seemed suspicious to Alan.
Looking around, Alan found more and more reasons to be wary of Alcor's
entire operation.

Inside Jerry Leaf's closet, Alan saw semiautomatic assault rifles alongside instructions on how to convert them to fully automatic weapons.
Alan also saw a collection of hand grenades and a claymore mine (an anti-
personnel mine used by the U.S. military primarily for ambushes, and as
an anti-infiltration device—a deadly booby trap).

Alan found human hearts, kidneys, entrails, fingers, and fetuses in various stages of development in Jerry Leaf's closet, all preserved in jars of
formaldehyde.

He also found stores of canned water and army rations around the Riverside facility. "It looked like Alcor was preparing for Armageddon," Alan told
me. "Their attitude was that they were the best humanity had to offer. They
were the ones who must survive in order to carry on human civilization."

The more I spoke with Alan, the more I thought: *These people haven't
changed in the past two decades.*

As Alan was looking through Alcor's filing cabinets for the videotape
and missing Dora Kent documents, he heard a commotion. He walked
outside to find that Rick Bogan had taken a group of Alcorians into cus-

tody. Bogan had asked Darwin to open up a freezer so he could look inside for Dora's head, and Darwin had refused. Some other Alcorians objected, including Hugh Hixon, David Pizer, and Mike Perry. Alan cautioned Bogan not to arrest them but Bogan said the Alcorians weren't cooperating, and they weren't being forthcoming regarding the whereabouts of Dora Kent's head. Alan thought they had no probable cause to arrest these people yet and told Bogan to wait, but Bogan insisted. Ultimately Mike Darwin, Hugh Hixon, David Pizer, Mike Perry, and Carlos Mondragon were taken into custody.

Alan said he knew that was a mistake. "Already I felt this case going downhill fast," he told me.

Meanwhile, the pathologist who had recently performed the autopsy on Dora Kent's headless body told Alan, "Concerning the incision I would say that the individual or individuals that did this were very sloppy, very messy. Amateurish. Didn't know what they were doing."

In my experience, not much had changed around Alcor in that regard either.

But the pathologist found evidence of more than amateurish surgery. Alan showed me Dora Kent's toxicology report. It confirmed what Charles had told me in my pickup truck that day as we drove back from Saul Kent's house: two barbiturates were found in great, lethal quantities in Dora Kent's bone marrow, pentobarbital and secobarbital. These are the two most common drugs doctors have used to euthanize people (either in countries where suicide isn't illegal or in doctor-assisted suicides). Pentobarbital is likewise commonly used by veterinarians to euthanize animals. Most notable, and most disturbing, pentobarbital and secobarbital are part of the drug cocktail used to kill death-row inmates who are sentenced to die by lethal injection.

Alan returned a third time to Alcor, this time with a "media warrant." He wanted to keep looking for the videotape, and he wanted to confiscate the UCLA medical equipment, as well as Alcor's computers. Still, due to the premature arrest and subsequent release of the Alcorian leaders, as well as the missing head and hands, Alan did not have a good feeling about this investigation.

COLTON, CA 92324
F.R. MODGLIN, MD, DIR.

RIVERSIDE COUNTY CORONER   500
PO BOX 113   RO
RIVERSIDE, CA 92501

KENT, DORA					02427
ACCESSION NO.	AGE	SEX	TV/SOURCE	DATE RECEIVE
42040139	83	F	BONE MARROW	01/14/8
REFERRING PHYSICIAN			CLIENT NO.	DATE REPORTE
DEP. BOGAN			803379	1/20/88
ORDER STATUS	COLLECTION DATE/TIME			CLIENT DATA
COMPLETE	12/18/87			FRM

TEST	OUTSIDE RANGE	WITHIN RANGE	UNITS	REFERENCE RANGE
COMPREHENSIVE DRUG PNL		PENTOBARBITAL: 4.8 MG/KG		
		SECOBARBITAL: 5.8 MG/KG		
		SPECIMENS ARE ANALYZED BY GAS CHROMA-		
		TOGRAPHY & RIA FOR THE FOLLOWING DRUGS:		
		AMITRIPTYLINE, AMOBARBITAL, AMPHETAMINE,		
		CHLORDIAZEPOXIDE, COCAINE, DIAZEPAM,		
		DIPHENHYDRAMINE, DOXEPIN, FLURAZEPAM,		
		IMIPRAMINE, MEPERIDINE, METHADONE,		
		METHAMPHETAMINE, METHAQUALONE, OPIATES,		
		PENTOBARBITAL, PHENCYCLIDINE,		
		PHENOBARBITAL, PROPOXYPHENE, SECOBARBITAL,		
		AND THIORIDAZINE.		

Dora Kent's toxicology report.

"When Carrillo came in and said we're not taking the head that first day, that right there would have caused a major issue in court. Unfortunately, at the time, our offices were already being investigated by a grand jury because of other things Carrillo had been doing, terminating people illegally . . . the press got into it. Carrillo was referred to as a buffoon. He gave some ridiculous press conferences."

The flamboyant celebrity Liberace had recently died in Carrillo's jurisdiction and he made a mess of that as well, Alan said. Everyone knew Liberace was suffering from AIDS. He was under doctors' care. Carrillo ordered an autopsy anyway. It made the whole office look awful, like they were somehow singling out the dead pianist for special, abusive treatment. "It was a horrible time," Alan recalled.

The ineptitude of Alan's boss was so breathtaking that Alan began suspecting him of collusion, of being crooked. Alan eventually dropped this theory, though, and started believing Carrillo was just grossly incompetent. If Carrillo hadn't intervened right then, in a way he never had before, Alcor would probably not be in business today, Alan told me. It was an open-and-shut case. Saul Kent, Mike Darwin, and other Alcor leaders would have gone to court, and probably on to jail.

Alan and I both believe that as soon as Carrillo let Alcor off the hook during that first visit, they gathered the head, hands, videotape, and files, and drove them, hell-bent, to Saul Kent's house. It was their only safe haven. During my time at Alcor I heard rumors that these things were hidden in a warehouse in southern Florida, where they may still remain. I can picture Saul Kent with his sunken eyes and wild white hair driving through the countryside with his mother's head on ice on the passenger seat, whistling all the way to Florida.

According to Alan, Carillo continued to botch the case so badly that no prosecutor was willing to take it to court. The negative and embarrassing press regarding the coroner's incompetence in Dora's case began to have detrimental effects on morale around the office and throughout the whole county government.

"When I went to court, no one from the county discussed the case with me beforehand," Alan told me. "Prosecutors never go into court without doing that. I was the lead investigator and they never asked me

anything. I would always, always sit down to counsel with the county attorney to discuss the case. Never happened here. I never even got a phone
call. So how can you go into the case and argue a point of law without
knowing what the case is? All the mistakes being made by Carrillo and the
younger deputies made the prosecutors run far and fast from the case.
They knew they didn't have a case, so they made it go away. They had already filed a petition, so they had to appear in court, but they were only
going to put forward the least amount of effort possible. The judge allowed it to happen.

"And then I found out the judge was involved with Carrillo. I felt like I
was in a box trying to fight my way out. The whole thing was just swept
away out of sight as quickly as possible." Alan considered it the biggest
travesty of justice he has witnessed in his entire career. He quit his job
fourteen months later.

─────────────

"That case was a slam dunk," Alan told me. "I never had a case where
things were so well documented by the people who committed the crime.
Not even close."

The Alcorians were so talkative, so egomaniacal, so convinced of their
own invincibility that they gave every piece of damning evidence right to
him. "They believe they're better than everybody else. They believe they're
in the upper crust of society, intellectually. And for that reason, they're
better suited to head this cryonics movement so they can preserve themselves. I've interviewed every type of criminal from serial killers to
shoplifters in my career. I have never run across a group of people that
were so easy to interview. They loved to talk."

I knew from my own experience that they loved to write. They believed they were documenting events of tremendous importance to all of
mankind, for now and into the remote future. Alan saw it too. "They
each rewrote the same event," he told me. "They were in competition
with each other, to see who could write the better account." What they
were creating would be read and revered thousands of years hence, they
seemed to be telling themselves. They were pioneers and scribes at the

same time. They were their own biographers, writing the history of the future. It disturbed me when I reflected on the fact that the Nazis, from the arrogant heights of their presumed superiority, also meticulously and thoroughly documented virtually all of their evil deeds. As with Alcor's reams of record-keeping, examples of which I've presented in this book, the Nazis employed an early form of punch-card technology that had been developed by IBM and leased to the German government. They conducted medical experiments on people they'd forcibly detained; cataloged the identities of their victims; photographed the theaters of death they created; and carefully kept records of it all. The analogies to Alcor chilled me. Like the Nazis, the Alcorians also seemed oblivious to the self-incriminating nature of all their obsessive documentation.

Alan told me he found conclusive evidence in Mike Perry's diaries that he couldn't use in court because Carrillo had had the diaries returned to Perry and, like Dora Kent's head and hands, they then simply disappeared. Alan became very familiar with Mike Perry's diaries while he had them, though, and took detailed notes on their contents. Alan described to me how Mike Perry would write about something in his diary, then rewrite the same thing almost word for word a few pages later. In fact, Alan found entire copies of Mike Perry's notebooks, which Perry had taken the time to duplicate by hand. I've heard of deliberate redundancy, but this was ridiculous.

According to Alan, Mike Perry described in his diary how Dora Kent was deprived of food and medicines, injected with barbiturates, and died. Right there in his diary, Mike wrote that Dora's "deanimation" was "performed" by Mike Darwin and Jerry Leaf. In Perry's later "Our Finest Hours" online account of the Dora Kent case, that statement does not appear. But, said Alan, there it was, plain and simple, in black and white.

After decapitating Dora Kent, Mike Perry wrote, the Alcor team went out to Pizza Hut. There, Mike Perry told everyone he had written about the Dora Kent case in his diary. They all joked about how he should shred his diary, just in case.

Mike Perry actually wrote in his diary about all the files and materials Alcor hurried out of the building between the time Carrillo told Alan

Kunzman he couldn't take anything from Alcor, and the time Alan came back with the search warrant.

Alan found evidence in Mike Perry's diaries of another case of what could be labeled with a dark euphemism as "unrequested euthanasia." Mike wrote about an Alcor member in Madison, Wisconsin, who had taken days longer to die than the response team wanted. The Alcor team had to live in a hospital waiting room for days, sitting the death watch, washing in the men's room sink. Then, when they were finally rushing the woman from the hospital to the airport in a U-Haul, the woman revived. In Mike Perry's words, in the back of the truck, they "had been forced to put her down." It was as if he were writing about an old dog.

Inside Alcor, Kunzman found a Polaroid of Mike Darwin as a boy, dressed in a lab coat, cutting up a cat. He also found documents in which Alcor employees recounted answering want ads for cats and dogs. They would go to people's homes to adopt their animals, claiming they intended to give them a good home, and then performed their ghastly experiments on them. I had heard rumors of the same thing when I had visited CCR in California. Alan corroborated what I had also heard, that Alcor actually placed their own ads and people were bringing their pets straight to Alcor themselves. "They preferred larger animals," Alan told me.

Alan saw several dogs living at Alcor, including Dixie, the famous zombie dog. Kunzman read files describing how Dixie and another dog named Slinky had been experimented on in Riverside. Alan said Dixie appeared to be suffering from brain damage when he met her and could hardly move on her own. Alan learned from Mike Perry's diary that she had to be physically taken outside to relieve herself. That's how badly they screwed those animals up with their experiments. I can only hope that PETA and other animal rights organizations take a good, hard look at Alcor and CCR someday soon.

In his diaries, Mike Perry wrote about his hopes that scientists of the future would reconstruct Alcorians' brains inside computer matrixes so that they would not have to be resurrected inside flesh-and-blood bodies. It was no surprise that a man who had removed his own testicles with a razor and then intentionally severed the nerves to his penis would have disdain for the human body.

Mike Perry also wrote in detail about some of Mike Darwin's loud, all-night gay sex parties in the Alcor operating room. Alan read a diary entry where Mike Perry wrote, "Mike [Darwin] had a rough night last night, fucking till 5:30 in the morning. Cliff, his partner, had to get up at 6 to go to work so he made what for him was a difficult decision, to call in sick as Mike . . . put it, he was ill with swelling of the groin and pain in the ass."

I don't care what two consenting adults do. It's just a little freaky to be doing it on the operating tables of a self-proclaimed medical facility—the same tables where Alcor decapitated people.

Alan found a note written by Mike Perry that described his self-castration and asked surgeons of the future not to reconnect any genitalia to him when they reanimated him. He referred to his former sex drive as burdensome. Everything attached or not attached to Mike Perry was on purpose and it was the way he wanted it, thank you very much. The handwritten note began, "I, R. Michael Perry, Alcor suspension member A-1064, being of sound mind and memory," and went on to include the language, "it is my wish, desire, and preference that upon my revival I shall be revived without gonads." Alan Kunzman saw over thirty identical handwritten copies of this note placed all over Alcor. Mike Perry clearly wanted to leave nothing to chance.

In his diaries, Mike Perry described media preparation meetings. Alcor officers sat behind closed doors and practiced answering any questions that could be posed by the public or by police. Kunzman called it "Hitleresque." Indeed.

Alan also found pages, handwritten on both sides by Mike Perry, in writing smaller than any word processor or typewriter could create, describing how to make fake IDs, how to set up mail drops, how to buy land with a false name, what to say to government officials, how to answer questions, and how to get a new driver's license.

Alan corroborated my suspicion of Alcor improperly dumping chemicals and potentially AIDS-infected blood. It was standard operating procedure in Riverside, Alan noted, for them to dump the blood and chemicals down the sinks inside the building. Just as in Scottsdale, there were no chemical sinks, no biohazard containment storage units. Alan read documents in which Alcor members actually described the dumping of toxic materials. So they'd been doing this for over two decades, at least.

In his account of the Dora Kent case I had found in the online Alcor archives, Mike Perry also wrote about a meeting with Alcor's lawyers and a joke Darwin made: "Mike [Darwin] asked me to leave during this meeting, which started at 7:30 p.m., mainly because, he said, legal counsel advised it for my own protection. I said I wasn't much worried about personal danger. Mike smiled and said, 'Oh yeah? Then I have a job for you—just say you did it'—meaning I caused the death of Dora Kent." Pretty dark—and revealing—humor.

In his diaries, Mike Perry also recounted other conversations he had with Mike Darwin, in which Perry suggested that some particular Alcor members were getting old and should have "assisted deanimations." Darwin agreed with Perry's suggestions and said some members would benefit from that. They named a few and then Darwin said it could be "handled through Venturism."

Alan took note of millions of dollars' worth of medical equipment and machinery around Alcor's Riverside facility. Just like the pricey-looking microscope I found at Alcor in Scottsdale fifteen years later, many of the state-of-the-art medical supplies and machines Alan saw were tagged with little UCLA stickers. He consulted the UCLA police. Sure enough, some, if not all, of it was UCLA's equipment and had gone missing from the university. It was a very embarrassing situation for the UCLA police. As far as Alan knows, they have never investigated it. He figured that UCLA had so much stuff, it was impossible to keep track of it all.

Dr. Steve Harris was on the staff of the UCLA Medical School at the time. Jerry Leaf also worked at UCLA. According to the UCLA police sergeant Alan spoke to, Leaf had keys to storage warehouses and had actually been caught taking supplies from there in the past. Even the jars of human organs in Jerry Leaf's closet had little blue UCLA stickers on them.

(Ironically, Alan told me about this UCLA equipment the day we met on the UCLA campus. Still paranoid, I got a bit creeped out as people walked by. I warily lowered my voice and kept looking over my shoulder.)

Mike Darwin was proud of all that equipment around Alcor, Alan said. He even showed it off to Alan, bragging. Alan had been both a paramedic and navy medic, and he could not imagine a good reason for Alcor to have all that stuff. "They just grabbed everything they could," Alan said. "They had things in there they could never possibly use." Just like Alcor in Scottsdale, they were better outfitted than many hospitals.

Then Alan found receipts from a dummy company Jerry Leaf had created called Blaylock. According to Alan, through the name Blaylock, Leaf was taking the UCLA medical equipment, storing it at Alcor, and then renting it to television and film production studios for use as props.

But Alan also found that there were still piles and piles of expensive equipment that did not look like they had come from UCLA.

"I worked on a drug task force prior to my time in the coroner's office," Alan told me. "When I first walked into the Alcor facility in Riverside and saw the millions and millions of dollars in equipment and supplies, and that they had three or four heads in there that they had charged $35,000 for as their only source of income, it didn't take a genius to figure out the money was coming from somewhere else."

Alan wrote about an ex-employee of Saul Kent's in Florida who came forward and contacted Alan during his investigation of Alcor.

"Listen, I can't give you my name," the informant told Alan, "but I can tell you some things about Alcor. Some things which will bring them down . . . I'm afraid either they might kill me or hire someone to have me killed."

"I've interviewed thousands of people over the years," Alan told me. "This guy was absolutely scared to death. He knew he was going to die if he got caught talking to me." The informant would call from a pay phone, scared of being followed, then jump off the phone without warning, Alan said. It seemed to me like Alan's informant and I had this paranoia in common.

Prior to taking the job in Florida, Alan's informant was working as a biochemist in Colorado. He told Alan, "I flew down there and originally was impressed with their operation, which they call the Life Extension Foundation. . . . At first I thought it was a legitimate company interested in producing vitamins, which had the potential to perhaps extend life. I went down there and was introduced to all of the big wigs. I met Saul Kent, who is the godfather of this bunch. . . . They were touting their vitamins as helping to fight diseases such as AIDS and cancer when what they were doing was selling nothing more than placebos. I tried to convince Kent that we could make money honestly by legitimately researching life extension drugs, but he wanted nothing of it."

The informant said he left partially because he "suggested we do things on the up-and-up. But almost as much because I just didn't fall into line. They want followers—true believers. . . . They especially don't want people who can think for themselves."

Alan tested his informant by asking him Mike Darwin's real name. He passed the test. The informant knew Darwin well. He even mentioned Darwin's "messiah complex." "The only thing Mike Federowicz is a genius at is hustling," the informant said to Alan.

Alan, his informant, myself—it seemed to me like every non-cryonicist who came in contact with these people left with the same impressions of them.

The informant went on to describe an alleged international illegal drug trafficking operation that he claimed had earned Saul Kent and his partner Bill Faloon millions of dollars. According to the informant, people associated with Alcor had been arrested in Florida on cocaine smuggling charges.

"When the Dora Kent case started to build," Alan told me, "and we conducted our search, in one of their [Alcor's] filing cabinets I found a newspaper story describing how their building had been seized in Florida and someone there was arrested because he was trafficking cocaine. As the Riverside investigation broadened and the story broke wider, my informant gave me more details of their drug operation.

"They were ordering Mannitol in bulk, in big drums," Alan said. Mannitol is a type of sugar alcohol used to reduce swelling after brain trauma. It is also, however, commonly used in the illegal drug trade as a cutting agent for heroin, methamphetamines, and other illicit drugs. On the street, it's referred to as "baby laxative."

"They would have the Mannitol shipped out of the country, to their own offshore businesses in Argentina and Brazil," Alan said. "Where they got the cocaine from, I don't know, but my informant told me they would then mix the cocaine in with the Mannitol overseas, and then ship it to themselves in Florida. There, they would extract the cocaine and it would hit the streets through their organized crime contacts." I had seen containers of Mannitol myself while working at Alcor in Scottsdale, though at the time I couldn't guess what they were for.

The idea of Alcorians having contacts in organized crime was new to me but Alan clarified. Alan's informant told him about a guy named Stephen Ruddel, who was a cryonicist in so deep, he not only gave Saul Kent and Bill Faloon the initial $100,000 seed money to start their Life Extension Foundation, he also gave Saul his Florida office space for free. Indeed, Ruddel was at one point charged by the U.S. government with cocaine trafficking. (Ruddel was described in a local Florida newspaper's cover story as "a regular Howard Hughes and an eccentric real estate mogul with a 'penchant for cocaine and cryogenics and a fear of intruders'; he is said to have laced the air ducts of his building with barbed wire.")

The building Saul Kent and Bill Faloon had occupied in Florida was raided and seized. Ruddel was fined $80,000 and placed on probation (he avoided jail time by agreeing to be part of a sting operation). The seizure of the building was big news.

Through my own research, I later discovered that Ruddel had tried to write off his fines as "charitable contributions" to the Florida police. His petition was rejected, but I found the details of Ruddel's arrest in the U.S Tax Court decision, published online:

On August 28, 1986, the Hollywood, Florida, police department (Police Department), with the assistance of the United States Marshals (collectively referred to as Officers), searched petitioner's home pursuant to a valid search warrant. The Officers found 334 grams of cocaine, $7,362 in United States currency, various gold and silver coins, and jewelry in a safe. They also uncovered drug paraphernalia, weapons, ammunition, and other miscellaneous items. These items were seized and inventoried by the Police Department. Petitioner was arrested for cocaine trafficking.

"But," the informant told Alan, "even with all of the fines, to this day they're still running the vitamin scam out of the back of a bingo parlor." A guy with the improbable name of Marty Bogus ran the bingo parlor. He was connected with Florida organized crime as well, Alan's informant said.

The informant also gave Alan the name of Saul Kent and Bill Falloon's offshore operation, the Hauptmann Institute, saying this was the company they were using to import the drugs.

Of Saul Kent and Bill Falloon, Alan told me, "The money people stay one step ahead, keep one foot outside the circle. That's how I perceived Saul Kent and Bill Falloon in Florida." That's why, Alan believed, Saul and Bill had never been charged, themselves, with cocaine trafficking.

At first, it sounded pretty fantastic to me, the idea that Saul Kent could have been in charge of a cocaine smuggling operation. However, with decades of police work behind him, I trusted Alan's instincts and assessments. And, after working for Saul Kent and the other Alcorians, I believed they would do anything to further their cause and to protect themselves, the self-styled saviors of humanity who would lead mankind into the future.

"There are umpteen cases of drug trafficking ongoing in Florida all the time," Alan said. "This would be a tougher one to pursue. The DEA [Drug Enforcement Administration] would have to really get in there and work and investigate and interview people and dig up records and look into overseas companies. This kind of investigation gives the DEA pause, as opposed to taking out a truck down the road filled with $2 million worth of cocaine, which happens all the time in Florida. So they walked away from it. Plus, there was all this lunacy and bad press going on with the Riverside coroner's office that sure made it seem it was going to be a dead-end case filled with law enforcement mistakes. Again, nobody wanted to get involved with it. A bad rep, a black mark was promised for all names involved. This case was easy for the DEA to walk away from. What government agency wants to be associated with that?"

———————

Through my own research, I realized that a different agency, the Food and Drug Adminstration, probably ended up asking itself the same question. According to a 1994 article in the *Miami New Times,* Saul and his Life Extension Foundation partner, Bill Faloon, had a history of, in this journalist's words, "shady dealings." A former LEF employee (and then federal witness against Saul and Bill) told the reporter, "Back in 1985 Bill and Saul reported $300,000. They actually took in more like four or five million." The reporter revealed that, to date, they had not filed tax returns for seven years. The two men had been fighting with the FDA ever since it first raided the LEF warehouse in 1987, ten months before the Dora Kent affair. The FDA alleged that the LEF "shipped unapproved drugs into the U.S. and sold them to foundation members through two overseas companies . . . that amounted to little more than mail drops." What the FDA called "unapproved" and potentially "lethal" drugs, Saul and Bill called anti-aging supplements.

In 1991 the battle escalated into a twenty-seven-count federal criminal indictment. Saul and Bill were jailed and then released after each raised $825,000 bail. Over the next four years, they spent at least $1.2 million on their legal defense. Faloon told the *New Times* reporter that the money for their defense came primarily from the foundation's $50 annual membership dues. "Though we are nonprofit, we do generate a surplus here, a healthy surplus," he said, thanks to their sale of "books and tapes and vitamins." Their lawyers filed thousands of pages of motions, delaying the proceedings again and again. In 1996 the FDA finally gave up after the case was bounced from judge to judge, apparently unable to make anything stick. Bill Faloon said, "We're not afraid of the government."

Saul's colleague, Ben Best—a former Alcorian and president of Cryonics Institute, another cryonics facility—wrote that "It was the first time in the history of the FDA that the agency had given up on a criminal indictment against a political opponent." To me, it seemed like Saul Kent was well practiced in getting away with "shady dealings."

———————

While Alan Kunzman was working the Dora Kent case, his informant told him all about a cryonicist "fortress" owned by a David Pizer. This apparently wasn't the Creekside Preserve location near Prescott I had visited; in some postings online I gathered there had been an earlier version of Ventureville in the Phoenix area. The informant claimed there were stores of survivalist gear buried out there. Guns, bombs, medical supplies, cryonics equipment, everything they'd need to hole up prior to Armageddon and prepare for its aftermath. There were underground bunkers, he said, surrounded by barbed wire and claymore mines.

Alan read documents that corroborated his informant's claim, describing how buses had been purchased and modified and then joined together underground. These were filled with water and supplies, and the entire area was mined.

Alan's informant also talked about desert locations where he believed bodies could be found. Teenage runaways and homeless people. Alan's informant suspected Alcorians and David Pizer's Venturists had kidnapped "people who wouldn't be missed" and then experimented on them until they died.

That was a very serious and shocking allegation. However, after having spent time with Pizer and his followers, I believed it could be true.

In fact, I had heard rumors of the exact same thing while I was at Alcor in Scottsdale, almost twenty years after Alan's informant came forward. That was one of the reasons I had wanted to stay even longer at Alcor, bugging my colleagues, to get proof of those rumored kidnappings and alleged murders. Hearing that Alan's informant had the same suspicions was extremely frightening.

In his book Alan quotes his informant: "These people will literally stop at nothing to insure their survival. They are ruthless in the sense that they don't care what laws they break as long as they can continue their mission. . . . They almost don't think of themselves as humans, but as a superior life form. . . . I believe Kent and the others want to recruit followers, set themselves up as the leaders, and make these people subservient to them. They say they believe there's going to be an apocalypse, and they are going to be the only ones who survive, the only ones who deserve to survive, and through their science they are going to repopulate the earth through cryonics and cloning. And, they believe that how they prepare for that eventuality is not restricted by law. Only their survival matters. The ends justify the means."

It all sounded too familiar to me.

"These people are completely without scruples," Alan's informant said. "If they needed to, they'd have no compunction against lying, stealing, or whatever. I think they might even . . . might even kill to do what they thought necessary. If not to survive, after some cataclysm, then to protect their organization. I'm telling you these people have no souls. No conscience."

One day the informant told Alan his apartment had been broken into and torn apart. Someone was looking for something. The informant was very afraid for his safety and felt like he was being watched.

The next time Alan spoke to him, he told his informant the case was over. Because of the bunglings of Alan's boss, it would never go to court. The informant kept in touch with Alan off and on for about another year, then quit calling.

After the case was dropped, Alcor filed two lawsuits against the Riverside coroner's office. One had to do with the privacy of Alcor's "electronic correspondence" and the interruption of its e-mail services when the computers were confiscated. It was settled out of court and Alcor officers claimed they were paid $30,000. The other suit was for what they claimed had been their false arrest and detainment. This one was also settled out of court. According to Alcorians, they got an additional $90,000 in that settlement.

Alcor saw an immense increase in requests for information from potential members after the Riverside coroner's office dropped the case. The whole fiasco only succeeded in driving their membership up. After that, the Riverside coroner's office received a Christmas card from Alcor.

The card's caption read: "During the Holiday season more than ever, our thoughts turn gratefully to those who have made our progress possible." Underneath the caption was a single handwritten word: "Thanks."

TWENTY

"WHEN WILL IT END?"

As a result of my coming forward in *Sports Illustrated* and then providing further information to local authorities, including Arizona state representative Bob Stump, HB 2637 was drafted in the Arizona House of Representatives in February 2004. The bill was designed to force cryonics facilities operating in the state to be regulated under the Arizona Board of Funeral Directors and Embalmers. The bill's target was obvious. Alcor was, and is, the only cryonics organization operating in Arizona. The House Health Committee gave the bill a do-pass recommendation.

The lawmakers behind the bill weren't aiming to shut down Alcor. They didn't even plan to force cryonics storage facilities to comply with the same rules as funeral homes. But fairly, they wanted to come up with a new, unique code of conduct under which cryonics facilities would be regulated. The state funeral board would be the regulating body, overseeing Alcor's adherence to these new rules.

Cryonicists blistered Bob Stump with e-mails. It was obvious they hadn't even read the bill, because they accused him of wanting to thaw out frozen Alcorians. Mr. Stump displayed what I consider impressive restraint and patience in actually replying to those long, fanatical e-mails. At times, though, Representative Stump seemed to become understandably exasperated, writing, "Have you read the bill? . . . Do you believe the cryonics industry should have no oversight whatsoever? This bill simply provides oversight of an industry that has none. . . . This bill does NOT cast judgment, pro or con, on cryonics contrary to what you may have heard. The misinformation regarding this bill is breathtaking."

Alcor hired a full-time lobbyist to fight the bill.

From personal experience, I know Alcor and its members are strongly opposed to any regulation at all. They have good reason to worry what could happen if the outside world got a thorough look at their past and present practices.

Then, on the cryonics Internet bulletin boards, it seemed Alcor was going to respond by playing the religion card.

On CryoNet.org, David Pizer and other cryonicists posted messages suggesting that Alcorians could save themselves from government regulation by turning Alcor into a church. Pizer had done it by starting the Church of Venturism. If they were successful, they could claim religious freedom and cry religious persecution whenever anyone opposed them. In Alcor's case, the "opposition" came in the form of the government's trying to regulate them.

We all know that anyone can mail in paperwork and a little money and become registered as a minister in his or her own religion. People use it as a tax shelter or so they can perform marriages. But to me, Alcor's using religion as a tool would be real Thomas Jefferson–spinning-in-his-grave-type stuff.

Some Alcorians ultimately took a different track to derail the legislation that would regulate them, though.

Shortly before the bill came to a vote, Representative Stump pulled it himself. Stump killed the legislation that would regulate Alcor because he started receiving death threats.

"They had a ruthless campaign," he said in a newspaper interview. "I'm not a glutton for punishment." One phone call was so serious, Stump felt so personally threatened, he referred it to the Capitol Police.

Rudy Thomas, director of the Arizona Board of Funeral Directors and Embalmers, worked closely with Representative Stump, drafting the bill. Researching the fairest way to regulate Alcor, Thomas attended Alcor board meetings and was amazed at how widespread cryonics was: "There were people calling in from all over the world. . . . And if looks could kill, I'd be dead." Alcorians starting following him in their cars and harassing him. "I was labeled an archenemy of cryonics because I was looking into regulating them. They left me notes saying I had to stop what I was doing and I didn't know who I was dealing with." Previously, Thomas had been the assistant chief of police in Detroit. "I was the head of the Detroit narcotics and vice division," he told me, "so I took the threats I got from Alcor in stride. Representative Stump, though, was very scared at the threats against him and his family. We dropped the bill."

Several months after the bill was dropped, veteran political journalist Phil Riske wrote, "Disciples of cryonics . . . do not suffer critics well. Just ask Arizona State Rep. Bob Stump. He received threatening messages last year because he sponsored a bill that would have established state regulatory authority over Alcor Life Extension Foundation, the Scottsdale facility that is the cold graveyard of baseball immortal Ted Williams."

Alcorians actually posted physical threats against Stump on CryoNet.org. After that, Stump said he had "no plans" to bring the bill back to life.

It's apparent from the postings on CryoNet.org and other discussion groups that hard-core cryonicists, and the Venturism disciples, are getting dangerously close to the world of Waco, Koresh, and the Branch Davidians. Some of those postings are hair-raising. It's all "We'll do things our own way," and "If we need to separate ourselves from the rest of the world, so be it," and "We know best so why adhere to the laws of lesser men?" They have to keep up the struggle against those they call the "deathists." One such post reads:

> We don't need to agree with the normals, but only to find a way to work with them—we might be able to do something about it.
>
> We need to create a class of people to tend our bodies when we've deanimated. Employees won't do it—anyone whose loyalties depend on the highest bidder isn't someone I want my existence to rely on for several decades. We need a class of people who are fundamentally and psychologically locked in to doing it. We need them to be mindfucked into doing it. We need a class of true-believers, thralls, people who would actually die to keep the nitrogen topped up in the dewars.

I was at Waco. I've seen the carnage that can result from these kinds of fanatics. Based on that experience, I believe Pizer's Ventureville is every

bit as much a cult compound, a stronghold of fanaticism, as David Koresh's Davidian complex was. I've tried to hold the brains of ATF officers
inside their skulls while choppering them to the hospital. Let me tell you,
it is much smarter to try to nip these things in the bud.

Of Alcor, the legitimate cryobiologist Kenneth Storey has said, "They
are more or less a theology; there is no real difference between cryonics
and any other religious organization. They have the truth with no proof,
you must have faith but you can never see a real example of it, you must
do what they say without any hesitation (give large amounts of money to
them every so often) and they have this key to eternal life."

───────────────

Months after meeting with Detectives Carr and Garcia regarding the death
of John Dentinger, I called Detective Carr on the phone. I wanted to check
on the progress of the case, see if there was anything else I could do to
help the LAPD. I was told the homicide investigation was "ongoing."

"We appreciate your coming forward. We will look into it. But Mr.
Johnson," Detective Carr said, "I'm going to be honest with you. That
case is over ten years old. Right now we're working on the half-dozen murders that happened last night. Tomorrow, it'll be the same thing. We'll be
in touch."

Dejected, I sat down and idly Googled Detective Carr. I was surprised
and impressed to find out that he had been assigned the Black Dahlia murder case in the late '90s. I read an interview where he pretty much said
this exact same thing about the Black Dahlia case: that it was important,
but that the daily homicides in Los Angeles took precedence. I knew the
kind of workload these guys were under. I couldn't blame Detective Carr.
But I was disappointed in the system. We're talking about murder.

MARCH 14, 2004, 8:00 P.M.

I was leaving the Glendale property, on my way to pick up Beverly from
work. The sun had recently set. Bev's car, an early 1990s Ford convertible,
was parked out in the street. As I unlocked the door I noticed an SUV
parked down the street. It was three or four houses back, far enough away

that I couldn't make out whether anyone was inside. What caught my eye was that the vehicle was parked illegally in front of a red curb. That struck me as odd because there were plenty of open parking spaces on the street. The headlights were off but the parking lights were on. Unusual. Then I realized its engine was running.

Okay, they must be picking someone up.

As I pulled away from the curb, though, the SUV's headlights flicked on. I looked in my rearview mirror. The SUV also pulled away from the curb.

Suddenly it was on my tail and FLICK—the high beams came on.

This was a residential area atop a hill. The roads were twisting and lonely; there was nobody else around. There were plenty of side streets that could have been this driver's destination but no, he stuck right to me. We navigated around some turns. He was right on my bumper, dangerously close.

We straightened out on a stretch of road leading down to a traffic light. I accelerated. He kept right up with me, and I mean right on top of me. He was so close all I could see was his bumper as I squinted into the wash of his high beams. His engine was roaring. There was no more than a foot or two between us. This was no Glendale soccer mom running late to fetch Junior from practice. This person was trying to terrorize me, or worse.

Without taking my eyes off the road, I reached down to the left side of my waist where I always have my cell phone clipped on. Great. This was one of the extremely rare times I didn't have my phone with me.

We were racing down the hill. If I had touched the brakes, he would've slammed right into me. A few times I was able to get a couple feet between us and see a bit of his grill. It looked like a Jeep grill, maybe a late model Cherokee, but I wasn't positive. The headlights were so bright I couldn't make out the driver at all. I also couldn't tell whether or not there was someone in the passenger seat.

At the bottom of the hill, the traffic light was red and I came to a stop. The SUV stopped so close I still couldn't see anything but bumper and a tiny bit of grill. I normally turned left at this intersection on my way to Bev's job. I figured, *Let me take a right, just to see if he follows me.*

He did. So I made another turn onto an even smaller residential side street. He followed me again.

All right, I figured, *this has to be someone from Alcor, or a hired gun.* There was no way I was going to let them see where my wife worked.

I made a few turns, doubling back. I turned onto Colorado, one of the main streets in Glendale, and approached the big and busy intersection of Colorado and Brand. There were four lanes of traffic on my side of Colorado and the same number of lanes facing me. Brand was several lanes across as well. Normally I would have stayed on Colorado and shot across Brand toward Bev's job. I had an idea. I got into the left-hand-turn lane, as if I was going to turn left onto Brand.

The light was red. Everybody was stopped. I put on my left blinker. I watched the cross traffic for a minute . . . wait for a break . . . wait . . . wait . . . a small hole was coming and . . . NOW! I gunned the engine, raced out into the intersection, and yanked the wheel hard right, cutting straight across the three lanes of cars on my right. I zoomed past all of them, taking the surprise right turn, right through the red light.

It's an old ambulance trick. Forget about left lane, right lane, take the path of least resistance. Of course in an ambulance you have the benefit of a wailing siren and flashing lights.

I timed it right. It was too tight for the SUV to stay with me. There was no way the driver could have followed me without slamming into traffic.

I flipped my finger to the Jeep and banged a few quick turns, angling through side streets. I was shaking. I pulled over for a minute to calm myself, my eyes glued to the rearview mirror. I have to admit, I had another moment of wondering whether or not I was doing the right thing, staying involved in all this. I thought about Karen Silkwood, driven off the road after blowing the whistle on her company. Was all this really worth being threatened and terrorized?

I waited a few more minutes to make sure the coast was clear, and then went and picked up Beverly.

She knew right away that something was wrong. I told her what had happened. It frightened her terribly. We drove around awhile, making sure no one was following us. Bev kept looking out the back window. I couldn't stop thinking about the danger I was placing her in.

We circled the block a few times before going into the house. There was no sign of the SUV.

I got inside and called John Heer. He couldn't believe what I had done, roaring through a red light like that. John said he never would've thought of doing that. I told him I didn't recommend it.

The next day, on John's advice, I drove to the local police department. You should've seen the looks on those cops' faces when I told them what I had done at Colorado and Brand. I was sure they didn't like guys playing *Starsky and Hutch* on their city streets, so I told them I was a paramedic. They knew what kind of training and driving situations veteran paramedics have behind them. Still, they were skeptical, so I asked them if they had heard of "the whole Ted Williams thing." They had.

"Have you heard about the guy who fled the company that cut off Ted's head and was making trouble for them in the news?"

"Oh yeah," they said. "We heard about that guy."

"That's me."

"Really?!"

They Googled Larry Johnson and Alcor while I sat there. They were already pretty knowledgeable about the whole story, actually. They had been following it.

I told them I was glad they knew I was in town. I wanted them to know about everything in case they found my corpse out in the desert somewhere. I told them about my recent death threats. I told them LAPD detectives Carr and Garcia were investigating the death of John Dentinger.

"Larry, thanks for coming in, but listen. If you notice you're being followed again, just drive to the police station."

Several days later, Beverly and I were getting into my truck.

"What's that?" Beverly asked.

There was another note under my windshield wiper. I read it and then handed it to Beverly. Her hands started shaking, then Bev started to cry. It broke my heart.

Beverly looked up at me through her tears and asked, "When will it end?"

I didn't know what to say.

FOr tHE
ATTEMPtED
muRder OF OUR
PATienTs
U wiLL
dIe

Threat Letter #3.

EPILOGUE

In July 2002, the scandal involving the treatment and handling of Ted Williams's remains brought Alcor into the national spotlight for a short time. Connie Chung called it "macabre" and "terrible"; Tucker Carlson on CNN's *Crossfire* called it "grotesque, ghoulish, and revolting." And it was all happening in violation of Ted's will, they informed viewers. Bioethicists debated cryonicists on TV, calling Alcor a scam that "doesn't even meet the silliness threshold."

Ted Williams once said, "A man has to have goals—for a day, for a lifetime—that was mine, to have people say, 'There goes Ted Williams, the greatest hitter who ever lived.'" This was a far cry from the type of immortality his troubled son and the people at Alcor had planned for him.

In 2005, a sculptor displayed what he called Ted Williams's "Death Mask" at a New York art gallery. To gain publicity, he claimed at first it was a true cast of Ted's frozen face at Alcor. It was gruesome. Frankly it made me sick that someone would do that. The *New York Times* called me for verification that it was Ted's actual face. I declined comment. The truth is, Ted's frozen face looked much worse.

Ted Williams answered the call to serve his country, not once, but twice. He put his life in jeopardy and came close to losing it. That's enough for me, as an American, to be grateful to him.

In an essay titled "Achieving the Impossible Dream," Harvard evolutionary biologist Stephen Jay Gould wrote, "Williams's .406 [season] is a beacon in the history of excellence, a lesson to all who value the best in human possibility." Perfection was more than an attitude for Ted, it was a lifelong ambition. With hard work and determination, he proved anything is possible.

Ted Williams was a baseball legend and an American hero. Now he's just "that guy who was frozen."

Personally, Ted Williams has always been a role model for me. I still have my Sears Ted Williams bicycle. I still have my Little League Ted Williams baseball bat. To this day, I am a starry-eyed kid and Ted Williams is a hero to me.

Right now Ted's bodily remains are inside Alcor, frozen in pieces, upside down in cold steel cans, cracking, all against his stated wishes. It doesn't escape me that my name is now in one small, sad way associated with that of Ted Williams. I have become an unfortunate footnote to his great name. I only hope I can one day look back and say I was part of the team that got him out of Alcor and helped fulfill his last wish, to be cremated and "sprinkled at sea off the coast of Florida where the water is very deep."

I fled Alcor six years ago. As of July 2009, here is a rundown on where some of the people discussed in this book are now.

Because of her settlement agreement with her brother, John Henry Williams, **Bobby-Jo Ferrell** and her husband, Mark, can no longer participate in the efforts to release Ted's body from Alcor.

John Heer continues the fight.

Ted Williams's nephews still insist that their uncle never wanted cryonics for himself.

John Henry Williams died of leukemia in March 2004. He must have worked something out with Alcor regarding the debt for his father's bungled cryonic suspension, because he's currently residing inside a dewar or two. From what I can tell, John Henry is now A-2063.

Two weeks after my story appeared in *Sports Illustrated* in August 2003, **Jerry Lemler** resigned as president and CEO of Alcor citing health problems. Jerry had been receiving treatment for cancer for some time, but the resignation came without warning. The timing made me think he got out of the kitchen before it got too hot in there. Jerry continued to be active in cryonics, though, retaining the title of Alcor's medical director.

Jerry's cancer went into remission and he accepted a position as a psychiatrist and medical director at a behavioral health services center in a very small town ninety miles north of Alcor—Jerry once more went to work as the head of a mental health facility. He returned to Phoenix in 2007 to work in private practice for general adult psychiatry.

Joe Hovey also retired from Alcor shortly after I left. He owns a house in Scottsdale and, as far as I can tell, has continued to work with Alcor sometimes officially, sometimes unofficially.

Charles Platt left Alcor but continued "pissing out" for a while from a new position as consultant at Suspended Animation, a smaller cryonics organization in Boynton Beach, Florida. Suspended Animation's CEO is **Saul Kent,** who remains extremely active in cryonics and at Alcor, both personally and financially. I don't believe Charles is an official employee at SA; I think he calls himself a "cryonics consultant."

I hope I'm wrong, but I believe Todd Huffman is still active in cryonics. I heard rumors that he left Scottsdale with Charles and went down to SA in Florida, yet remained a field team member for Alcor. Todd once told me he wanted to be a neurosurgeon. I believe Todd can do anything he sets his mind to.

Mathew Sullivan has left Alcor as well and, last I heard, was also working at Suspended Animation.

Tanya Jones, the woman who—according to Hugh Hixon's eyewitness account—drew up the injection Mike Darwin used to kill John Dentinger, got promoted a few times. First, she got my old job, Alcor's chief operating officer. Then, in mid-2008, she became Alcor's president and executive director (apparently Alcor no longer uses the title CEO).

Jennifer Chapman is still at Alcor as well. She's also been promoted a few times. When Tanya was bumped up to president and executive director, Jennifer was promoted to COO. Then Tanya Jones left Alcor in early 2009 (amid rumors of being fired by Saul Kent), and Jennifer Chapman, Helmet Girl, became Alcor's president and executive director. On the cryonics Internet bulletin boards, Jennifer's promotion to president is a joke. They make cracks about her sitting at her desk doing her nails all day. Worse, it's common knowledge among Alcorians that Jennifer has a phobia about dead people. When I was at Alcor, she refused to be in the building when a suspension was in progress.

Because of me, Alcor has apparently battened down the hatches and reorganized its management structure. Cryonicists complain online that since I left, Saul Kent has basically taken the place over, squashed all opposition, and rendered the board powerless. The company can't come out and say it but, because of my whistle-blowing, Alcorians vow never to let a nonmember reach a high-ranking position again.

I've read that the Alcor building itself has been given a facelift since I've been there. For instance, they have replaced the plaques under the patient photos on the lobby wall. They no longer contain the words "First Life Cycle." According to Alcor's online news reports, they were getting too many "odd looks" from people taking the tours. I haven't been inside the facility since I fled Scottsdale, of course, but my feeling is they're trying harder and harder to appear more "normal."

Mike Perry and **Hugh Hixon** continue to live and work at Alcor.

Mike Darwin pops up on cryonics Internet bulletin boards once in a while. Although he's secretive about his whereabouts, he is rumored to be in Florida, working with Saul Kent, Mathew Sullivan, and the other ex–Alcor leaders who left Scottsdale for SA.

David Pizer continues to build up the ranks of his followers at the Ventureville compound.

As strongly as I feel about Ted Williams and the serious wrongs he and his family have suffered, I know there are more important issues to be investigated at Alcor: For starters, from what I've heard with my own ears, there are the questionable human resources practices, environmental waste and dumping issues, and seemingly unlawful storage of human bodies. If Rudy Thomas, the director of the Arizona Board of Funeral Directors and Embalmers, is correct, what they've been doing to their members' bodies—

including Ted Williams's body—qualifies as mutilation. If I am to believe what Alan Kunzman and Alcor's own OR technician James Sikes have told me is status quo, they have been dumping toxic chemicals as well as AIDS- and cancer-ridden blood down the drain into public water systems and into the plant beds outside their back door—for decades. If I am to believe what company officers have told me, including the recording I have of Hugh Hixon's firsthand account of what happened in that North Hollywood garage, Alcor's past leaders have literally gotten away with murder.

I never set out to close down Alcor. Even now, that's not what I want. The company should, however, be regulated. This is for the good of its own members. Hospitals and funeral homes are regulated. To date, cryonics seems to have been too far out on the fringe to attract enough government attention. But the people at Alcor have in my view been abusing the fact that they've always slipped through the cracks. And then, the one time they were faced with regulation, they avoided it by threatening the life of the Arizona state representative who wrote the reform bill. As for Alcorian attitudes toward regulation, Saul Kent, the most powerful man in cryonics, calls the FDA a "terrorist organization" that "will stop at nothing to destroy its enemies."

After all of my horrible experiences with Alcor, I still have no problem with people who choose cryonic suspension instead of burial or cremation. If that's what you want, good luck, go for it. That's fine with me. In a free country, I believe that people should be able to have their earthly remains handled as they wish. There are some pretty smart people putting their hopes in cryonics. Personally, I got real swept up with the incredible possibilities at first. What they're doing at Alcor, though, is not that kind of science.

When nefarious marketing combines with shady business practices and a willingness to hasten the demise of "patients," it shocks the conscience and cries out for reform. When in March 2009 President Barack Obama announced the lifting of the ban on federal funding for research with embryonic stem cells, the regulations simultaneously forbade human cloning.

I don't believe a blanket prohibition like that should be adopted for cryonics, but a good place to start would be a federal statute modeled along the lines of Bob Stump's ill-fated bill in Arizona, creating a unique code of conduct under which cryonics facilities would be regulated. I don't think anyone wants to spend the money creating a new government body to oversee cryonics facilities—the code of conduct could be enforced by state funeral boards.

I know this isn't tobacco or Enron or a national security issue. I know it affects only a small group of people. But murder is murder. I was at Waco. When I say these prominent Alcorians are cultlike fanatics, I am not exaggerating. They consider themselves the hope of mankind, the intellectual elite who deserve to be frozen into the coming millennia. What are the laws of twenty-first-century society to them, the immortals? I've seen them lord their delusions of godlike control over their frozen comrades, wielding the power of what they believe is eternal life and death. I've seen them act completely without conscience, feeling justified in anything they do. I've watched them apathetically slaughter animals in experiments with no scientific value whatsoever.

I believe I did everything a decent human being should do, placed in that situation at Alcor. The LAPD Homicide Division didn't have the manpower to follow through on the John Dentinger homicide investigation. The Florida state attorney's office let the Ted Williams case die on the vine. An Arizona state representative folded under Alcorian death threats. I put my wife and myself in danger to gather proof against these people and these are the results?

In 2006, someone called my dad and told him I had been killed in a motorcycle accident. This was meant to terrorize him and to send me a message: They were willing to go after my family.

After telling my father that I was dead, the caller asked him for my current address.

My dad, though worried by the call, didn't fall for it. He wrote down the number that showed up on his caller ID and gave it to me. It was from inside Alcor.

In 2007, an anonymous caller reached me at my new job. The call came straight to my phone, not through the company switchboard. Somehow they had my direct number, a line that had been connected only a few days before. Even I didn't know that number by heart. When I answered, the voice said, "Larry Johnson?"

"Yes."

The voice stated my exact street address, then said, "I can see that Beverly is home alone right now. You two sleep well tonight." Click.

Running through the halls toward my truck, I called home and told Bev to crouch down in the center of the kitchen, between the island and the sink. I raced home with my 9mm Beretta shaking in my hand. Beverly was sobbing when I got there, lying on the floor, clutching the handgun I had shown her how to use. She had almost shot me in blind terror. I had to pry the gun out of her hand. Several days later, Beverly saw a car outside our house with someone inside taking pictures of her. She called me, crying. Again, I rushed home.

I know that by writing this book to finally tell the whole bizarre story I am still doing the right thing. I am convinced that Alcor should be investigated and regulated. I can only hope this book encourages more people—and the authorities—to act and not let these horrible deeds stand.

If my previous experience serves as an example, Alcor officials will sue me over this book. Perhaps, as before, they will file frivolous lawsuits to try to distract the public eye from what I have reported here.

How truthful were they in response to the *Sports Illustrated* article and the questions raised in it?

After the *SI* article, Carlos Mondragon denied all my allegations to the press, saying Alcor had "nothing to hide." Then several months later, after an OSHA walk-through of the facility, Alcor actually admitted to four violations in its own News Bulletin, each of them "serious," OSHA's second highest order of risk.

Mondragon told the press I had stolen my company cell phone—after Alcor had signed for its return.

Alcor sent John Heer a jumbled packet of paperwork, claiming it constituted Ted Williams's Document of Gift—yet the only piece of paper in the entire mess with Ted's signature on it was the, shall we say, highly dubious oil-stained note.

Carlos Mondragon, Paula Lemler, and Charles Platt each denied in the press that Ted Williams's DNA samples could not possibly be missing because Alcor never takes DNA samples from their members—and then in a news bulletin four months later, Tanya Jones reminded members to provide DNA samples so that Alcor could keep them on file.

This time, though, I have my recordings.

I don't know how Charles Platt could deny telling me that he was afraid some *National Enquirer* photographer would snap a picture of an Alcorian dumping AIDS-contaminated blood, as well as toxic chemicals, into the shrubs out back. I don't know how Hugh Hixon could deny saying Alcor used powerful paralytic drugs to "put them down and make sure they stay that way. We did not want anyone waking up and causing problems." I don't know how Joe Hovey could deny saying, "He killed her."

Still, I have no doubt that they will go back to calling me a liar and a thief. More important, though, I have to take the death threats seriously, for my wife's sake and for my own. As of July 2009 there are at least 888 active Alcorians who consider me a mortal enemy. Some of them are worth millions, hundreds of millions, even billions of dollars. Some of them believe that I am a threat to their everlasting life. This group includes David Pizer and his militant cult at Ventureville.

Today in Scottsdale, Alcor remains in business, smug in its victories, operating without any regulation whatsoever. I know that if nothing is done, this book, like the Dora Kent and Ted Williams scandals, will only serve to boost hits on Alcor's Web site and increase their membership. That is quite a thought.

I don't think things will ever return to normal for my wife and me. Thanks mostly to Bev's understanding, trust in me, and her core belief that one should do the right thing even in the face of danger, we are still together. But I still can't answer Beverly's question—I don't know when it'll end, or how. I do know Alcor should be regulated, and I know those responsible for the misdeeds reported in this book should be held accountable for what they've done. Doing the right thing is not always easy.

Beverly carries mace everywhere she goes.

I still carry my gun.

CAST OF CHARACTERS

The job titles of Alcor employees and company officers changed quite often—before, during, and after the time I worked there. Some had previously been Alcor presidents, vice presidents, board members, and advisors to the board, etc. It was never easy for me to keep track of their official titles, and some of them may have held multiple titles while I was there. The Alcorian job titles listed below are—to the best of my knowledge—as they were when I was working at Alcor, from January through August 2003. Some Alcor employees have since left, others have new titles, and a few have been promoted (see Epilogue).

Aido: The cat.

Alan Kunzman: The investigating detective from the Riverside coroner's office when Alcorians including Mike Darwin, Hugh Hixon, Mike Perry, Carlos Mondragon, and David Pizer were arrested (by a different investigator) during the homicide investigation of Saul Kent's mother, Dora. Alan tells of the experience in his book, *Mothermelters*. From Alan's perspective, "they got away with murder."

Beverly Johnson: My wife.

Bill Faloon: A longtime associate of Saul Kent's, Bill was prominent in the development of the TimeShip project.

Bill Haworth: A public relations professional hired by Alcor.

Bobby-Jo Williams Ferrell: Ted Williams's daughter who fought to have Ted's body released from Alcor in order to provide him with the cremation he requested in his will. Bobby-Jo's husband is Mark Ferrell.

Bobby June, Louise Gold, Peter Voss, and Regina Pancake: Alcor's Los Angeles–area emergency response team/volunteer transport team. Regina now works full-time at Alcor.

Bob Stump: The Arizona state representative who drafted the bill to regulate Alcor, then dropped the bill after receiving threats.

Brian Carr: The LAPD detective investigating John Dentinger's death. His partner in that investigation was John Garcia. Detective Carr is also known for his work on the notorious Black Dahlia murder case.

Carlos Mondragon: Senior board member and one of the Alcorian leaders arrested during the Dora Kent homicide investigation. Carlos was an ex-president of Alcor and acted as Alcor's spokesman when I first came forward in the press, blowing the whistle on the organization's practices.

Charles Platt: During my time at Alcor, Charles went from being called independent contractor to chief operating officer to consultant. In my opinion, Charles was the one Alcor employee who kept the place together, organizationally. Even after he asked me to take over for him as acting COO, Charles was very active at Alcor for the rest of my time there.

Claudia Williams: Ted Williams's younger daughter, who sided with her brother, John Henry, claiming that Ted Williams wanted cryonic suspension for himself.

Cynthia Pilgeram: Cynthia's was the one case I knew of where a body was successfully removed from Alcor. Family members knew Cynthia didn't want cryonic suspension for herself. She had requested a Christian burial, but her husband, Laurence, put her into Alcor against her wishes.

David Hayes: An Alcor representative contracted mainly to assist in the transport of deanimated members. David was the Alcorian who took possession of Ted Williams's body on behalf of Alcor from Ted's son, John Henry, in Florida.

David Pizer: Founder of the Church of Venturism, David is a past Alcor vice president and remains very active at Alcor. He was one of the Alcorian leaders arrested during the Dora Kent homicide investigation.

Dick Clair: A television writer/producer, pioneer cryonicist, and Alcor member; Dick's Emmy Award awaits his reanimation in Alcor's lobby.

Dixie: The mentally and physically impaired German shepherd I met at Saul Kent's house. Dixie was one of the many unfortunate dogs that have been experimented on at Alcor and its affiliated research facilities over the years.

Dora Kent: The woman who was allegedly euthanized with a lethal injection of barbiturates—the same exact drugs used to carry out the death sentence in prisons—by the Alcor surgical team led by Mike Darwin, under the orders of her son, Saul.

Erico: Charles Platt's girlfriend, who took the OR notes during Ted Williams's decapitation surgery.

Frank Brothers: Friend and live-in nurse of Ted Williams who believed it was never Ted's wish to be put into cryonic suspension at Alcor. George Carter and Jack Gard were other domestic employees of Ted's who felt the same way.

Futureman 2030: A prominent Alcor member who changed his name to Futureman and believed he would be reanimated in time to celebrate his hundredth birthday in the year 2030. Hence, he identified himself as "FM-2030." His picture was on the wall in Alcor's front lobby.

Greg Fahy: A cryonicist and cryobiology researcher at Saul Kent's CCR facility in Rancho Cucamonga, California.

Hugh Hixon Jr.: Facilities engineer and senior board member. Hugh jury-rigged Alcor's machines and developed many of the chemical formulas used in cryonic suspensions. His father, also named Hugh, was in cryonic suspension at Alcor. Hugh was one of the Alcor employees arrested during the Dora Kent homicide investigation.

James Sikes: Jerry Lemler's son-in-law, James is married to Jessica Sikes. A computer systems technician, James tended to Alcor's computers and was paid extra as a lab assistant during cryonic suspensions. I've seen him referred to as technical support staff and as facilities operations manager.

Jennifer Chapman: As director of membership services, Jennifer was in charge of helping prospective members with their Alcor applications. She was also active in marketing and recruitment.

Jerry Leaf: Now in cryonic suspension, Jerry was at one time an Alcor vice president. An ex–Green Beret and cryobiology researcher at UCLA, Jerry is considered a cryonics hero by many Alcorians.

Jerry Lemler: Alcor president and CEO during my tenure.

Jerry Searcy: An unpaid, elderly Alcor volunteer who did administrative work and ran errands.

Jessica Sikes: Jerry Lemler's daughter, who was hired as Jerry's administrative assistant. She was also paid separately to assist in cryonic suspensions, for example, as note-taker for the OR logs.

Joe Hovey: Alcor treasurer and secretary, previously Alcor vice president and comptroller.

Joe Klockgether: Active in cryonics since the 1960s, Joe worked with pioneer cryonicist Bob Nelson and was sued as a result of the Chatsworth Incident. Joe was the mortician who assisted Alcor officials by helping them obtain death certificates and by allowing Alcor transport teams to use his Orange County funeral home for initial suspension procedures for members who deanimated in Southern California.

John Dentinger: A gay rights activist, John was the Alcorian Mike Darwin allegedly euthanized in North Hollywood in order to hurry up the cryonic suspension process.

John Garcia: The LAPD detective investigating John Dentinger's death. His partner in that investigation was Brian Carr.

John Grigg: David Pizer's right-hand man and general manager of the Creekside Preserve Lodge (Ventureville).

John Heer: Attorney for Ted Williams's daughter Bobby-Jo and then Ted Williams's nephews in their efforts to free Ted Williams's remains from Alcor. John became my "whistle-blowing confidant" while I was gathering information at Alcor.

Jose Kanshepolsky: The retired surgeon Alcor hired to decapitate deanimated members.

Keith Henson: An active cryonicist and hero to many at Alcor, Keith vehemently fought against the Church of Scientology. At Alcor, before my time, Keith assisted in cryonic suspensions and for several years wrote a column for Alcor's *Cryonics* magazine.

Mathew Sullivan: Director of suspension readiness. I still don't know exactly what that meant, though Mathew had a hand in ordering supplies, organizing patient files, and, I suppose, keeping Alcor in a state of readiness for cryonic suspensions.

Michael Riskin: Alcor chief financial officer. Riskin lived in Orange County, California, and visited Alcor roughly every two weeks.

Mike Darwin (Mike Federowicz): An Alcor ex-president, Darwin was active in cryonics from a young age. He has been called Saul Kent's protégé (hired by Saul to perform a cryonic suspension when Mike was seventeen years old) and was the first to develop and implement some of the suspension protocols still used at Alcor. He at times held the title team leader, called in to perform cryonic suspension surgery, as in the case of Ted Williams. Mike was the leader of the team of Alcorians who were arrested during the Dora Kent homicide investigation.

Mike Perry (R. Michael Perry): Patient caretaker. Mike was technically responsible for patients' safety inside the Patient Care Bay, though he lent a hand in a variety of other capacities. A prolific writer, Mike also penned many articles for Alcor's *Cryonics* magazine and Web site. Mike was another Alcorian arrested during the Dora Kent homicide investigation.

Paula Lemler: Jerry Lemler's wife, who was hired as his typist.

Ray Carrillo: The Riverside County coroner and bungling boss of Detective Alan Kunzman. Ray stopped Kunzman from confiscating Dora Kent's head and hands during Kunzman's first visit to the facility and ordered that they remain at Alcor—whereupon they promptly disappeared. As a result, formal homicide charges could not be brought against the Alcor leaders.

Rick Potvin: A very active and flamboyantly dressed Alcorian who hosted several cryonics online bulletin boards and discussion groups.

Robert Ettinger: The "Father of Cryonics."

Robert F. (Bob) Nelson: Pioneer cryonicist and author of *We Froze the First Man,* Bob is demonized by those at Alcor for allowing some of the first people he placed in cryonic suspension to thaw and melt in what came to be known as the Chatsworth Incident.

Rudy Hoffman: The Alcorian insurance agent who set up the insurance policies Alcor members were required to purchase, naming Alcor as the beneficiary to help pay for the members' long-term storage.

Rudy Thomas: The director of the Arizona Board of Funeral Directors and Embalmers who in February 2004 helped Arizona state representative Bob Stump draft a bill that would have regulated Alcor. As a result, Thomas was dubbed a cryonics archenemy. Alcorians followed him and left him threatening notes. He has called what Ted Williams's body has endured at Alcor "mutilation" and illegal under Arizona state law. After his personal experience with Alcor, Rudy feels that it needs to be regulated.

Saul Kent: Saul was one of the original cryonics pioneers. Saul exerts much control over happenings at the facility, financial and otherwise. His other enterprises include his Life Extension Foundation, through which he sells vitamins and supplements. Saul also founded CCR, Critical Care Research (aka 21st Century Medicine), in Rancho Cucamonga, California.

Sid Horwitz: The attorney representing Alcor in the lawsuit brought against me following publication of Tom Verducci's *Sports Illustrated* article.

Steve Bridge: The Alcor board member and ex-president who objected, via teleconference, to my becoming COO, because, to his knowledge, I wasn't an official Alcor member.

Steve Harris, MD: A CCR employee during my tenure at Alcor, Steve conducted animal experiments and research there. Steve was the medical doctor who took Dora Kent into his care just before her son, Saul, took her from her nursing home and brought her to die at Alcor's facility in Riverside, California.

Steve Rude: A local mortician Alcor hired to collect and cremate members' bodies when they were not signed up for full-body suspensions.

Tanya Jones: The Alcorian who drew up the syringe Mike Darwin allegedly used to end John Dentinger's life, Tanya Jones replaced me as acting COO and was eventually promoted to president. .

Ted Williams (A-1949): An American hero and sports legend whose remains, sadly, are still frozen inside Alcor. In his will, Ted left instructions for his body to be cremated and his ashes "sprinkled at sea off the coast of Florida where the water is very deep."

Thomas Donaldson: The Alcorian who unsuccessfully sued California in an attempt to achieve a premortem, "elective cryo-preservation." Thomas wanted Carlos Mondragon to euthanize him to have his body frozen before his cancer further damaged his brain.

Todd Huffman: An active Alcorian and member of the Los Angeles–area volunteer response team. Todd was twenty years old when I met him and had already been working with Alcor for several years.

Tom Verducci: The *Sports Illustrated* writer who worked with me on the article that was my first step in making Alcor's misdeeds public.

GLOSSARY

First, the word "cryonics" is commonly confused with "cryogenics" and "cryobiology," so to be clear:

Cryogenics: The study of low temperatures and how they affect materials. A branch of physics, cryogenics is defined by the *Encyclopedia Britannica* as the production and application of low-temperature phenomena. Many people mistakenly use the term "cryogenics" when they are really referring to cryonics.

Cryobiology: The study of the effects of low temperatures on biological matter or organisms. The definition from the Society for Cryobiology Web site reads: "The word cryobiology literally signifies the science of life at icy temperatures. In practice, this field comprises the study of any biological material or system (e.g., proteins, cells, tissues, or organs) subjected to any temperature below normal (ranging from cryogenic temperatures to moderately hypothermic conditions)."

Cryonics: The application of the cold-temperature sciences with the intention of freezing people or animals in the hopes of one day reviving them. Alcor's Web site defines cryonics as "the speculative practice of using cold to preserve the life of a person who can no longer be supported by ordinary medicine. The goal is to carry the person forward through time, for however many decades or centuries might be necessary, until the preservation process can be reversed, and the person restored to full health."

Other Terms:

Alcor Life Extension Foundation: Alcor's full name; I worked there from January to August 2003.

Alcorian: The name the more dedicated Alcor members have given themselves.

Anticoagulants/heparin: After icing the head and body, the first step in cryonic suspension protocol is to inject anticoagulants such as heparin, to stop the blood from clotting, so that the subsequent injections of cryo-preservants can circulate throughout the body.

A-number: A-numbers are how Alcor refers to patients, especially the majority who wish to remain anonymous outside the facility and keep their membership secret. It is Alcor's version of a social security number; for instance, my number was A-2032. The "A" stands for Alcor, and the following four digits are for identification.

Barbiturates: A class of drugs that depress the central nervous system, achieving effects ranging from mild sedation to anesthesia. Dora Kent's toxicology report revealed toxic levels of two barbiturates, pentobarbital and secobarbital, the exact drugs used to euthanize people and animals, as well as execute criminals sentenced to lethal injection.

Blaylock: According to Alan Kunzman, the dummy corporation created by Jerry Leaf while Alcor was in Riverside, California, through which they made a profit by renting stolen UCLA medical equipment to film and TV studios for use as on-camera props.

Blood washout/partial washout: The process by which Alcor replaces a deanimated member's blood with anticoagulants and cryo-preservant chemicals in the hopes of protecting body tissue during cooling to extremely low temperatures during his or her long-term storage.

Cannulation: The process of attaching tubes to arteries so that chemicals can be pumped into the bloodstream.

CCR (Critical Care Research), aka 21st Century Medicine: Although I refer to this facility as CCR throughout this book, many know it as 21st Century Medicine. CCR, in Rancho Cucamonga, California, is run by Saul Kent and staffed by cryonicists who are also cryobiologists whose research focuses on improving Alcor's cryonic suspension techniques and chemical formulas. It was here that I witnessed Dr. Steve Harris perform what I believed was senseless and cruel animal experimentation. Recently deanimated Alcor patients from

Southern California often lay over at CCR when being transported to the Alcor facility in Scottsdale, to begin the "blood washout"—replacing the patient's blood with anticoagulants and/or cryo-preservative chemicals—the initial stages of Alcor's cryo-suspension procedure.

Cephalic isolation box: The Plexiglas box in Alcor's OR inside which newly decapitated Alcorian heads ("cephalons") are screwed into a "halo" and begin the freezing process.

Chatsworth Incident: The name cryonicists have given to the unfortunate series of events when cryonics pioneer Bob Nelson eventually could not afford to replenish the dry ice keeping his first suspended bodies frozen, and allowed them to thaw and melt into each other.

Church of Venturism (renamed the Society for Venturism): Prominent Alcorian David Pizer formed this "religion" based on "the physical pursuit of immortality." Venturists believe mankind will eventually achieve immortality, and they are the ones—the elite visionaries—who deserve to live forever. Pizer owns and operates the remote Arizona desert resort known as the Creekside Preserve Lodge, although Pizer and his devotees refer to it as "Ventureville" and use it regularly for Venturist and Alcorian seminars and training sessions.

Cool-Down Bay: The large room inside Alcor that houses the cooling machines—such as the CryoStar and LR-40—where heads and bodies are cooled down to super-low temperatures before storage. "Patients" normally stop off inside the Cool-Down Bay for several days on their way from their decapitation surgeries in the OR, to their long-term cold storage in the Patient Care Bay.

CPS (as opposed to CPR): Since Alcorians do not want patients to resuscitate, when they perform chest compressions to circulate chemicals through the bloodstream of a deanimated body, they call it cardiopulmonary support as opposed to cardiopulmonary resuscitation.

Crackphone: A modified electrocardiogram machine/computer rig Alcor uses to measure the inevitable brain cracking that heads endure while cooling down to −321 degrees Fahrenheit. The computer measures "acoustic events" from microphones drilled into the skull and resting on the brain. The readouts look like earthquakes on a seismograph. Cryonicists believe that by mapping these incidents, scientists in the future may be able to repair the damage sustained during the freezing process.

Cryonic suspension: The process of icing, injections, surgery, freezing, and cold storage through which Alcor prepares its deanimated members to await re-animation in the future.

Cryo-preservatives/cryo-protectants: Chemicals or substances used to protect biological tissue from freezing damage.

CryoStar: Alcor's malfunctioning CryoStar looked like a big blue, waist-high ice chest, maybe five feet in length and three feet wide—like a refrigerator lying on its side. Alcor obtained its faulty CryoStar from CCR. It was never intended for storing human heads—which are highly susceptible to temperature changes. Still, Alcor kept two heads in their CryoStar without even testing it first. One of these heads was "A-1949." For fear of someone coming to carry away its celebrity head, Alcor protected the CryoStar with a thick chain and padlock.

CryoWars: The name Alcorians have given to their internal power struggles.

Deanimation: Since they consider their frozen patients to still be alive, Alcor officials do not call their patients dead (though they are clinically dead). They refer to them as being "deanimated," and the event of "death" is called "deanimation."

Dewar: A large container for storing extremely hot or cold substances, consisting of two flasks, one inside the other, separated by a vacuum. Most famously used in the distilling of Scotch whisky, the tall silver dewars are used at Alcor for the long-term storage of frozen bodies.

Diprivan: A sedative agent commonly used for the induction of general anesthesia. Seeing Diprivan stored at Alcor was at first a mystery to me—why would anyone need to sedate a corpse?

Document of Gift: The mechanism (paperwork) for donating organs under the Uniform Anatomical Gift Act.

Femoral cutdown: A procedure in which veins in the legs are opened and tubes slid in, one in the femoral vein, one in the femoral artery. The tube in the vein pumps the cryonics chemicals in; the one in the artery sucks the blood and chemical mixture out.

First life cycle/second life cycle: Alcorians believe this current life is only the first of several "cycles." What others call death, Alcor calls the end of the first life cycle. Alcorians believe they will one day be unfrozen and reanimated into their "second life cycle."

Life Extension Foundation: Saul Kent's company that provides paid members with what I would call dubious medical information, while offering supplements and vitamins for sale.

Liquid nitrogen: The cooling agent Alcor uses to bring heads and bodies down to −321 degrees Fahrenheit. Back in the early days, pioneer cryonicists like Bob Nelson used dry ice.

LR-40: A cylindrical aluminum cooling tank that was pumped full of liquid nitrogen and then, through a process of fans and valves, cooled heads down to optimal cryonics storage temperature.

Mannitol: A sugar alcohol commonly used to treat head trauma, and as a cutting agent for street drugs such as heroin (referred to in illegal drug culture as "baby laxative"). I never knew why Alcor stored Mannitol but Detective Alan Kunzman's informant alleged that some Alcorians had run an international cocaine smuggling venture.

Neuro Can: A stainless steel container that Alcor used to store heads. It looked like a lobster pot to me.

Neuro Vault: About three feet per side, Alcor's silver Neuro Vault was a cylindrical cold-storage tank accessed by a lid on top. The company kept heads, samples of patients' DNA, and frozen animal parts in it.

Neuro vs. full-body suspension: Alcorians had the choice to either store only their heads (referred to as a neuro-suspension) or their entire bodies (full-body suspension).

Oil-stained note: The highly contested scrap of paper and John Henry Williams's alleged proof that Ted Williams wanted cryonic suspension for himself.

Paralytic drugs: A class of drug that does just that: paralyzes the patient. When paralytics are administered, patients cannot breathe on their own. They can be fully awake and experience pain but will be unable to move. Vecuronium, stored at Alcor, was a paralytic drug.

Patient: Since Alcor considers the clinically dead people cryonically suspended on premises to be still "alive," what most people call a corpse, Alcor refers to as a patient. To Alcorians, the frozen people in the dewars are equivalent to patients in hospital beds.

Patient Care Bay: The room inside Alcor where the dewars and Neuro Vault are—where frozen Alcor members "reside," awaiting the day future technology will advance to the point of being able to reanimate them.

Perfusion: The process by which chemicals are delivered into the bloodstream. At Alcor, this meant connecting tubes to arteries and pumping in the cryoprotectant chemicals.

Reanimation: To Alcorians, reanimation is another word for their rebirth, perhaps centuries from now, after doctors of the future thaw them out and revive them. They will be "reanimated."

TimeShip: A proposed humungous "Cryotorium" facility large enough to store 10,000 or more cryonauts and transport them into the future. It was compared to an Egyptian pyramid, only much bigger, complete with amusement park–type attractions.

Tuna can: Alcor uses aluminum BumbleBee tuna cans as pedestals, placing upside-down human heads on them so they don't fall over and stick to the bottom of the freezer.

UAGA (Uniform Anatomical Gift Act): In the United States, the legal foundation upon which human organs and tissues are donated to science or medicine for transplantation or research. Alcor uses the UAGA as the legal "justification" for members' leaving their bodies to Alcor.

Vecuronium: A paralyzing agent commonly used to induce skeletal muscle relaxation during surgery or mechanical ventilation (intubation). Seeing vecuronium stored at Alcor was a warning flag to me—when vecuronium is administered, a patient becomes paralyzed immediately and will stop breathing within seconds. Why would anyone need to paralyze a corpse? I wondered.

Vitrification: A process of converting a material into a glasslike solid that is free from any crystalline structure. Alcor and CCR are working on a vitrification process to replace their current freezing process. The benefit would be the removal of water crystals that cause great cellular damage during freezing. I encourage those who read up on Alcor's vitrification process to keep in mind they may be exaggerating their results.

ACKNOWLEDGMENTS

LARRY JOHNSON:

First and foremost I would like to thank my coauthor and friend, Scott Baldyga. From the first time we met at Clancy's in Glendale, California, I knew (even in my paranoid state) I was in the presence of a very talented and caring individual. I was on the run from a group of fanatics and frightened beyond imagination, but he quickly gained my trust. Here (I'm lifting my beer glass) is to the hundreds of hours we sat and discussed my experiences at our frequent hangouts, Starbucks in Studio City and Killer Shrimp in Marina del Rey. You listened to my stories with great interest and enthusiasm and never lost sight of my desire to simply tell the truth in the form of a book. Next, I would like to thank my agent, Sharlene Martin, of Martin Literary Management, another truly talented person. An assiduous worker who continually encouraged me during this project, you are the true definition of determined and hardworking. Thanks so much for all of your support and for believing in me and in this book.

My sincere thanks go to my publisher, Roger Cooper, and to his dedicated staff at Vanguard Press, especially Georgina Levitt. Special thanks go to my publicist, Justin Loeber, and to our film agent, Jody Hotchkiss.

To my parents, thank you for your profound love and support. I would also like to thank attorney John Heer for the sound advice you gave me through my "hell year." Even though I sometimes did not listen to your advice, we quickly became friends and to this day share a common bond. I want to thank Larry Cano and some of the special members of the Ted Williams family, Gino and Andrea Lucero, and Mark and Bobby-Jo Ferrell. My heartfelt thanks go to some of my close friends who helped me keep my sanity during some trying times. Thanks go to Bryan and Emma Bledsoe, Rickey Reed, John Osborn, Marie and Wanda, John Wilson, and Sharon Henry. Oh yes, by the way, Sharon, you were right. A word of gratitude goes to a sports memorabilia dealer who wishes to remain anonymous: Thank you for your support and advice; words cannot describe how much I appreciated your help.

I want to thank the media personalities who treated me in a fair and dignified manner throughout a harrowing event. The list is long; however, I feel I need to mention a few: Tom Verducci and Lester Munson of *Sports Illustrated,* Bill Redeker of ABC and Diane Sawyer of *Good Morning America,* Bill Madden of the *New York Daily News,* and Richard Sandomir of the *New York Times.* Other newspaper writers and editors I would like to thank are Peter Corbett, Bill Bertolino, Greg Hardesty, Phil Riske, and Peter Kerasotis. You guys are fantastic. To Alan Kunzman (author of *Mothermelters*) and to Jack Polidoro (author of *Project Samuel* and *Brain Freeze −321*), thank you for publicly sharing your insight. To anyone who wants to find out more on this subject, I strongly suggest you pick up Alan's and Jack's books.

Finally, to my lovely wife, Beverly. Thank you for your love, patience, and support during some of the worst experiences of your life. I know this has not been easy for you. You have gone through more than any individual can be expected to endure. I love you!

SCOTT BALDYGA:

Larry, thanks so much for your courage in coming forward with this story, and for trusting me to help tell it. Most of all, thanks for your friendship.

Beverly, thanks for your hospitality and your strength.

I strongly echo Larry's thanks to our tireless literary agent, Sharlene Martin, for sticking with us through so many obstacles. I am extremely grateful to have had her at the rudder these long years.

Thanks also to Justin Loeber and his staff at Mouth Public Relations, and to Jody Hotchkiss and his staff—for believing in this project, and for all their hard work.

After having several publishing companies back out of our contracts because, ultimately, they were afraid of Alcor, I cannot say a strong enough thanks to Vanguard Press and the Perseus Books Group. Thanks to *everyone* there. Your support was a lifeline for this book. As for our intrepid publisher, Roger Cooper, and his hardworking associate Georgina Levitt, I remain appreciative for their talent and energy. Individual thanks also go out to Amanda Ferber and Renee Caputo. A few weeks after our initial meeting in New York, it struck me one night exactly what it means when someone says their book "finally found a home" with a publisher. Thank you.

And a big thank-you to our editor, Philip Turner. From his very first notes, I realized—after five and a half years—we finally had someone who'd help take this book to a higher level. This book—and my writing—are both the better for Philip's knowledge, experience, and hard work.

I'd like to extend overdue, special thanks to Mark O'Connor, Father Frank Murphy, and Larry Cano.

Thanks to Alan Kunzman, John Heer, and members of Ted Williams's family for everything they shared with us.

There are a few talented people who took great time and care in reading this book during its creation and were extremely helpful to me. I hugely appreciate their input, and this book is better for their comments: MB, RS, TG, OG, PW, George P., Todd L., and K . . . thanks!

Above all, thanks to my parents for their support. In the face of all adversity, my dad never stopped telling me, "Follow your bliss." And Mom: You're the one who never lost hope. With all my heart, thanks.

ABOUT THE AUTHORS

Larry Johnson has over thirty years of experience as a street paramedic, flight paramedic, and clinical director for major-city 911 services. He was chief flight paramedic at the Waco, Texas, Branch Davidian siege; has served as keynote speaker at national medical conferences and was a contributing author for Prentice Hall's 2005 *Critical Care Paramedic*, the most widely used textbook of its kind. After blowing the whistle on Alcor in late 2003 and receiving multiple death threats, Larry went into hiding.

Scott Baldyga grew up in West Springfield, Massachusetts. After graduating from Boston College in 1991, Scott spent four years as a volunteer, teacher, and professional musician in Kingston, Jamaica. Living in Los Angeles since 1996, Scott has written screenplays for hire and worked as a writer, script supervisor, casting associate, development assistant, editor, and composer for both film and TV. *Frozen* is Scott's first book. Visit him at www.scottbaldyga.com.

For further information about *Frozen,* visit www.frozenbook.com.

NOTES

Some references are made to Web pages hosted or posted by Alcorians and other cryonicists. Wherever possible, we have copied these original Web pages and posted them on our Web site, www.frozenbook.com. This is in the event that the people who originally posted them decide to take them off the Internet after, perhaps, reading this book.

2. JUST ANOTHER RESEARCH FACILITY OUTSIDE PHOENIX

16   *. . . celebrity Alcor members*: Charles Platt and Jerry Lemler mentioned all these names to me many times. Lemler would call them out while giving tours of the facility to visitors. Here are some other sources.

Larry Flynt and his late wife, Althea: Christine Quigley, *Modern Mummies* (Jefferson, NC: McFarland, 1998), 145; and Michelle Green, "Her Death Ends the Improbable Love Match of Porn Merchants Althea and Larry Flynt," *People*, July 20, 1987, www.people.com/people/archive/article/0,,20096764,00.html.

Don Laughlin publicly admits to Alcor membership in interviews: Antonio Regalado, "A Cold Calculus Leads Cryonauts to Put Assets on Ice," *Wall Street Journal*, January 21, 2006, p. A-1; Charlie Vascellaro, "Waiting to Awake," *AZ Business Magazine*, August-September 2007, www.azbusinessmagazine.com/azb/2007/ABAS07/ABAS07_1.html; and http://video.google.com/videoplay?docid=8801182148349147478&q=cryonics&hl=en.

Charlie Matthau also publicly admits to membership: Richard Sandomir, "Please Don't Call the Customers Dead," *New York Times*, February 13, 2005, www.nytimes.com/2005/02/13/business/yourmoney/13freeze.html

Timothy Leary's interest in and then backing out of Alcor is well documented, including: http://en.wikipedia.org/wiki/Timothy_Leary#Death; www.leary.ru/english/lasttrip; and www.cryonet.org/cgi-bin/dsp.cgi?msg=6156, as well as numerous other CryoNet.org postings.

Peter Sellers and Walt Disney are familiar names on lists of celebrities who expressed early interest in cryonic suspension; see, for example, "Cryonics: Freezing for the Future?" BBC News World Edition, July 18, 2002, http://news.bbc.co.uk/1/hi/world/2133961.stm.

Michael Jackson's interest in Alcor was something Charles Platt and Jerry Lemler told people about proudly. Those two, especially, were very quick to name celebrities associated with Alcor, even ones I personally never saw documented. For example, though I never saw any proof to support it, Lemler told my wife, Beverly, all about Michael Jackson's interest in Alcor at a luncheon—the one time Beverly attended an Alcor function.

3. WELCOME TO ALCOR

35   *I kill dogs and I hurt them . . . enormous pain:* Michael Darwin, "The Lone Wolf," CryoNet.org, October 27, 1999, www.cryonet.org/cgi-bin/dsp.cgi?msg=12648.

4. ACCLIMATING

54   *"The ice had been gathered . . . dressed silly":* Jerry Lemler, "'Twas the Night of My Suspension," *Cryonics,* 4th quarter 2000, 49.

54   *At the end of his second chapter . . . JFK's funeral services:* Jerry Lemler, *Alcor Life Extension Foundation: An Introduction* (online book), www.alcor.org/Library/pdfs/alefione.pdf, 1, 14, 16, 18, 73, 83–87.

63   *It got pretty heated between Rick and Alcor at times . . . dug a little too deep:*

Threat to Rick's suspension: www.network54.com/Forum/291677/message/1097115572/they+are+using+Rick+to+get+to+Alcor.

Online sparring between Rick and Group of Six: www.network54.com/Forum/291677/message/1090857558/The+Fall+of+Cryonet+Cafe, www.network54.com/Forum/291677/message/

1094396914/I%27ve+decided+to+take+Group+of+6+seriously
(same posting is archived at http://web.archive.org/web/
20050517023437/www.network54.com/Forum/message?forumid
=291677&messageid=1094396914), and www.network54.com/
Forum/291677/message/1094260048/Group+of+Six.

5. TURNING HAMBURGER BACK INTO A COW

70   *"the present rickety human model . . . give service indefinitely"*: Robert F. Nelson, *We Froze the First Man* (New York: Dell, 1967), 8.

71   *Cryonics is "the most profound revolution in human history" . . . his contribution to mankind, Ettinger claimed*: ibid., 7–9.

71   *Certainly if a person is ill . . . the freezing process as well*: ibid., 35.

73   *Ettinger appeared on* Steve Allen *. . . Johnny Carson was host*: ibid., 52.

73   *After the first suspension was completed,* Life *magazine was going to make it a lead story*: ibid., 95, 111.

73   *about 2 million copies of the magazine . . . had the story run in full*: ibid., 113–118.

74   *"Some day," Nelson wrote, "in the not too distant future . . . the team of Karloff and Lugosi"*: ibid., 38.

76   *the day when you would defrost a blonde . . . when you shut the refrigerator door*: ibid., 91–92.

77   *"Some went head first, some went feet first, and as an Alcorian later put it, 'it was like putting together a Chinese puzzle'"*: R. Michael Perry, "Suspension Failures: Lessons from the Early Years," http://www.alcor.org/Library/html/suspensionfailures.html. (The article in its original form appeared in the "For the Record" column in *Cryonics*, February 1992.)

78   *"Only with excellent vision . . . vision as regards life extension"*: Jerry Lemler, *Alcor Life Extension Foundation: An Introduction*, www.alcor.org/Library/pdfs/alefione.pdf, 98.

78   *Some mythologies do not paint the star Alcor kindly . . . amputated to protect the whole*: Constellations of Words, "The History of the Star Alcor, www.constellationsofwords.com/stars/Alcor.html, citing Richard Hinckley Allen, *Star-Names and Their Meanings* (New York: Stechert, 1889), 445.

79   *"To see the flaw in this system . . . This is your brain on cryonics"*: Dr. Michael Shermer, "Nano Nonsense & Cryonics," *Scientific American*, September 2001, www.michaelshermer.com/2001/09/nano-nonsense-and-cryonics.

80   *"Believing cryonics could reanimate somebody who has been frozen, is like believing you can turn hamburger back into a cow"*: quoted in Andrew Stuttaford, "Frozen Future," *National Review,* July 9, 2002, www.nationalreview.com/flashback/flashback-stuttaford070902.asp.

80   *"This doesn't pass the straight-face test," says Kenneth Goodman, director of the University of Miami's Bioethics Program:* Robert L. Steinback, "Frozen In Time," *Miami Herald,* September 17, 2002. Reprinted: www.cryonet.org/cgi-bin/dsp.cgi?msg=20112.

80   *The president of the National Council Against Health Fraud, William T. Jarvis PhD, calls cryonics "quackery's last shot at you":* Stephen Barrett, MD, "Is Cryonics Feasible?" Quackwatch.com, September 2, 2005, www.quackwatch.com/04ConsumerEducation/QA/cryonics.html, citing Jarvis's words in K. Butler, *A Consumer's Guide to "Alternative" Medicine* (Amherst, NY: Prometheus Books, 1992).

81   *The pursuit of cryonic suspension is "supreme egotism," said John Baust . . . that they would want them":* Steinback, "Frozen In Time."

6. GATEKEEPERS TO IMMORTALITY

85   *"I have never seen a public statement . . . Fortunately no journalists have investigated JL's Tennessee background":* Charles Platt, "A Petition to Alcor's Board of Directors" (memo distributed to Alcor officers), July 30, 2003, 14.

85   *The Tennessee Board of Medical Examiners Docket No. . . . controlled substances:* "Lemler, Jerry: Licensure Verification," Official Web Site of the State of Tennessee—Tennessee.gov Department of Health, http://health.state.tn.us/licensure/Discipline.ASP?prof=1606&licnum=9048.

87   *I found a movie "Written & Directed" by Michael Riskin . . . "prior to acquiring licensure and board certification":* "Our Experts" page, adult video retailer, http://lovingsex.com/ProductInfo.aspx?productid=D608 and http://lovingsex.i4vision.com/custom.aspx?id=1.

87   *"multimedia masturbation":* quoted in Robert Anton Wilson, "The Future of Sex," http://www.rawilsonfans.com/articles/futuresex.htm.

87   *"The sexual superwoman . . . continuous state of multiple orgasm"*:
Robert Ettinger, *Man into Superman* (1972), p. 88, reproduced at
www.cryonics.org/chapter5_1.html.

90   *"Back in college, he peeled the layers of his own scrotum off with a
razor"*: Mike Perry voluntarily shared this information with a
psychologist who published a paper on self-mutilation that
included Perry's own account of mutilating himself: John Money,
PhD: "The Skoptic Syndrome: Castration and Genital Self-
Mutilation as an Example of Sexual Body Image Pathology,"
Journal of Psychology and Human Sexuality 1, no. 1 (1988): 113–128. A
reprinted excerpt from Perry's account in the Money article:
www.eunuch.org/Alpha/E/ea_235824excerpt_.htm. The story of
Perry's self-castration is also corroborated by Alan Kunzman,
former Riverside County deputy coroner, who read many of Mike
Perry's handwritten letters, notes, and diaries. (See Kunzman's
Mothermelters, Bloomington, IN: 1st Books, 2004, pp. 176–177.)

91   *Greg was a cryobiologist who used to work for the Red Cross in Bethesda,
Maryland*: *Cryonics* newsletter, August 1986,
www.alcor.org/cryonics/cryonics8608.txt.

92   *"They do a good deal of animal experimentation here at CCR," Charles
explained*: In a 1997 posting, Dr. Steve Harris elaborated on the
subject: "I've frozen my share of dogs. We're hell on dogs, I admit
it" (http://yarchive.net/med/lef.html).

94   *she looked to me like a mentally retarded dog that had had a stroke . . .
Charles told me her name was Dixie*: Looking back, this would have
made Dixie over twenty years old when I met her, an awfully long
life for a German shepherd. Maybe Charles was somehow
mistaken or maybe in the old days Alcor used to rename their lab
dogs "Dixie." Either way, it didn't really matter. The important
thing was what they were doing to these dogs.

7. DEEPER

104   *"So, like I said, that Emmy Award . . . Isn't that exciting?"*: As
mentioned and noted in Chapter 2, Charles Platt and Jerry Lemler
were fond of naming celebrities who had joined or expressed any
interest in becoming Alcor members. They could have exaggerated.
Some specific references:

104   *"The famous publisher Larry Flynt is a member"*. By this time, Larry
Flynt may have given up membership in Alcor but I was present

numerous times when Jerry Lemler would perhaps exaggerate about who was and wasn't still an Alcorian.

105   *"Larry King—the CNN talk show host—has talked seriously to us about cryonics"*: Saul Kent claimed, on CryoNet among other places (www.cryonet.org/cgi-bin/dsp.cgi?msg=9601), that Larry King had interviewed him twice over the years. According to Kent, King told him during breaks that he was interested in cryonics for himself. That was enough for Jerry Lemler to use the name Larry King on tours.

105   *"Many science fiction writers . . . have been interested and sympathic to cryonic suspension . . . Gore Vidal"*: These are among the names listed in "Cryonics: Freezing for the Future?" BBC News World Edition, July 18, 2002, http://news.bbc.co.uk/1/hi/world/2133961.stm and at www.cryonics.org/prod2.html.

109   *After the interview, Charles circulated a memo . . . "we need a little more cooperation around here"*: Charles Platt, "CBS from LA" e-mail, April 9, 2003.

8. SUSPENSION 1: TOURISTS AT A MUTILATION

119   *"Dr. Munson had been a long-time Alcor member . . . willing to be associated with cryonics"*: Charles Platt, "Thomas Munson, MD: 1922–2003 (a personal account by Charles Platt on behalf of Alcor)," Alcor News Bulletin, no. 9 (February 26, 2003), www.alcor.org/Library/html/alcornews009.html.

9. SUSPENSION 2: REMEMBER THE ALAMO

136   *"The patient was delayed overnight by mortuary paperwork problems"*: Charles Platt, "Alcor's Oldest Member Enters Cryopreservation," Alcor News Bulletin, no. 10 (March 10, 2003), www.alcor.org/Library/html/alcornews010.html.

10. AN ADRENALINE JUNKIE, THE CULT AT VENTUREVILLE, AND SUSPENSION 3: THE HAMMER AND CHISEL

145   *Charles told me he was compiling a list of Jerry's bad decisions . . . "He wants to look good on a grand scale. . . . seem trivial and demeaning compared with his ambition"*: Charles Platt, "A Petition to Alcor's Board of Directors," memo, 18.

146   *Hugh Hixon believed that due to the long delays, clotting had occurred and the perfusion . . . was not as successful as in other cases:* ibid., 22.

152   *The Venturists had a Web site . . . "abolition of death and the establishment of a free society of immortals":* Society for Venturism, www.quantium.plus.com/venturist/bylaws.htm.

152   *Elsewhere, in their Web site's "About Us" section . . . "for example, of a physical threat to a cryonics patient)":* Society for Venturism, www.quantium.plus.com/venturist/about.htm.

152   *he'd be, according to what he told the* Wall Street Journal, *"the richest man in the world":* Antonio Regalado, "A Cold Calculus Leads Cryonauts to Put Assets on Ice," *Wall Street Journal,* January 21, 2006, p. A-1.

153   *"I'd like to come back and buy a big spaceship . . . maybe you could even get out of this galaxy":* John Dickerson, "Frozen Assets," *Scottsdale Times,* March 2006, www.scottsdaletimes.com/mar06-feature1.asp.

154   *Bobby June was "not entirely happy to be woken since he had been up partying for most of the night":* Charles Platt, "Yet Another Unexpected Case in Southern California," Alcor News Bulletin, no. 11 (March 23, 2003), www.alcor.org/printable.cgi?fname=Library %2Fhtml%2Falcornews011.html.

11. ALCORIAN A-2032

158   *I read comments on cryonicists' online bulletin boards . . . Alcor had sued the coroner's office and won settlements totaling $120,000:* Mike Darwin, "Keystone Coroners," *Cryonics,* October 1988, 8–16, and Mike Perry, "Alcor's Legal Battles," *Cryonics,* 1st Quarter 1999, www.alcor.org/Library/html/legalbattles.html.

162   *Jerry Lemler had written the following for the Alcor News Bulletin . . . "part-time status after he resigned from that position, has left the organization":* Jerry Lemler, Alcor News Bulletin, no. 1 (December 13, 2002), www.alcor.org/Library/html/ alcornews001.html.

162   *in Charles's words, two of those four ex-employees had "left Alcor under controversial circumstances, and subsequently initiated an expensive dispute." The third was fired for failing a drug test.:* Charles Platt, "A Petition to Alcor's Board of Directors," memo, 9.

164   *I learned that Jerry Lemler had convinced Alcor's board to pay Haworth a retainer of $10,000 a month for promotional services . . . he'd endangered*

the lives of the patients inside for a photo shoot: Charles Platt, "A
Petition to Alcor's Board of Directors," memo, 8–9.

168   I read an article . . . It sure was distasteful to read about the Alcorians
       fighting Dick's will in order to keep his money for their company and
       away from his family: James S. Kunen and Marie Moneysmith,
       "Reruns Will Keep Sitcom Writer Dick Clair on Ice—indefinitely,"
       People, July 17, 1989, http://www.people.com/
       people/archive/article/0,,20120770,00.html.

168   Timothy Leary . . . didn't want to "wake up in 50 years surrounded by
       humorless men with clipboards": quoted in R. U. Sirius, "Can Web Site
       Have a Life after Leary?" Wired, August 25, 1997, http://www.wired
       .com/culture/lifestyle/news/1997/08/6302).

168   Charles Platt was working with CryoCare at the time . . . Leary was so
       famous that his involvement would benefit all of cryonics: Charles Pratt,
       "The Strange Case of Timothy Leary," CryoCare Report no. 8, July
       1996, http://www.cryocare.org/index.cgi?subdir=&url=
       ccrpt8.html#LEARY.

169   On the inside cover of every Cryonics magazine . . . "easily restored to
       health": "What is cryotransport," inside cover of numerous
       Cryonics magazines, including 4th Quarter 2002, vol. 23, no. 4.

169   On the very first page of the Alcor Web site . . . "restoring the individual
       back to good health": home page, Alcor.org, February 1, 2003,
       http://web.archive.org/web/20030201195705/
       http://www.alcor.org/index.html.

169   "Cryonics may seem like a radical idea, but really it's just another way of
       giving people what they are already trying to get, and what they have
       wanted for thousands of years: a longer, healthier life": home page,
       Alcor.org, January 19, 1998,
       http://web.archive.org/web/19961029023710/www.alcor.org/
       01.html.

170   "Imagine the possibility of having more time . . . limitations of a
       twentieth-century lifespan": "Cryonics and the Alcor Life Extension
       Foundation Electronic Brochure," Alcor.org, 1996, http://web
       .archive.org/web/19970512081559/http://www.alcor.org.

170   "The Alcor Foundation is your ambulance to that future of advanced
       medicine": home page, Alcor.org, May 12, 1997, http://web.archive
       .org/web/19970512081559/http://www.alcor.org.

170   On the back of those Cryonics magazines was an advertisement . . . stops
       cancer cells from dividing: "Life Extension Foundation"

advertisement, back cover of numerous *Cryonics* magazines, including 4th Quarter 2002, vol. 23, no. 4. Original emphasis (bold) preserved.

172   *a posting on CryoNet from Mike Darwin explained, "She was not cryo-preserved because she was autopsied with subsequent refusal of the ME [medical examiner] to release her brain"*: Mike Darwin, "SCI.CRYONICS: Cryopatients autopsied and cryopreserved," posting on CryoNet.org, January 9, 1997, www.cryonet.org/cgi-bin/dsp.cgi?msg=7463.

172   *On the fightaging.org Web site, More posted . . . "Flip past the lovely Victoria to p.43 and you'll find it. Have fun"*: fightaging.org, January 21, 2006, www.fightaging.org/archives/000734.php.

172   *they had a habit of changing their emergency phone numbers and then not telling their members:* Apparently this continued to be a problem at Alcor even after I left. For instance, in 2005 Mike Perry reported: "Unfortunately, we are occasionally notified that an emergency number on an ID tag doesn't work." ("Medic-Alert ID Phone Numbers," Alcor News Bulletin, no. 37, April 8, 2005, www.alcor.org/Library/html/alcornews037.html.)

       And in a 2007 posting on CryoNet, one Alcorian reported: "The cryonics system is far from perfect. Alcor Phone Number not working in Canada. Alcor should contact every Canadian and change their bracelet for new and good phone number." (Jonano, "Alcor Phone Number Not Working in Canada," CryoNet.org, January 15, 2007, www.cryonet.org/cgi-bin/dsp.cgi?msg=28945.)

173   *Several articles were written about it:* e.g., Alec Wilkinson, "The Cryonic Castle," *New Yorker*, January 19, 2004.

173   *Typically, there was much Alcorian bickering over the TimeShip:* Brent Fox, "Pizer's comments on Platt's comments re: TimeShip," posting on CryoNet.org, August 27, 2001, www.cryonet.org/cgi-bin/dsp.cgi?msg=17402.

173   *"For those of you with a short memory . . . the first state to allow pre-death suspensions"*: David Pizer, "More on Platt's comment on TIMESHIP," CryoNet.org, August 26, 2001, www.cryonet.org/cgi-bin/dsp.cgi?msg=17388.

173   *Always at the center of any controversy, Charles chimed in . . . "Why not invest that money in perfecting the vitrification process?"*: Charles Platt, "TimeShip," CryoNet.org, August 25, 2001, www.cryonet.org/cgi-bin/dsp.cgi?msg=17970,

12. "THAT GUY WHO WAS FROZEN"

175   *Jerry Lemler told a Miami newspaper that before Ted Williams . . .*
      "raised the public's consciousness about cryonics": Robert L. Steinback,
      "Frozen In Time," *Miami Herald*, September 17, 2002.

176   *Throughout his life, Ted Williams dedicated himself to the pursuit of*
      perfection. . . . "John Henry, goddamn it, you finally did something
      right": I've been a Ted Williams fan all my life and have read many
      articles and books on the Splendid Splinter. The main source I
      drew on in compiling this short biography was Leigh Montville,
      Ted Williams: The Biography of an American Hero (New York:
      Doubleday, 2004).

      Apart from numerous online articles I read, other books I
      referred to while writing this short biography of Ted Williams
      include:

      Bill Nowlin, *Ted Williams at War* (Burlington, MA: Rounder
      Books, 2007).

      Ted Williams and David Pietrusza, *Ted Williams: My Life in*
      Pictures (Kingston, NY: Total / Sports Illustrated, 2001).

      Ted Williams and John Underwood, *The Science of Hitting*, rev.
      and updated (New York: Fireside, 1986).

      Ted Williams with John Underwood, *My Turn at Bat: The Story*
      of My Life (New York: Fireside, 1988).

      John Underwood, *It's Only Me: The Ted Williams We Hardly Knew*
      (Chicago: Triumph Books, 2005).

177   *At the end of World War II, Ted had been promised . . . Ted grumbled*
      about it, but he went: Nowlin, *Ted Williams at War*, 90.

178   *senator John Glenn, who has said, "Ted only batted .406 for the Red Sox.*
      He batted a thousand for the Marine Corps and the United States":
      Nowlin, *Ted Williams at War*, 301.

178   *As one description of the book* Ted Williams at War *recounts: . . .*
      "devoted nearly five full seasons to serving his country": Amazon.com
      "Product Description" of Nowlin's *Ted Williams at War*,
      www.amazon.com / Ted-Williams-War-Bill-
      Nowlin / dp / 1579401252.

178   *John Glenn has echoed that thought: "I was well aware of Ted Williams,*
      of course, and his records in baseball. Who knows what those records
      might have been if he hadn't had two hitches in the Marine Corps?":
      Nowlin, *Ted Williams at War*, 313.

178   *John Glenn has also said, "There's nobody, I swear, there's nobody that served in the Marine Corps that is any more proud of having been a Marine than Ted Williams"*: ibid., 324.

179   *"When Ted Williams died America lost one of her greatest heroes. Without Ted and the rugged code of honor he lived by, baseball is a lesser sport"*: Chip Ballard, "Baseball Great Ted Williams: An American Hero," *DeSoto Sun-Herald*, September 8, 2006, www.sun-herald.com/NewsArchive4/100806/tp10de10.htm?date=100806&story=tp10de10.htm.

180   *"my little girl, Bobby-Jo. You should see her. An iddy-biddy little thing, pretty and sweet, just as sweet as she can be. . . . Is she smart! She can do anything, that iddy biddy little thing . . . the most important thing in my life is my little girl"*: Montville, *Ted Williams*, 192.

180   *During his high school years at the Vermont Academy prep school, John Henry was caught robbing a video game on school property . . . ended up in a burn ward himself:* ibid., 388.

181   *Coach Winkin said of John Henry, "You had to watch him like a hawk. . . . I thought he was a sneaky guy"*: ibid., 391.

181   *John Henry even failed at an Internet porn business:* Lynn Burke, "Porn Scammers Calling the Shots," *Wired*, www.wired.com/techbiz/media/news/2000/05/36055.

182   *John Henry actually used to boast that he could forge his father's signature . . . no way to tell it wasn't the real thing:* Darren Rovell, "Williams Memorabilia Floods onto Market," ESPN.com, July 9, 2002, http://espn.go.com/sportsbusiness/s/2002/0708/1403337.html.

182   *"I would bet my life that there are autographs that he has authenticated and sold that he signed himself"*: ibid.

193   *"Security in the operating room during this case was grossly negligent . . . and most of the photographs (possibly all of them) have been stored outside of Alcor"*: Charles Platt, "A Petition to Alcor's Board of Directors," memo, 5–6.

196   *The bloodied surgical team waited in the OR . . . convince John Henry that his father really should be decapitated:* Charles Platt later described this tremendous mistake in his "A Petition to Alcor's Board of Directors" memo (p. 5). Although he wrote, "The surgeon waited with the scalpel in his hand" while Lemler "placed a hasty phone call to the son"—perhaps intending it to be inferred that surgery had not yet begun—privately Charles told me the full

story, of how the decapitation procedure had already progressed to
the point I've described before Hayes walked into the OR.

203   *"In trying to figure out what I can say and not say—which I suppose is*
going to be par for the course if I continue to write about cryonics—I
concluded that it's okay to talk about what a piece of junk the Cryostar
is": Rick Potvin's July 14, 2003, comment is quoted in Charles Platt,
Alcor News Bulletin, no. 14 (August 1, 2003),
www.alcor.org/Library/html/alcornews014.html.

204   *Potvin surmised, "So the moral of the story is don't get your head caught*
in a fluctuating temperature Cryostar freezer": Rick Potvin, "If Ted's
Head Was Vitrified, Was It Also Stored at Intermediate (Optimal)
Temp?" Cryonics Café, July 16, 2004, www.network54.com/
Forum/54032/message/1089991435/If+Ted%27s+head+was+vitr
ified%2C+was+it+also+stored+at+intermediate+%28optimal%2
9+temp-.

204   *"a technician visited Alcor and noted that the ambient temperature . . .*
even with Alcor's industrial-strength air conditioning running
constantly": Charles Platt, Alcor News Bulletin, no. 14 (August 1,
2003), www.alcor.org/Library/html/alcornews014.html.

14. HI, MY NAME'S LARRY AND I'M A WHISTLEBLOWER

235   *"New Chief Operating Officer—With the resignation of Charles Platt . . .*
wish him well, as we all do here in Scottsdale": Jerry Lemler, Alcor
News Bulletin, no. 13 (July 1, 2003),
www.alcor.org/Library/html/alcornews013.html.

15. "HE KILLED HER"

240   *I asked Joe about Keith Henson, a former Alcor board member . . .*
considered a hero by most Alcorians, including Joe Hovey, for his battles
with Scientology: I found out later that Canada didn't get around to
denying Henson's asylum petition until 2005, at which point he
slipped back into the United States and eventually landed in
Prescott, Arizona—coincidentally about five miles from David
Pizer's Creekside Preserve—where he lived until Arizona
authorities caught up with him in early 2007 and sent him back to
California for a four-month stint in jail.

      See Susan Gamble, "Scientology Foe Seeks Refugee Status
Here," *Brantford Expositor* (Ontario, Canada), July 2, 2005,

www.operatingthetan.com/expositor.htm. See also Mike Zapler, "In Jail for Protesting Scientology, Man Seeks Pardon, *San Jose Mercury News,* July 7, 2007, http://www.wwrn.org/article.php ?idd=25586&sec=45&cont=all and the Religious Freedom Watch Web article at www.religiousfreedomwatch.org/anti-religious-extremists/keith-henson/. For information from Keith Henson's daughter, see http://valerieaurora.org/keith.html.

240 *I had also heard talk . . . child molestation:* As for the child molestation allegations, in 2007, after Henson's release from jail, one of his daughters, Valerie Aurora, went public with her own corroboration of his molestation of "at least four girls," including "at least two" of her sisters. Some of the victims didn't want to relive the experience, she claimed, and had refused to testify in court at the time. According to Valerie, Henson confessed to a therapist and his wife that he had molested the girls. His wife, however, had refused to testify because she didn't want Keith assaulted in prison when other inmates learned he was a child molester. For more information from Keith Henson's daughter, see http://valeriequrora.org/keith.html.

257 *"A-1949 has had nine cracking events in the first 35 hours of cool-down." Later, he wrote that A-1949's head suffered a total of sixteen cracks during the cooling process:* Hugh Hixon, e-mail messages to Alcor staff, subject: "Re: A-1949 and Cryostar problem," July 17, 2003, and subject: "A-1949," July 18, 2003.

16. "FOR YOUR CRIMES AGAINST CRYONICS YOU WILL DIE"

272 *Charles sent me an e-mail saying I should contact him immediately: "I am probably the only person whom it is safe for you to talk to at Alcor right now," he wrote:* Charles Platt, e-mail message to Larry Johnson, subject: "Oh Larry!" August 13, 2003.

17. ON THE RUN

277 *Of the more than 620 Alcor members signed up for cryo-suspension at the time:* Alcor membership was 629 as of the end of the first quarter of 2003, according to Alcor's *Cryonics,* vol. 24, no. 1 (2003): 23, http://web.archive.org/web/20040729040201/www Alcor.org/cryonics/cryonics2003 1.pdf.

18. TED'S LAST WISH

291   *"SECTION 8, ARTICLE 11. PRESERVATION, TRANSPORTATION,*
       AND DISPOSITION OF HUMAN REMAINS" . . . At such time as it is
       further buried, cremated or removed, a disinterment permit shall be
       obtained: State of Arizona Administrative Code—Agency, Board &
       Commission Rules, Title 9, Article 11, R9-8-1102,
       www.azsos.gov/Public_Services/Title_09/9-08.htm#Article_11.

291   *B. When being removed, disinterred remains shall be deposited in a*
       casket . . . shall not be opened for viewing of remains, except in cases
       involving medical or legal investigations: ibid., R9-8-1108.

292   *On request of an interested person, on or after the donor's death, the*
       person in possession shall allow the interested person to examine or copy
       the document of gift—Ariz. Rev. Stat. Section 36-847(B): Arizona State
       Statutes, Title 36, Chapter 7, Article 3, archive is online at
       http://web.archive.org/web/20021217193634/
       http://www.azleg.state.az.us/ars/36/00847.htm.

293   *STATE OF FLORIDA 2002 STATUTES, SECTION 765.512 . . . shall not*
       accept the gift: Florida Civil Rights Code Section 765.512—Health
       Care Advance Directives, archive is online at
       http://law.onecle.com/florida/civil-rights/765.512.html.

294   *During my research I ran across a very similar court case . . . The judge's*
       final ruling was: "The will . . . must be honored": Judge Philip W.
       Marking, Superior Court County of Santa Barbara, ruling for
       Sharon Fields v. Laurence O. Pilgeram, State of California, Second
       Appellate District, Division Six, ruling filed January 29, 1994.

298   *When Ted had been faced with the idea of open-heart surgery . . . "If I*
       have to die on an operating table, so be it": Montville, *Ted Williams,*
       432.

299   *Furthermore, a nurse who was present at Shands Hospital . . . to correctly*
       date the oil-stained paper: ibid., 464–465.

300   *In one CNN interview, Lisa Bloom of Court TV pointed out that normally*
       in disputes like this . . . "an amendment to the will, to memorialize, in
       writing, his change of mind": Wolf Blitzer Reports, CNN, July 16,
       2002, transcript online at http://transcripts
       .cnn.com/TRANSCRIPTS/0207/16/wbr.00.html, video online at
       www.youtube.com/watch?v=XrO-Bvcd05Y&source=video.

302   *"Finally we must emphasize, contrary to news reports, that Alcor has*
       never collected 'DNA samples' from its cryopatients. Obviously Alcor has
       no need to collect 'DNA samples,' since a neuropatient already contains

billions of DNA molecules: Alcor News Bulletin, no. 15 (August 13, 2003), www.alcor.org/Library/html/alcornews015.html.

302 *"Alcor does, however, encourage its members to deposit a DNA sample in its dewars, and we even went so far as to send out sample kits to all our members some years back. . . . There are hundreds of those samples logged and stored in our vaults":* Tanya Jones, Alcor News Bulletin, no. 19 (December 7, 2003), www.alcor.org/Library/html/alcornews019 .html.

302 *Phil Riske of the* Arizona Capitol Times *interviewed Rudy Thomas, director of the Arizona Board of Funeral Directors and Embalmers. . . . "That to me is mutilation, if it happened," Mr. Thomas said:* Phil Riske, "Some Officials Want State Regulation of Cryonics Firm," *Arizona Capitol Times,* February 20, 2004. Article has been archived at http://web.archive.org/web/20050516151710/ http://www.cryonet.org/cgi-bin/dsp.cgi?msg=22570 and is referred to/refuted on another CryoNet posting: www.cryonet.org/cgi-bin/dsp.cgi?msg=22577.

19. "WE WILL GET YOU YOU WILL PAY"

311 *Dora Kent's suspicious death was one of the most persistent mysteries I had encountered at Alcor. . . . Underneath the caption was a single handwritten word: "Thanks":* This Dora Kent information is taken from my conversations with Alan Kunzman, from his book with Paul Nieto, *Mothermelters* (Bloomington, IN: 1stBooks, 2004), from conversations I had with my Alcor coworkers, and from my online research. Specific references to *Mothermelters* follow.

312 *She always thought he visited his mother on a "prescription label schedule":* Kunzman and Nieto, *Mothermelters,* 2.

313 *In his book, Alan Kunzman wrote, "Once Dora was wheeled inside . . . died without ever knowing what had happened to her":* ibid., 6.

315 *I had found an online account written by Mike Perry . . . experiment on them with a new chemical perfusion formula:* Michael Perry, "Our Finest Hours: Notes on the Dora Kent Crisis," *Cryonics,* October 1992, www.alcor.org/Library/html/DoraKentCase.html.

319 *Meanwhile, the pathologist who had recently performed the autopsy on Dora Kent told Alan, "Concerning the incision I would say that the individual or individuals that did this were very sloppy, very messy, Amateurish. Didn't know what they were doing":* ibid., 87.

326   *In his account of the Dora Kent case I had found in the online Alcor
       archives . . . "meaning I caused the death of Dora Kent":* ibid.

329   *"an eccentric real estate mogul with a penchant for cocaine and cryogenics
       and a fear of intruders . . . laced the air ducts of his building with barbed
       wire":* Colleen Dougher, *City Link* Magazine,
       www.citylinkmagazine.com/cover/coverstory060502.html.

330   *"On August 28, 1986 . . . Petitioner was arrested for cocaine trafficking":*
       United States Tax Court, STEPHEN D. RUDDEL, Petitioner, v.
       COMMISSIONER OF INTERNAL REVENUE, Respondent,
       "Memorandum Findings of Fact and Opinion,"
       http://law.onecle.com/tax/1996/ruddel.tcm.wpd01.html.

331   *had a history of, in this journalist's words, "shady dealings" . . . "We're
       not afraid of the government":* Steven Almond, "They're Gonna Live
       Forever," *Miami New Times,* June 8, 1994,
       http://www.miaminewtimes.com/1994-06-08/news/they-re-
       gonna-live-forever/1.

332   *Saul's colleague . . . wrote that "It was the first time in the history of the
       FDA that the agency had given up on a criminal indictment against a
       political opponent":* Ben Best, "The FDA versus the Life Extension
       Foundation," http://www.benbest.com/polecon/
       fdalef.html.

20. "WHEN WILL IT END?"

335   *Cryonicists blistered Bob Stump with e-mails. . . . "The misinformation
       regarding this bill is breathtaking":* A reprint of one such e-mail
       exchange is found at the Immortality Institute Web site,
       www.imminst.org/forum/index.php?s=&act=
       ST&f=56&t=3153&st=20&#entry27130.

336   *On CryoNet.org, David Pizer and other Alcorians posted messages
       suggesting that Alcorians could save themselves from government
       regulation by turning Alcor into a church:* David Pizer, "Weekly
       Services?" CryoNet.org, March 14, 2004, www.cryonet.org/cgi-
       bin/dsp.cgi?msg=23623.

       Several other CryoNet postings from Pizer, Robert Ettinger, and
       others discuss organizing Alcor as a religion, including
       http://cryonet.org/cgi-bin/dsp.cgi?msg=23485,
       http://cryonet.org/cgi-bin/dsp.cgi?msg=18713,
       http://cryonet.org/cgi-bin/dsp.cgi?msg=10356, and
       http://cryonet.org/cgi-bin/dsp.cgi?msg=18694.

336   *"They had a ruthless campaign," he said in a newspaper interview. "I'm not a glutton for punishment." One phone call was so serious, Stump felt so personally threatened, he referred it to the Capitol Police*: Phil Riske, "Lawmaker Says He Won't Reintroduce Bill to Regulate Cryonics Firm," *Arizona Capitol Times*, September 9, 2005.

336   *Researching the fairest way to regulate Alcor . . . "Representative Stump, though, was very scared at the threats against him and his family. We dropped the bill"*: personal conversation with Rudy Thomas, February 12, 2009.

337   *Several months after the bill was dropped, veteran political journalist Phil Riske wrote, "Disciples of cryonics . . . do not suffer critics well. Just ask Arizona State Rep. Bob Stump. He received threatening messages last year because he sponsored a bill that would have established state regulatory authority over Alcor Life Extension Foundation, the Scottsdale facility that is the cold graveyard of baseball immortal Ted Williams"*: Phil Riske, "Brain Freeze −321° F," book review for the *Arizona Capitol Times*, October 25, 2005, www.longtailpublishing.com/jackgraphics/AZreview.pdf.

337   *"We don't need to agree with the normals . . . people who would actually die to keep the nitrogen topped up in the dewars"*: Peter Merel, "The White Lodge of Cryonics," CryoNet.org, September 27, 2003, www.cryonet.org/cgi-bin/dsp.cgi?msg=22591.

338   *Of Alcor, the legitimate cryobiologist Kenneth Storey has said, "They are more or less a theology . . . they have this key to eternal life"*: Kevin Miller, "Life as a Popsicle," *Carleton University Catalyst*, Spring 2004, www.carleton.ca/catalyst/2004/sf/km/km-cryonics.html.

EPILOGUE

343   *Connie Chung called it "macabre" and "terrible" . . . a scam that "doesn't even meet the silliness threshold"*: *Connie Chung Tonight*, CNN, July 8, 2002; *CNN Crossfire*, July 9, 2002, transcript online at http://transcripts.cnn.com/TRANSCRIPTS/0207/09/cf.00.html. The bioethicist quoted is Jonathan Moreno, director of the University of Virginia's Center for Bioethics. Videos available online: www.youtube.com/watch?v=GvfL4p87DCQ and www.youtube.com/watch?v=p_9nnJrUKcA.

345   *Tanya Jones, the woman who— according to Hugh Hixon's eyewitness account . . . (apparently Alcor no longer uses the title CEO)*: "The Alcor Team" page, Alcor.org,

www.alcor.org/AboutAlcor/meetalcorstaff.html, accessed
September 20, 2008.

346   *they have replaced the plaques under the patient photos . . . too many
       "odd looks" from people taking the tours:* Steve Van Sickle, "Patient
       Photos," Alcor News Bulletin, no. 51 (May 2006),
       www.alcornews.org/weblog/2006/05/alcor_news_51.html.

347   *Saul Kent, the most powerful man in cryonics, calls the FDA a "terrorist
       organization" that "will stop at nothing to destroy its enemies":* Saul
       Kent, "FDA Tyranny In Action," Life Extension Report, vol. 14, no.
       4, April 1994, www.realgh3.com/tyranny.html.

349   *Then several months later, after an OSHA walk-through of the facility,
       Alcor actually admitted to four violations in its own News Bulletin, each
       of them "serious," OSHA's second-highest order of risk:* Tanya Jones,
       Alcor News Bulletin, no. 18 (November 2, 2003),
       www.alcor.org/Library/html/alcornews018.html.

INDEX